Antisemitism and Anti-Zionism in Turkey

The Jewish community in Turkey today is very diverse with extremely different views as to whether Jews are reluctant or enthusiastic about living in Turkey. Many see themselves primarily as Turks and only then as Jews, while some believe quite the opposite. Some deny there are any expressions of antisemitism in Turkey while others would call it xenophobia and claim that the other non-Muslim communities in Turkey share the same antagonism.

Antisemitism and Anti-Zionism in Turkey provides a comprehensive history of the extent of antisemitism in Turkey, from the time of the Ottomans, through the establishing of the Turkish Republic, and up to recent times and the AK Party. It also provides an in-depth analysis of the effect of Israeli military operations on antisemitism, from the Second Lebanon War in 2006 to Operation Protective Edge in 2014. Much emphasis is given to the last decade, as scholars and local Jews assert that antisemitism has increased during this period. An illustrated overview of antisemitism in Turkish media, covering newspapers, books, entertainment, and education, is provided. The book also analyzes Turkish society's attitude toward Jews in contrast with other minorities, and examines how the other minorities see the Jews according to their experience with Turkish society and government.

A unique poll, data collected from personal interviews and the use of both Turkish and Israeli research resources, all help to provide a fresh insight into antisemitism in Turkey. This book will therefore be a key resource for students and scholars of antisemitism and anti-Zionism studies, Turkish studies and Middle East studies.

Efrat Aviv is a lecturer in the Department of Middle Eastern Studies at Bar Ilan University, Israel. She was a fellow at the Vidal Sassoon International Center for the Study of Antisemitism between 2012 and 2015, and a research fellow at Begin-Sadat Center for Strategic Studies, Israel.

Israeli History, Politics and Society
Series Editor: Efraim Karsh
King's College London

This series provides a multidisciplinary examination of all aspects of Israeli history, politics, and society, and serves as a means of communication between the various communities interested in Israel: academics, policy-makers, practitioners, journalists, and the informed public.

53 **Politics of Memory**
 The Israeli Underground's Struggle for Inclusion in the National Pantheon and Military Commemoralization
 Udi Lebel

54 **Moment in Palestine in the Arab/Israeli War of 1948**
 On the Israeli Home Front
 Moshe Naor

55 **Britain's Moment in Palestine**
 Retrospect and Perspectives, 1917–1948
 Michael J. Cohen

56 **Israel and the Palestinian Refugee Issue**
 The Formulation of Policy, 1948–1956
 Jacob Tovy

57 **Jihad in Palestine**
 Political Islam and the Israeli–Palestine Conflict
 Shaul Bartal

58 **Ralph Bunche and the Arab–Israeli Conflict**
 Mediation and the UN, 1947–1949
 Elad Ben-Dror

59 **Muslim/Arab Mediation and Conflict Resolution**
 Understanding Sulha
 Doron Pely

60 **Antisemitism and Anti-Zionism in Turkey**
 From Ottoman Rule to AKP
 Efrat Aviv

Israel: The First Hundred Years (Mini Series)
Edited by Efraim Karsh
1 Israel's Transition from Community to State, edited by Efraim Karsh
2 From War to Peace? edited by Efraim Karsh
3 Politics and Society since 1948, edited by Efraim Karsh
4 Israel in the International Arena, edited by Efraim Karsh
5 Israel in the Next Century, edited by Efraim Karsh

Antisemitism and Anti-Zionism in Turkey
From Ottoman Rule to AKP

Efrat Aviv

LONDON AND NEW YORK

First published 2017
by Routledge
2 Park Square, Milton Park, Abingdon, Oxon OX14 4RN

and by Routledge
711 Third Avenue, New York, NY 10017

Routledge is an imprint of the Taylor & Francis Group, an informa business

© 2017 Efrat Aviv

The right of Efrat Aviv to be identified as author of this work has been asserted by her in accordance with sections 77 and 78 of the Copyright, Designs and Patents Act 1988.

All rights reserved. No part of this book may be reprinted or reproduced or utilized in any form or by any electronic, mechanical, or other means, now known or hereafter invented, including photocopying and recording, or in any information storage or retrieval system, without permission in writing from the publishers.

Trademark notice: Product or corporate names may be trademarks or registered trademarks, and are used only for identification and explanation without intent to infringe.

British Library Cataloguing in Publication Data
A catalogue record for this book is available from the British Library

Library of Congress Cataloging in Publication Data
Names: Aviv, Efrat, author
Title: Antisemitism and anti-Zionism in Turkey from Ottoman rule to AKP / Efrat Aviv.
Other titles: Cass series–Israeli history, politics, and society; 60.
Description: Milton Park, Abingdon, Oxon: Routledge, 2017. | Series: Israeli history, politics and society; 60 | Includes bibliographical references and index.
Identifiers: LCCN 2016040342 | ISBN 9781138231795 (hardback) | ISBN 9781315314136 (ebook)
Subjects: LCSH: Antisemitism–Turkey–History. | Jews–Turkey–History. | Minorities–Turkey. | AK Parti (Turkey)
Classification: LCC DS146.T87 A93 2017 | DDC 305.892/40561–dc23
LC record available at https://lccn.loc.gov/2016040342

ISBN: 978-1-138-23179-5 (hbk)
ISBN: 978-1-315-31413-6 (ebk)

Typeset in Times New Roman
by Wearset Ltd, Boldon, Tyne and Wear

To my late parents Regina Kalomiti and Hayim Abravaya

Contents

Preface ix

Introduction 1

PART I
From Ottoman rule to modern times 7

1 Jews between Ottoman rule and the Turkish Republic: the Ottoman law and the Jews 9

Tolerance and violence 14
Jews and sultans 17
Social status 18
Greeks and Christians 20
Communal administration and taxes 22
Modern times 23
The War of Liberation and onwards: the formative years 24
Who is a Turk? The first years of the Republic 25
Policy of the unified Turkish society 28

2 From the 1920s to the 1990s 35

1923–1933 35
1933–1943 36
Varlık Vergisi 41
Post-war to the late 1960s 44
Late 1960s–1970s 48
1980s–1990s 57

PART II
Antisemitism under AK Party rule   67

3 The rise of the AK Party   69

   International politics: relations with Israel and Zionism 72
   Criticism of Israel 78
   Political approaches: Islamists 81
   Leftists 87
   Nationalists and ultranationalists 88
   The Kurdish issue 90

4 Israeli military operations and their impact on antisemitism   100

   Second Lebanon War 2006 100
   Operation Cast Lead 2008–2009 103
   Mavi Marmara 2010 and the aftermath 107
   Operation Protective Edge 2014 114
   Hate speeches and their impact: Jews and other minorities 127

5 Antisemitism in the Turkish media   140

   Newspapers 141
   Books 145
   Entertainment 151
   Education 157
   Daily life 157
   The discourse of Erdoğan as reflected in the Turkish media 167
   Jews' responses 176
   Reflections of awareness 186

Conclusions   212

Bibliography   215
Index   227

Preface

Both of my parents were born in Turkey. My mother was born in Izmir in 1943 and moved to Tire (known as 'Tiriya' by the Jews) with her family. She made Aliyah in 1960. My father was born in Ezine, Çanakkale in 1931 and made Aliyah in 1949. Though my parents' childhood was a very happy one, my late father did tell us about his troubles with the non-Jewish youngsters in his neighborhood. A few times he was attacked by kids calling him "korkak yahudi" (a coward Jew), which was the common derogatory name for Jews. His younger brother told me years ago that during World War II, municipality clerks approached their house to conduct a population census. When a young Muslim boy who was my uncle's friend followed them into the house and asked why they did not conduct the census in their house as well, they kicked him to shut him up. On the other hand, during the famine years of the war, my father never forgot the assistance and basic food products that were given to his family by the villagers who resided in the mountains. From my mother's side I have never heard any reference to antisemitism, but there was always the belief that Jews could live freely only in Israel.

When I was doing research work in the Ottoman Archive in Istanbul in 2010, one of the librarians used an antisemitic saying within my hearing. It was a terrible feeling that one who has never experienced racism would never understand. I emailed the archive director and I will never forget his kind apology.

The Jewish community in Turkey today is very diverse and thus one cannot reach a definite conclusion as to whether Jews are reluctant or enthusiastic about living in Turkey. Some see themselves as Turks first and only then as Jews, while some believe quite the opposite. Some would declare there is no antisemitism in Turkey at all and others would argue that antisemitism exists in Turkey but only as a general phenomenon and that they themselves as individuals have never experienced it first- or second-hand. Some would oppose the discourse on antisemitism in Turkey from the beginning and deny there are any expressions of antisemitism in Turkey, while others would call it xenophobia and claim that the other non-Muslim communities in Turkey share the same antagonism. Some would like to make Aliya or already have and some would never agree to leave 'their home' in Turkey. This research investigates these various viewpoints thoroughly and it gives me great pleasure to credit the following.

x *Preface*

I would like to thank the Vidal Sassoon International Center for the Study of Antisemitism (SICSA), for their fellowship and assistance, and especially Professor Robert Wiestrich who passed away while I was writing this research, for his strong belief in this research and for his support. I'd like to thank BE-SA (Begin-Sadat Center) from Bar Ilan University for their kind support, and its chairperson Professor Inbar for pushing me into this research. I would like to also thank the American Research Center (ARIT) in Istanbul for their kind hospitality throughout all the years I have been working on this. I'd like to thank Dr. Shlomit Levy from the Hebrew University for her professional and kind help with the poll I took in Turkey and all my interviewees, those who are mentioned by name and those who requested to be kept anonymous, to Beyazıt and Atatürk Libraries in Istanbul and Israel State Archives in Jerusalem. Last but not least, my dear family who have been there for me all along with everything I do, and everyone else who helped make this research study become a reality.

Introduction

The purpose of this document is to provide a practical guide to identifying incidents, collecting data, and supporting the implementation and enforcement of legislation dealing with antisemitism.

A working definition of antisemitism, and the one used in this book is:

> Antisemitism is a certain perception of Jews, which may be expressed as hatred toward Jews. Rhetorical and physical manifestations of antisemitism are directed toward Jewish or non-Jewish individuals and/or their property, toward Jewish community institutions and religious facilities.

This definition is used by the European Parliament Working Group on Antisemitism, which is based on the European Union Monitoring Center on Racism and Xenophobia (EUMC) in collaboration with NGOs and representatives of Democratic Institutions and Human Rights (ODIHR). The U.S. State Department has also adopted this definition.[1]

In addition, such manifestations could also target the state of Israel, conceived as a Jewish collective. Antisemitism frequently charges Jews with conspiring to harm humanity, and it is often used to blame Jews for 'why things go wrong.' It is expressed in speech, writing, visual forms, and action, and employs sinister stereotypes and negative character traits.

Taking into account the overall context, contemporary examples of antisemitism in public life, the media, schools, the workplace, and the religious sphere, could include, but is not limited to, the following:

- Calling for, aiding, or justifying the killing or harming of Jews in the name of a radical ideology or an extremist view of religion.
- Making mendacious, dehumanizing, demonizing, or stereotypical allegations about Jews as such or the power of Jews as a collective – such as, especially but not exclusively, the myth about a world Jewish conspiracy or of Jews controlling the media, economy, government, or other societal institutions.
- Accusing Jews as a people of being responsible for real or imagined wrongdoing committed by a single Jewish person or group, or even for acts committed by non-Jews.

2   *Introduction*

- Denying the fact, scope, mechanisms (e.g., gas chambers) or intentionality of the genocide of the Jewish people at the hands of National Socialist Germany and its supporters and accomplices during World War II (the Holocaust).
- Accusing the Jews as a people, or Israel as a state, of inventing or exaggerating the Holocaust.
- Accusing Jewish citizens of being more loyal to Israel, or to the alleged priorities of Jews worldwide, than to the interests of their own nations.

Examples of the ways in which antisemitism manifests itself with regard to the State of Israel, taking into account the overall context, could include:

- Denying the Jewish people their right to self-determination, e.g., by claiming that the existence of a State of Israel is a racist endeavor.
- Applying double standards by requiring of it a behavior not expected or demanded of any other democratic nation.
- Using the symbols and images associated with classic antisemitism (e.g., claims of Jews killing Jesus or blood libel) to characterize Israel or Israelis.
- Drawing comparisons of contemporary Israeli policy to that of the Nazis.
- Holding Jews collectively responsible for the actions of the State of Israel.

Antisemitic acts are criminal when they are so defined by law (for example, denial of the Holocaust or distribution of antisemitic materials in some countries).

Criminal acts are antisemitic when the targets of attacks, whether they are people or property – such as buildings, schools, places of worship, and cemeteries – are selected because they are, or are perceived to be, Jewish or linked to Jews.

Antisemitic discrimination is the denial to Jews of opportunities or services available to others, and is illegal in many countries.[2]

However, criticism of Israel similar to that leveled against any other country cannot be regarded as antisemitic. In this book 'antisemitism' will be used in accordance with the aforementioned definition, whereas anti-Israeli expressions will also be discussed but separately from antisemitism. Anti-Zionism is further discussed in the section 'Relations with Israel and Zionism,' but basically criticism against Israel and Zionism is not antisemitism. However, when ideological references are made which denounce not only the Zionist Jews' deeds but also stereotyped negative characteristics such as being evil, greed, and deviousness, these references become antisemitic.

The main manifestations of Turkish antisemitism are verbal and through publications such as newspapers and, in recent years, social networks. Yet, there are several manifestations of antisemitic deeds which are discussed in this research.

It is commonly believed that antisemitism is not encountered in Turkey and that Turkey has one of the few 'fortunate' Jewish communities because, historically, there has been little antisemitism in Turkey, an exception to the communality, universality, and historicism of the phenomenon. Turkish Jews have never been the victims of organized pogroms and did not experience the atrocities of the Holocaust as their counterparts did in most of Europe.[3]

Turkey's prime minister, Erdoğan, stated in a response letter he sent to the Anti-Defamation League's (ADL) national director Abraham Foxman on August 21, 2014:

> Whether practicing Judaism or any other religion, to feel enmity toward someone just because they are different has never and will never gain acceptance in this land. Even during the first half of the 20th century when antisemitism reached its vicious peak, our country never allowed this ideology to enter our lands. On the contrary, we opened our borders to many people of Jewish descent who were subject to grave atrocities during and prior to World War II.[4]

Antisemitism in Turkey is of a discrete nature and it is expressed without a steady recurrence, being unsystematic, irregular, and not widespread. As Mümtaz'er Türköne described it in *Today's Zaman*:

> Turkish society is not an antisemitic society. There are no anti-Jewish factors present in either religious or popular culture. This situation is particularly clear when one compares our culture to Western Christian societies or, in particular, Arab societies. In fact, the term 'antisemitic' is relatively new, and was taken from the West.[5]

Talip Küçükcan, Professor of Sociology at Marmara University and a politician from the AK Party, who has served as a Member of Parliament for Adana since June 7, 2015, agrees, saying: "neither Turkey nor the Islamic world is the motherland of antisemitism. Turkey has opened its arms towards the world's Jews during the wars. Antisemitism occurred in Europe, it is a European creation."[6] Turks often feel as if antisemitism does not exist in their homeland. Sabahattin Ali describes in his famous 1943 novel *Kürk Mantolu Madonna* (The Fur Coated Madonna) a love story between a young Turkish student named Raif and a Jewish cabaret singer named Maria Puder, which takes place in Berlin in 1928. In one of their dialogues, Ali writes what many Turks tend to believe – that antisemitism is not a problem encountered in Turkey:

> "My father was Jewish" she said. "My mother is German, but she is not a blond either."
> "You are therefore Jewish?"
> "Yes ... might you too be antisemitic?"
> "What's the connection? Those things do not exist in our country."[7]

Following the murder of the Israeli consul general in Istanbul in 1971, Efraim Elrom, İnönü, who served as the President of Turkey from 1938 to 1950 and who led the Republican People's Party (CHP), expressed the same opinion, saying that throughout history the "plague of antisemitism" did not exist within the Turkish nation.[8]

Turkish intellectuals tend to view antisemitism as a problem that Turkey does not suffer from, and which preoccupies only Turkish Jews. Subsequently, these Turkish Jews do not research or even read in this area, preferring instead to repeat the pat phrases of their respective ideological positions. For instance, Davut Şahin says: "The discourse of Zionism is not allowed in Turkey. I do not believe there is antisemitism in Turkey."[9] Many people I have spoken with noted the same thing: Antisemitism does not exist in Turkey and if it ever did, it was only during the first centuries of the Turkish Republic, and even then was not exclusive to Jews but to all other minorities. Fatih Gökhan Diler, a journalist from *Agos*, the Turkish-Armenian daily, can understand it. He said that the Turks are not even aware of antisemitism or anti-Armenianism.[10]

Unlike them, Jews feel differently: İvo Molinas, chief editor of *Şalom* newspaper, mentions that not only does antisemitism exist in Turkey, it grew stronger after Operation Protective Edge. This antisemitism is expressed not only through printed newspapers, as in the past, but it rambles within social media as well. According to Molinas, Jews who used to declare that antisemitism did not exist have changed their minds and have realized it does. That is why the community is currently panicking.

> The Turkish authorities express their objection towards antisemitism at every opportunity, emphasizing that Israelis and Turkish Jews should not be mixed, but the flip side is that even if this is what they declare, the hate speeches continue, resulting in frustration.[11]

Does antisemitism not exist in Turkey, or is it part of Turkey's official politics so that, as human rights activist Ayşe Günaysu describes,[12] it is not even sensed? Despite the fact that the term 'antisemitism' appears in the official dictionary of the Turkish language association (Türk Dili Kurumu), it is not in extensive use in Turkish society nor does it have a meaning that is equally understood by all parts of Turkish society. Other terms, such as 'Yahudi Aleyhtarlığı' and 'Yahudi düşmanlığı' or even 'Yahudi Karşıtlığı' all denote hostility or enmity toward Jews. Even those who are familiar with the term 'antisemitism' sometimes do not fully understand its meaning. In recent years, for example, a television channel that advertised for a debate program on the topic of antisemitism received calls from viewers complaining of a misunderstanding of the term 'antisemitism.'[13] Bali explains that the Turkish way of noting the adjective "anti-Semite" – antisemitisit – is inspired by and created as a sort of linguistic equivalent of the term 'communist.' The language expresses how alien the topic of antisemitism is to the Turkish intelligentsia.[14]

According to the Turkish constitution, Jews are protected like any other minority, but there has never been a specific law banning antisemitism. Some of the reasons for the absence of such a law are Turkey's fear of similar demands from other minorities, as well as ethnic minorities such as Kurds.

Introduction 5

This research attempts to examine the place antisemitism occupies within Turkish history and society, especially since the rise of the AK Party. Concurrently, it attempts to elucidate and analyze the various actors, factors, and changes that the term and the phenomena of 'antisemitism' have gone through. In addition, this research attempts to present the Turkish regime's relations, attitude, and approach toward the Turkish-Jewish community in Turkey.

Notes

1 www.state.gov/j/drl/rls/fs/2010/122352.htm, retrieved April 4, 2015.
2 www.antisem.eu/projects/eumc-workinGodefinition-of-antisemitism, retrieved May 12, 2015.
3 Şule Toktaş, "Perceptions of antisemitism among Turkish Jews," *Turkish Studies*, 7, 2 (June 2006), p. 203.
4 www.adl.org/Israel-international/Israel-middle-east/content/l/letters-adl-Erdoğan.html, retrieved September 10 2014.
5 Mümtazer Türköne, "Israel's attack on Gaza and antisemitism in Turkey," *Today's Zaman*, July 19, 2014 www.todayszaman.com/columnist/mumtazer-turkone_353475_ Israels-attack-on-gaza-and-Antisemitism-in-Turkey.html, retrieved July 22, 2014.
6 No author, "Prof. Dr. Talip Küçükcan'dan çarpıcı İsrail analizi," *Stargazete*, August 2, 2014, http://haber.stargazete.com/guncel/turkiye-neden-yahudi-karsiti-olarak-gosterilmeye-calisiliyor/haber-920926, retrieved August 3, 2014.
7 Sabahattin Ali, *Kürk Mantolu Madonna*: 58th (Istanbul: Yapı Kredi Yayınları, 2013), p. 90.
8 No author, "Elrom'un öldürünler Türk olamaz," *Tercüman*, May 24, 1971, p. 7.
9 Quoted in: Yunus Emre Kocabaşoğlu, "Antisemitizm Korkusu, İsrail'in Eleştirilmesine Engel mi?," *Bianet*, January 30, 2010: www.bianet.org/biamag/biamag/119754-antisemitizm-korkusu-israil-in-elestirilmesine-engel-mi, retrieved September 1, 2012.
10 Interview in Istanbul, February 22, 2015.
11 İvo Molinas, "Yeni Türkiye'de antisemitizm olmasın," *Şalom*, August 27, 2014: www.salom.com.tr/haber-92162-yeni_turkiyede_antisemitizm_olmasin.html, retrieved September 1, 2014.
12 Ayşe Günaysu, "İstanbul'da Hamas, Karako cinayetleri ve "Ölen Bayan," *Sendika.org*, August 26, 2014: www.sendika.org/2014/08/istanbulda-hamas-karako-cinayetleri-ve-olen-bayan-ayse-gunaysu-ozgur-gundem, retrieved September 23, 2014.
13 Rıfat N. Bali, *Antisemitism and Conspiracy Theories in Turkey* (Istanbul: Libra Kitap, 2013), p. 9.
14 Ibid., p. 99.

Part I
From Ottoman rule to modern times

1 Jews between Ottoman rule and the Turkish Republic

The Ottoman law and the Jews

As a Muslim empire, the judicial law toward religious minorities[1] is based on Sharia (religious Muslim law), the Kanun law (Sultanic law), and the customary law, which manifested in customs and precedents toward the non-Muslims in previous Muslim countries and in the Ottoman Empire. This framework enabled the existence of Jewish communities in certain conditions, set their judicial position, and formed the public and private life until the nineteenth century. In the seventeenth century, Jews, known as Francos, were included in the treaties and contracts signed between the Empire and Christian countries, where clauses related to Christian citizens. In addition, Jews who served European ambassadors and consuls enjoyed limited protection.

Ottoman attitudes toward minorities were, at first, rooted in the Islamic tradition. The Islamic state regarded its relations with non-Muslim subjects as "people of the book" (*Ahl al-Kitāb*) as protégés (Ahl al-dhimma, Zimmet in Turkish), meaning that in return for recognizing the superiority of Islam and its adherents, the Dhimmi would have the right to exist and be protected, to practice their own religion, enjoy freedom of movement and occupation, maintain their houses of worship, and run their own affairs to a large extent.

The relations between Muslims and non-Muslims can be summed up in three words: separate, unequal, and protected.[2] However, the Ottoman Nizam relied not on the principle of equality but on a certain version of justice (adalet) that did not recognize equality between the rulers and the ruled or among the different sectors of the ruled. Instead, the Ottoman adalet meant to secure for each of the communal groupings the legal status they deserved. This was a system of accepted inequality that existed between believers and non-believers. Despite the protection and communal autonomy granted, non-Muslims had a lower sociopolitical and legal status compared to Muslims. For example, their testimony was inadmissible, they were exempted from political and military affairs, they were prohibited from constructing new places of worship, and they were required to dress in group-specific colors and style.[3]

However, the main manifestation of the Dhimmi's inferiority was the poll tax (Jizya in Arabic, Cizye in Turkish), a special Islamic tax paid by non-Muslim adult males. The tax was formally abolished with the Imperial Reform Edict in 1856. The restraints were aimed at differentiating and creating boundaries between believers and non-believers. Some other restrictions leaned on the Pact of Umar, and others were imposed with time. Among other restrictions, as mentioned, was a prohibition to build new houses of worship; their residences' height was limited, and they could not be built with stone. Non-Muslims were not allowed to live near mosques and they were required to keep their worship far from the public sphere. They were not allowed to own Muslim slaves, ride horses, or carry weapons. There were also restrictions regarding non-Muslims' clothing: Only specific raw materials, models, and colors were allowed to be worn by non-Muslims, although some sultans, such as Murat II, did not insist on Jews dressing in a particular manner but allowed them to dress and live as they pleased.[4] The qāḍī and Muhtesib (public moral and markets trade inspector) were in charge of enforcing these rules on the minorities.

The principle inferiority of non-Muslims was also expressed in their judicial position: Sharia (Islamic law) did not accept Dhimmi's testimony against a Muslim and the punishment of a Muslim who murdered a non-Muslim was not equal to Dhimmi who murdered a Muslim. Furthermore, Dhimmi were not allowed to marry Muslims and Dhimmi heirs were also discriminated against, including converted Dhimmis. Even the official discourse allegedly used a humiliating terminology pertaining to non-Muslims.[5] On the other hand, this corpus of religious rules made it easier for the non-Muslim to integrate within general society, because Islam tolerated the Empire's impact on diversity. Islam had a script for how to deal with Jews and Christians, whereas Christianity, especially after the Crusades, conducted itself as an exclusive religion with an organized body ideally unified with public authorities. In Christendom, religious and secular leaders administered in tandem, whereas in the Ottoman Empire Islam was subordinated to the will of polity.[6]

The Ottoman Empire was one of the most tolerant Muslim states to ever exist, since Ottomans followed the Hanafi rite of jurisprudence, the most liberal of the four rites. The Hanafis assigned greater relative importance to consensus and legal reasoning, in addition to tradition and precedent, than the other rites; thus, their system was more flexible and allowed change, reinterpretation, and adoption of new elements. Thus, Ottomans treated non-Muslims more liberally and with greater equality with Muslims.[7] However, İçduygu and Soner claim that the non-Muslims were tolerated, with their belief systems and religious practices, but only at the expense of unequal obligations and responsibilities. In other words, privileges and obligations were not based on political membership in the Ottoman state but on the basis of people's communal membership, and subsequently, the religious affiliation of an Ottoman subject dictated his or her sociopolitical and legal position.[8] According to Barkey, Ottoman tolerance was also a result of the pragmatic policy of governance that the Ottomans developed over the centuries. Ottoman pragmatism was born out of necessity, as during the fourteenth and fifteenth centuries non-Muslims were the majority in the growing empire. During these centuries, new converts as well as non-Muslims played a prominent role in administration and the military. Their firm presence in the ruling class, and the great diversity of religions and ethnicities in Ottoman society made it pluralistic, tolerant, and open. It also forced the Ottoman rulers to recognize early on that in order to effectively govern a heterogeneous society, they needed to be tolerant. In the sixteenth century, with the conquest of Arab lands in the Middle East and North Africa, Muslims became the majority, which was one of the reasons that Ottoman society became more conservative.[9] Jews who served as court physicians, translators, advisers, government officials, and military personnel were even part of the tax-exempt class (askeri) in the fifteenth century and to a lesser degree in later centuries. All others, Muslims and non-Muslims, were taxpayers (Reaya). In general, Jews trusted the Ottoman judicial system and used it even in their own internal affairs, despite strong opposition by rabbis.[10]

The Sunni Muslim authorities preferred to run its administrative relations with the population under its rule through mediating organizations; as a result, there was no free existence of individual Ottoman subjects, who were considered members of their millet parts. The term 'millet' in the Ottoman Empire was used to determine a non-Muslim religious community. The Turkish term 'millet' (from Ar. milla; Ott. Tur. pl. milel; mod. Tur. pl. milletler) originally meant both a religion and a religious community. In the Quran, 'millet' frequently refers to the 'millat Ibrahim,' meaning the religion of Abraham, and rarely as milla for only Judaism or Christianity. There are also references to millet as "religion, confession, or rite" from 1158 to 1833 in various internal and international communications between the Ottoman Empire and other, mostly non-Muslim empires. Occasionally, millet was translated in the West as 'sovereign nations,' especially in terms of rebellion. Commonly, the definition of millet has been 'religious community.' Millet has its roots in early Islam and the Ottomans used this system to deal with the different religious communities living in their empire, giving minority religious communities a limited amount of power to regulate their own affairs, under the overall supremacy of the Ottoman administration.

According to the Quran, as stated, Christians and Jews are the people of the Bible, also referred to as Dhimmi, who were protected, and not violently forced to convert to Islam. They were given the right to live under the Muslim arrangement and practice their religion, paying the cizye and military exemption tax while having certain prohibitions. Although the Ottoman Empire was predominantly Muslim, it allowed non-Muslims to practice their religion and conduct their community affairs, provided they exhibited loyalty to the Ottoman rulers and paid their taxes. The Ottomans allowed the 'religions of the book' to be organized in millets: the Orthodox Christians or Rums, the Armenians, and the Jews. Non-Muslims had to be part of a millet in order to be considered citizens of the Ottoman Empire. In the nineteenth century, while retaining its original meanings, it also came to denote such modern concepts as nation and nationality. In connection with the reforms in the Ottoman Empire in the nineteenth century, the structure of the millet organization underwent many changes. The regulations of the Greek community (millet-i Rum) were finally drafted and approved in 1862, and those of the Armenian community (millet-i Ermeniya) in 1863. The submission of proposals for the reorganization of the Jewish community (millet-i Yahudiyan), as required by the Khaṭṭi humayun (imperial decree) of 1856, was delayed due to internal dissent. The "Organizational Regulations of the Rabbinate" (ḥakham Khane niẓamnamesi) was eventually approved in 1865 (ḥakham Başı). The nature of the regulations reveal a desire to limit the powers of the ḥakham Başı, and they remained in force as long as the Ottoman Empire existed; only under the Republic did they lapse de facto – without being officially replaced.

In recent years there has been an academic discussion regarding the general attitude toward non-Muslims in the Empire and in regard to the millet in particular, either as an example of tolerance or oppression, using the Ottoman millet system theory as a model of interpretation.[11]

No manifestation of equal rights or the practice of citizenship appeared in the Ottoman Empire before the nineteenth century. On the contrary, the classic policy of separation of elements means bestowing privileges and obligations not on the unifying basis of law and politics, but on the dividing force of religion.[12] Jews were initially organized into multiple small congregations (kahal/cemaat), usually consisting of members who knew each other from their original towns of immigration and who congregated around a synagogue. These congregations operated as religious and secular units of administration in which elected leaders handled issues of religion, education, taxation, and communication. In larger towns, smaller units were organized into a larger organization (kehilla, the Hebrew term for community). Ottoman authorities adapted to this multilayered system without undermining its autonomy. This is one manifestation of the Ottomans' flexibility and the expediency of their rule. Unlike any other group, Jews early on had penetrated the imperial palace as high government functionaries, doctors, and advisers, thus creating an open channel between rulers and communities, as well as a clear notion regarding how the Jews were organized, which was brought to the governors' attention.

The Ottomans negotiated with each community separately. The lay leaders were responsible for managing internal affairs and for negotiating with state authorities. The Ottomans stipulated a set amount of taxation from the Jewish communities and were indifferent to the manner in which it was divided between the communities.[13] The condition of the Jews in the Ottoman Empire was in stark contrast to the conditions imposed on them in various parts of Christendom in the fifteenth century, when there was a large influx of Jews into Empire territories, especially after they were expelled from Spain in 1492. The Jews fleeing Spain became joint members with the Christians and Muslims in industrial and commercial guilds. Maranos, who had outwardly converted to Christianity to escape persecution in Spain, soon reverted to Judaism in Ottoman lands and specialized in weapons manufacturing. Others engaged in large-scale trade by land and sea, and the Jews of the medical school of Salamanca worked as doctors and became influential court physicians. In addition, Jews were employed as interpreters due to their connections in Europe. The Ottomans welcomed the migrating Jews, so the image of Ottoman authorities in Jewish historiography has been a very positive one. They were free to settle wherever they wished (except for the times when the Sürgün (expulsion or simply obligatory transfer from one place to another) was imposed on them, as well as other populations (whether Muslim or non-Muslim), and they could pursue almost any occupation; they were able to travel freely and were free to practice their religion and run their own educational and social institutions.[14]

Since the founding of the Ottoman state in 1299 and particularly during its ascendance in the sixteenth century, the ethnic and religious minorities living within its boundaries, regardless of their origin, culture, or religion, enjoyed tolerance and relative security in corporate life, liberty, estate, social, educational autonomy, and economic prosperity, and preserved their ethnic and religious identity in peace and order within the Ottoman millet system. Following the Islahat Fermanı (Islâhat Hatt-ı Hümâyûnu, a royal decree which reaffirmed the stipulations of the 1839 Gülhane Hatt-ı Şerif Tanzimat decree, and which introduced sweeping changes in Ottoman law and administration) of 1856, the non-Muslim minorities began to be employed in government service. More and more historiographers claim that the Ottoman Empire was not a despotic theocracy that oppressed its non-Muslim subjects, but rather that it allowed a large degree of local communal and regional autonomy and expressed tolerance toward the numerous ethnic and religious groups living in it. In fact, the non-Muslim subjects of the Empire were no more oppressed than the Muslims. In many respects they were in a better position than the latter. For instance, from the nineteenth century they were exempt from military service in return for a tax, Bedel-i Askeriye, while Muslims were forced to fight in wars.[15]

This argument contradicts the impression given by Western travelers, scholars, and diplomats, who broadly described the Ottoman rule as oppressive, cruel, and ineffective. Jews and Christians did suffer from maladministration from time to time, especially in times of decline. According to Sonyel, Jews and Christians sometimes suffered from Ottoman maladministration, but they suffered even more so from the actions of their own leaders and from persecution inflicted by various non-Muslim creeds upon one another. They also suffered a great deal from fanaticism from Christians who converted to Islam and vied with one another to express their devotion to their new-found religion. Regardless of this, autonomy and freedom of the masses were much better displayed in Turkey than in most developed countries in the West. Edgar Granville says that the minorities owe the protection and continuation of their history, religion, and culture to Turkey and the millet system. One more reason for the insecure feeling of Jews and intolerance toward them in the Empire stemmed from nationalism and revolutionary ideas that began to make inroads into the Ottoman fabric early in the nineteenth century.[16]

Like the Armenians and Greeks in the nineteenth century, an official millet was defined for the Jews in 1865, and included the Jewish communities in all Ottoman territories, headed by the chief rabbi. Some scholars claim that the millet system already existed in the seventeenth century,[17] and that even following the conquest of Istanbul in 1453 the different millets were recognized by the Ottomans.[18] In contrast, recent scholars believe that the Ottomans did not develop uniform structures for their minorities but enabled diverse structures of self-government. These arrangements were the balance between the state's interests and the particular needs of every community.[19] Thus, there was no chief rabbi for the Jews and, unlike some claims in Jewish history, the Jews were not invited to Istanbul upon its conquest by the Ottomans but were forcibly taken there. The Jews who already lived in Istanbul prior to the conquest were sold into slavery. Braude claims there was no post in the fifteenth century such as chief rabbi, with powers similar to those enjoyed by the Ottoman patriarch over all his coreligionists in the Empire.[20] Even the term 'Haham Başı' belongs to a much later period; it came into official use only in the nineteenth century. However, the absence of the title 'Haham Başı' in the fifteenth century cannot indicate that this term was not in use in earlier periods, as before the migration of Jews from Spain and their settlement in Istanbul, Romaniot, Ashkenazi, French, and Italian Jews used the term Rav in Hebrew.[21]

Ottoman rule endowed the Dhimmis with religious, organizational, and somewhat judicial autonomy in managing their inner domestic affairs. As long as the law was enforced and tax collected in an orderly fashion, the Ottoman state refrained from intervening in community matters. In fact, the Ottoman sultans, who saw themselves as heirs of the Caliphate, felt obliged to protect their non-Muslim subjects according to Sharia law. This conception was one aspect of their commitment to justice (adalet).[22] This principle guided the sultans in their attitude toward the Dhimmi. Religious and ethnic heterogeneity that characterized the Empire created a tolerant affiliation toward the Dhimmi. Sunni Islam was much more convenient than the Shia form. In the Ottoman Empire, coerced conversions to Islam were rare and usually took place in times of zeal by individuals.[23] In other words, conversion as a state policy was not institutionalized (except for the Devşirme, a periodic levy by the Ottoman administration of a limited number of male Christian village children for service to the sultan) and increased at times of imperial uncertainty or turmoil, such as during the reign of Mehmet VI (1648–1687), known to be a period of religious zealotry and purification, which led to the conversion of Jews in the capital. Sultan Beyazid II (1447–1512) is also known for putting pressure on Jews to convert. In the Ottoman Empire, conversion also involved voluntary communal or individual conversion for better economic and social status, less taxation, and the privilege of belonging to the victorious class.[24]

Tolerance and violence

Karen Barkey argues that the toleration, as developed in the Ottoman Empire, was a way to qualify and maintain the diversity of the Empire, to organize the different communities, to establish peace and order, and to ensure the loyalty of these communities. Barkey claims that "Ottoman tolerance" had little to do with ideals or with a culture of toleration. Tolerance in the Ottoman period does not mean multiculturalism but means extending rule and consolidating and enforcing state power. Tolerance, then, was only one of many policies of incorporation, such as persecution, assimilation, conversion, or expulsion. Toleration in the imperial setting means absence of persecution of certain groups but not their acceptance into society as full members. Toleration therefore refers to the relations among various religious communities and secular authorities, and it is the outcome of networked and pragmatic forms of rule.[25] Yet, tolerance cannot be understood as a single narrative on the value system ranging from toleration to persecution. A period of high insecurity and even persecution did take place, especially in the seventeenth century, but they can be understood as particular historical and localized cases. Ottoman sultans, for example, were coerced by the zealot Sunni preachers (Kadızadeler) who tried to cleanse the realm of Jews, Christians, and even Sufi orders. It took place during periods of political and economic insecurity and especially after wars, deportations and conversions took place, but it was far from being a uniform, organized, or premeditated policy.[26] Toleration emerged as the negotiated outcome of intergroup relations and was maintained in the first three centuries of Ottoman rule from the top down by the state and from the bottom up by the communities whose interest was to maintain the inter-communal peace and order. Out of the communities' desire to maintain their religious autonomy and community existence free from interference, the community's leadership negotiated on agreements with Ottoman rulers. The result was integration of the non-Muslim communities into the state, although a degree of separation was retained as well, as desired by both parts.[27]

The distinction between Dhimmi and Muslims was manifested in semantics and orthography. Sometimes, in the case of some names that were used by both Muslims and Jews, official certificate writers intentionally used faulty writing when mentioning Jews' names, e.g., Ibraham instead of Ibrahim, Salomon instead of Süleyman, and so on. In general, contemptuous language was used for Dhimmis, men or women. Honorary titles preceding Jewish names were not written, and Jewish and Christian women never gained the title Hatoun, which accompanies a Muslim lady's name. The term öldü, which has a negative connotation, was placed next to a Dhimmi who passed away. For Muslims the Islamic 'rahmetli oldu' is used, whereas for non-Muslims 'toprağı bol olsun' is used, referring to non-Muslim funeral ceremonies. The statement 'öldü' is very impolite for both Muslims and non-Muslims. The Dhimmis' rituals and religious beliefs were described with disgraceful words, and the registration of a convert to Islam in the Sharia court was an 'opportunity' to describe Judaism as the subordinate religion.'

Nonetheless, the enforcement of Islamic law was not consistent and within the Ottoman Empire changes were made according to political and economical circumstances:

1   Gizye, or poll tax, symbolized the subordinate position of the Dhimmi and was a fundamental condition in the patronage between Dhimmis and their Muslim governors. Although the authorities collected it, the policy of debit

and the manner of collection were changed. Only by the end of the seventeenth century was personal collection according to property, under Sharia orders, reinforced again.
2 Segregation rules: The main opposition to coexistence referred to coed living and even more to the existence of Dhimmis' worship houses near mosques. Throughout the Empire, demands to distance Dhimmis by claiming that their presence bothered Muslims and disturbed their prayers were voiced. Constant tension and sometimes conflicts arose in places that were sacred to two or three religions, like the Tomb of Samuel near Jerusalem, where Jews were eventually forbidden from entering. In the Hamams there was no distinction between Muslims and non-Muslims, although sometimes a certain separation was required and in some cities Jews were forbidden from entering the Hamams.
3 A restriction that aims to humiliate and mark non-Muslims: The construction of new synagogues/churches was prohibited and their renovation was allowed only after strict examination assuring no size deviations occurred. A violation of this law entailed heavy penalties. Status symbols were revoked from Dhimmis; their residences' height was restricted; and they were not allowed to build them with stone. Owning Muslim slaves or servants was highly forbidden. Dhimmis were required to wear certain colors, which changed throughout the years. Sometimes specific fabrics and furs were prohibited and restrictions to their head covers and length of cloaks and width of their sleeves, which were status symbols, were in place.[28]

However, in reality many rules were broken and as was the case with the Jewish community, new synagogues were built and white turbans (special to Muslims) were worn, at least in non-Muslim lands.[29] Sources prove that despite its importance, enforcement of Sharia law was not at the top of Ottoman rulers' priorities. When done, it was a result of two influences: the sultan or local ruler on one hand, and religious scholars (ulema) and the masses on the other. A ruler's enthusiasm to enforce religious law was a consequence of religious zealousness, but also due to internal political reasons, such as recruiting public opinion and especially religious staff to the ruler's side. A ruler's weakness usually resulted in a stricter policy toward non-Muslims, and the greater the crisis and decline, the higher the level of intolerance. As mentioned above, the attitude toward non-Muslims reflected the relationship between the ruler and the ulema. Sometimes, when religious leaders considered a moral religious weakening as a cause of various problems, they toughened their attitude toward Dhimmis in an attempt to revive Islam's glorious idealistic past. Therefore, in Istanbul, where ulemas were located, as well as in provincial capitals such as Cairo and Jerusalem, much more adherence to Islam prevailed.[30] Violence against minorities was also inflicted by individual Ottoman officials who took advantage of their position to exploit and damage the communities.[31] Large-scale, state-sponsored ethnic and religious massacres occurred only in the eighteenth century, when it was clear that the Empire was not sustainable and expectations for future interactions by all elements fell. These massacres were administered and organized from the center and carried out at the eastern periphery of the Empire.[32] According to recent analyses, the more communities engage in interethnic relations, especially of a formal and organized sort, the better the chances for peace among the different groups. Thus, ethnic conflict is more likely to occur when communities are insular, separated from others, and when political agendas manipulate ethnic differences for their own advantage. However, since religious identity determined a subject's legal and political status, boundaries were essential and therefore relations within and across communities, brokered by a boundary manager (community leaders) and state officials, were a key to peace.[33]

As for the concept that the law did not discriminate between the Dhimmis, some official documents seem to mention that Jews were preferred over Christians. Jews have always been fewer in number than other minorities, they were an urban and peaceful element who always preferred Ottoman rule and, thus, were loyal to it,[34] although Joseph R. Hacker, in an article dealing with the fifteenth century, argued that even though the description of the Jews in recent historiography has been that of the "authorities' favorites" he had great difficulty tracing the roots of the Jews in the transition period between the Byzantine and Ottoman rule.[35] It should be noted here that the Christian population was much larger than the Jewish one, and from the eighteenth century onwards it gained more political power than the Jews and enjoyed a strengthening European patronage. This did not necessarily work to the benefit of the Christians and sometimes even provoked the Muslims. We might carefully say that in some circles this was because they had never identified with any foreign power. Moreover, from the fifteenth century the Jews were renowned for their efficient and productive existence, as well as for their quiet and adherent attitude toward the Ottomans. Yet, there is no tangible evidence to support this.

Jews and sultans

The sultan and the grand vizier, who ran the state from the seventeenth century, held a specific policy that stemmed from Sharia law, Kanun law, and the custom law. As the defenders of the 'holy law' the sultans were obliged not only to impose order and laws but also to enact justice and trials. They considered strictly retaining the social distinction between Muslims and non-Muslims as highly important, as it was one of the fundamental engagements of the ruler toward his subjects.[36] Sharia was seen as the framework and the source from where guiding principles stemmed for the entire legal system. In reality, however, much of the detail and daily management of political and societal affairs was governed by the Kanun, which produced a complementary legal system of a secular character. The system was pragmatic and flexible; it took into consideration prevailing conditions, practices, customs, and traditions, and it could be changed often, according to given circumstances.[37]

The Jews trusted the sultan, who is always mentioned in Jewish sources along with the title "His Royal Highness" (Yarum Hodo), and every Sabbath and holiday a special prayer for the sake of the sultan was said and even printed in prayer books. As loyal citizens, the Jews identified with the Empire in its constant conflicts with enemies from within and without, and in some Christians' eyes the Jews indeed were identified as loyal adherents of the Ottomans.[38] Even throughout World War I and during the Turkish War of Liberation, the Jewish community in Turkey remained loyal to the Turkish government and Turkey as a whole.[39] However, the perception of the Jews as more loyal than other non-Muslims has changed throughout Ottoman history: The period during which the Ottoman Empire began to decline also witnessed the decline of the Jewish millet within it. Not only the increasing role of European traders, with their capitulations weakening their ability to play a primary role in international trade, but also the growing conservatism of Muslim institutions and the revival of attempts to enforce the conditions imposed on non-Muslims caused the Jews' power to weaken, casting them in the same light as other non-Muslims. This had not been the case until the sixteenth century.[40] According to Sonyel, the Jews did not necessarily feel miserable. They were an integral part of the urban society and very involved in their environment. Wealthy Jews imitated the general society's elite and thus proved their own will to integrate within it. Over the years, Jews occupied government posts as well. The peak was in the nineteenth century, when between 1850 and 1908, 12 Jews served in the Ottoman civil service, among them members of Sephardic, Ashkenazi, and Karaite communities.[41]

Even though Jews benefited from many aspects of Ottoman rule and from favorable, even supportive, attitudes on the part of the authorities, they were affected to some degree by their relations with the general population among whom they lived. These relations differed from one place to another and over time. Except for some individual Jews, the community was seen as weak and vulnerable. The military was a good example. Jews suffered from attacks by the Janissaries as well as other military units, especially in times of unrest. These attacks were not only directed at Jews, but the frequency of these acts implies that Jews were regarded as particularly easy targets.[42]

Social status

Although most attacks on Jews were caused by Christians, and despite the Jews' efficiency and financial status in medium and large cities, they suffered from negative stigma and attacks by Muslims as well. The main characteristic of the social relations between Muslims and Dhimmis in general, and Jews in particular, was the scorn, disgust, and abhorrence Muslims demonstrated toward the Dhimmis. The insults were usually literal or financial, and only seldom were physical. The Jews were apathetic to these insults, which surprised the Europeans, who described sadly the gap between the Jews' good services and the derisive attitude they received from their masters. The Jews' loyalty despite this treatment is also mentioned.[43] Yet, constant psychological and economical pressure was enough to erode their security in the seventeenth century, so the Jews gave a peaceful impression but really felt they were a persecuted and unprotected minority.[44] In fact, in the Arabic-speaking provinces the attitude toward the Jews was more hostile than in Anatolia and the Balkans. One possible reason is that the Jews were culturally and religiously different to the local Arabs, who were not accustomed to the Jews. In addition, the Jews were considered privileged or even a preferred minority by the Ottoman rulers.[45]

Reflections of the Muslim masses on the Dhimmis are widespread in folklore and literature – Turkish and Balkan prose and poetry, proverbs, and allegories. In Turkish proverbs, the Jews were perceived as cautious and calculated, intelligent and perceptive, greedy and despised. More evidence as to how the Jews were perceived by the masses was saved in the *ludicrous* image shadow theater called 'Karagöz.' The figures seemed to have 'typical Jewish' occupations such as rabbi, usurer, midwife, old witch, magician, and others. The Jew is portrayed as a bearded man with faltering Turkish whose prominent characteristics are: up to no good, hostile, cowardly, miserly, and lowly. In other sources the Jew is perceived as isolated and distant. This distance was provoked by fear and made the Jews suspected of having malicious intentions toward all others. Also, the gap between the impression that Jews are in charge of all commerce and their 'tendency' to hide their wealth by living in crowded neighborhoods probably created the perception of Jews' sick miserliness, an explanation that was repeated until the nineteenth century. Very often, successful rich Jews were ignored, whereas poor Jews were often defamed. This treatment had a pure theological meaning, for Jews were 'supposed' to be poor and lame. In the fifteenth and sixteenth centuries, many Jews served as lessees and in fact it was the highest administrative position that a Jew could reach.[46]

However, the Jews were not incapable of defending themselves; the first line of defense would normally be an appeal to the local authorities; if this step was ineffective they could appeal to the central government in Istanbul. The influential Jews in Istanbul were often used as mediators, spokespersons, and protectors of their fellow Jews. This meant that in times and places where the government's effectiveness waned, Jews' status was jeopardized.[47]

The supremacy the Turks felt was aimed at all strata. The Ottomans' negative patronizing attitude toward Christians began to change among small circles of courtiers by the end of the seventeenth century due to military defeats. Muslim festivals, Haj convoys, and successful or unsuccessful military journeys were all reasons for incitement against Dhimmis. The masses' scorn toward the Dhimmis manifested mainly in derogatory names such as Çifit. Sources do not portray a clear picture regarding physical injuries of Jews, but killing Jews on the roads is not mentioned as a rare or unusual thing. It is not surprising, as the Jews were a preferred target and thus many Jewish merchants were robbed and killed. Wearing typical Muslim clothing or hiring security guards (yasakçılar), as Europeans did, was not always successful.[48] Jews were more protected in the cities but, again, in times of turmoil they were easy targets. European travelers testified that Muslims' grudge toward Christians was much worse than the grudge toward Jews. In addition, they testified that the Jews' position in the provinces was the worst of all Dhimmis, but this description is not necessarily accurate.[49]

Greeks and Christians

In the fifteenth and sixteenth centuries, the loathing of Greeks, Armenians, and other Christians toward Jews stemmed from religious and financial motives and was thus probably stronger than that of Muslims. Jews were subject to attacks by Christians, and particularly Greeks, who were generally hostile to Jews. For example, Jews passing through Christian neighborhoods occasionally risked physical assault; sometimes Jews were accused of ritual murder. In the case of the Greeks, religion-based hostility was intensified by economic and social rivalry. As a result, Jews generally preferred to settle near or within Muslim neighborhoods, where they felt more secure, even though they were not completely safe there either.[50]

The emergence of Greek merchants in the Empire in the last third of the seventeenth century and their manning of high positions in the capital contributed to the existing hostility between them and the Jews. In the Balkans, the Jews were identified as the Ottoman conquers' supporters; along with the rise of Greek nationalism in the eighteenth century, this led to another layer of hatred.[51]

The insults were usually verbal and only seldom deteriorated into physical violence and blood libel. The hostility between Christians and Jews was not absolute, but it manifested at the personal and community levels. Hebrew sources mention libels and Christians informing on Jewish communities, as well as drawing attention to Jews' wealth, causing their tax burden to be increased. The blood libels and antisemitic harassment were mainly a phenomenon of the nineteenth century, but also occurred before this period; it is impossible to attribute these harassments to certain populations, either Christians or yeniçeriler who were formerly Christians themselves, but it is clear that low strata, which had religious hatred toward Jews or felt economically inferior or even oppressed by them, were a breeding ground for these sentiments. The central authorities acted strongly against the libels and already in the sixteenth century there were decrees requiring a direct transfer to the royal Divan in such cases, where the judgment would be conducted with no local influence. Many documented libels are dated to the end of the sixteenth century and the 1640s, and it seems that the emergence in this period is related to increased zealotry and inter-community tension, against a background of an unstable political and economic situation.[52]

This problem was enhanced since Jews' occupations in commerce, translation, and brokerage created close ties with Christians. These ties highly affected Christians. In the nineteenth century, Jews still fled to Ottoman lands, especially from Russia where they fled persecution. During the first half of the nineteenth century, Jews still dominated finance, together with Greeks and Armenians, but they started becoming less prosperous than the Greeks or Armenians since they lost their positions in commerce, banking, manufacturing, crafts, and the learned professions, although they still occupied an important place in the economic life of the Empire. This fierce competition, especially with the Armenian sarraf, resulted in violent clashes and even deaths.[53] However, the opponents of the Jews were also the Greeks, with whom they were in direct competition. The Greeks were hostile toward the Jews and became more so following the Greek rebellion of 1821. When the Greek Orthodox patriarch Gregory V was executed on April 22, 1821, his body was dragged through the streets by Jews, after three days of suspension from the gate of Patriarchate. The Greeks never forgot this incident and, perhaps as a result, on October 5, 1821, the entire population of Tripolitsa, where the Ottoman governor of Morea resided, was exterminated in a barbaric way. There were 35,000 Jews among them. A Jew who tried to leave the town of Nauplia in December 1922 (besieged by Greek rebels) was stripped naked and castrated, and then driven around the town and hanged.[54] There are numerous examples of religious antisemitism coming from Greeks but, despite the aforementioned, the greatest example of antisemitism inside the Ottoman Empire was the Damascus blood libel of 1840. Many Jews lost their lives during this incident, and it led to a huge outcry among European Jews to take urgent measures to protect the lives and property of their brothers in the Ottoman Empire.[55] However, in the nineteenth century, when antisemitism raised its head in the Russian Empire, the Balkans, and especially in Western Europe and before the United States gained worldwide recognition as the greatest Jewish haven of modern times, the Ottoman Jews could consider themselves among the most fortunate Jewish communities in the world.[56]

Jews continued to suffer from enmity and hostility from the Greeks and Armenians of the Empire in the nineteenth and twentieth centuries. For instance, in 1885, in Haydarpaşa during the riots of April 1885 caused by the discovery of a desecrated cross on the doorstep of a Greek grocer, the windows of most Jewish houses were broken and passersby were stoned in the street. The riots were so remarkable that Osman Paşa, the minister of war, had to intervene in person in order to stop the fighting. During the Turco-Armenian conflict of the nineteenth century, the Jews supported the Ottoman government and remained loyal to the Empire until the emergence of the Zionist movement. Even Zionism had only a slight effect on the Jews; although the Zionists ran an office in Istanbul, they could only find feeble support among local Jews.[57]

Despite the aforementioned, Barkey claims that although many emphasize the potential for conflict between groups, the intense animosity between Christians and Jews and the visible and invisible rivalry in demographic, economic, and trading terms, the centuries of Pax Ottomanica were relatively calm and free of ethnic or religious strife. Furthermore, according to court records, when local incidents occurred they were not allowed to get out of control; even in cases where members of different communities engaged in fighting across boundaries, their actions did not get out of hand.[58]

The modernization of Ottoman Jewry, which occurred in the nineteenth century, helped the emergence of a new and growing Jewish middle class, especially by the end of the century. The social mobility and cultural integration and modern education ensured Jews' access to liberal professions, new sectors of commerce and finance, government service, and trade. This economic emergence went hand-in-hand with antisemitic sentiments among the Greek and Armenian communities, which resulted in acts of violence against Jews, such as anti-Jewish agitation, blood libels, and physical violence. The Jews therefore emphasized their sympathy toward the state as it protected them in times of such violence.[59]

Communal administration and taxes

The historical examination of the Ottoman Empire and maintenance of relations with the multiethnic and multi-faith communities throughout the first three centuries of rule demonstrates that toleration was the preferred solution to imperial rule over diversity. It was the Ottoman nature to find an intermediate organizational solution with which it could exploit the manpower and skills of the various populations by enlisting local elements into the imperial way of life. Ottomans usually paid much more attention to administrative boundaries of rule than to any markers of difference. Only during periods of state zealotry did physical markers become critical to maintaining boundaries. As long as everyone was controlled, paid taxes, and was accountable to the state through a 'unit,' the Ottomans were satisfied. Difference and separation was a value pursued by the state and the communities themselves. From the sixteenth century, records of community show the degree to which they responded to Ottoman government in collective terms. Every Jew paid taxes within two main frameworks: guild and community.

The cizye, a tax that originates in Islam, symbolized more than anything the inferior legal and constitutional status of the Dhimmis living in a Muslim country. Every foreigner who stayed within the Empire for more than a year had to hold an exempting Berat (an imperial diploma signed with the official seal of the sultan; the Berat gave its holder special rights, privileges, and immunities). Cizye aimed to fund: the royal court and kitchen; army and administration maintenance in the provinces; purchase of wool fabric for the yeniçeriler's uniforms; repair of fortresses in border regions; and maintenance of holy cities and clerks. Sometimes, certain communities' cizye was dedicated to the sultanic Waqf (Vakif in Turkish, sacred property) and so some of the cizye given by a portion of the Jews of Istanbul was dedicated to Mehmet the Conqueror's Waqf. The same holds true for the Jews of Jerusalem, whose cizye was partly donated to the Temple Mount's Waqf.

Another tax the Jews paid was Yave. It was probably first imposed in 1653 as a sort of cizye that immigrants needed to pay during the first decade of their new settlement. This was how Ottoman rule solved the problem of "negative immigration."[60] A tax that was related directly to Jews was the Rav Akçesi, the only unique tax imposed on Jews, was for the right to nominate rabbis and to run a restrictive judicial authority.[61] Since the Jews were segregated in communities, leaders found that the authorities were not interested in the community details of taxation; they were interested in taxes but not in how the Jews paid them.

Modern times

By the time Abdülhamid II was on the throne, the Jewish bourgeoisie of large towns had become more established. At the end of the century, Christians surpassed Jews in many fields, but Jews gradually began to catch up with them. Some of the Jews continued to be employed in Ottoman official service, e.g., Salomon Hatem Efendi, a Jew, was appointed in 1879 by Sultan Abdülhamid's aides de camp in the non-Muslim civic guard, where he established an order to defend the Empire from the Russians. Other Jews were employed at the state council, as professors at the college of medicine, and in governmental service between 1850 and 1908. Jews took part in Ottoman governmental service even after the Young Turk revolution of 1908.[62] The reforms, Tanzimat, of 1876 welcomed an atmosphere of toleration from which the Jews benefited. The guarantees granted to minorities by the Hatt-ı Hümayun of Gülhane, confirmed by the constitution of 1876, were not lip service. Unlike their brothers in Russia, Romania, and most of the Balkan states, Jews in Turkey did not suffer from persecution, which encouraged Jewish migration into Turkey. This migration occurred especially in times of conflict between the Empire and its neighboring states, which increased the number of refugees flocking into Turkish territory.[63]

The Tanzimat reforms were designed to create an Ottoman society consisting of equal individuals connected directly to the state, lacking the segregation of the millet. In other words, the Ottoman administration sought to dispense with the structure of the classical system in favor of creating both a centralized state and a community of equal individuals integrated in the notion of Ottomanism (İttihad-ı anasır), surpassing ethno-cultural distinctions, on the one hand, while on the other hand, non-Muslim minorities would no longer seek separation from the Empire so the tendency for ethnic disintegration would be directed from liberation toward personal emancipation and social integration.[64] Later on, it was not the 'Ottoman nation' (Ottomanism) of citizens that replaced millet inequalities, but rather national states of non-Muslim minorities. The dilemma of duality that prevailed between the notion of Ottoman citizenship and equal accommodation of minority distinctions remained unresolved. The Christian communities in particular moved out of the millet notion directly into a national understanding without ever having accepted Ottoman citizenship.[65] One of the outcomes of Ottomanism was the grudge created among the Muslim people and the rulers of the Empire, particularly the Turks who had invested great hopes in the principle of citizenship equality to save the state from collapse. The failure of Ottomanism, in other words, created the legal and political domination of the Muslim millet.[66]

One of the most important libels that took place in the border period between the Ottoman and Turkish Republic eras was the Sami (Samuel) M. Günzberg trial. Günzberg was a renowned Jewish dentist who worked in the Ottoman court; he was Atatürk's private dentist. He was also a community activist from Istanbul, and was attacked by the Turkish journalist Ebüzziya Tevfik as part of the latter's campaign against the Jews, starting from 1909 when he translated antisemitic materials to Turkish. Günzberg was accused of being a spy against the Ottoman Empire and that his clinic served as a meeting spot between German officers and Muslim women – the officers received confidential information this way. Günzberg sued Tevfik, who was convicted; however, following his appeal the trial was reopened and lasted until 1928, when Günzberg finally won the case. However, during these years the trial served as an open stage for attacks against Jews.[67]

The Günzberg trial was the last significant and influential antisemitic incident before the formative years of the Turkish Republic.

The War of Liberation and onwards: the formative years

As seen in the previous sections, antisemitism was not common in the Ottoman Empire, at least not in the same form or quantity as in some Christian lands in Eastern and Western Europe during the same era. If antisemitism existed, its manifestations were part of the skepticism regarding 'foreigners' that the ruling Turks felt. This skepticism was mainly within the range of economy and culture. During the last periods of the Empire, a political element was added, which turned this skepticism into pure xenophobia. In the economic sphere, middle class Turks' hatred of minorities increased. In the cultural sphere, there is much evidence of non-Turks being ridiculed, as expressed in the Karagöz Theater, discussed earlier, which mocks the clothing, accent, and behavior of Greeks, Armenians, Arabs, Europeans, and Jews. In the political sphere, suspicion by the ruling Turks increased mainly at the end of the nineteenth century and during the first two decades of the twentieth century toward all ethnic groups that aspired to national autonomy by dismantling the Empire, including Jews in the land of Israel. Criticism was directed at Jews and actions aimed at restricting Zionist activity, but usually with less violence and hatred than against Armenians, Arabs, or Greeks.[68]

Once the Turkish Republic was established, it became a smaller country but with much more homogeneity regarding origin, culture, and religion: the majority consisted of Turks and Muslims. There were three main religious minority groups, and the smallest among them was the Jews, after the Armenians and the Greeks. Also, the Turks had no collective historical memory of armed strife with the Jews, such as was the case of the other minorities, who before and during the Turkish War of Independence collaborated with the Allied Forces in invading and carving up Anatolia. This betrayal came to dominate the general perception toward all non-Muslim groups, although the Jewish minority had traditionally been known as the 'loyal nation' (millet-i sadıka). Since the Ottoman era, the general view of them had been influenced by the negative image attributed to Greeks and Armenians.[69] In addition, until 1948 there was no foreign state to support the Jews, unlike the case of the Greeks and Armenians. Minorities were called upon to undergo Turkification for their integration. It is interesting to note that, compared to other minorities, Jews have been seen as the most reliable minority. Yet, the conditions that characterized the minority–majority relations in the Turkish Republic were different from those of the Ottoman era. First of all, a Turkish nationalist ideology arose even toward the end of the Ottoman era but was nurtured by the educational elite only. In the Turkish Republic, Mustafa Kemal Atatürk cultivated a spirit of national pride among the entire Turkish society, even though he consistently abstained from referring to nationalism against Turkey's minorities. Despite that, it was quite natural that the Turks saw the minorities as a stumbling block on the path to creating a homogeneous state. Second, the economic system operated against the minorities' interests. In the Ottoman Empire, specific spheres were almost exclusively defined as 'minority oriented,' such as bureaucracy and parts of trade, where minorities could utilize their knowledge of languages and ties outside the Empire. Already in the last decade of the Empire, the Young Turks leaders called for the transfer of governmental and financial power to Turks and also did this themselves. In Turkey, a generation of educated Turks took over the financial power centers at the expense of the minorities. However, there has never been an official policy of discrimination in Turkey toward its minorities and their socioeconomic status has usually been stable.[70]

Another significant component that differentiates between the Ottoman period and the Republican one is the number of Jewish citizens. During the first two decades of the Republic, the Jewish population decreased from 100,000 to an estimated 20,000.

Who is a Turk? The first years of the Republic

When the Turkish republican state was founded, the deep resentment the Ottoman statesmen felt toward the failure of the equal citizenship policy was reflected in its founders' political, social, and cultural viewpoint. The effects of the failure of Ottomanism were evident in the attitudes of nationalist leaders during the Turkish War of Liberation (1919–1922). The new leaders, who 'learned the lesson' from Ottoman experiences, seemed to have lost their belief that reconciliation would be achieved by different treatment of minorities and that the nationalist equality of citizenship in a national unity framework could succeed. The nationalist leaders adopted a strong policy of union of the Muslim elements (Ittihad-ı anasır-ı İslamiyye). In other words, the new national form was sought from within the Muslim elements. This meant that non-Muslim minorities were excluded from the early stages of the nation-state building process. The founders of the republican state agreed on the terms of the Treaty of Lausanne (signed on July 24, 1923), which included paragraphs on citizenship equality, but the Turkish conceptualization of the term minority was expanded from minority protection on a religious basis to a notion that was ethnic and linguistic in nature. According to the Turks, there was no ethnic or linguistic minority in the country except the historical non-Muslim communities. This is how the Turkish minority rights regime established a strong continuity between the sociopolitical and legal stratification of the Ottoman millet system and minority/majority classification of republican Turkey. This way, the issue of minority rights was exclusively associated with millet status in the Turkish regime. The Lausanne framework therefore aimed at constituting legal equality without neglecting distinct circumstances of non-Muslim Turkish citizens. Accordingly, minorities were granted equal treatment in education, religious practices, and cultural foundation spheres.[71] According to Aktürk, the term millet has been kept in place by the Turkish Republic as the definition of the modern nation, which evades and suppresses any ethnic distinctions among Muslims. This policy prevented the Turkish Republic from cataloging the ethnic background of its Muslim citizens but by the same token individuals or groups that emphasized their ethnic identity in public, such as Kurds, were suppressed and their political, cultural, ethnic, and linguistic rights were firmly rejected. In other words, the Turkish nation is identified as a Muslim nation. According to Aktürk, the definition of Turkish nationhood is neither territorial nor mono-ethnic but rather mono-religious (despite the secular agenda of its founders) and anti-ethnic, continuing the legacy of the Islamic millet under the Ottoman Empire.[72] The definition of nationalism is not civic versus ethnic and the supremacy of religious over ethnic categories in Turkey, as a historical legacy of the Ottoman millet system might be comparable to most post-Ottoman states in the Islamic Middle East and North Africa, in contrast to the supremacy of ethnicity and religion in Western Europe. Therefore, Turkish identity with reference to the Islamic millet and Ottoman legacy conceptions leads to Turkey's exclusive policies on issues such as immigration, citizenship, public employment, and minority policies.[73]

Despite this, or perhaps because of it, the Jews assisted Turkey in diplomatic ways; in January 1919 the grand rabbi of Turkey, Haim Nahum (1872–1960), was sent by İsmet Paşa (İsmet İnönü), who served as the chief of the Turkish delegation to the Lausanne talks, and by the minister of finance, Cavit Bey, to go to America to encourage the American government to renew its relations with Turkey. Rabbi Nahum was involved in Turkish politics and he made pro-Turkish statements while interacting with foreign powers.[74] Nahum is actually credited by the Islamists and ultranationalists in Turkey as the one who convinced İsmet to accept the imposition of secularism in Turkey as well as the abolition of the Caliphate.[75] In other words, Jews were to blame for secularism in Turkey.

Among the opponents who appealed against the internationalism of Istanbul and the relegation of the Turkish state to the interior of Anatolia in 1919 were Jewish academics such as Professor Abraham Galanté and Michon Ventoura. During the War of Liberation, the majority of the Turkish Jewry supported Mustafa Kemal Atatürk with all their resources. The Jews supported the Kemalists during the elections that took place in Turkey in 1923. The Jews also participated in the general joy and celebrations following the signing of the Treaty of Lausanne. According to the Lausanne Treaty, the Turkish government was obligated to recognize the rights of religious and ethnic minorities in Turkey (Article 39), who were allowed to run social institutions, funds, and schools (Article 40). In fact, the Lausanne Treaty excluded sectarian Muslim minorities like the Alevis, as well as several ethnic and linguistic groups such as Kurds, Arabs, and even the Assyrian community in Turkey, who up until today has no legal capacity to teach its liturgical language. The Western powers accepted these limitations only in order to protect the remaining non-Muslim portion of the population, which was reduced after two wars (the 1915 incidents involving the Armenians and the forced population exchange in 1923–1924 between Turkey and Greece). The Jews, however, were recognized as a protected minority. The Turkish leadership was dissatisfied with these articles as it harmed its attempts to create a homogeneous society. Thus, young educated Turkish Jews who feared hostility pursued a rejection of this recognition. The government itself pressured the Jews, portraying them as Spanish citizens.[76] Consequently, on September 15, 1925, the Jewish community renounced its rights granted by paragraphs two and three of Article 42 of the Lausanne Treaty. This triggered a chain reaction and the Armenian and Greek communities also renounced similar rights. The renouncement declarations resulted in harsh criticism at the international level, including from the American Jewish Committee. It seemed that the young nation-state rejected any sign of the old millet system. It had unwillingly accepted the minority provisions at Lausanne in order not to prolong and obstruct the negotiations and was not particularly enthusiastic about implementing them, as they constituted propitious grounds for foreign intervention.

However, despite the Jews' optimism and the Turkish leaders' pro-Jewish rhetoric (such as praise that was published in the booklet released during the Lausanne Committee, claiming that the Jews had always proved their loyalty to the motherland), this did not go well for the Jews. Although the Lausanne Treaty provided non-Muslim minorities with a substantive right to ethno-cultural and religious diversity as well as citizenship equality, the imprints of the millet system were still in effect in two ways: (1) one's faith continued to determine the criteria of 'inclusion' or 'exclusion' when it came to minority/majority classification. In other words, the non-Muslims were considered 'the others.' (2) The understanding of non-Muslims during the war as a fifth column caused a loss of confidence in both minorities' rights and the minorities themselves in the eyes of the regime, as well as the Turkish public. Non-Muslim Turkish citizens were perceived as 'perilous,' 'suspect,' and 'foreign' within the general Turkish society. This perspective mainly rested on non-Muslims' collaboration with the occupying powers during World War I, especially Armenians, in their aspiration to obtain the right to self-determination over territories from Ottoman land, as appeared in the Sevres Treaty and was superseded by the Lausanne Treaty. In addition, non-Muslim minorities often found themselves in a vulnerable position. Century-long traditions, concepts, and confrontations continued to poison the plausibility for citizenship equality for non-Muslims, as well as their integration within the new Turkish society. The minorities were perceived as amorphous by the Muslim Turks: They were included in the Turkish citizenship category (tabiiyet) but were excluded from the Turkish nationality (milliyet), as the latter was a privilege reserved for Turkish Muslim citizens alone. Throughout the years, the formula of national citizenship denied ethno-linguistic and cultural differentiations. The Turkish regime could not reach a compromise between the universal aspect of citizenship equality and the particular treatment of non-Muslim minorities. At this stage, the basis of exclusion or inclusion was no longer the legal political and social implication of the millet system but the legal political conceptualizations and practices of the republican citizenship when Turkish politics created equivalence between citizenship equality and national uniformity while simultaneously serving as an exclusivist instrument toward ethno-cultural others.

The Turkish constitution recognized the equality of all citizens before the law, regardless of language, religion, ethnicity, political affiliation, etc., but it was also affirmed that differential treatment would not be given to any segment of the Muslim population (Article 10). Both the 1961 and 1982 constitutions stressed the "indivisible unity of state with its nation and territory" (Article 3), which would be subjected to amendment under no condition (Article 4). To this end, state authorities were constitutionally charged with the task of preserving national integrity (Article 5), which is why the exercise of constitutional rights and freedoms, including freedom of religion, thought, expression, communication, press, and association were conditional upon the preservation of this foundational unity. It was clearly laid down that fundamental rights and freedoms would be curtailed if they were used in contravention of the principle of national unity and territorial integrity of the state (Articles 13–14).

Policy of the unified Turkish society

The first blow to the Lausanne Treaty came from the new Civil Code adopted in 1926. While it approved the establishment of new religious, social, and charitable foundations, it excluded non-Muslim foundations. Article 74 (2) of the new Civil Code stated: "foundations that aim to support members of a certain race or a community cannot be registered."[77] Generally speaking, in the 1920s, educational and cultural policies were subjected to unitary requirements and a homogenization process of the state and nation, what is also known as the process of 'Turkification.' For instance, the right to learn or receive instruction in mother tongues was prohibited for the non-Muslim minorities. The Turkish language was stipulated as the sole language of instruction in schools, in accordance with Article 42 of the constitution. The Law on Foreign Language Education stipulated that only Turkish would be taught to all Turkish citizens as their mother tongue.[78] It should be noted that the Turkification process is seen as the main reason for discrimination against minorities in Turkey. For example, Erdal Doğan, one of the lawyers representing the plaintiffs in the Zirve murder case,[79] believes that the problem of ethnic and racial discrimination is deeply rooted in Turkey: "Since the founding of the Turkish Republic, our country had been built according to the concept of 'oneness.' To 'Turkify' everyone, governments normalized hate speech and did not recognize ethnic or religious differences." According to the lawyer, the goal of such policies was to label as an enemy all those who were not Sunni Muslim Turks. That is why, according to Doğan, even criminalizing discrimination is ineffective due to the lack of emphasis on constitutional equality.[80]

As stated, the anti-Jewish stance of the Turkish public could be seen as part of a hostile attitude that prevailed toward all minorities at that time. During the 1920s, the Turks were frustrated due to their losses in the Italo-Turkish War (1911), Balkan Wars (1912–1913), World War I (1914–1918), and the War of Independence (1919–1922). From the remains of the Ottoman Empire, on torn, poor, burnt, and demolished lands, an independent Turkey arose. The Turks felt themselves betrayed and blamed the world, especially their minorities, for collaborating with the enemies during wartime. The masses did not see any differentiation between the Jews and Greeks/Armenians. In some cases the Turks adopted an apologetic stance toward the Greeks and Armenians as they confronted assertions of massacres coming from both minorities, and thus were obliged to express decency toward them. Furthermore, the Turks believed that both Armenians and Greeks 'had paid enough,' whereas Jews had not been hurt by any means. Furthermore, it was much easier and less perilous as the Jews had no backing support, whereas the Armenians and Greeks had patronage in Christian states. The Turks strived to cleanse their state of strangers and thus directed the bulk of their rage against the Jews. The masses have always disrespected the minorities from the Ottoman era until today.[81] It still exists in proverbs in use today. One of the famous proverbs against Jews are: "Yahudi züğürtleyince eski defterleri açarmış" (When a Jew goes bankrupt he opens up his old books). Another allegedly typical character of the Jew is greed. Many examples exist: "Sarı Yahudi" (Yellow Jew) figuratively means a Jew who is greedy for money, "Yahudi pazarlığı" (a Jewish bargaining).[82] An example of an antisemitic publication in the years preceding the establishment of the Republic of Turkey is the writings of Ebüzziya Tevfik, which were published in *Tasvir-i Efkar* (*Picture of Ideas*), which he started editing in 1910.[83] This journal showed some photos of Atatürk from the front in Çanakkale during World War I, despite the prohibition and call for censorship of those times by Enver Paşa. Tevfik is known as "the first professional anti-Semite in Turkey." He interviewed the chief rabbi of Izmir, Rabbi Moshe Levy, and in his article he used prejudiced and mocking language regarding Jews. From this interview onward, some local journals, especially humoristic journals, started attacking Jews. One example is *İleri*, whose owner, Celal Nuri İleri, was also a member of parliament (1920–1935), and whose publication began in December 1922. In one of its articles it referred to Jews and called them "blood mongers." Jews were depicted as hypocrites that do not deserve to be called "loyal" due to having a pro-Greek attitude during the Greek occupation of Thrace.[84] A similar press campaign also took place in Edirne, a city with a significant Jewish population. The local newspaper *Paşaeli* criticized Jews for speaking Ladino. A similar stance was encountered in the Izmir press: A local newspaper, *Türk Sesi* (Turkey's Voice), called on Muslim merchants to cooperate with each other to fight against the "Jewish menace," and to avoid working in Jewish-owned trade houses. All these campaigns incited the Turkish public against Jews, and the masses chanted "Jews get out" in street gatherings.

In addition to the external affairs tingeing the relations between Muslims and non-Muslims in Turkey in the 1920s, the regime itself was not very stable and

30   *From Ottoman rule to modern times*

needed to defend itself. This situation was much more significant for the Jews, as usually it was the authorities who protected them. Military emergency situations, clashes, and political executions prevailed in Turkey at that time, and the Jews, who were protected under Kemalist rule, were assaulted as a surrogate for protesting against the government. Also, the raging antisemitism in Europe after World War I infiltrated Turkey and young nationalists sometime absorbed its echoes.[85] Actually, despite no declared or official antisemitism in Turkey, until the 1960s a Jew could not own a weapon in the Turkish military, could not be accepted as a policeman, and could not gain any governmental position. Jews owning factories were discriminated against via government allocation of funds or import permits. A veiled discrimination also existed in academic institutions, where concealed 'numerus clausus' existed.[86] Bali adds that the Kemalist xenophobic policy had an economic manifestation as well; within the nationalization process, the non-Muslim population, including the Jews, faced the above-mentioned discrimination and exclusion from public service as the Republic's founding cadres viewed them as foreigners to the Turkish body, politically and socially. In their eyes, the true owners of the country were the 'real' Turks, the Muslim population who fought for the independence of Turkey in the Turkish War of Independence. For them, the non-Muslims did not shed their blood for their country and also took advantage of the situation to amass wealth. Thus, trade and industry should be given to the authentic children of the nation, the Muslim Turks.[87]

Avner Levi divides the history of Jews in Turkey, from their relations with the Turkish authorities and society's point of view, into four periods, 1923–1933, 1933–1943, post-war to the end of the 1960s, and the 1960s onwards.[88]

Notes

1 Non-Muslim millets should not be described as 'minorities.' The communities did not see themselves as such and nor did the Ottomans. They were religious communities. There was no word for minority in Ottoman Turkish. The term was introduced with the Treaty of Lausanne along with the modern Turkish 'azınlık,' and therefore an anachronism if used before 1923.
2 Karen Barkey, *Empire of Difference: The Ottomans in Comparative Perspective* (New York: Cambridge University Press, 2008), p. 120.
3 Ahmet İçduygu and B.A. Soner, "Turkish minority rights regime: between difference and equality," *Middle Eastern Studies*, 42, 3 (2006), pp. 449–450.
4 Salahi R. Sonyel, *Minorities and the Destruction of the Ottoman Empire* (Ankara: Turkish Historical Society Printing House, 1993), p. 48.
5 Yaron Ben-Naeh, *Jews in the Realm of the Sultans* (Jerusalem: Magness Press, 2007), pp. 77–78.
6 Barkey, *Empire of Difference*, p. 153.
7 Avigdor Levy, "The Ottoman–Jewish symbiosis in the fifteenth and sixteenth centuries," in: Avigdor Levy (ed.), *The Jews of the Ottoman Empire* (Princeton, NJ: Darwin Press, 1994), p. 16.
8 İçduygu and Soner, "Turkish Minority Rights Regime," p. 450.
9 Levy, "The Ottoman–Jewish Symbiosis," pp. 16–17.
10 Ibid., p. 18.

11 This discussion can be found in: Benjamin Braude and Lewis Bernard, *Christians and Jews in the Ottoman Empire: The Functioning of a Plural Society* (New York: Holmes & Meier, 1982). Other classic statements include: H.A.R. Gibb and H. Bowen, *Islamic Society and the West: A Study of the Impact of Western Civilization on Moslem culture in the Near East, Vol. 1, Islamic Society in the Eighteenth Century Part 1* (London: Oxford University Press, 1950); Aron Rodrigue and Nancy Reynolds, "Difference and tolerance in the Ottoman Empire," *Stanford Humanities Review*, 5 (1995), pp. 81–92; Kemal Karpat and Yetkin Yildirim, *The Ottoman Mosaic: Exploring Models for Peace by Re-exploring the Past* (Seattle, WA: Cune Press, 2010); Zachary Karabell, *Peace be Upon You: The story of Muslim, Christian and Jewish Coexistence* (New York: Alfred A. Knopf, 2007); Mark Haberlein, "A 16th century German traveller's perspective on discrimination and tolerance in the Ottoman Empire," in: Guðmundur Halfdanarson (ed.), *Discrimination and Tolerance in Historical Perspective* (Pisa: Pisa University Press, 2008), pp. 71–84; Halil İnalcık, "The status of the Greek Orthodox patriarch under the Ottomans," *Turcica*, 21–23 (1991), pp. 407–435; Suraiya Faroqhi, *The Ottoman Empire and the World Around It* (London: Tauris & Co, 2004); İlber Ortaylı, "Osmanlı'da Tolerans ve Tesamuh," in İlber Ortaylı, *Osmanlı Barışı* (İstanbul: Timaş, 2007), pp. 53–60; Stefanov Svetoslav, "Millet system in the Ottoman Empire: example for oppression or for tolerance?" *Bulgarian Historical Review*, 2–3 (1997), pp. 138–142.
12 İçduygu and Soner, "Turkish Minority Rights Regime," p. 450.
13 Barkey, *Empire of Difference*, p. 139.
14 Levy, "The Ottoman–Jewish Symbiosis," p. 19.
15 Sonyel, *Minorities and the Destruction*, pp. 445–446.
16 Ibid., pp. 446–448.
17 Ben-Naeh, *Jews in the Realm of the Sultans*, p. 78.
18 Barkey, *Empire of Difference*, p. 131.
19 Levy, "The Ottoman–Jewish Symbiosis," p. 43.
20 Sonyel, *Minorities and the Destruction*, p. 52.
21 Levy, "The Ottoman–Jewish Symbiosis," pp. 54–55.
22 'Justice' in this context means having every religious/social group in its place and keeping a segregation between all groups.
23 Ben-Naeh, *Jews in the Realm of the Sultan*, pp. 78–79.
24 Barkey, *Empire of Difference*, pp. 122–123, 126.
25 Ibid., p. 110.
26 Ibid, p. 113.
27 Ibid, p. 114.
28 Ben-Naeh, *Jews in the Realm of the Sultans*, pp. 81–82.
29 Barkey, *Empire of Difference*, p. 121.
30 Ben-Naeh, *Jews in the Realm of the Sultans*, p. 83. On times of religious zealousness, see: ibid., pp. 84–86.
31 Barkey gives an example of Şeyhüllslam Hocazade Mesut who became the judge of Bursa in 1642 and ordered a newly built church's closure according to the Sharia injunction against building of new worship houses which are not mosques. When the grand vizier heard about it he dismissed the judge. In response, Muslim mobs vandalized the city but were punished and arrested afterward. See: Barkey, *Empire of Difference*, pp. 113–114.
32 Ibid., p. 114.
33 Ibid., pp. 117–118.
34 Levy, "The Ottoman–Jewish Symbiosis," p. 45.
35 Joseph R. Hacker, "Ottoman policy toward the Jews and Jewish attitudes toward the Ottomans during fifteenth century," in Benjamin Braude and Lewis Bernard (eds.), *Christians and Jews in the Ottoman Empire* (New York: Holmes & Meier, 1982), pp. 117–126.

36 Ben-Naeh, *Jews in the Realm of the Sultans*, p. 91.
37 Levy, "The Ottoman–Jewish Symbiosis," pp. 17–18.
38 Ben-Naeh, *Jews in the Realm of the Sultans*, p. 105.
39 The Jews did not hesitate to use some of their own publications to help Turkey come out of the war with a minimal loss. Yet, some Jews served the cause of the Entente powers, especially in the sphere of espionage: Sonyel, *Minorities and the Destruction*, pp. 430, 439.
40 Ibid., p. 133.
41 Ibid., p. 221.
42 Levy, "The Ottoman–Jewish Symbiosis," p. 40.
43 Ben-Naeh, *Jews in the Realm of the Sultans*, p. 90.
44 Ibid., p. 106.
45 Levy, "The Ottoman–Jewish Symbiosis," p. 41.
46 Ben-Naeh, *Jews in the Realm of the Sultans*, pp. 98–99, 114.
47 Levy, "The Ottoman–Jewish Symbiosis," p. 41.
48 Ben-Naeh, *Jews in the Realm of the Sultans*, p. 197.
49 Ibid., pp. 96–97.
50 Levy, "The Ottoman–Jewish Symbiosis," pp. 40–41.
51 Ben-Naeh, *Jews in the Realm of the Sultans*, p. 99.
52 Ibid., pp. 100–101.
53 Sonyel, *Minorities and the Destruction*, p. 221.
54 Ibid., p. 221.
55 On Damascus blood libel, see: Jonathan Frankel, *The Damascus Affair: "Ritual Murder," Politics, and the Jews in 1840* (Cambridge: Cambridge University Press, 1997); Ronald Florence, *Blood Libel: The Damascus Affair of 1840* (Madison, WI: University of Wisconsin Press, 2004).
56 Avigdor Levy, "Ottoman Jewry in the modern era, 1826–1923," in: Avigdor Levy (ed.), *The Jews of the Ottoman Empire* (Princeton, NJ: Darwin Press, 1994), p. 123.
57 Sonyel, *Minorities and the Destruction*, pp. 310–311. On the Ottoman Empire and Zionism, see: Esther Benbassa, "Zionism in the Ottoman Empire at the end of 19th century and the beginning of 20th century," *Studies in Zionism*, 11, 2 (1990), pp. 127–140; Mim Kemal Öke, "The Ottoman Empire, Zionism and the Question of Palestine," *International Journal of Middle East Studies*, 14, 3 (1982), pp. 329–341; Esther Benbassa and Aron Rodrigue, *Sephardi Jewry: A History of the Judeo-Spanish Community, 14th–20th Centuries*, second edition (Berkeley, CA: University of California Press, 2000), pp. 116–159; Yuval Ben-Bassat and Eyal Ginio (eds.), *Late Ottoman Palestine: The Period of Young Turk Rule* (London: I.B. Tauris, 2011); Michelle Campos, *Ottoman Brothers: Muslims, Christians, and Jews in Early Twentieth-Century Palestine* (Stanford, CA: Stanford University Press, 2011); Avigail Jacobson, *From Empire to Empire: Jerusalem Between Ottoman and British Rule – Space, Place, and Society* (Syracuse, NY: Syracuse University Press, 2011); Rashid Khalidi, *Palestinian Identity: The Construction of Modern National Consciousness* (New York: Columbia University Press, 1997); Salim Tamari, *Mountains Against the Sea: Essays on Palestinian Society and Culture* (Berkeley, CA: University of California Press, 2009).
58 Barkey, *Empire of Difference*, p. 146.
59 Levy, "Ottoman Jewry in the modern era," pp. 115–116, 541.
60 Ben-Naeh, *Jews in the Realm of the Sultans*, pp. 116–117.
61 Ibid., p. 118. On other taxes, see: ibid., pp. 116–123.
62 Sonyel, *Minorities and the Destruction*, pp. 308–309.
63 Ibid., p. 310.
64 İçduygu and Soner, "Turkish Minority Rights Regime," p. 451.
65 Ibid., p. 451.

Between Ottoman rule and the Republic 33

66 Ibid., p. 452. Some scholars refer to the Muslim community as a millet as well, even though the organizing principles of the Muslim community were different and were divided according to Askeri (military) and reaaya/raya (the flock). Some scholars claim that the term millet for Muslims was in use only in the late Ottoman Empire.
67 Avner Levi, *History of the Jews in the Republic of Turkey* (Jerusalem: Lafir Press, 1992), p. 17 [Hebrew]; Rıfat N. Bali, "The banalization of hate: antisemitism in contemporary Turkey," in: Alvin H. Rosenfeld (ed.), *Resurgent Antisemitism: Global Perspectives* (Bloomington, IN: Indiana University Press, 2013), pp. 313–314. See also: Rıfat N. Bali, *Sarayın ve Cumhuriyetin Dişçibaşısı Sami Günzberg* (Cağaloğlu, İstanbul: Kitabevi, 2007). The book was reprinted in 2014.
68 Jacob M. Landau, "Al Dmuta Shel Haantishemiyut BaRapublika Haturkit" [On the Form of Antisemitism in the Turkish Republic], in: *Ninth World Congress of Jewish Studies, Division B, Vol. II, The History of the Jewish People* (Jerusalem: World Union of Jewish Studies, 1986), p. 77 [Hebrew].
69 Toktaş, "Perceptions of antisemitism," p. 205.
70 Landau, "Al Dmuta Shel Haantishemiyut," p. 78.
71 İçduygu and Soner, "Turkish Minority Rights Regime," pp. 452–453.
72 Sener Akturk, "Persistence of the Islamic *millet* as an Ottoman legacy: mono-religious and anti-ethnic definition of Turkish nationhood," *Middle Eastern Studies*, 45, 6 (2009), pp. 900, 904.
73 Akturk, "Persistence of the Islamic *millet*," p. 906. On Turkish nationalism and identity, see: Soner Çağaptay, "Citizenship policies in interwar Turkey," *Nations and Nationalism*, 9, 4 (2003), pp. 601–620; Soner Çağaptay, "Race, assimilation, and Kemalism: Turkish nationalism and the minorities in the 1930s," *Middle Eastern Studies*, 40, 3 (2004), pp. 86–101; Kemal Kirişçi, "Disaggregating Turkish citizenship and immigration practices," *Middle Eastern Studies*, 36, 3 (2000), pp. 1–22; Faruk Birtek, "Affiliation to affinity: citizenship in the transition from empire to the nation-state," in: Seyla Benhabib, Ian Shapiro, and Danilo Petranovic (eds.), *Identities, Affiliations, and Allegiances* (New York: Cambridge University Press, 2007), pp. 17–44.
74 On Nahum, see: Esther Benbassa (ed.), *Haim Nahum: A Sephardic Chief Rabbi in Politics, 1892–1923* (Tuscaloosa, AL: University Alabama Press, 1995).
75 Bali, "The banalization of hate," pp. 312–313. According to Bali, the Islamists believe that "Secret Protocols of Lausanne" exist, a paraphrase of the Protocols of the eldest of Zion.
76 Ever since Spain's Law on Citizenship for Sephardic Jews came into force, scholars and journalists have discussed the possibility of Turkish Jews fleeing to Spain as a result of growing antisemitism. See, for example: http://forward.com/opinion/320352/will-Antisemitism-drive-turkeys-sephardic-jews-to-spain and www.Hürriyet.com.tr/dunya/29125234.asp, retrieved September 6, 2015.
77 Füsun Türkmen and Emre Öktem, "Foreign policy as a determinant in the fate of Turkey's non-Muslim minorities: a dialectical analysis," *Turkish Studies*, 14, 3 (2013), p. 5.
78 İçduygu and Soner, "Turkish minority rights regime," p. 457.
79 The Zirve affair is the Zirve Publishing House massacre, which took place on April 18, 2007 in Zirve Publishing House, Malatya, Turkey. Three employees of the Bible publishing house were attacked, tortured, and murdered by five Sunni Muslim assailants. See: Erkan Acar and Çetin Çiftçi, "Malatya'daki vahşi cinayete 'terör'den tutuklama," *Zaman*, April 24, 2007: www.zaman.com.tr/_malatyadaki-vahsi-cinayete-terorden-tutuklama_530979.html, retrieved March 10, 2014.
80 Meltem Naz Kaşo, "Minority groups face increasing discrimination in Turkey," *Today's Zaman*, March 20, 2014: www.todayszaman.com/news-342607-minority-groups-face-increasinGodiscrimination-in-Turkey.html, retrieved March 24, 2014.
81 See, for example: Abraham Galanté, "The Jew in Folk Proverbs," *Reshumot*, n.s 7 (1947), pp. 163–166 (nos. 26–49) [Hebrew].
82 http://ayrimcisozluk.blogspot.co.il, retrieved on September 12, 2012.

83 On Tevfik, see: Özgür Türesay, "Antisionisme et antisémitisme dans la presse ottomane d'Istanbul à l'époque jeune turque (1909–1912): L'exemple d'Ebüzziya Tevfik," *Turcica*, 41 (2009), pp. 147–178.
84 Mücahit Düzgün, "Cumhuriyetin İlanından İsrail'in Kuruluşuna Kadar Türkiye'deki Yahudiler," *Çağdaş Türkiye Tarihi Araştırmaları Dergisi*, 3, 9–10 (1999–2000), p. 68.
85 Levi, *History of the Jews*, pp. 15–16.
86 David Achi-Yaakov, "Al Yehudey Turkiya [on the Jews of Turkey]," *Gesher* [Bridge], 4, 61 (1969), pp. 82, 84 [Hebrew].
87 Bali, "The banalization of hate," p. 309.
88 Avner Levi, "Yahas HaShiltonot ve HaChevra HaTurkim Klapey HaYehudim Agav Parashat Aliza Niego [The attitude of the Turkish authorities and society toward Jews in the aftermath of the Aliza Niego Incident]," in: Avraham Hayim (ed.), *Chevra VeKehilla: MiDivrey Hakongress HaBenleumi HaSheni LeCheker Moreshet Yahadut Sfarad ve HaMizrach 1985* [Society and Community: Proceedings of the Second (International) Congress on Sephardi and Oriental Jewish Heritage] (Jerusalem: Misgav Yerushalayim, 1991), p. 237 [Hebrew].

2 From the 1920s to the 1990s

1923–1933

After four centuries in which an Islamic code for minorities recognized Ottoman Jews as a specific part of the nation, in 1923 Jewish community officials exchanged differentiated special status for universal citizenship in the Turkish Republic, effacing communal autonomy for the promise of emancipation.[1] This period was characterized by intolerance toward minorities, including Jews. In this period, Turkish society made an effort to recover from the tragic results of World War I and the War of Independence that followed it. On the other hand, Turkish society was committed to the Kemalist reforms in education, language, law, secularism, etc. on its way to rapid modernization. Thus, the minorities were called to join these missions, although they were occasionally condemned for maintaining their communal uniqueness. From the beginning of this decade there was a palpable sense of hostility in some parts of Turkish society. As a consequence, Jews migrated from Turkey to Egypt and South America mainly.[2] One important example of intolerance is the Aliza Niego Affair:[3] On August 17, 1927, Aliza Niego, a young Jewish girl from Istanbul, was murdered in Galata, Istanbul. The murderer, Osman Ratib, a married man, a father and grandfather, fell in love with Elza, courted her for a long period, and even threatened her and tried to kidnap her. The Niego family consequently filed a complaint against him with the police; he was arrested for a few days but then released. When Ratib was informed of Aliza Niego's engagement to a Jewish man, he murdered her in the street. Ratib was arrested and convicted. Jewish and Turkish newspapers expressed sympathy for the victim, not mentioning the fact that the murderer had been a Muslim and the victim a Jew. However, the day after Elza's funeral the Turkish newspapers, including *Vakit*, *Son Saat*, and others, changed their attitude and accused the Jews of using the funeral as an excuse to demonstrate against the Turkish Republic and national Turkish honor (Türklük), resulting in rampaging, disorder, attacks on Turks, and resisting the policemen who tried to impose order.[4]

According to the newspapers, during the funeral Jews called for justice and cursed the Turks. As a result, the police arrested several Jews and nine were brought to trial. During the trial, the journalists continued to incite against the

36 From Ottoman rule to modern times

Jews and the campaign against the Jews continued. Parallel to the anti-Jew campaign, some Turks defended the Jewish community. One of them was Yunus Nadi Abalıoğlu, owner and chief editor of *Chumhuriyet*, who made a decision to cease the anti-Jewish campaign in his paper.[5] During this period, minorities, including Jews, were forced to serve a full military service but could not receive a rank. They could only serve as non-commissioned officers and were forbidden from carrying a weapon.[6] The Aliza Niego Affair stemmed from several journalists' agitation against the Jews, which fell on attentive ears, especially among urban, educated young people who had already adopted antisemitic ideas and escalated hostility. Yet, the violence against the Jews was mainly verbal and not physical. The authorities avoided intervening until the attacks became more radical. It seems that the authorities did not consider attacks against minorities a good enough reason to take action during this period, but when violence escalated they immediately intervened.[7]

1933–1943

After the rise of the Nazi regime in Germany, criticism against Jews among the Turkish intelligentsia grew stronger. References to Nazi antisemitic policies were strengthened as if to threaten the Jews regarding their fate unless they Turkified themselves or, alternatively, as a benchmark against the benevolent and tolerant attitude of the Turks toward its own recalcitrant Jews. Prominent figures who expressed themselves against Jews included Asaf Belge, Hüseyin Nihal Atsız, Sadri Etem, and Muhittin Bergen.[8]

This period is characterized by pressures and restrictions, especially against the Jews. Unlike the previous decade when antisemitism and xenophobia were intertwined, this period is characterized more by a standalone antisemitism which partially stemmed from the financial crisis (part of the world crisis) and from Nazi propaganda.[9] On one hand, after the crisis of the Niego affair, a more tolerant stance was taken toward the Jews. The regime became more stable and established; the rivals of Kemalist rule were wiped out; and most of the new reforms were accomplished. Thus, the military emergency situation was ended. Some other domestic problems, such as debts that remained from Ottoman times, vanished and population exchange was resolved. Turkey began getting closer to the West. This affected the attitude toward minorities, which although far from ideal, was a noticeable change.[10] Moreover, after 1933, a new law was put into effect in Nazi Germany for the mandatory retirement of officials of non-Aryan races. Thus, the law required all Jewish scientists in Germany to be fired. Unemployed scientists, led by Albert Einstein, formed an association in Switzerland. Professor Schwartz, the general secretary of the association, met with the Turkish minister of education in order to provide jobs for 34 Jewish scientists in Turkish universities, especially at Istanbul University.[11] It should be noted, though, that the Turkish government granted the right of asylum to an elite cadre of Jewish experts only, and withheld the same right from the rest of the Jews fleeing the Nazi regime. On the other hand, these years included another violation of the Lausanne Treaty: The 1930 Municipality Law transferred control of cemeteries, including non-Muslim ones, to municipalities, in violation of Article 42 of the Lausanne Treaty. As stated, Article 40 granted non-Muslim minorities the right to establish and administrate religious, social, and charitable foundations, but this article was violated by the 1935 Law on Foundations. In 1936, through Law no. 2762, all foundations were requested to submit a property declaration listing their property's ownership. The so-called 1936 Declaration was later to be considered by the judiciary as well as the administrative authorities as the charter (vakıfname) of the foundation. In case that these declarations did not carry a special provision entitling the foundation to acquire immovable property, the Directorate General of Foundations (DGF) would expropriate all the immovable property acquired after 1936. The Court of Cassation not only upheld this policy but also considered minority foundations as "non-Turkish legal persons" (1971 and 1974 rulings).[12] Many other laws and regulations enacted in the 1930s included the requirement of "being of Turkish race" or "Turkish ascendance" in order, for example, to apply for civil service positions, establish a military career, or even study abroad. The Law on Professions and Services Assigned to Turkish Citizens in Turkey, dated 1932, prohibited the performance of a broad scope of professions by foreigners: barber, hat and shoe makers, singers, waiters, servants, actors in hotels, hammams, caravanserails, cafes, dance clubs, and bars (all refer to men and women). As being Turkish meant necessarily being a Muslim, this law reduced the presence of non-Muslims in economic or political life. In fact, until the 1940s, non-Muslim citizens were registered as foreigners in the registry office. This law was only abolished in 2003.[13] According to Çağaptay, the incidents in the 1930s were not evidence of antisemitism or racism but of intolerant nationalism and security perceptions, which seemed to play a role in these incidents. Evidence is Ankara's several permissions given to Jews to come to Turkey from Europe in 1939, a tolerant step in a very intolerant time for Jews. In other words, it was Turkish nationalism that shaped Turkey's attitude toward Jews in the 1940s, as Ankara hoped to assimilate Jews within Turkish society by making them adopt Turkish names and the Turkish language as their own. This was expressed by enacting bills or proposals of a law such as Sabri Toprak's proposal aimed at punishing every citizen who spoke any language other than Turkish, on the one hand, and to restrict Jewish migration to Turkey, on the other hand.[14] Unlike Europe during this period, race did not separate Jews from the majority in Turkey, and antisemitism was impotent in the country at the outbreak of World War II.[15]

Yet, some facts paint a different picture: In June 1938, the Turkish Grand Assembly formalized a discriminatory policy by enacting the Passport Law, which restricted the entrance of Jews to Turkey. This step was enhanced during World War II as the Council of Ministers took stronger measures to prevent Jewish immigration to Turkey. Furthermore, this decree issued by the council also regulated the transit of Jews through Turkey to other countries, especially to Palestine. As a result, migrants wishing to pass through Turkish territory had to comply with both the Passport Law (1938) and the Council of Ministers' Decree

38 *From Ottoman rule to modern times*

(1941), which required a legal permit for the entrance or residence of non-citizen Jews.[16] These examples only manifest the rising trend of nationalism in Europe, which affected Turkey directly in the 1930s. As a consequence, Turkish nationalism shifted from Muslim Turkish culture to Turkish-ethnic cores. An immediate manifestation of this tendency was the new Settlement Law, enacted in 1934 (İskan Kanunu), which restrained living conditions especially for non-Muslims who inhabited strategic regions of the country. The law closed certain parts of the country to non-Muslim settlers. The Jewish residents of Turkish Thrace, for instance, were forced to evacuate the region as 10,000 of them sought refuge in Istanbul.[17] "Trakya olayları," the Thrace Pogroms, began in June–July 1934. Turkey saw Thrace, with its relatively high number of Jews (13,000 in Thrace; 8,000 in Edirne), as the underbelly of the Republic. The majority of the Thracian Jewish community did not speak Turkish and had not assimilated as part of the "vatandaş Türkçe konuş" ("citizen, speak Turkish") campaign. In addition, Ankara did not enjoy military control over the Straits in this period as the Lausanne Treaty had created an international regime and a non-militarized status for the Dardanelles, Bosphorus, and the adjoining areas in Thrace, which were populated by Jews. Ankara perceived the great presence of Jews in these sensitive areas as a hazard in the event that the Jews became disloyal.[18]

The term 'Thrace Incidents' refers mainly to the 3,000 of the 13,000 Thracian Jews who were forced to leave Thrace, according to the government, or 7,000–8,000 according to British documents,[19] and who escaped to Istanbul while leaving their property behind.[20] The Jews who stayed suffered from personal attacks or burglary, which forced them to eventually leave their homes in Çanakkale, Kırklareli, Edirne, and other places. They also witnessed a fair number of antisemitic publications that circulated at that time. The Turkish authorities turned a blind eye toward antisemitic publications when they surfaced in Thrace, hoping that intimidating the Thracian Jews would perhaps convince them to be more loyal citizens. The antisemitic publications at that time included *Orhun*, which was issued in November 1933 in Edirne by Nihal Atsız (1905–1975),[21] a young schoolteacher and one of the ideologues of Turkish racism. Atsız labeled the Jews and the communists as Turkey's two main rivals, and also claimed in the May 25 issue that "Germany has become the first country to solve the Jewish problem."[22] As stated, it could be that the main intention was to remove non-Turkish elements from a highly important frontier from a military standpoint. It is also unclear whether this affair was an initiative of the Turkish authorities in Thrace only. Regardless, the government intervened and encouraged Jews to return to their homes. However, the turmoil continued; for instance, a small political group in Çanakkale called for the Turkish Youth League in August that year to boycott Jewish businesses.

This period was accompanied by a popular antisemitic cartoon series titled *Salamon Fıkraları* (Anecdotes of Salomon) that was published in the 1930s in the Turkish press, such as *Akababa*, *Karikatür*, and *Şaka*, portraying a Jewish man named Salomon (a name that iconically represents Jewishness), his wife Rebeka, and his friend Mişon (a paraphrase of Moshon, the version of Moses for

From the 1920s to the 1990s 39

Sephardic Jews) as foolish, greedy, and ugly.[23] All Jewish characters possessed stereotypical physical characteristics such as a large nose and curly hair. An example is the cartoon shown in Figure 2.1, which implies Jews' wealth and greed, saying:

> "Salomon, also this year, Republic Day will be luminous." [In Turkish 'parlak olacakmış' also means 'wonderful']
> "Of course, I sold 50 thousand bulbs..."[24]

In another cartoon (Figure 2.2), Salomon is sinisterly depicted as sitting in his safe room, counting his money and treating it as his/Jews' real "weapon":

> "They say that all the countries must decrease their weapons, I wonder, will they decrease my money?"[25]

Others depict Jews as cowards ('korkak yahudi' [coward Jew] is a well-known phrase in Turkish). Salomon is shown saying:

> "Salomon, if someone curses you, what would you do?"
> "I can't answer this question without seeing the guy's size, weight and height."[26]

Figure 2.1 Salomon sitting in his safe room.

40 *From Ottoman rule to modern times*

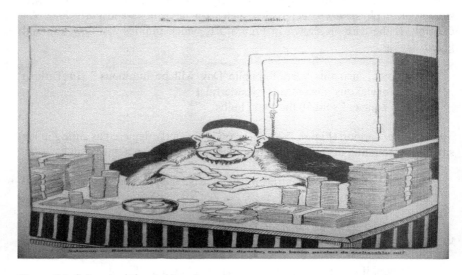

Figure 2.2 Salomon sitting in his safe room.

It should also be noted here that Salomon and actually all Jews that appear in the cartoons are presented as speaking poor Turkish from their selection of words and grammar.

The fact that Jews are greedy is represented also by a cartoon showing Salomon carrying his friends' newborn, while his friend says:

"Salomon look, my son was born tonight."
"maşallah maşallah [a common saying against the Evil Eye], what sort of trade would he do?"[27]

Another example of the Jews' greed is the following dialogue, which appeared in another cartoon (Figure 2.3):

"Salomon, will you make me laugh with strange words?
"Leave me alone, I'm not in the mood, I don't have money, I came here to borrow money from you."
"Ohh stop ... don't make me laugh any more...."[28]

In 1933 and 1934 one of the mainstream newspapers, *Akşam* (Evening), not a caricature journal, ran weekly "Saturday caricatures" by a famous caricaturist named Cemal Nadir Güler, who mainly ridiculed Jews, especially on Saturday, the Jewish holy day of rest. Although the satirical press contained cartoons almost identical to the ones found in the Nazi press in Europe, translations of classic antisemitic books were not published until 1943, when Nazi agents active in Turkey found Turkish publishers willing to translate and publish them.[29]

This period also featured the antisemitic Varlık Vegisi.

From the 1920s to the 1990s 41

Figure 2.3 Example of Jews' greed.

Varlık Vergisi

In 1940–1941, a general mobilization of reserve soldiers took place in Turkey. The Jews who were recruited as reserve soldiers were concentrated in several units consisting only of Jews. Most of these units were posted on a base in Maltepe in Istanbul in very difficult conditions. The Jewish soldiers more closely resembled prisoners in concentration camps rather than soldiers in national service. Armenians and Greeks were not treated the same way.[30] Later, it worsened. The greatest inequality perhaps in Turkish history is the capital tax known as the Varlık Vergisi.

The law was created in 1942 in order to levy an extraordinary tax on wealth earned through exploiting the ongoing wartime conditions. Although unofficially the law was supposed to levy off the non-Muslim presence in the country's commercial life, some assurances prove that the government recognized no distinction between the citizens of the country; the taxpayers were categorized on the basis of the traditional duality. Again, one's faith determined the amount of tax to be paid. Non-Muslims paid up to ten times more than the amounts levied on their Muslim neighbors. Objective reports of consular representatives and others described that Turks were lightly taxed, while minorities, especially Jews, whose occupations (such as lawyers, industry, trade, and seamanship businesses) were equal but more heavily taxed than their Turkish counterparts. For instance, a Jewish lawyer was obligated to pay 225,000 Turkish lira, whereas his Turkish partner was required to pay only 115,000.[31] In order to pay the tax, most non-Muslims were forced to sell their property. It is estimated that 98 percent of the real estate owned by non-Muslims was either bought by individuals, mostly Muslims, or made property of the state.[32] Those who were incapable of paying were forcibly taken to labor camps established in the remote corners of Anatolia, like Aşkale, where they were supposed to pay by working for the tax. Muslim Turks refused to be taken to these camps. Toward the end of World War II, the Turkish government ended capital tax and forced labor, but the breach already existed and the trust of non-Muslims toward the Turkish government began to fail.[33]

The Varlık Vergisi law was allegedly a fiscal step taken to improve the national budget, but was planned in an exceptional way: There were no clear criteria regarding who and how this tax would be imposed. Every settlement had a special committee manned by administration clerks so it could estimate every citizen's property and determine the tax rate accordingly. A high rate was set for all Jews. Sometimes they could not afford to pay it. It was discovered later that these committees were instructed to charge Jews a tax five times higher than was imposed on the Muslim Turks. The committee's decision was final. As noted above, those who could not afford to pay the tax were deported to Aşkale province (East Anatolia, where difficult weather conditions prevailed) and enslaved in difficult conditions. Some Jews who lived in the same period testify that concentration camps designed for Jews were planned. The Turks, who wanted to strengthen ties with Germany, thought that hurting Jews would be an easy way to appease the Germans.[34]

Eventually, in 1944, the Varlık Vergisi was replaced with a new law, No. 4530, ending the levies and forgiving former tax debts.[35] The Varlık Vergisi plays an important role in Turkish–Jewish history; in addition to the economic calamity it also allegedly included an encouragement to xenophobia. The press justified the Varlık Vergisi, and it was one step away from a verbal attack on minorities. The antisemitic tendencies in the press and literature were backed as Nazi propaganda in Turkey increased, and since then has become part of the Turkish discourse.[36] In 1943, for instance, the 'Jewish anecdotes' book was published. This book describes Jews negatively and depicts them as greedy, stingy, and as producing ludicrous pronunciations of the Turkish language.[37] Pan-Turkish elements, influenced by Nazi race theory, emerged in 1943 to preach against foreigners, especially Jews. The nationalistic journalism of these cycles began even before World War II. Cevat Rıfat Atilhan, a retired army officer who Jacob Landau describes as the "first professional anti-Semite in Turkey," and who "was the person most centrally responsible for the spread of antisemitic thought in Turkey" according to Rıfat Bali,[38] published in 1934 a journal entitled *Milli İnkılap* (National Revolution), to be followed by more than 50 books, inspired by the Nazis and probably sponsored by them, after spending some time in their circles in Germany in 1934.[39] Atilhan was invited to Germany after Hitler's rise to power, where he met Julius Streicher, editor of *Der Stürmer*. Upon his return to Turkey he started publishing an antisemitic journal entitled *İnkılap* (Revolution) in 1933 in Izmir. He accused the Jews of betraying the Turks during the Balkan Wars and World War I, and of hostility toward Turkish culture, civilization, and nobility, among many other accusations. In 1934 he moved to Istanbul and started publishing his antisemitic newspaper under a new name, *Milli İnkılap*.[40]

Milli İnkılap was banned on July 16, 1934, less than two weeks after the Thracian incidents. Among others, Atilhan wrote two novels, pretending to be documentary books, where he expressed his antisemitic ideas. One of them, *Musa Dağ*, is a reply to Franz Werfel's famous book, *The Forty Days of Musa Dağ*. Atilhan presents Aaron Aaronsohn and a mysterious Jewish spy named Rachel Rabinovitz who is being punished for her secret actions against the Ottoman Empire.[41] The other is *Suzy Liebermann, Jewish Spy* (Suzi Liberman'ın Hatira Defteri),[42] which was first published on May 26, 1935 and purchased by the Office of the Turkish Chief of Staff; 40,000 copies were purchased for Turkish Armed Forces officers. The book was reprinted four more times after 1935 and the most recent edition was published in 1995.[43]

Nihal Atsız, the main ideologist of pan-Turkism,[44] wrote that the Turkish race is equal to the Turkish nation, and also mentioned that the Jews are not part of the Turkish nation despite their living in its territory. According to him, a distant kirghiz is a Turk since Turkish blood flows through his veins, but the close Jew is like a dog. This perspective was repeated in pan-Turkish journalism to different degrees and using various metaphors and images. Atsız wrote several articles accusing Jews of being unrestrainedly greedy and nationally disloyal, and of being communist and cosmopolitan at the same time. From here, this links straight to the nationalistic circles of the 1960s and the 1970s, when MHP (Milliyetçi Hareket Partisi, Nationalist Action Party, the Turkish far-right political party) members republished the Turkish translation of *Mein Kampf* (Kavgam) and the memoirs of Goebbels. Of course, they attacked the Jews again.[45]

Another group that incited against Jews during this period was fundamentalist Muslims. These circles became marginal during Atatürk's regime and only in the 1950s, along with religious resurrection in Turkey, became more active and vocal. They enjoyed the liberalization of the press in the 1960s and through Erbakan's Islamist Millî Selâmet Partisi (National Order Party) entered the Turkish political system. The party's daily, *Milli Gazete*, which has been published from 1973 until today, agitated against Jews in the same way as other journals. The daily attempts to link Turkish Jews with the State of Israel (which controls some Islamic holy sites) by slamming Zionism, Jews, and Turkish Jews. Sometimes they use translations from the Arab press. In addition to nationalistic and financial arguments, antisemitism against a religious background is promoted. As the daily pretended to be the moral and ethical protector of Turkey, it is easy for it to present Christians and, even more, Jews as the corrupters of Turkish national morals and Muslim virtues.[46]

Post-war to the late 1960s

From the mid-1940s to the late 1960s, Turkish society became more tolerant toward minorities. The established democratic processes were accompanied, except for specific periods, by freedom of speech and freedom of assembly that were expanded following the establishment of the new constitution in 1961. This constitution and the one replacing it in 1982 prohibited the establishment of either leftist or rightist radical movements, but authorities were not always strict in preventing viewpoints expressed by and within Islamic circles, including fundamental Islamic expressions.[47] Past hostility toward Jews stemmed from the Kemalist elites' Turkification process, and as these circles controlled the national discourse within Turkish society, current hostility stemmed from previously silenced nationalistic Islamist circles in Turkey. As their press institutions and organizations became much freer than in the past, antisemitic expressions flourished. The antisemitic themes and motifs found in these publications echoed those found both in the Western world and throughout the rest of the Islamic world.[48]

The establishment of the State of Israel, which occurred in this period, was seen positively in Turkey, which increased the local Jewish community's prestige in the eyes of Turks. On the other hand, massive immigration to Israel took place and in a short time the community in Turkey was noticeably reduced. The mass immigration gradually made it impossible to run independent institutions, which led to the integration of Jews into general Turkish society and culture like never before, according to Levi.[49] Weiss disagrees with Levi regarding the impact of Israel's establishment on Turkish Jews. According to Weiss, starting from 1948, with the establishment of the State of Israel, an anti-Israel element was added so the differentiation between antisemitic feeling and anti-Israel sentiment in Turkey became blurred.[50] According to Düzgün, during the Israeli–Arab War in 1948, Turkey remained neutral but public opinion was mostly in favor of the Arabs. There were quite a few new, marginal, and particularly humorous magazines (*Bomba*, *Dava*, *Davar*) or antisemitic journals and newspapers that dealt mainly with the Israeli–Arab conflict. These newspapers made no distinction between Israel and the Turkish Jews. Some of the papers depicted the Jews as communists, since communism was the embodiment of everything that was wrong due to the poor relations between the Soviet Union and Turkey at that time.[51] The pro-Arab and later pro-Palestinian attitude of the Turks has dictated, in many cases, the official and unofficial Turkish attitude toward Israel and Jews throughout the years.

This was also expressed in regard to Aliyah. In 1948, articles calling for the condemnation of Aliyah were widely published in Turkish newspapers, claiming that Aliyah might undermine the Turkish economy and that the communists were the ones organizing it.[52] But the Turks' opposition was not only based on financial reasons. As 4,000 Jews made Aliyah, Hasan Saka's government (1947–1949) prohibited Jews from leaving Turkey. The prohibition was later changed and Jews were allowed to leave for any country other than Israel. This decision was made due to pressure from Arab countries. The law was abolished in 1949. At the same time, Turkey adored the young State of Israel, which arose from the desert, serving as the only democracy in the Middle East.[53]

Generally, the Jews' status improved and Jews began serving in all sorts of units, including combat units, carrying weapons and serving as officers. Preceding the change in the military service law, Recep Peker, the Turkish prime minister (1946–1947), said right after he was elected that Turkish minorities must be treated equally and receive all the rights they deserve: "if there were some restrictions and accidents in the past, we have to fix it as soon as possible." He also added that "Antisemitism is the disgrace of the 20th century."[54] But antisemitism did not vanish, even during this relatively tolerant period. Rıfat Atilhan, for instance, continued publishing his antisemitic articles until his passing in 1961, and he was praised by ultranationalists in Turkey even long after his death. For instance, Suat Gün wrote in the nationalist daily *Önce Vatan:*

> Cevat Rıfat Atilhan was an officer, much valued by the great Atatürk. His units fought in important [...] battles [during World War I]. When the Arab–Israel war started in 1948, he joined that front with the 300 volunteers he gathered, and was successful in capturing a Jewish settlement from the enemy. Cevat Rıfat Atilhan is an unequalled patriot, who informed the Turkish public of the "Jewish threat." [...] This present day espionage [in the United States] is an operation undertaken by the Jews [...] who like a cancer virus have spread everywhere, destroying the American governmental system. In reality, the U.S. has been infected with a "Jewish cancer," and the Jews will bring about its death, demise, or destruction [whichever term you choose].[55]

Others published antisemitic books in the 1940s, continuing the previous decades of antisemitic narratives. One of them is Hilmi Ziya Ülken's book, *Yahudi Meselesi (the Jewish Problem).*[56] The book attempts to trace the "Jewish problem" and to answer the question of why the Jews are so "problematic." According to Ülken, every race and nation can change its character. For instance, the British were fanatics, emotional and intemperate in the seventeenth century but nowadays they are cold blooded. The Turks are not the same Turks as in the Ottoman Empire period.[57] The Jewish religion has always been waiting for the Messiah, thus they attempt to bring about Doomsday.

In 1950, when the Democrat Party (Demokrat Parti) replaced the Republican People's Party (Cumhuriyet Halk Partisi), which put an end to a longlasting single-party regime, great hopes were raised among minority groups as well. The Democrat Party asserted that any religious, linguistic, or cultural distinctions would no longer be subjected to inequality. However, in the mid-1950s, ethnocultural differences continued to be associated with sociopolitical and economic aspects of unequal treatment. Non-Muslims were still perceived as 'unreliable' and 'undesirable' in the eyes of the authorities as well as the public. However, according to İçduygu and Soner, and unlike previous decades, the position of minorities began to be defined not by nationalist aspirations of internal politics but by diplomatic crises of external relations. Since non-Muslim minorities were considered agents of external forces, namely enemies, they lost sociopolitical and economic security in Turkey whenever the latter faced diplomatic disputes outside the country. Excluding the establishment of the State of Israel, the first example is Cyprus, which surfaced in the mid-1950s, since Turkey and Greece could not reach an agreement on the final status of the island. As the conflict escalated in 1954, Turkey adopted a hardline foreign policy against Greece. The Greek minority living in Turkey was accused of siding with Greek Cypriots. Members of the Greek minority, in particular, began to be treated as 'foreign' and even 'hazardous' to the country. In addition, the house where Mustafa Kemal Atatürk was born was burned in Salonika. As a result, on September 6–7, 1955, anti-Greek violence erupted in Istanbul and Izmir and this violence expanded to the burning of Jewish-owned businesses and threats to Jews and Armenians.[58] A mass riot in Istanbul and Izmir destroyed the cultural, religious, and economic presence of the minorities, and surprisingly not just the Greek minority. In Istanbul alone, the damages were estimated at $60 million. Over 100 people were injured, probably 15 lost their lives.[59] According to Türkmen and Öktem, the continuity of the affinity between Turkish foreign policy and its treatment of its non-Muslim minorities was embodied mainly in a negative way.[60]

It is interesting to note that the 1955 incidents are still vivid in the Turkish consciousness. For instance, during Operation Protective Edge in 2014, Faruk Köse approached Rabbi Haleva, Chief Rabbi of the Jewish community in Turkey, through his column in *Yeni Akit*, notifying him that if Haleva did not condemn Israel's actions, a Kristallnacht, or in his words "1955 incidents," against the Jewish community in Turkey could result.[61] In 1955 and 1964, in the riots against Greeks, which extended to other minorities, more than 5,000 buildings, including churches, schools, and shops belonging to minorities, including Jews, were damaged. The total damage from these incidents amounted to $300 million. In 1964, 24 Jews who held Greek citizenship were expelled from Turkey along with other Greeks whose rights were denied.[62]

In the 1950s and the 1960s, antisemitic articles were still quite common in Turkish journalism. Sometimes the Turkish government intervened, especially due to pressure from the Jewish community. However, this interference wasn't always useful or even implemented; *Büyük Doğu* by Kısakürek, for instance, which was one of the notorious antisemitic newspapers of this period, continued to exhibit an antisemitic approach.[63] The antisemitic themes expressed in Turkey's media and political arena during this period changed. Whereas the previously expressed hostility toward Jews seemed to stem from the dominant Kemalist elites, in the new, more open society, antisemitic expression became identified more with Islamist and ultranationalist camps. These groups felt free to express their own particular hostility toward the Jews after two decades of censorship by the Kemalists.[64]

Since the 1950s there have been no non-Muslim members of the Turkish parliament, except for İsak Altabev and Cefi Joseph Kamhi (son of the Jewish tycoon Jak Kamhi), who by representing the Doğru Yol Party (True Path Party) was elected a deputy from the second district in Istanbul in the general elections, held on December 25, 1995, and entered the Turkish parliament in 1995.[65] The lack of a fellow Jew in a high position that would be able to both represent and assist the Jewish community was perhaps another reason for the increased insecurity of the Jews. This feeling of insecurity was also sensed by the JDC (Joint Distribution Committee), as evident from the correspondence and reports written by JDC clerks. In a report dated April 14, 1958, S. Shnidell writes about the precautions that must be taken into consideration while corresponding with Turkey. Free, open correspondence might put the Jewish community in danger according to Shnidell's report:

> They request specifically that any correspondence carry no other destination on the envelope, that the letter inside be addressed to the Chief Rabbinate's council, and that no reference be made at any time to either my visit or previous correspondence or conversations. If any material is to be sent to Turkey it must be sent as a completely unsolicited gift, and any evidence that the community had made a request would jeopardize both their position and their ability to accept the material shipped to them. They are prepared, of course, to pay any customs that may be required on any of the items that the JDC send them.[66]

In the same document, Turkish Jews are reported as a community which holds no expectations of being able to obtain civil service or regular military appointments, holds inferior positions only with the faculty of the university, and in general has disadvantages in business contacts. Interesting to note is that, according to the document, German and Austrian professors who established their life anew in Turkey following the rise of the Nazi party in Germany were referred to as "German professors," and were not considered in the same way as the "native" Istanbul Jews.[67] It was not only a feeling of insecurity that emerged from the correspondence with the JDC clerks, but even a feeling of fear. Shnidell later wrote:

> while I was most cordially received and while information was given freely on the activities of the community, there was an apparent undercurrent of fear in many of the conversations, especially if discussion turned to the political status of the minorities in general and the Jews in particular ... expressions of caution on the manner of future contact or correspondence were made.[68]

The fear stems from the community's reluctance to be associated with a 'foreign' or 'international' organization. Turkey had this sort of fear in the 1950s, but Jews were even more fearful than the general Turkish society as they were already seen as 'foreigners.' Two years later, though, in correspondence between Henri Elfenbein and Harold Trobe, the picture seems more positive. İsak

Altabev, who was the president of the Jewish community and also the Democrat Party's Istanbul representative in parliament, described the attitude toward the Turkish Jews as "tolerable and certainly not worse than the situation and the treatment of the other minorities."[69] He even mentioned that Jews from Syria fled their homeland to Israel through Turkey and that the Turkish government was aware of this activity but had voiced no objection as long as it was kept quiet.

Late 1960s–1970s

From this period onward, religious nationalist parties that espoused antisemitism as part of their platforms existed in Turkey mainly due to the establishment of the new constitution in 1961 which, as mentioned, was more liberal during this time, and defended freedom of speech. The first to appear was the moderate Islamic newspaper *Tercüman*, which was published in 1961. A year later, a radical rightist Islamic daily newspaper, *Yeni İstiklal*, appeared. Islamic journalism, especially the radical kind, took advantage of the Turkish regime's failure to take any administrative or judicial stand against newspapers expressing antisemitic, anti-Zionist, and anti-Israeli attitudes in order to express themselves freely and harshly and to even goad the government for its attitude toward Israel, Zionism, and Judaism in general. Those articles merged Western Christian antisemitic elements with antisemitic elements based on Islamic traditions, all accompanied by suspicion, hostility, and allegedly decisive stereotypes. As typical of radical Islamic journalism even today, the journals deliberately created contradictions depicting Israel and Zionism differently in their different articles, but the writers believed and still believe that the more attacks and accusations against Israel are made, the better it is, even if the attacks contradict one another or are based on lies.[70] Thus, even if Islamic journalism harshly criticizes a phenomena taking place in Israel, it is depicted as a positive one if it assists in goading secular political elements in Turkey itself.

Except for a rare organization located in Izmir known as the Association for Combating Zionism in Turkey (Türkiye Siyonizmle Mücadele Derneği),[71] which was active between 1969 and 1970 and which published a few sources against Zionism and the Jews, probably inspired by Arab sponsors, there has not been any organized antisemitism in Turkey and it was usually beneath the surface.[72] In the 1970s and the 1980s, using the conflict with Cyprus and Greece, non-Muslim minorities were concentrated in several units in inner Anatolia in some cases. It should be noted here that the military academies where career officers were trained were never opened to minorities in Turkey. Yet there is no such official policy or expression of this except an announcement of the military academy's opening year, published by the Turkish Ministry of Defense, that the candidates were required to be of the "Turkish race."[73]

In these years, and especially after 1967, the number of antisemitic publications in Turkey increased and they became more aggressive. These years were characterized by the dissemination of radical ideologies, crises of confidence in the regime, dissention within political parties, the rise of violent groups, and increasing deterioration of the economic situation, all phenomena that opened the road to military interventions in 1971 and 1980. Under these conditions, and in light of Israel's victory in the Six Day War, propaganda against Jews was bound to increase.[74] Among the more popular antisemitic themes published in this period are: (1) Capitalism and communism are systems that serve Zionism's goal of establishing world domination and control. (2) Communism is depicted as a Jewish ideology as it was formulated by Marx, a Jew. Even the Bolshevik Revolution was carried out by Jews. (3) The Rotary and Lions clubs, as well as Freemason lodges, are tools to embody the aims of Zionism. (4) Israel's goal is to implement the biblical promise of its territory "from the Nile to the Euphrates" and covet the lands of Anatolia, which are included within the borders of "the Promised Land." (6) The Dönme, Sabbateans control Turkey.[75] One example of how these themes were expressed in the 1960s was Pirzade's book, *Türkiye ve yahudileri (Turkey and its Jews)*,[76] which was published in 1968 and serves as a good example of the atmosphere in those days.

On the first page of his book, Pirzade writes: "I believe that every citizen who carries the same national and religious responsibility shares the same feeling as me and to those I present this book."[77] In this book, the cover of which contains a picture of a hand holding the globe, there is a so-called historical-religious explanation of the character of the Jews. On page 6, when the writer discusses the ancient history of the Jews, he claims that the Jews have rebelled against both Moses and Jesus. In the case of the latter, the Jews subjected him to gruesome torture, which "justly" caused Rome, and later on the whole of Europe, to exact hatred and revenge.[78]

On the next page, when he examines the affinity between Judaism and Islam, he claims that: "today as well, the exploiting Jews in the Middle East nullify Islam which causes the Islamic people to live in a terrorized and fearful atmosphere, and ruin their houses of worship."[79]

With regards to Israel, Pirzade involves the "overall" Jewish power as well as the local Turkish Jewry's strengthening and immersion. Pirzade notes, for example, that many Turkish Jews have relatives in Israel. The Jews attempt to establish large families all over the world. As a consequence, Jews manage to own real estate assets....[80]

Another characteristic attributed to Jews is a lust for money: "it doesn't matter what the Jews lose or have to pay, as long as money isn't lost."[81] In addition, Jews are accused of being rich but concealing it from the Turkish public. The Jews exploit the Turks' religion and country and operate against it. On page 24, for example, he says: "Israel is the most prosperous industrial country in the Middle East and the objective of the Imperialist Jews is to exploit the surrounding countries." Further down the page he says that Jews should be prevented from developing industry inside Turkey because the Jews exporting from Turkey to Israel do not return all their profits to Turkey but leave some of it in Israel, and in other cases they export their goods to countries other than Turkey. This is the result of Israel's financial support of the Turkish Jews who develop industrial facilities inside Turkey.

The author attempts to prove that world trade is controlled by Jews, mentioning many famous brands and companies owned by Jews, such as Singer and Unilever in Holland. He does not hesitate to utilize Ford's antisemitic quotations regarding American Jews in his antisemitic book *The International Jew*.[82] The Turkish Jews play a significant role in damaging the Turkish economy by preferring the State of Israel as an import and export destination.[83] Furthermore, the ultimate goal of imperialist Jewish thought and action is to exploit other countries in the Middle East. When he discusses Israel, he describes Israel's war as a scam against "our Arab brothers," which was planned with "crusader" colonial powers. He calls Israelis dishonorable people, stating that the "great Jewish economic power" treats every Jew as a king but sees those who belong to other congregations as servants. These dishonorable people are found in any economical and political activity in order to carry on their control and exploitation of the honorable people.[84]

In some cases, Pirzade refers specifically to the Jews of Turkey in the 1960s. On page 33, for example, he says: "we shouldn't forget that the Jews of our time do not show any respect for our society, religion, and nation, for a profit of 3 cents they count our holy things as nothing." According to him, the Jews of Turkey and especially the Istanbul community, have a special position among other communities in the world as their community is one of the four strongest social and economical powers in the world (along with the Tel Aviv, New York, and London communities), whose activities control and guide international Zionist efforts. The Jews of Turkey exploit their country in favor of their Zionist imperialist activities. The Turkish Jews have a special position in world Zionism. Ever since World War I they have been serving as the executors of global Zionist decisions.[85] The Jews are compared and condemned along with Communists and Freemasons, Rotary, Lions, and other representatives of "Jewish capitalism and its servants."

The Jews brainwash their children through instruction organizations; they introduce profit as the best friend their child can have. A Jew does not and cannot consider anything but serving the Jewish cause.[86] It was not incidental that World War I and the war of Israel were mentioned. The Jews, according to Pirzade, were the cause and motive for both World Wars, and others. He quotes the Zionist leader Jabotinsky as pushing the Jews to keep up a constant fight against Germany because Germany endangers the Jews.[87] Thus, Jews are a danger to the entire world.

As hypocrites they jeopardize all religions, as that has always been their objective. The Jews are the ones that began the anarchist movement and the reason for inner rivalry within Muslim and Christian societies.[88] The book contains a cartoon presented on page 52, depicting Moshe Dayan, a former Israeli defense minister, as Hitler, raising his arm, leading his soldiers. The caption says: "Those who were cruel to others shall not complain when they are being treated cruelly (Hitler)."

The rest of the book discusses Israel's faults and atrocities against the Palestinians. There is even a historical survey of Jerusalem, maps of Israel before and after 1967, and pictures of so-called tortured Arabs who suffered at the hands of Israel. However, the most disturbing part of the book is the lists at the end of the book, containing names of Jews living in Istanbul who allegedly belong to the Freemasons and other international organizations (such as Rotary, Lions, etc.), some of which are supposed to be discreet. There is also a list of Jews who "play a significant role in export and import," including their office addresses.[89]

Books were not the only example. In 1969, as part of the election campaign, ultranationalist groups distributed antisemitic propaganda and the government not only disregarded this activity but also expressed a tolerant attitude toward it as part of its tolerant attitude toward Islamic religious activity as a whole. During this period, Jews were mainly accused of exploiting the Turkish economy, fraud, and black market trade.[90]

Antisemitic assertions, such as the ones disseminated in the previous decade, were even more popular in the following decade, usually by pan-Turkists or radical nationalistic circles. Some antisemitic events in the late 1960s and early 1970s were related to the Arab population residing in Turkey, which contained elements of fanatical Palestinian guerilla organizations. Turkish citizens were trained in Al Fatah camps in Syria and Lebanon, and during this period Palestinian and Arab terrorists were active inside Turkey. In 1969, for instance, a Jordanian student was killed and another one was injured when their car was bombed before they could enter the Israeli stand at the Izmir international fair. The Israeli consul, Efraim Elrom, was murdered after being kidnapped and held captive in 1971.[91]

During the trial against Elrom's murderers, some Turks took advantage of the delicate situation and committed antisemitic actions, like the muhtar (*muhtar* is the elected village head in Turkish villages) belonging to the Izmir province, who threatened the lives of Jewish merchants for money. This case was the first verdict of the military court (following the military coup d'état) in Izmir in 1971. The muhtar was jailed for eight years.[92]

Another example is the American consul's report, which was written on September 18, 1972, and was based on information supplied by an American officer of Jewish origin, that five Jewish leaders in the Adana community received death threats by telephone on September 17, 1972. The American officer, stated that the Turkish gendermerie (*Jandarma*) placed guards around the synagogue. This information was confirmed by several members of the Adana Jewish community, who indicated that threatened individuals stayed at home, presumably with police protection: "They did not believe the threat was real but in light of the incidents in Munich and elsewhere, thought it prudent action to take."[93] This was the first known threat against the local Jewish community in a long time. Also, the local Turkish authorities took the incident seriously due to the large Arab population in Adana at that time.

The newspapers also published antisemitic articles in this decade, especially at the end of it. *Bugün*, for instance, started a series of articles on Judaism and international Zionism, as well as on Turkish Jewry and its "taking control" of various elements of Turkey's financial life. The newspaper distributed pamphlets calling for boycotts of merchant Jews and their exclusion from Turkey's economy (Figure 2.4). The popular publications in *Bugün* stirred the pot and fell on attentive ears in some cases.[94] However, this was not the only newspaper encouraging antisemitism in the 1960s. According to *Maariv*, dated August 22, 1968, a new antisemitic organization was established in Izmir in 1968 by seven merchants who did not belong to any party. Its name was "The Association for Combating Zionism in Turkey" and its goals were "to combat Zionism and similar subversive ideologies, and to rescue our national culture and national morals." The association aimed to spread throughout Turkey.[95] Another example of the rampant antisemitism in the 1960s was the systematic marking of apartments belonging to Jews in Istanbul in March 1969. It was clear that only apartments populated by Jews were marked, because when some Jews attempted to mark non-Jewish populated apartments in the same way they were immediately erased. The Jews in this period were tense and some reported work absenteeism due to this fear.[96]

According to Kerim Balcı, a prominent journalist from *Zaman*, the reason for the rising antisemitism in the late 1960s stemmed from different religious interpretations. Whereas during the Ottoman era, the main religious source the Islamic clerics leaned on was the Hadith, the tradition in the late 1960s, along with Necmettin Erbakan's appearance in the Turkish political arena,[97] was for the Quran to become the main religious source at the expense of the Hadith. Erbakan followers adopted the Quranic sayings, some of which are quite rough and, thus, the link between Erbakan's religious antisemitism, national antisemitism, and anti-Westernization agenda was created. Erbakan's preaching was popular in light of the 3.5 military revolts (1960, 1971, 1980, 1997 – known as the "post-modern coup," it is not considered a full coup) and due to the Turkish military's strengthening of religion at the expense of the communist/socialist left that was popular in Turkey.[98]

Erbakan's repeated demonization of Israel and Zionism throughout the years included the principle that Zionism is an evil ideology that was responsible for the fall of the Ottoman Empire. Israel was an artificial state that should be uprooted, according to Erbakan. Zionism also means imperialism, and is a movement that runs Wall Street and America. But Erbakan's most concerning viewpoint was the one claiming that Zionism's "great plan" is to conquer the territories of the biblical promised land, which are currently Turkish territories, as stated in the Old Testament: "On that day the Lord made a covenant with Abraham and said, 'To your descendants I give this land, from the Wadi of Egypt to the great river, the Euphrates.'" One of the ways to control Turkey, according to Erbakan, was to oblige Turkey to enter the Common Market in 1970. In other words, Israel stands behind all of Turkey's problems (including why Erbakan was removed from the Turkish government).[99]

Even today, on one of my own trips to Turkey I took a connecting flight from Ankara. At the airport I approached one of the security men regarding a bracelet that I forgot during the scanning check. While trying to assist he started conversing with me. When I replied I was an Israeli, he asked with all seriousness:

Figure 2.4 An antisemitic poster.

54 From Ottoman rule to modern times

"Do you still want to fulfill your dreams of the Kingdom of Israel at the expense of Turkey?"

Despite the ongoing antisemitism in Turkey in the 1960s, the Israeli Consulate in Istanbul reported that the Turkish authorities' attitude toward Turkish Jews had not deteriorated due to the Six Day War. This impression was given, said the report, due to the growing antisemitic activity in Turkey by reactionary people/ groups that were sponsored by Arab countries. Right after the Six Day War, an antisemitic and anti-Israel campaign took place with the assistance of extremist newspapers such as *Bugün* and *Yeni Istanbul*. These activities were partly sponsored and encouraged by Arab countries. A report from the Israeli Consulate revealed the fact that some of those who assisted this anti-Israel and antisemitic propaganda, such as İsmet Belgeç, who ran the antisemitic campaign in *Bugün* using the pseudonym Piroğlu, did it for money and even agreed to 'withdraw' their antisemitic publications for money.[100] Among them, says the report, reserve duty Major Şahap Tan,[101] who arrived in Israel in September 1958 in order to spy for Egypt, was arrested by the Israeli security forces and, after confessing, was sentenced to five years' imprisonment. He was released two years later and deported from Israel. Tan published several antisemitic books and was one of the two people who initiated and were in charge of the anti-Israel, antisemitic campaign in *Bugün* during this period.[102] Two other reports from the Israeli Consulate from April 24 and 29, 1969, confirm that during the previous six months less evidence of antisemitism was received by the Consulate compared to the first six months of 1968. This report also reinforced the fact that antisemitism in this period was namely due to newspapers such as *Bugün*. Even the fascist organization of Bozkurts led by Alparslan Türkeş was not depicted as purely antisemitic by the Israeli diplomats, but also as xenophobic; it was active mainly among students.[103]

In the 1970s, the number of antisemitic publications written by radical nationalists increased. In their eyes, the three main threats to Turkey were: Zionism, Communism, and Freemasonry. Some of them saw the greatest threat as Zionism. Sometimes, when the communists were attacked in these publications, the link between Jews and every central position of the communists is clear (according to Ismail Hakki Yılanlıoğlu, for instance, even Lenin was Jewish).[104] Other authors link Jews and Freemasons, and even proved that King Solomon is admired in Freemason circles. Jews were also accused of causing every possible problem of the Ottoman Empire and the Republic of Turkey, including the Kurdish movement. Jews, like other minorities, were depicted as Turkey's enemies whose agents are educated and trained in the non-Muslim community's schools in order to destroy Turkey from within. The most interesting publication from the 1970s is Hikmet Tanyu's book *Tarih Boyunca Yahudiler ve Türkler I–II* (Jews and Turks throughout History).[105] Tanyu was a theology professor at Ankara University, and even studied Hebrew at Ulpan Etziyon in the 1950s in Israel. In his two-volume book, containing more than 1,000 pages, Tanyu expresses the aforementioned antisemitic ideas under a scientific cloak, using twisted and irrelevant quotations.[106] Antisemitism was expressed in ultranationalist and Islamist publications as well in the 1970s.[107]

From the 1920s to the 1990s 55

The antisemitism of the 1970s is related also to the affinity the Turks saw to occurring between the United States and Israel. As the United States was seen as the main evil in the world, and the Jews were seen as those who control America, it was easy for antisemitism to prevail. In addition, Israel was seen as the United States' proxy in the Middle East. Thus, according to Corry Guttstadt, the leftists' approach did not target Jews specifically but was part of an overall world perspective.[108]

As for specific incidents against Jews, some Jews received threatening printed letters (Figure 2.5). The Jews, out of fear, refused to report receipt of such letters, so their remains unknown. According to a report by the Israeli Consulate in Istanbul, Jewish leaders were advised to complain to the police but they did not seem to take any such steps at the time.[109]

According to Weiss, antisemitism in modern Turkey up to the 1980s can be categorized into four manifestations:

1 Government aggression against Jews as part of its attitude against all minorities and foreigners in Turkey.
2 Laws against the Jewish religion and education as part of the government's policy to emphasize secularization.

These two categories mostly prevailed in the first decades of the Turkish Republic.

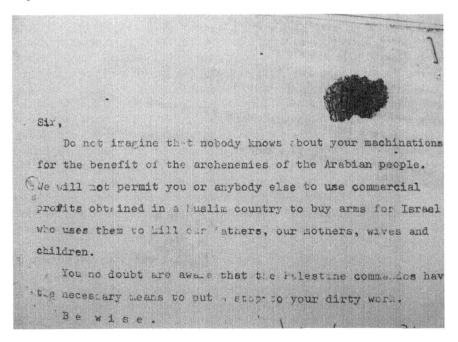

Figure 2.5 A threatening letter.

56 *From Ottoman rule to modern times*

3   Unveiled antisemitic steps due to the relative wealth of the Jewish community.
4   Anti-Israel actions.[110]

In this period, antisemitism was also displayed by Fethullah Gülen and his movement, which came together almost irrespective of concurrent events, excluding the influence of the social atmosphere in Turkey during that time. Fethullah Gülen (born in 1941) is a moderate Turkish Muslim scholar, a prolific writer (he has authored more than 80 books), philosopher, and leader of a self-named movement. His critics accuse him of undermining Turkish secular values, while his followers claim he is a moderate religious scholar and a victim of baseless and recurring attacks. Gülen and his movement promoted dialogue as one of the movement's central principles. From the mid-1990s onward, Gülen's movement began to shift public attention to discussions of dialogue, tolerance, and multiculturalism. The community began to hone its public image more intensively using the Gazeteciler ve Yazarlar Vakfı. The name of the foundation is compatible with the community's hegemonic goals, covering virtually all writers in Turkey. The foundation's activities were also all-inclusive, from Ramadan meals, to organizing soccer games and interreligious dialogue conferences, or bestowing a prize on a popular Turkish celebrity. The foundation publishes books that deal with coexistence, for example, but the landmark of the foundation's activities was covering Gülen's meeting with the former Pope, Jean Paul II. The foundation went to great efforts to present the Gülen movement in a positive light to the world.[111]

According to Gülen, the idea of tolerance does not aim to confine itself in a narrow space. On the contrary, you must begin with the immediate environment, and then spread to more distant circles. Gülen sees great importance in disseminating tolerance because of the fact that the world is a global village, and it is imperative to lay the foundation for communication without making Christian/Jew/atheist/Buddhist distinctions. However, you must still begin with your immediate circle, since without it you cannot move onward and outward. In this way you can radiate tolerance from your immediate environment to more distant ones.[112] Gülen states that tolerance is occasionally interpreted superficially by specific individuals, since they are attempting to change those around them under the guise of dialogue, but the idea that stands behind tolerance is to accept everyone as is, regardless of faith or beliefs. Beyond this, tolerance also includes the ability to connect with each other, to make a connection, to talk and communicate.[113]

Gülen apparently slandered the Jews in the 1970s. Rabbi Haleva testified that he saw a televised speech that Gülen gave against Jews in one of the mosques, but Haleva claims that he was not affected by the speech since he is accustomed to hearing defamation against Jews. Apparently, these things even appeared in print, on tapes, and in books that contained various declarations Gülen made against the Jews. Zali De Toledo, a Turkish Jew, head of the Association of Turkish Jews in Israel, who served as the Israeli cultural attaché to Turkey from

1993 to 2003, stated that Gülen's first books, which contained numerous passages against the Jews, were removed from stores and can no longer be found.[114]

Attempts to find Gülen's books from that period were mostly futile, though some examples still exist.[115] Gülen denies it, saying that prior to the 1990s he wrote and preached against those that disguised political aims with religion, but he was never involved in an active or open conflict with any Jewish group, and he is interested in pursuing a line of tolerance toward Jews. He even claims to be the first Muslim in Turkey that initiated a dialogue with the Jewish community and its leaders in Turkey in the 1990s.[116] Haleva explains this by saying that during that period (seemingly the late 1970s), Gülen was familiar with Jews through books alone. Another possible reason, in his opinion, is the desire to win wide and sweeping public approval, and it was common knowledge that among the extremist Muslims in Turkey, as Haleva said, anyone that exhibits anti-Jewish sentiments wins greater acclaim. In other words, in order to be accepted and create legitimacy among the religious community, Gülen had to initially express populist opinions, which he distanced himself from later, after gaining sufficient legitimacy. On the other hand, it is possible, as Haleva proposed, that Gülen simply underwent a true spiritual transformation (or maybe material as well) when he got closer to the world outside of Islam. According to Haleva, the change that Gülen underwent was so great that he began to speak very positively about Jews. Perhaps it is no surprise that he mentions Kısakürek, among others, as a source of inspiration.[117]

1980s–1990s

In the 1980s, Turkey–Israel relations reached a diplomatic low due to the Israeli government's declaration of Jerusalem as Israel's "eternal and indivisible capital" on July 30, 1980, and Ankara's decision to lower its level of diplomatic representation in Israel to advisory status. Consequently, and in light of the 1973 oil crisis, Turkey attempted to diplomatically distance itself from Israel, counting on the Gulf petrodollars to assist Turkey in overcoming its shortfall in foreign reserves.[118] Since the 1980s, new twists in antisemitic themes have appeared: (1) The U.S. administration was controlled by the Jewish lobby. The Jews of America were depicted as controlling the Hollywood film industry. This is one of the reasons why American films show Israel in a positive light and also make films on the Holocaust. Not only is the film industry controlled by the Jews, but also the American media. In the following years, even the Jewish neocons were depicted as taking control of the White House and attempting to create a favorable foreign policy toward Israel. (2) The Holocaust is a fabrication. (3) Israel treats Palestinians like the Nazis treated Jews, which is why it is known for being 'colonialist,' 'rogue,' and 'terrorist.' (4) Sympathy toward Hitler. (5) The PKK is supported by Israel. (6) Israelis are attempting to purchase southeastern Anatolia through the framework of Turkey's Southeastern Anatolia Project (GAP, or Güney Anadolu Projesi).[119] However, as the Soviet Union fell in 1991, the consistent theme of "Communism is a Jewish invention" began to disappear from the Turkish rightist discourse, but Freemasonry continued to be depicted as a Jewish tool "to control the world."[120] Just like Gülen, in the 2000s Oktar changed his viewpoint and became a great advocate of interfaith dialogue and a pro-Israel religious leader.[121]

One of the main reasons for the antisemitism of the 1990s was Turkey's gradual transformation into a more liberal society in which, among others, Islamist groups and individuals could more openly express their views, which they were prohibited from doing military rule in Turkey. As part of the liberalization of Turkish society, two marginalized groups, the Islamist movement and the Kurdish nationalist movement, both acted to increase their strength within Turkish society. In response, the left and the liberals started debating the need for a multicultural society. This liberalization was part of a domestic discourse on liberating Turkish society from the Kemalist establishment and the Turkish armed forces. This is when an alliance was forged between leftists and Islamists, as both movements support liberalization. The leftists supported liberalization so much that they turned a blind eye to antisemitic expressions. The result of this process was the legitimization and transformation of once marginal Islamist journalists and others into mainstream Islamist intellectuals who openly expressed their minds.[122]

Another significant thing occurred in the 1990s: despite the peak in political military relations between Israel and Turkey, from this point onwards antisemitism was no longer manifested only through words. In 1993, a number of Islamist terrorists threatened the life of the president of the Quincentennial Foundation (500. Yıl Vakfı; formed in the 1980s to commemorate the 500-year anniversary of the expulsion of Jews from Spain in 1492, and their arrival and settlement in the Ottoman Empire), Jak Kamhi, whose car was targeted. In March 1992 Ehud Sadan, the Israeli top security officer of the Israeli Embassy in Ankara, was killed by a powerful car bomb. Two militant Islamic groups took responsibility for the murder, one of them referring to the assassination as a revenge for Israel's killing of Sheik Abbas Musawi, the head of the Hizbullah organization in southern Lebanon, on February 16, 1992.[123] But Islamic Jihad and the previously unknown Islamic Revenge Organization believed to be associated with Islamic Jihad separately claimed credit, although Hizbullah denied involvement.[124] In 1995, Professor Yuda Yürüm's (the head of the Jewish community in Ankara) car was bombed by Turkish Islamists, who received approval for this attack from Iran.[125] Yürüm was only injured, but no official governmental condemnation was expressed. These incidents were followed by murders that continued into the 2000s.[126]

In the 1990s, a prominent religious leader named Adnan Oktar published numerous antisemitic books as well as an antisemitic journal, *Rönesans* (Renaissance), which was published between 1991 and 1992, and an antisemitic newspaper *Son Mesaj* (Last Message) under the pseudonym Harun Yahya ('Harun' refers to the biblical Aaron and 'Yahya' refers to the New Testament John the Baptist). First, by acquiring a following as the leader of a small religious group at Istanbul University in the 1980s, Oktar sought to attract wealthy and influential Istanbul youths with a materially fulfilling brand of Islam. He made a name for himself penning antisemitic, anti-Freemasonry, anti-Communist, conspiracy theory-laden tracts, which culminated in his 1987 book *Yahudilik ve Masonluk* (Judaism and Freemasonry).[127] This book argued that Jews and Freemasons had infiltrated state institutions in Turkey, aiming "to erode the spiritual, religious, and moral values of the Turkish people and make them like animals." It was printed close to 100,000 times, but soon after the book's appearance Oktar was prosecuted in Turkey on charges of promoting a theocratic revolution. He ended up serving 19 months in jail, ten of which he spent in a mental institute when he was diagnosed with obsessive-compulsive personality disorder and schizophrenia. Nevertheless, after Oktar's release his group continued to expand.[128]

As for Oktar's antisemitic publications, although the claims against him said that he "made serious accusations about the Jews and incited the population to hatred and enmity [against them]" the prosecutor decided not to continue the investigation due to lack of proof that Oktar had "consciously published incendiary material against the Jewish community."[129] In 1995, BAV[130] distributed its first book, entitled *Soykırım Yalanı* (The Holocaust Lie),[131] which sparked controversy but is still available in Turkey. This book basically 'refutes' the existence of the Holocaust and the murders of six million Jews. As Bali says, the book, which was distributed in Germany, promotes ideology not unlike that of the neo-Nazi organizations in Europe.[132] The Stephen Roth Institute for the Study of Contemporary Antisemitism and Racism at Tel Aviv University listed Oktar as a Holocaust denier due to the publication of *Soykırım Yalanı* (*The Holocaust Lie*). The Institute referred to Oktar in its 2000–2001 report on antisemitism as a "Turkish anti-Semite."[133] Yet, in the 2000s, Oktar changed policy, increasing his tolerance toward non-Muslims, especially Jews. In 2006, a book affirming the Holocaust, titled *Soykırım Vahşeti* (The Holocaust Brutality),[134] was published after the transformation in Oktar's attitude toward Jews and Judaism. In fact, Oktar has become an advocate of Israel, hosting many political or religious and non-religious Jewish leaders from Israel and all over the world, meetings which were screened on the movement's Channel 9.[135] He has also published numerous books to promote tolerance and peace between Christians, Muslims, and Jews.[136] He himself in an interview with *Der Spiegel* claimed that *Soykırım Yalanı* had been written by a friend of his who had published his own essays using Oktar's pen-name, Harun Yahya, as his own:

> The book, "The Holocaust Lie," is by one of my friends, Nuri Özbudak. It is not one of my books. He published his own essays under that title. Later, we protested against this through the Public Notary and declared that fact to the public. I did not take any other legal action but only protested through the Public Notary because he used my name. My book expressing my own ideas was published later.[137]

Sinem Tezyapar, an executive producer and program director on Channel 9, as well as a close disciple of Oktar's, denied the fact that Oktar wrote antisemitic books. Regarding his viewpoints on Jews, she says:

Adnan Hoca is not rigid. He is very open minded and he constantly encourages progress. If he learns something is incorrect, he instantly, at that moment, can change his whole view with humility. When he realizes there is a better style, way, argument, he makes necessary changes. So his books are also in constant editing. He no longer publishes some of his books. Having said that his views changed as he interacted with Jews and Israelis is true. He does not deny that he was critical of Zionism back then but he has never been antisemitic. But later he learned what Zionism IS for Israelis and that happened especially after people from Israel came to visit him and explained what Zionism is for Israelis. Then he changed his views regarding that.[138]

Tezyapar herself is an advocate of tolerance and fights antisemitism.[139]

Notes

1 Marcy Brink-Danan, *Jewish Life in 21st Century Turkey: The Other Side of Tolerance* (Bloomington, IN: Indiana University Press, 2012), p. 10.
2 Landau, "Al Dmuta Shel Haantishemiyut," p. 79.
3 Sometimes spelled Elza Niyego.
4 Levi, *History of the Jews*, pp. 43–44.
5 Levi, "Yahas HaShiltonot ve HaChevra HaTurkim," p. 245; Soner Çağaptay, *Islam, Secularism and Nationalism in Modern Turkey: Who is a Turk?* (New York: Routledge, 2006), p. 149.
6 Levi, "Yahas HaShiltonot ve HaChevra HaTurkim," p. 239.
7 Ibid., p. 246.
8 Bali, *Antisemitism and Conspiracy Theories*, pp. 209–214.
9 On Turkey and the Jews during World War II see: Corry Guttstadt, *Die Türkei, die Juden und der Holocaust* (Hamburg: Assoziation A, 2008); Corry Guttstadt, *Turkey, the Jews and the Holocaust* (New York: Cambridge University Press, 2013); Izzet Behar, *Turkey and the Rescue of European Jews* (New York: Routledge, 2014); Tuvia Friling, "Nazi–Jewish negotiations in Istanbul in mid-1944," *Holocaust and Genocide Studies*, 13, 3 (1999), pp. 405–436; Esther Benbassa and Aron Rodrigue, *Sephardi Jewry: A History of the Judeo-Spanish Community, 14th to 20th Centuries* (Berkeley, CA: University of California Press, 1999); Dalia Ofer, *Escaping the Holocaust: Illegal Immigration to the Land of Israel 1939–1944* (New York: Oxford University Press, 1990).
10 Levi, *History of the Jews*, p. 49.
11 Çağaptay, *Islam, Secularism and Nationalism*, p. 151.
12 Türkmen and Öktem, "Foreign policy as a determinant,"p. 5.
13 Ibid., p. 6. See also: Mustafa Alp, "Yabancıların Çalışma İzinleri Hakkında Kanun," *Ankara Üniversitesi Hukuk Fakültesi Dergisi*, 53, 2 (2004), pp. 33–59.
14 Landau, "Al Dmuta Shel Haantishemiyut," pp. 74–75.
15 Çağaptay, *Islam, Secularism and Nationalism*, p. 155.
16 Şakir Dinçşahin and Stephen R. Goodwin, "Towards an encompassing perspective on nationalism: the case of Jews in Turkey during the Second World War, 1939–1945," *Nations and Nationalism*, 17, 4 (2011), pp. 847–848.
17 İçduygu and Soner, "Turkish minority rights regime," p. 459.
18 Çağaptay, *Islam, Secularism and Nationalism*, pp. 141–142.
19 Ibid., p. 144.
20 On the Thracian Incidents, see: Avner Levi, "Hapra'ot BeYehudeyTrakaya, 1942" [The pogroms against the Jews of Thrace, 1942], *Pe'amim* 20 (1984), pp. 11–132;

From the 1920s to the 1990s   61

Rıfat N. Bali, *1934 Trakya Olayları* (İstanbul: Bayrak Matbaası, 2008); Berna Pekesen, *Nationalismus, Türkisierung und das Ende der jüdischen Gemeinden in Thrakien, 1918–1942* (München: R. Oldenbourg Verlang, 2012); Hatice Bayraktar, *"Zweideutige Individuen in schlechter Absicht," Die antisemitischen Ausschreitungen in Thrakien 1934 und ihre Hintergründe* (Berlin: Klaus Schwarz, 2011).

21 On Atsız, see: Umut Uzer, "Racism in Turkey: the case of Nihal Atsiz," *Journal of Muslim Minority Affairs*, 22, 1 (2002), pp. 119–130; Jacob M. Landau, *Exploring Ottoman and Turkish History* (London: C. Hurst & Co., 2004), pp. 58–61.
22 Çağaptay, *Islam, Secularism and Nationalism*, p. 142.
23 Brink-Danan, *Jewish Life in 21st Century Turkey*, p. 75. On Jews in Turkish cartoons, see Hatice Bayraktar, "Türkische Karikaturen über Juden (1933–1945)," *Jahrbuch für Antisemitismusforschung*, 13 (2004), pp. 85–108.
24 *Akbaba*, October 25, 1934.
25 Ibid., August 16, 1934.
26 Ibid., March 16, 1937, p. 8.
27 Ibid., March 19, 1937, p. 8.
28 Ibid., January 15, 1937, p. 4.
29 Bali, *Antisemitism and Conspiracy Theories*, p. 216.
30 Levi, "Yahas HaShiltonot ve HaChevra HaTurkim," p. 239.
31 Landau, "Al Dmuta Shel Haantishemiyut," p. 80.
32 Toktaş, "Perceptions of antisemitism," p. 207.
33 İçduygu and Soner, "Turkish minority rights regime," pp. 459–460.
34 Levi, "Yahas HaShiltonot ve HaChevra HaTurkim," pp. 237–238.
35 Toktaş, "Perceptions of antisemitism," p. 207.
36 Landau, "Al Dmuta Shel Haantishemiyut," p. 226.
37 *Yahudi Fıkraları: Akbaba Yayını Mizah serisi I*, (İstanbul: Cumhuriyet Matbaası, 1943). See: Jacob M. Landau, "Tofaot shel Antishemiyut BaSifrut, uva'Itonut shel Harapublika Haturkit," [Expressions of Antisemitism in the Turkish republic literature and journalism] in: Abraham Haim (ed.), *Society and Community: Proceedings of the Second International Congress for Research of the Sephardi and Oriental Jewish Heritage 1984* (Jerusalem: Misgav, 1991), p. 227 [Hebrew].
38 Bali, *Antisemitism and Conspiracy Theories*, p. 13.
39 On Milli İnkılap, see: Erdem Güven and Mehmet Yılmazata, "Milli İnkilap and the Thrace Incidents of 1934," *Modern Jewish Studies*, 13, 2 (2014), pp. 190–212; on Atilhan, see: Rıfat N. Bali, "Cevat Rıfat Atilhan-I," *Tarih ve Toplum* 30, 175 (1998), pp. 15–24; Rıfat N. Bali, "Cevat Rıfat Atilhan-I," *Tarih ve Toplum* 30, 176 (1998), pp. 21–30; Mustafa Murat Çay, "Cevat Rıfat Atilhan-Askerî, siyasî ve fikrî yönleriyle," unpublished dissertation submitted to Selçuk University, Konya, 2013: http://acikerisim.selcuk.edu.tr:8080/xmlui/handle/123456789/1205?show=full, retrieved October 10, 2014; Jacob M. Landau, *Radical Politics in Modern Turkey* (Leiden: Brill, 1974), pp. 185–186. On Atilhan's antisemitic ideology, see: Celil Bozkurt, *Yahudilik ve Masonluğa karşı Cevat Rıfat Atilhan* (Istanbul: Doğu Kütüphanesi, 2012); Özen Karaca, "The theme of Jewish conspiracy in Turkish nationalism: the case of Cevat Rıfat Atilhan," unpublished thesis submitted to the Graduate School of Social Sciences of Middle East Technical University, Ankara, 2008: http://etd.lib.metu.edu.tr/upload/12609505/index.pdf, retrieved September 1, 2013.
40 Çağaptay, *Islam, Secularism and Nationalism*, pp. 142–143.
41 Landau, "Tofaot shel Antishemiyut," p. 232. On Atilhan's other antisemitic publications, see: Çağaptay, *Islam, Secularism and Nationalism*, p. 149.
42 Cevat Rıfat, *Suzi Liberman* (İstanbul: Türkiye Matbaası, 1935). The book's title has had several small changes throughout the years. The author's name appeared in full in future editions.
43 Bali, *Antisemitism and Conspiracy Theories*, p. 103, fn. 215.

62 From Ottoman rule to modern times

44 Pan-Turkism is a movement that emerged in the 1880s among the Turkic intellectuals of Azerbaijan and the Ottoman Empire, with the aim of cultural and political unification of all Turkic peoples. On Pan-Turkism, see: Yusuf Akçuraoğlu, *Türk Yılı 1928* (Istanbul: Yeni Matbaa, 1928); M. Şükrü Hanioğlu, *Preparation for a Revolution: The Young Turks, 1902–1908* (New York: Oxford University Press, 2001); David Kushner, *The Rise of Turkish Nationalism: 1876–1908* (London: Frank Cass, 1977); Jacob M. Landau, *Pan-Turkism: From Irredentism to Cooperation* (Bloomington, IN: Indiana University Press, 1992); Jacob M. Landau, *Tekinalp – Turkish Patriot 1883–1961* (Istanbul: Nederlands Historisch-Archaeologisch Institut, 1984).
45 Landau, "Al Dmuta Shel Haantishemiyut," p. 81.
46 Ibid., pp. 81–82.
47 Aryeh Shmuelevitz, "Emdat HaItonut HaIslamit BeTurkiya Klapey Israel [The attitude of the Turkish Islamic press toward Israel]," *HaMizrah HeHadas* [The New East], 39 (1997–1998), p. 114.
48 Bali, *Antisemitism and Conspiracy Theories*, p. 66.
49 Levi, "Yahas HaShiltonot ve HaChevra HaTurkim," p. 239.
50 Although the calls for Jews ("illegal citizens of Turkey") to get out of Turkey "maybe to Palestine" were made long before the State of Israel was established. See: Levi, *History of the Jews*, p. 46.
51 Düzgün, "Cumhuriyetin İlanından," p. 81. On Israel–Turkey relations in 1948, see: Umut Uzer, "Turkish–Israeli relations: their rise and fall," *Middle East Policy*, 20, 1 (2013), pp. 97–110; Ofra Bengio, *The Turkish–Israeli Relationship: Changing Ties of Middle Eastern Outsiders* (London: Palgrave, 2009).
52 Adina Weiss, "Yehudey Turkia: Misgeret Datit BeMishtar Stagrani" [The Jews of Turkey: religious framework in closed regime], *Tfutzot Israel* [Israel diaspora], 12, Choveret [booklet] Bet (March–April 1974), p. 105 [Hebrew].
53 Düzgün, "Cumhuriyetin İlanından İsrail'in Kuruluşuna," p. 82.
54 Ibid., pp. 80–81.
55 www.memri.org/report/en/print1388.htm#_edn9, retrieved September 1, 2012.
56 Hilmi Ziya Ülken, *Yahudi Meselesi* (Istanbul: Üniversite Kitabevi, 1944).
57 Ibid., p. 122.
58 Toktaş, "Perceptions of antisemitism," p. 207.
59 İçduygu and Soner, "Turkish minority rights regime," p. 460.
60 Türkmen and Öktem, "Foreign policy as a determinant," p. 2.
61 Faruk Köse, "Hahambaşı'na çağrı," *Yeni Akit*, July 15, 2014: www.habervaktim.com/yazar/65969/hahambasina-cagri.html, retrieved July 17, 2014.
62 Weiss, "Yehudey Turkia," p. 106; Türkmen and Öktem, "Foreign policy as a determinant," p. 7.
63 Weiss, "Yehudey Turkia," p. 105.
64 Bali, "The banalization of hate," p. 310.
65 Akturk, "Persistence of the Islamic *millet*," p. 899.
66 AJJDC, Box 55B, file: C.85010, April 14, 1958, p. 24.
67 Ibid., p. 3.
68 Ibid., p. 2.
69 AJJDC, Box 55B, file: C.85010A, January 11, 1960, pp. 1–2.
70 Shmuelevitz, "Emdat HaItonut HaIslamit BeTurkiya," p. 115.
71 This association was first mentioned in: Landau, "Al Dmuta Shel Haantishemiyut," p. 82. It was later mentioned by Bali. See: Rıfat N. Bali, "Irkçı Bir Dernek: Türkiye Siyonizmle Mücadele Derneği" [A racist association: Turkish Association for Fighting Zionism], *Toplumsal Tarih*, 29 (1996), pp. 32–36.
72 Landau, "Al Dmuta Shel Haantishemiyut," p. 82.
73 Levi, "Yahas HaShiltonot ve HaChevra HaTurkim," p. 239.
74 Landau, "Tofaot shel Antishemiyut," p. 229.

75 Bali, "The banalization of hate," p. 310. It is interesting to note that young urban Turkish males who migrated to Europe were not aware of the accusations in Turkey that some politicians are not truly Turkish but actually Dönme. See: Günther Jikeli, *European Muslim Antisemitism: Why Young Urban Males Say They Don't Like Jews* (Bloomington, IN: Indiana University Press, 2015), p. 278. On the Dönme and conspiracy theories involving Dönme, see: Cengiz Sisman, *The Burden of Silence: Sabbatai Sevi and the Evolution of the Ottoman–Turkish Dönmes* (New York: Oxford, 2015); Cengiz Sisman, *Transcending Diaspora: Studies on Sabbateanism and Dönmes* (Istanbul: Libra Kitap, 2016); Gershom Scholem, *Sabbatai Sevi: The Mystical Messiah* (Princeton, NJ: Princeton University Press, 1973); Marc David Baer, *The Dönme: Jewish Converts, Muslim Revolutionaries, and Secular Turks* (Stanford, CA: Stanford University Press, 2009); Rıfat N. Bali, "Bir Dönmenin Hikayesi: Nazıf Özge kimdir?" *Tarih ve Toplum* 38, 223 (2002), pp. 15–22; Rıfat N. Bali, *A Scapegoat for all Seasons: The Dönmes or Crypto-Jews of Turkey* (Istanbul: ISIS, 2008); Paul Bessemer, "Who is a crypto-Jew? A historical survey of the Sabbatean debate in Turkey," *Kabbalah: Journal for the Study of Jewish Mystical Texts*, 9 (2003), pp. 121–122; Turkay Selim Nefes, "The history of the social constructions about Dönmes," *The Journal of Historical Sociology* 25, 3 (2013), pp. 413–439; Cengiz Şişman, *Sabatay Sevi ve Sabataycılar: Mitler ve Gerçekler* (İstanbul: Aşina Kitaplari, 2008).
76 The book was first published in a serialized version in the newspaper *Bugün*.
77 İ.H Pirzade, *Türkiye ve Yahudileri* (Istanbul: Ark Matbaacılık, 1968), p. 1.
78 Ibid., p. 6.
79 Ibid., p. 7.
80 Ibid., p. 11.
81 Ibid., p. 12.
82 Henry Ford, *Beynelmilel Yahudi* (Ankara: Serdengeçti Neşriyatı, 1961).
83 Pirzade, *Türkiye ve Yahudileri*, pp. 17–19, 20, 23.
84 Ibid., p. 27.
85 Ibid., pp. 37–39.
86 Ibid., p. 45.
87 Ibid., p. 46.
88 Ibid., p. 48.
89 Ibid., pp. 69–96.
90 Weiss, "Yehudey Turkia," p. 105.
91 On Efraim Elrom's murder, see: Efrat E. Aviv, "Turkey and Elrom affair: a unique affair or a link in a chain of terrorist events in 1970s Turkey?," *Hamizrah Hehadash: The New East*, 52 (2013), pp. 286–308 [Hebrew]; Efrat E. Aviv, "The Efraim Elrom affair and Israel–Turkey relations," *Middle Eastern Studies*, 49, 5 (2013), pp. 750–769.
92 No author, "Pakid Machoz Turki Sheiyem al Yehudim Nidon Lishmone Shnot Maasar" [A Turkish clerk, who threatened Jews was sentenced to eight years in prison], *Maariv*, June 10, 1971, p. 2 [Hebrew].
93 MND 969045 US NARA ADANA 00165 181742z (Department of State Archive).
94 Israel State Archive, TUR 351.1/registered 212/Ministry of Foreign Affairs/4245/21 CHETZ/Istanbul/February 21, 1968 [in Hebrew].
95 Sh. Cohen, "Admiral Turki: Ha'aravim yilmedi lekabel et Israel" [A Turkish admiral: the Arabs will have to accept Israel]," *Maariv*, August 22, 1968, p. 16 [Hebrew].
96 Israel State Archive, registered 109/Ministry of Foreign Affairs/4245/21 CHETZ/Istanbul/March 19, 1969 [in Hebrew].
97 Necmettin Erbakan (October 29, 1926–February 27, 2011) was a Turkish politician, engineer, and academic who was the prime minister of Turkey from 1996 to 1997. He was pressured by the military to step down as prime minister and was later banned from politics by the Constitutional Court of Turkey for violating the

64 *From Ottoman rule to modern times*

separation of religion and state as mandated by the constitution, a ban that was later upheld by the European Court of Human Rights (ECHR).The political ideology and movement founded by Erbakan, Millî Görüş (National View), called for the strengthening of Islamic values in Turkey and turning away from what Erbakan perceived to be the negative influence of the Western world in favor of closer relations to Muslim countries. Erbakan's political views led to conflict with the core principle of secularism in Turkey, culminating in his removal from office. With the Millî Görüş ideology, Erbakan was the founder and leader of several prominent Islamic political parties in Turkey from the 1960s to the 2010s, namely the Milli Nizam Partisi (National Order Party) (1970–1971), the Millî Selâmet Partisi (National Salvation Party) (1972–1980), the Refah Partisi (Welfare Party) (1983–1998), the Fazilet Partisi (Virtue Party) (1998–2001), and the Saadet Partisi (Felicity Party) (2001–). On Millî Görüş, see: Hakan Yavuz, *Modernleşen müslümanlar: Nurcular, Nakşiler, Milli Görüş ve AK Parti* (İstanbul: kitapyayınevi, 2003); Efecan İnceoğlu, "Türkiye"de Siyasal İslamcılığın Evrimi," MA thesis submitted to Ankara University, 2009. Erbakan, in whose honor Konya University was renamed in 2010 (now: "Necmettin Erbakan University"), is an example of anti-Semites who are considered as intellectuals in Turkey, where he is still called 'Hoca' (learned teacher). See: Bali, *Antisemitism and Conspiracy Theories*, pp. 14, 45.
 98 Interview, Istanbul, February 2, 2013.
 99 Bali, *Antisemitism and Conspiracy*, p. 86.
100 Israel State Archive, registered 996-351/Ministry of Foreign Affairs/4245/21 CHETZ/Istanbul/August 21, 1968 [in Hebrew].
101 On Şahap Tan, see: Rıfat N. Bali, *Model Citizens of the State: The Jews of Turkey during the Multi-Party Period* (Lanham, MD: Fairleigh Dickinson University Press, 2012), p. 129.
102 Israel State Archive, TUR 351.1/registered 387/Ministry of Foreign Affairs/4245/21 CHETZ/Istanbul/July 7, 1968 [in Hebrew].
103 Israel State Archive, TUR 351.1/registered 257/Ministry of Foreign Affairs/4245/21 CHETZ/Istanbul/April 24, 29, 1969 [in Hebrew]. On Türkeş, see: Alparslan Türkeş, *Dava* (İstanbul: Kamer Yayınları, 2013); Alparslan Türkeş, *Savunma* (İstanbul: Kamer Yayınları, 2013); Landau, *Exploring Ottoman and Turkish History*, pp. 58–61.
104 Ismail Hakki Yılanlıoğlu, *Üç büyük tehlike Siyonizm-komünizm-farmasonluk* (İstanbul: Güven Basımevi, 1968).
105 Hikmet Tanyu, *Tarih Boyunca Yahudiler ve Türkler I–II* [Jews and Turks throughout History] (İstanbul: Yağmur Yayınları, 1976). The book was reprinted in 2005 in Elips Kitap Press.
106 Landau, "Tofaot shel Antishemiyut," pp. 230–231. For more on antisemitic publications in the 1960s and 1970s, see: Bali, *Antisemitism and Conspiracy Theories*, pp. 25–35.
107 Islamism is also known as a political Islam, a political ideology which strives to establish a state and society under Islamic Sharia law. For the place that antisemitism occupies in Islamist doctrine, see: Bassam Tibi, *Islamism and Islam* (New Haven, CT: Yale University Press, 2012).
108 Interview, Jerusalem, February 3, 2015.
109 Israel State Archive, registered 996-351/Ministry of Foreign Affairs/4631/26 CHETZ/Istanbul/November 9, 1970 [in Hebrew].
110 Weiss, "Yehudey Turkia," p. 105.
111 Mucahit Bilici, "The Fethullah Gülen movement and its politics of representation in Turkey," *The Muslim World*, 96 (2006), p. 15.
112 Fethullah Gülen, *İnsanın Özündeki Sevgi* (İstanbul: Da Yayıncılık, 2003), p. 165.
113 İsmail Ünal, *Fethullah Gülen'le Amerika'da Bir Ay* (İstanbul: Işık Yayınları, 2001), p. 89.

114 An interview with Zali De Toledo, Ramat Hasharon, March 4, 2004. Attempts to obtain these books through various libraries and different sources were futile.
115 www.flickr.com/photos/eksib612/sets/72157631747801352, retrieved January 12, 2015.
116 An email interview with Fethullah Gülen, November 14, 2006.
117 M. Hakan Yavuz, "Search for a new contract in Turkey: Fethullah Gülen, the Virtue Party and the Kurds," *Sais Review*, 19, 1 (1999), p. 121.
118 Bali, *Antisemitism and Conspiracy Theories*, p. 226.
119 Bali, "The banalization of hate," p. 310.
120 Bali, *Antisemitism and Conspiracy Theories*, p. 111.
121 See, for instance: Adnan Oktar, "Turkey's unforgettable Jewish history," *Ynet*, November 3, 2014: www.ynetnews.com/articles/0,7340,L-4497490,00.html, retrieved December 15, 2014.
122 Bali, *Antisemitism and Conspiracy Theories*, pp. 90–91.
123 Alan Cowel, "Car bomb kills an Israeli Embassy aide in Turkey," *New York Times*, March 8, 1992: www.nytimes.com/1992/03/08/world/car-bomb-kills-an-israeli-embassy-aide-in-turkey.html, retrieved September 12, 2012.
124 Edward Mickolous and Susan L Simmons, *Terrorism 1992–1995: A Chronology of Events and a Selectively Annotated Bibliography* (Westport, CT: Greenwood Press, 1997), pp. 129–130.
125 Gareth H. Jenkins, "Occasional allies, enduring rivals: Turkey's relations with Iran," Central Asia-Caucasus Institute, Silk Road Studies Program, Johns Hopkins University, May 2012, p. 20: www.silkroadstudies.org/new/docs/silkroadpapers/1205Jenkins.pdf21, retrieved May 23, 2013.
126 Bali, *Antisemitism and Conspiracy Theories*, p. 227.
127 See: Harun Yahya, *Yahudilik ve Masonluk* (Istanbul: Sezgin Neşriyat, 1992). This book is still available in Turkey.
128 William Armstrong, "The mahdi wears Armani: the bizarre world of Adnan Oktar," *Hürriyet Daily News*, October 2, 2014: www.Hürriyetdailynews.com/the-mahdi-wears-armani-the-bizarre-world-of-adnan-oktar.aspx?pageID=238&nID=72412&NewsCatID=474, retrieved November 12, 2014. For more on Adnan Oktar, see: Anne Ross Solberg, *The Mahdi wears Armani: An analysis of the Harun Yahya Enterprise* (Stockholm: Södertörn University, 2013).
129 Bali, *Antisemitism and Conspiracy Theories*, p. 19. Bali also mentions the antisemitic publications of Oktar. See: ibid., fn. 30.
130 Oktar was allied with the Science Research Foundation in Turkey (Bilim Araştırma Vakfi, or BAV), which is said to be headed by him.
131 This edition is still available in Turkey: Harun Yahya, *Soykırım Yalanı* (Istanbul: Alem, 1995).
132 Bali, *Model Citizens of the State*, p. 387.
133 Dina Porat and Roni Stauber (eds.), *Antisemitism Worldwide 2000/2001* (Lincoln, NE: Nebraska University Press, 2002), p. 308.
134 See: Harun Yahya, *Soykırım Vahşeti* (Istanbul: Araştırma Yayıncılık, 2003).
135 http://a9.com.tr. A partial list of the rabbis that have visited Adnan Oktar in Istanbul: Chief rabbi of Tel Aviv, Yisrael Meir Lau, former chief rabbi of Israel, Rabbi Haim Meir Drukman, former vice-minister of religious affairs, Rav Avraham Yosef, the chief rabbi of Holon in Israel, son of former Israeli chief rabbi, Harav Ovadia Yosef. Some of the leaders that were part of the Israeli delegation that have visited Mr. Adnan Oktar in Istanbul: Ayoob Kara, deputy minister of the development of the Negev and Gallilee in Israel, Likud (twice with a delegation), Knesset member Rabbi Nissim Zeev, one of the founders of Shas Party, chairman of the Joint Knesset Committee on Interior Affairs and Education, Shimon Shetreet, former minister of religious affairs, finance, science and technology, Labor Party; some pro-Israeli politicians that Oktar's representatives met in the U.S. Capitol regarding the security of

66   From Ottoman rule to modern times

  Israel: Jon Kyl, U.S. senator from Arizona, member of the Republican Party; Mike Lee, U.S. senator from Utah, member of the Republican Party, and many others.
136 The book can be downloaded from www.harunyahya.com/en/Books/2954/a-call-for-unity, retrieved October 24, 2013.
137 Daniel Steinvorth, "Interview with Harun Yahya: 'All terrorists are Darwinists,'" *Der Spiegel*, September 23, 2008: www.spiegel.de/international/world/interview-with-harun-yahya-all-terrorists-are-darwinists-a-580031.html, retrieved March 10, 2012. Michael Hopkins listed on "talksorigin" some reasons why Oktar's denial of authoring the antisemitic books is untrue: www.talkorigins.org/faqs/organizations/harunyahya.html, retrieved January 12, 2014.
138 I met Sinem in Istanbul on February 24, 2014. The quoted opinion was sent to me by email.
139 For example: On February 23, 2013, Sinem's article urging Muslim leaders to stop using antisemitic slogans, either for political reasons or out of ignorance, was published in the London-based *Al Quds Al Arabi*, the third largest circulated offshore pan-Arab newspaper according to the Carnegie Endowment for International Peace. See: www.alquds.co.uk/?p=137066, retrieved November 10, 2014.

Part II
Antisemitism under AK Party rule

3 The rise of the AK Party

Turkey's domestic politics experienced an earthquake on November 3, when the AK Party, established on August 14, 2001, won the elections. *Millî Görüş* (National View) formed the ideological basis for the political Islamist movement founded by Necmettin Erbakan, who pursued an Islamist agenda through a number of political parties. These began with the National Order Party in 1970, and subsequently three more Islamist parties led by Erbakan (Refah Partisi and Fazilet Partisi) who were able to get the support of the majority of Islamic circles, including the İskenderpaşa, a branch of the Nakşibendi order, and politically active Nur communities (communities inspired by Said Nursi, a Kurdish Sunni Muslim theologian, and his writings, the Risale-i Nur Collection, a body of Quranic commentary), and which continued the Millî Görüş political Islamist line. A split developed within Millî Görüş between the first-generation leaders loyal to Erbakan, who moved to the newly founded Saadet Partisi (Felicity Party), and a younger generation, which was led by Erdoğan, Gül, and 69 others who founded the AK Party in August 2001. The AK Party (AK means white, unblemished) claims to have abandoned the mission of Millî Görüş and has become a conservative Democrat Party.[1]

The party platform avoided reference to Islam and expressed support for laicism as a fundamental requirement for democracy and freedom. Laicism, however, was defined in the party principles as state impartiality toward Islam, and politics in contemporary Turkey toward religion, rather than state control of religious affairs. The AK Party government faced a number of immediate challenges, including veiling and the American invasion of Iraq through its bases in Turkey but, importantly, the AK Party began to assert that it no longer made policy decisions on the basis of Islamic philosophy, that its platform was secular, and that it had no intention of changing the secular nature of the state it governed. Rather, it presented itself as a conservative Democrat Party running a secular government apparatus. Government officials took pains to point out, however, that they retained their Muslim ethical values. Some prominent members of the AK Party are influenced by Islamic philosophy developed by a group of scholars from the Department of Theology at Ankara University. It calls for a rejection of Arab reformist Islam and links between Islamic law and the state. Instead, it views religion as human nature or an internal state, and the secular state as an administrative mechanism, thus assuming there is no contradiction in political leaders of a democratic secular government holding personal Muslim values.

These scholars faced criticism from more orthodox Muslims and radical Islamist intellectuals, but their ideas were brought into the mainstream within the AK Party's core.[2]

Despite the founding leaders having come from banned Islamist parties, the AK Party rejected the label 'Islamist' and defined themselves as a 'conservative democratic' party; they likened themselves to Christian democratic parties in Western Europe. They insist they are "committed to the secularism of the Turkish state," and they only oppose "the petty exclusion of religious symbolism from public life," such as the headscarf in public buildings. The goal of Islamist parties now is to "build an Islamic identity without openly violating the constitutional principle of secularism," and critics of the AK Party argue this is their hidden agenda. It is important to note, though, that when the Virtue Party collapsed, the AK Party split from the Felicity Party not only from the leadership but also from the ideology of the old pro-Islamic circles. The Felicity Party marketed itself as a religiously oriented party, with a program to match. However, in an effort to distance itself from Islamist beliefs, the AK Party rejected any ideological liaison with the Felicity Party, as well as the old Welfare Party; the AK Party has subsequently depicted itself as a national party not based solely on regional, ethnic, or religious support. To add weight to the AK Party's claims that they are not an Islamist party threatening to destabilize the secular Turkish state, their actions concerning the EU are important. Efforts to get Turkey accepted into the EU lend support to the claim that they stand for "democratic conservatism"; the EU's requirements of democracy, human rights, and pluralism hardly support the principles of Islamism. It is ironic, however, that while secularists in Turkey favor EU membership in order to contain the Islamists and secure the modernization of Turkish society, the Islamists favor joining the EU to contain the state.

The party, highlighting its anticorruption agenda and its roots in "Islamic Conservatism" (which was coined by the AK Party), sought to balance its commitment to Turkey's secular constitution with its Muslim worldview and faith.[3] The rise of the conservative AK Party in 2002 and its Muslim worldview as a dominant force in Turkish politics, as demonstrated by its successful passing of the constitutional referendum on September 12, 2010 and the party's third consecutive electoral victory 11 months later has heightened fears among many in the West, claiming Turkey is "lost" and turning its back on the historical United States–Turkey alliance, especially after reducing military and secular elites in Turkey.[4] The main concern was and still is that while Turkey is regarded as an important Islamic actor, it will lead to a more radical, undemocratic, antisemitic, and anti-Western brand of Islam.[5] In a broader perspective, scholars labeled the AK Party's new foreign policy, especially in the Middle East, as "Neo-Ottomanism," "re-Islamization" or even as "Middle Easternization of Turkey." According to Davutoğlu, instead of dissociating itself from the past, Turkey should embrace its diverse Ottoman past and culture and combine it with contemporary republican values. His famous "strategic depth" notion meant tackling Turkey's historical and geographical depth as sources of political capital that can make Turkey a global influential factor in the post-Cold War era.[6]

Not only the Islamic background of the AK Party members but also the AK Party's relative lack of foreign policy experience left the United States and the West suspicious.[7] But above all, the rise of the AK Party proved that Turkey's national interests were no longer completely compatible with America's interests, yet the importance of this relationship cannot be overestimated. With the victory of the AK Party, the U.S. administration immediately began courting Turkey. Official visits were made by U.S. Deputy Secretary of Defense Paul Wolfowitz and Undersecretary of State Marc Grossman to Ankara in 2002 to make official requests for Turkish cooperation in the Iraqi war-planning efforts. However, the Turkish prime minister and minister of foreign affairs made it clear that despite the importance of their commitment to the United States, the importance of receiving "international legitimacy" meant securing a UN mandate before any action in Iraq. The term "cooperation" now gained a different understanding in the eyes of the Turks and the Americans.[8]

Since the AK Party government was established, Turkey has positioned itself as a rising soft power that cannot be ignored.[9] Turkey, a former non-permanent member of the UN Security Council, former secretary general of the Organization of Islamic Conference (OIC), member of the G-20 group of nations, the world's eighth strongest military, NATO member, with multilateral relations with various political actors, sees itself as an emerging soft power in the regions extending from the Balkans to the Middle East and Central Asia.[10] Also, although Turkey's image in the Middle East has deteriorated somewhat, the Turks still attribute to their country a growing influential political role. For example, 64 percent of Turks claimed in TESEV's (Türkiye Ekonomik ve Sosyal Etüdler Vakfı – The Turkish Economic and Social Studies Foundation) poll in 2013 that its political role in the Middle East becomes more influential with every passing day.[11]

The rise of the AK Party gave the Islamist press a boost of self-confidence. An example of this is the reporters from the daily *Anadolu'da Vakit*, a newspaper that for years had been publishing antisemitic articles including Holocaust denial, who have been part of the press corps to accompany Erdoğan and Gül during their travels, legitimizing their viewpoints and newspaper. The same thing happened with Islamic NGOs, who, after Israeli military operations, protested violently in front of the Israeli Embassy and Israeli ambassador's residence in Ankara, as well as the Israeli Consulate in Istanbul, besieging them for several days.[12] Generally speaking, Turkish Jews have always had an affinity for the Kemalist ideology and, from the 2000s, to the CHP (Cumhuriyet Halk Partisi – Republican People's Party), although some Jews voted for the AK Party at least in the early years. As a representative from the Rabbinate said, they had a "good, proactive relationship with the AK Party" and that it is "wise to keep lines of communication open between us, we live in the same country and are willing to give them a chance," but Jews still see their future in Turkey linked to the maintenance of secular law.[13] During the last decade, Jews stayed calm even while government-endorsed antisemitic rhetoric in Turkey increased, because they were certain that the Turkish military would not allow any movement from Kemalism. After the AK Party de-militarized politics and created strict political control of the army, this hope vanished.

International politics: relations with Israel and Zionism

The affinity between the Ottoman Empire and Zionism has been discussed widely by several scholars.[14] Generally, there are two approaches addressing whether the Young Turks were pro- or anti-Zionist. The first approach asserts that the Young Turks were openly or secretly Zionist. According to the Committee of Union and Progress' understanding, Zionism and the Dönme stood behind the Committee of Union and Progress' revolution against Sultan Abdülhamid II in order to punish him for refusing to accede to Herzl's requests regarding the Charter on Israel.[15] That the Committee of Union secret meetings were held in the Freemason lodges in Salonika, where the majority of the population was allegedly Jewish, and that Emmanuel Carasso, the Ottoman Jewish parliamentarian, was a member of the delegation that announced his abdication to the sultan, allegedly proved the "Zionist scam."[16] This approach was common among Turkish and Arab politicians and journalists, as well as some government circles, in the years before World War I. It was embraced by the generation following Mustafa Kemal Atatürk's passing and until the modern day, as part of the ongoing trend to cling to the memory of Abdülhamid II, and to vilify the Young Turks. Among those were Cevat Rıfat Atilhan, an army officer who became an antisemitic journalist. The second approach claimed quite the opposite; the elite of the Committee of Union and Progress were prominent in their persistent anti-Zionist positions. Some Young Turk leaders suspected that the Zionists would establish a great concentration of Jews in the land of Israel (or in the Middle East) and later on a state that would split from the Ottoman Empire. Various anti-Zionist steps were taken, like the prohibition on Jews purchasing lands in Israel, anti-Zionist speeches conducted in the Ottoman parliament, and the closure of Zionist organizations in Istanbul in April 1914.[17] However, on the eve of World War I, the Ottoman policy became more moderate as the Ottomans were hopeful of recruiting the 'Jewish fortune' as resources for the war. Despite this change, the anti-Zionist policy of the Young Turks was quite consistent.[18] In order to understand the anti-Zionist sentiments of the Young Turks it must be noted that the first 20 years of the twentieth century were years of survival for the collapsing Ottoman Empire. Trying to save the Empire, the Young Turks' attitude toward national movements became suspicious and, at the same time, a critical element in portraying their policy toward minorities. Whereas pan-Islamism dictated the Empire's relations with the Arabs and other Muslims, and Ottomanism continued to be the guiding line in domestic policy, dictating the approach toward all minorities in the Empire, pan-Turkism served as the basis for connecting other Turkish groups (in tsarist Russia and other places). The Jews, as non-Turks and non-Muslims, as well as Zionists, could not integrate into any of the aforementioned ideologies. Thus, public Zionist activities enhanced the Ottoman suspicion that they would establish a separate political unit, a state of their own.[19]

Throughout the years, Zionism has been considered a secret agenda of the Jews and has always been a reason for not trusting them. Bali notes that at least between 1965 and 1980 the nationalist and Islamist press were directly targeting Turkish-Jewish industrialists and merchants in Istanbul, but later on many of the antisemitic expressions in Turkey were not directed at Turkish Jews per se but at every Jew, and one of the most distinguishing features of this was "Zionism."[20] In other words, Zionism has been used to describe evil Jews. The Jews in Turkey are considered 'good Jews' as long as they are not Zionist. Anti-Zionist Jews, such as Noam Chomsky, Norman Finkelstein, Neturei Karta members, and others, are considered 'good Jews' in the eyes of the Turks, just as those who condemn antisemitism or publicly support the Jewish leadership in Turkey are called 'Zionists,' 'Israel lovers,' or 'pro-Israelists.'[21] Being a Zionist or having any affinity to Israel is a 'crime' in Turkey.[22] For example, Ersoy Dede from *Yeni Akit* clearly states that he expected famous figures from the Turkish-Jewish community, such as the singer Can Bonomo, the actor Yossi Mizrahi, and others, to clearly condemn Israeli policies. Dede spoke against including Mario Levi's (the Jewish writer who serves as a professor at Yeditepe University) book in the campaign to boycott Israeli products during Operation Protective Edge in 2014, due to Levi's expressions against Israel and in favor of Erdoğan during *Mavi Marmara*.[23] In other words, even if a Jewish figure would like to distance himself/herself from politics, they will be criticized for not criticizing Israel,[24] but even when they express no sympathy toward Zionism, they still feel different. B, who wished to conceal her identity while being interviewed for Max Blumenthal's blog, expresses her feelings regarding being a Jew in Turkey:

> In the social world you are aware that you are different. In the business world being Jewish is sometimes positive because we are seen as good at commerce and Jews almost always repay their debts here. But to be honest I would say I'm putting in more effort than ever at work because the moment I slip up, I become the foreigner. At work there are always a few people I have to win over. I have to prove my Turkishness to them somehow. And then these people see me as 'the good Jew.' But they don't represent the general consensus. And I wouldn't say there is any anti-Jewish movement in the country even though we are an easy target when people look for someone to blame.... I can give you an example. I was importing lingerie for five years. When Israel started bombing Gaza, I was importing all these brands from the States, and a trade magazine for the lingerie retailers [in Turkey] put out a boycott list that focused on Jewish owned brands. My brands were on the list. I'm not a public person so it's hard to know that I'm Jewish at all. But my brands were listed because I'm Jewish. Who am I?

How do you know who I am? The magazine was a small publication in some rural city. I only knew about the boycott list because some salesman found it and showed it to me.... Who knows if it distinguished between Jewish and Israeli? The page said, "The owners of these brands help Israel in its efforts against Gaza." What the hell do I have to do with Israel? These people don't know the difference between Jews and Israelis. And the extremists take advantage of this [lack of distinction].[25]

Faik Tunay, a member of parliament from the CHP, explained the existence of antisemitism in Turkey by noting that, for the masses, Jews are equated with Israel and vice versa. The ignorant mob believes that every Jew is a Zionist, but the truth is, said Tunay, Turkish Jews don't always support Israel's policies.[26]

And E. says:

The discriminatory laws were all related to the Kurdish situation and the Muslim minorities. They never really applied to us. At the same time we are often seen as strangers, even in Istanbul. I will sometimes be asked, "Are you Turkish or not?" People would call my grandmother, "Madam," which is how you refer to a foreigner in Turkey, instead of calling her by the Turkish way, which is "Lady." Another way discrimination plays out is through building laws. There was a rule – I'm not sure if it's still in effect – against building non-Muslim places of worship. So all the synagogues we have, come from the Ottoman times. And if we fill up a Jewish cemetery the state will seize it on the grounds that it is no longer usable. So the Jewish community here never lets its cemeteries fill up. To get buried in one you have to pay 25 thousand liras. But that law seems to have changed – I'm not really sure.[27]

A similar response was given by a Turkish Jew following the accusations of Turkish-Jewish participants in IDF combat with the *Mavi Marmara*: "As a Jew, I can attest that there is a difference between being a Turk and an Israeli," Ediz, a Turkish Jew, told *Al-Monitor*. "But whenever there is fighting between Israel and the Palestinians, the atmosphere in Turkey turns against us, and people start acting as if we've committed a crime." "The media paints such an image that many won't even consider us human," Leri, another Turkish Jew, told the paper.[28] It's no wonder the Jews of Turkey feel intimidated when the word "Zionism," or its various derivatives, is used to taunt them, even when they deny that it bothers them. For instance, IHH (İnsan Hak ve Hürriyetleri İnsani Yardım Vakfı – Humanitarian Relief Foundation) chairperson Bülent Yıldırım, while responding to the Marmara incident, said that the case was not against the Jewish nation but against Zionists and murderers. If one understands that the State of Israel was established on the basis of Zionism in order to offer an asylum to the Jews, making this odd differentiation between Jews and Zionism expresses a misunderstanding of the Jewish state. Sometimes, even the synagogues in Turkey are attributed to hostile Zionist activity, as Nurettin Şirin wrote in *Vakit* on September 2, 2004:

Firstly, the Chief Rabbi who uses his synagogues as Zionist bases must learn that no Jew has the right to teach a lesson on 'human rights' to [us], the children of the Ottomans. These [Jews], who fled Spain's massacres and found shelter thanks to Ottoman tolerance, have carried out nothing but treason and plots on Ottoman territory, and have [always] carried out the ugly designs of Zionism on this [Turkish] land.[29]

Following this matter, Kenan Kıran from *Vakit* ramped up the tension by saying, on August 27, 2004: "Haleva, if you do not stop Sharon, anti-Jewish voices may turn into anti-Jewish action."[30] Except for the direct violence the statement suggests, it is obvious that in order to enact 'revenge' on Israel, the Turkish Jews are the ones who will be the victims. The separation between Israel and Jews does not exist within the Islamist media and, as always, Jews are perceived as agents of Zionism or the State of Israel. Furthermore, when Turkey judged in absentia the four senior Israeli commanders due to their so-called part in the *Mavi Marmara* incident, demonstrators in front of the court building carried placards equating Zionism and Israel with Hitler.[31]

The boundary between rational criticism and irrational claim is contested and difficult to define. Sometimes the same claim may be either a rational criticism or a blunt weapon, depending on how it is mobilized and in what combination. Sometimes rational criticisms and irrational libels combine in toxic, angry swirls that are difficult to disentangle and that assume an inappropriate style and tone.[32] Accordingly, even if antisemitism is not clearly expressed, Turkish society can create a correlation between Israel, Zionism, world-ruling aspirations, and evil in general. In many cases it is not even necessary to connect Jews and evil. The public links the threads by itself. This is even harder for the Turkish Jews when Erdoğan himself calls Zionism "a crime against humanity," but also mentions fascism and antisemitism as crimes similar to Zionism.

In the Fifth Alliance of Civilizations Forum in Vienna's Hofburg Palace in 2013, Erdoğan underlined the rising trend of fascism across Europe:

> we are facing a world in which racist attacks have gained momentum … in a similar vein I must state that rising racism in Europe is a serious problem for the Alliance of Civilizations Project … we witness very frequently the alienation of the "other" in various countries instead of efforts to understand the culture and beliefs of the "other."[33]

"The same goes for Zionism," continued Erdoğan "Antisemitism and Fascism, it is inevitable that Islamophobia be considered a crime against humanity."[34] Despite the fact that Erdoğan was criticized for saying this on March 20, he did not regret his sad comparison, but said: "I stand behind every word that I said."[35] Shay Cohen, Israel consul general in Istanbul, mentions that for the Turks every sort of racism is equal to Islamophobia: "Just two days ago I attended the ceremony commemorating the Struma tragedy and the Minister of Culture said the same thing. Prime Minister Davutoğlu said the same while meeting minority leaders."[36]

The aforementioned is part of a large discourse on what antisemitism means, especially when discussed in reference to anti-Zionism. Anti-Zionism is often called "the new antisemitism."[37] Following the Holocaust and the rise of postwar anti-racist movements, there was a space left in public discourse for open antisemitism. One of the foundation blocks of post-war Europe was the narrative of the defeat of Nazism, the Holocaust, and the creation of a new human rights-based settlement. Europe was shocked out of its antisemitic ways of thinking by the Holocaust, but the 'new antisemitism' theorists argue that antisemitism continues to manifest itself in more subtle ways, specifically in both the quality and the quantity of hostility toward Israel.[38] But at the same time, this term is considered controversial by theorists and scholars, who claim that it stems from a Jewish nationalist exaggerated viewpoint that often covers for justified criticism of the State of Israel.[39] In his article David Hirsh highlights three key theoretical aspects of antisemitism:

1 Antisemitism is a social fact that is produced through shared meanings and exclusions; it is not an individual moral failing.
2 Difficulties of understanding are raised by the shift from explicit and self-conscious racism and antisemitism to discursive and institutional forms of racism and antisemitism.
3 Anti-Zionism tends to understand Israeli nationalism in a spirit that diverges from standard sociological approaches to nationalism. Israeli nationalism is often singled out as uniquely racist. Narratives of nationhood are usually not examined only for their truth or falsity, but understood also as social phenomena with particular trajectories and functions, but Israeli nationalism is often denounced in simplistic binary terms as an artificial construct as though all the others were in some sense authentic. Contradictions are usually examined and their consequences traced, but regarding Israel they are often employed to construct essentialist patterns of thinking to denounce the idea and reality of a Jewish state.[40]

Within a decade, Turkey has changed its foreign policy from one pole to another: from an inward-looking, regionally isolated country uneasy with the challenges of post-Cold War globalization, to being a respected member of the international community in terms of its economy. Turkey has completed its transformation into an export-oriented, industrial producer, characterized by a vibrant marketplace that ranks sixteenth among the world's largest economies. This economic rise was assisted by the start of accession negotiations with the EU in 2005. For the first time since Atatürk, Turkey has been basing its foreign policy on a homegrown doctrine shaped by the two key concepts of "strategic depth" and "zero problems with neighbors." This proactive outlook was carried even into international institutions when Turkey became one of the members of the UN Security Council for a two-year term between 2009 and 2010.[41] Due to this change in foreign policy, as well as the AK Party's Islamic orientation, Turkey became more supportive of the Palestinian side in the conflict between

The rise of the AK Party 77

Israel and the Palestinian Authority. The support grew so strong during the second half of the 2000s that even documents from the Ottoman Archive in Istanbul have often been transferred to the Palestinian Authority in Ramallah. Following Erdoğan's direct instruction, millions of documents dealing with Ottoman Palestine's soil have been transferred to the Palestinian Authority as part of what seems to be an attempt to create an evidence file that could be used by the Palestinians in future negotiations with Israel regarding refugees' property.[42] However, Uzer claims that the bilateral relations between Israel and Turkey did not deteriorate due to the Islamist ideology of the AK Party, something that the party does not openly embrace in any case, but due to Palestinian casualties, both militants and civilians, as a consequence of Israel's operations in Gaza and the West Bank.[43]

Turkey has always been sympathetic to the Palestinian struggle in Israel, and this sympathy was expressed not only by Islamists but also by secular politicians such as former President Ahmet Necdet Sezer (2000–2007) and former Prime Minister Bülent Ecevit (served as prime minister of Turkey in 1974, 1977, 1978–1979, and 1999–2002).[44] Even Israeli diplomats were aware of this sympathy. Zvi Elpeleg, who served as the Israeli ambassador to Ankara from 1995 to 1997, characterized the Turks as extremely sensitive to the plight of the Palestinians. Many Turks perceived the Palestinians as defending their rights and were critical of Israelis who called them 'terrorists.'[45] This sympathy has been encouraged by the Turkish media, which was a functional factor in its intensive and dramatic coverage of the Israeli so-called atrocities against Palestinians. This extensive coverage throughout the past decade has created massive general protests against Israel and made some civil society organizations more sensitive to the Palestinian question.[46] By constructing Palestinians as universally symbolic, their actual needs for solidarity and freedom go largely unconsidered. Rather than actual people finding a multiplicity of ways to live and to struggle in difficult circumstances, 'the Palestinians' are portrayed as a single heroic victim of the homogeneous and evil 'Zionism.' They become romantic and enraged carriers of our own anti-Western fantasies.[47] But it seems that under the AK Party, Turkey decided to take an active role in supporting the Palestinians. As a result, political and strategic relations with Israel have been deteriorating since 2008, after Turkey attempted to mediate between Damascus and Jerusalem following the Second Lebanon War in the summer of 2006, and after the triumph of the resistance. This involvement yielded positive results, and Israeli Prime Minister Ehud Olmert (served as prime minister of Israel from 2006 to 2009) stressed to the Turkish prime minister his willingness to return the Golan.[48] However, as Operation Cast Lead (December 2008–February 2009) took place right after Turkey's attempt to mediate between Israel and Syria, Erdoğan became outraged and blamed Israel for ruining Turkey's peace efforts. Twelve days before the Davos incident, Erdoğan made the following statement regarding Operation Cast Lead:

> There is a world media under the control of Israel. This has to be pointed out. As a matter of fact, if their publications were objective then the incident

would be seen in a very different light, but nobody says anything. Nobody says stop this inhumanity.... I'm reading from the Torah. The sixth of the Ten Commandments says "thou shall not kill." In Hebrew it's "Lo Tirtsach." Under which law, which religion, with what conscience can they justify the killing of innocent children?[49]

On January 29, 2009, Erdoğan walked out of a panel at the World Economic Forum in Davos after harshly criticizing Israeli President Shimon Peres over the fighting in Gaza. "Mr. Peres, you are older than me," Erdoğan said. "Your voice comes out in a very loud tone. And the loudness of your voice has to do with a guilty conscience. My voice, however, will not come out in the same tone." Later on Erdoğan described Peres as a man who "knew very well how to kill."

He continued by saying: "I remember two former prime ministers in your country who said they felt very happy when they were able to enter Palestine on tanks," Erdoğan then told Peres, speaking in Turkish. "I find it very sad that people applaud what you said. There have been many people killed. And I think that it is very wrong and it is not humanitarian."[50] Eventually Erdoğan walked off the stage, vowing never to return. One of Turkey's Jewish community representatives saw Davos as the turning point in Erdoğan's attitude toward the Jews: "I think that that day was Erdoğan's strategic decision to take a separate path from the Jews."[51] Relations with Israel deteriorated further when Israel's Deputy Foreign Minister Danny Ayalon berated Turkish Ambassador Ahmet Oğuz Çelikkol in Tel Aviv in 2010 by sitting him on a low chair as an act of humiliation. Ayalon had delivered a rebuke to Çelikkol regarding an anti-Israel television show in Turkey. At the beginning of the conversation with the Turkish envoy on Monday, Ayalon told cameramen in Hebrew: "Note that he is sitting in a lower chair ... that there is only an Israeli flag on the table and that we are not smiling." The Turkish ambassador and the Turkish government were furious at the envoy's humiliation. In a sharply worded ultimatum to Israel the following day, Ankara demanded an apology for what it described as Ayalon's demeaning treatment of its ambassador.[52] Ayalon apologized to the Turkish ambassador right after this incident, but the damage had already been done.

Criticism of Israel

Hirsh claims that subconscious antisemitism may be recognized by the use of racist stereotypes in an allegedly non-racist discourse. The same happens when opponents of Israeli human rights abuses find themselves embracing ideas stemming from classic antisemitic blood libels or theories.[53] In other words, while attempting to oppose anti-Israel policy or antisemitism, in some cases opponents use the exact terms they claim Israel uses in order to express their criticism. Images and tropes that resemble those of antisemitism also appear in the anti-Israel agitation of antiracists, of people who strongly oppose antisemitism. But even while doing that, it should be emphasized here that not all criticism of Israel is indeed antisemitic. The concrete positions against the State of Israel and Zionism, even those calling for their elimination, do not necessarily express antisemitism; but when they are supported by ideological reasoning that deny not only the deeds of the Zionist Jews but also the Jews themselves for their permanent negative 'characters' – e.g., immorality, greediness, deviousness – and for what these characters stand for, they certainly become antisemitic. Not all criticism of Israel is free from antisemitism. The question of antisemitism, therefore, must necessarily be one of judgment and interpretation rather than of proof or refutation. It is up to the public to judge whether a saying or a deed is hostile toward Israel and elicits antisemitic sentiments. Hirsh claims that the relationship between hostility to Israel and antisemitism is complex and difficult to pin down. It requires sociological and political judgment to recognize significant antisemitism. It is no accident that one of the nodes of particular controversy is around the issue of definitions of antisemitism, and there is nothing close to an agreed upon definition among scholars and activists. The proposed definitions are controversial. Some people are content to demonstrate that there is a contradiction between the requirements for Israel to be a democratic state for all its citizens and for Israel also to be a Jewish state. They find that contradiction to be sufficient to pronounce that Zionism is essentially a form of racism. Other people equally and triumphantly demonstrate that because anti-Zionism finds Israel as a Jewish nation to be the only illegitimate nation in the world, then anti-Zionism is by definition antisemitic.[54]

Criticism of Israel takes many forms. One might say that the occupation of Palestinian territory is oppressive and requires a regime of racist violence and humiliation to sustain it. One might say that Israel uses targeted assassinations against its enemies and practices imprisonment of Palestinians without trial, which is contrary to international human rights norms. Sometimes, antisemitic themes and images are put to work to help this process. Some anti-Zionist movements employ antisemitic tropes to explain Israel's bad behavior, to exaggerate it, and to bind people into an emotional commitment against it. Instead, there must be a subconscious drawing upon the antisemitic motifs that reside in the collective cultural reservoir. The rational type of criticism of Israel outlined above is joined in public discourse by a swirling mass of claims of a different kind, such as that Israel has a policy of killing children; the Israel lobby is immensely powerful; Israel is responsible for the Iraq War; Israel exaggerates the Holocaust and manipulates its memory for its own instrumental purposes; Israel steals the body parts of its enemies; Israel is an apartheid state; and Israel is essentially racist. As stated, the border between rational criticism and irrational claim is contested and difficult to define, but totally given to the context, atmosphere, and rhetoric style in which anti-Israeli criticism is expressed.[55]

In Turkey, just as in many other places, criticism of Israeli policies and hostility to Israel come from a number of different political traditions: liberal-left and socialist, nationalist and fascist, and Islamist-conservative. In parallel, those who hold antisemitic approaches are mostly part of the Turkish ultranationalist groups, radical Islam, and the radical left. These traditions are distinct, but they are also intertwined. Elements of rhetoric, especially from the 1990s onward, when communication and media became more open and more public in Turkey, evolved and switched easily from one to another. Yet, many of the critics of Israel do not seem to understand the link between anti-Zionism and antisemitism. In other cases they strive for the right to distinguish between criticism of Israel and antisemitism. This approach was defined by Talip Küçükcan as follows: seeing someone who criticizes Israel as an anti-Semite is an approach that is no longer in fashion. According to Küçükcan, every time Israel is criticized, Jewish organizations call it "antisemitism." In his eyes, there is a clear distinction between Jews and the State of Israel. Not only Muslims criticize Israel; it is also criticized on the streets of London and New York. There are even Jews who criticize Israel's politics. Are they also anti-Semites? No. On the other hand, the fear of being called antisemitic for criticizing Israel is starting to disappear.[56] Yunus Emre Kocabaşoğlu agrees on that. In a lengthy article he claims that criticizing the "atrocities in Gaza does not make the critic an anti-Semite." Kocabaşoğlu quoted several Turkish thinkers and journalists, such as Ümit Kıvan, who claimed that "the danger of antisemitism does not exist in 2004," and said that Israel cannot be challenged without declaring those who challenge it as anti-Semites.[57]

A plausible proof of the claim that antisemitism is an integral part of Turkey's attitude toward Israel is the statement made by the Turkish chief of staff between 1998 and 2002, Hüseyin Kıvrıkoğlu. He participated in a press conference following the decision to cancel a tank modernization contract with Israel (after Israeli soldiers besieged Palestinian President Yasser Arafat's headquarters in May 2002). In his speech, Kıvrıkoğlu described the politicians who opposed the contract with Israel as "those who were born anti-Semites and those who want to take a piece of the cake but cannot."[58]

Another example of the confusion between Zionism, Israel, and Judaism is an article published in *Milli Gazete* on January 8, 2013. After Operation Pillar of Defense, a few Israelis created accessories from the remains of rockets launched at Israel from Gaza during the operation. The accessories were sold online. The newspaper did not mention the word "Israelis" but "Zionists" in describing the sellers, and deplored the fact that "the Jewish mind" could come up with artwork as a "service for Zionism." The article used descriptions such as "Jewish minds," "Jewish merchant mind," "ferocious Zionist," and others.[59] It is interesting to note that even the Turkish Jews feel that the Turkish regime does not distinguish between Jews and the State of Israel, and it is interesting to witness that this feeling prevailed in Turkey long before the rise of the AK Party. In 1971, shortly after the murder of Efraim Elrom, Yigal Lavie from the Israeli Consulate in Istanbul, wrote to Jerusalem in a classified wire that the local Jews sensed a positive change in their general position in Turkey. As the regime felt guilty for the tragedy, it attempted to atone for that crime. An Israeli construction company representative to Turkey even told Lavie that whereas in the past he had been successful in selling apartments in Israel to Turkish Jews, that year (1971) he failed to repeat the same success. He was often told: "it is worthless to invest abroad now, when Jews begin to feel good here."[60] The Jews, who had usually denied any affinity with Israel, were enthusiastic to exploit this lack of distinction between Israel and Turkish Jews.

Political approaches: Islamists

Anti-Zionism was a constitutive element of Islamic political ideology, and in the crystallization of Islamism as a political ideology in the 1970s and 1980s. Islamic discourse was based on a dichotomy between 'us' and 'them' (the West). This dichotomy was also seen as the manifestation of a struggle between the forces of 'good' and 'evil.' The 'other' of Islamist discourse has mostly been the United States and Israel. The critique of American and Israeli imperialism was supported by the call for a front against the forces of Zionism. The distinction between anti-Zionism and antisemitism has always been blurred in these circles. Especially in the last two decades, religious-conservative establishments have gained prominence in political, social, economic, and intellectual fields in Turkey. The advent of religious-conservative publishing houses and Islamist journals and newspapers indicates a new chapter in Turkish intellectual and political history,[61] a chapter, which if not encouraged, is at least not prevented by the AK Party government. AK Party members frequently stress the antisemitism in the Kemalist regime and its army as, for example, Hüseyin Çelik, former deputy chairman in charge of publicity and media in the AK Party, stated following the *Mavi Marmara* incident. Çelik mentioned the purchase of Atilhan's antisemitic books by the Turkish army in the 1940s. Çelik admits that antisemitism does exist in Turkey, but not in AK Party circles:

> There is a history of antisemitism in Turkey. But with us there is no antisemitism and such. Look at the other side; if it weren't for our Prime Minister's reactions [Erdoğan who served as Prime Minister in 2010], antisemitism in Turkey would be far greater.[62]

For most of the Islamist intelligentsia, Palestine is considered a former Ottoman province. It recalls for the Turks Herzl's request in 1901 from Sultan Abdülhamid II for permission to settle Jewish immigrants in this territory and the sultan's refusal. A good example of the importance Islamist Turks give to Abdülhamid's anti-Zionist approach is the article by Mustafa Armağan from *Zaman*, which was published during the *Mavi Marmara* crisis and was titled: "How did Abdülhamid make the Chief Rabbi apologize?"[63] In this article, Armağan describes at length how Moshe Levy, the Chief Rabbi (served between 1872 and 1908), was forced to apologize to Sultan Abdülhamid II for introducing him to Theodor Herzl. Armağan calls on his readers to learn from Abdülhamid II regarding how to elicit an apology from either the Jews or Israel. Since Herzl was interested in having Israel (or Palestine as mentioned in *Zaman*) as a national home for the world Jewry, the meeting with the sultan, which was arranged by the chief rabbi, made the sultan angry. In response, he humiliated the chief rabbi by letting him wait for three days for a personal meeting. In those days, making someone wait for the sultan was considered as if the person was jailed. When the sultan finally met with the chief rabbi, he reprimanded him for being the mediator of such a meeting with Herzl, whose aim was to gain permission to settle Israel with Jews. According to the writer, the chief rabbi said:

"My Lord, I swear I did not know he [Herzl] would mention the word 'Zionism'! Herzl did not inform me of any such thing. Please do not make me responsible as if I was a part of it. I am innocent, my people are innocent" and afterwards he stood up, and fell at the sultan's feet, crying and asking him to forgive him and his people ... the Sultan stood up and angrily said: "You say that you did not know about his visit. However, in your letter, you write that he wanted to talk to me about a subject related to the Jewish nation! What is that supposed to mean?!" Moshe Levy, bursting into tears, answered as following: "Our Majesty, that man is a journalist, I assumed that he wanted to learn the opinion of your Majesty on the subject of the Jewish issue in general." The Sultan, touched by an elderly 70 something year old weeping before him, said: "I now understand that you are innocent." He called the Chamberlin [Mabeyinci – person responsible for the Sultan's external affairs] and ordered him to have the Chief Rabbi rest.[64]

According to Joshua Ashkenazi, Moshe Levy's grandson, who revealed his family story, his grandfather had become sick and spent 15 days in bed following this scolding. Armağan ends his article by saying:

he was indeed the last sultan. This word's sparkle is relevant still "if I accepted one percent of this man's request [Herzl], who knows what would have happened to me and to my state." We know what happened to you for not accepting this request, my sultan.[65]

Islamists also see the Turkish Republic's founder, Atatürk, as a Dönme, a descendant of the Jewish devotees of Shabtai Zvi, though law No. 5816 on crimes committed against Atatürk, which criminalizes the slandering of his memory and which was passed on July 31, 1951, prohibits that.[66]

Although the Dönme are not considered Jewish, in Turkey they are often perceived to be Jews. Marc Baer claims that when the Dönme arrived in Turkey they were perceived as Jews, whereas in Salonika they were perceived as Muslims. From the very beginning, the Dönme were seen as "hidden Jews."[67] The Islamist perception of Israel is of a 'robber' country that expelled the Palestinians from their homeland. In their eyes, both Turkey and Israel were established due to the 'Jewish' revolution. From this point, it is easy to realize that Zionism is a scam to conquer the world and this is why it is a satanic expansionist ideology that threatens not only the Arab world but Turkey as well. The Islamists reject Turkish nationalism because they believe that nationalism, as a secular ideology, cannot embrace Islam, since according to the religious ideology all Muslims belong to a single nation (Umma). Turkish nationalism damages this unity and divides Muslims' interests. This is why there is hostility toward Moiz Kohen, known as Munis Tekinalp, who was a Jew who called for general Turkification in the 1930s and 1940s in Turkey He is considered as the Jew who "planted the virus of nationalism" within Turkish society as a plan to destroy the unity of the Islamic nation. Tekinalp is held up as further evidence of the Jews' part in dooming the transformation of the Turkish Republic into the Turkish Islamic Republic and, in particular, the crypto-Jewish Dönme who established and have also been controlling Turkey behind the scenes, though Tekinalp was not a Dönme.[68] İhsan Dağı, a professor in the Department of International Relations at the Middle East Technical University, said in an interview with *Radikal* on February 25, 2005, that anti-Dönme propaganda is the common base for several groups in Turkey that are united by this conspiracy theory. They create a social problem in Turkey as well as they create unity and homogeneity by declaring that they must unite against "the people among us who hold sinister plans." These groups include nationalistic-conservative circles, Millî Görüş, pro-Third Word Kemalists, leftists, and security-centered sectors. According to Dağı, this anti-Sabattaist propaganda is considered antisemitism.

> It is a new and broad alliance against the Jews and the Dönmeö who are allegedly secretly plotting not only in the world but also in Turkey, who control Turkey and who need to be stopped ... in this alliance you have groups from AK Party, the Left, Kemalists, CHP, and Alevi's, a whole world of people.

(Alevism is the term used for a large number of heterodox Muslim Shia communities with different characteristics and a mystical branch of Islam whose adherents are followers of Ali, the Twelve Imams and their descendant. The Alevis in Turkey regard Hacı Bektaş Veli as their patron.)[69]

Generally, according to Islamist journalism, Zionism is related to organizations that share a common mission: To eliminate all other religions and impose the Jewish religion upon the world. These organizations are B'nai Brith, Freemasons, Mossad, and the CIA. According to Islamist journalism, B'nai Brith is the organization that influences world politics and the economy, and receives immediate reports and updates from the UN through friends who occupy key positions. B'nai Brith is active everywhere in the world and pretends to be a nice organization by fulfilling humanitarian missions. In Turkey, for instance, it is titled "The Association of Protecting the Poor" (Fakirleri Koruma Derneği). One of the examples encouraging positive echoes and sympathy toward B'nai Brith was the establishment of the Quincentennial Foundation organization. The foundation aimed to demonstrate the welcoming attitude of Ottoman rulers toward the expelled Jews, but Islamist journalism stressed that the expelled Jews took over the Empire through their economic resources (trade and interest), which led to the Empire's destruction. It is a repeated argument that Zionism was Judaism's messenger to destroy the Ottoman Empire.[70] Judaism is ascribed as the source of capitalism, socialism, and communism, and social-economical ideologies that aim to serve Zionist interests.[71]

Another way to prove Zionism's great power is related to Germany. The Jews are accused of planning the genocide conducted by Germany in order to bolster immigration to Israel. As for the Holocaust, the number of victims was exaggerated. The newspapers claimed that those who were transported to the extermination camps were Jews of Khazar-Turkic origin. Islamic Turkish journalism adopts the theory that eastern European Jews have a Khazar origin and blame Israel and Zionism for sacrificing these Jews for the sake of increasing immigration to Israel. Even among the Jewish people, there is a hostile attitude toward Turkish Jews and Muslim Turks. Islamic journalism always attempts to link the Jewish–Zionist–Israeli power to Turkey and the Turks.[72] In many cases, just like the example referring to the Khazars, Islamist scholars and journalists are eager to involve pseudo-theological discourses. Such a statement is made by the Millî Görüş member Dr. Recai Yahyaoğlu regarding the release of Gilad Shalit, the Israeli soldier who had spent five years in Hamas captivity. The fact that Israel was forced to release 1,000 Muslim Palestinians for only one soldier expresses the Jew's perspective of themselves as a superior race and chosen people.[73]

Even the Gulf War in 1992 was presented to readers as a scam created by the Jews. The latter, it was said, created the crisis in order to establish Greater Israel, whose borders were set by Herzl. Behind every world action stands Israel, Zionism, or Judaism in the eyes of Islamic journalism. The burning of the Al Aqsa Mosque in 1969, made Islamic journalism in Turkey publish allegations that the Zionists planned to do away with the Mosque of Al Aqsa, the holiest Islamic shrine in Jerusalem, and replace it with the Third Temple. This claim has repeated itself throughout the years.[74] The ostensible scams of the Jews are widely based on stereotypes familiar from European literature. For instance, Jews are accused of being tricksters, mega-swindlers, hypocrites, spies, and black market traders. The Jews, according to Islamic journalism, were known for these traits, but were not too noticeable as they have been scattered throughout many countries. But now that all Jews have gathered in Israel it seems like Israel has broken a record in forgery and fraud. The newspaper *Bugün*, for example, suggests being aware of these people, who Allah and Muhammad cursed as they are the "hyena of history:[75]

> If it were not for the Jews, world forgery wouldn't exist in the world's dictionaries. Only people like Sultan Abdülhamid II, Hitler, and De Gaulle were truly aware of their character, one that they hide well behind a mask of misery, forlornness, and cowardice.

As stated, Jewish control of the world is an economic, political, and scientific control. Jews are also the ones behind the establishment of international organizations such as the UN, IMF (International Monetary Fund), World Bank, and big international firms. Through these organizations Jews progresses toward their goal of world domination. In addition, the Jews caused the destruction of religious faiths in the name of science, which is a sham. Through their financial power they enacted revenge upon Europe: the Vatican surrendered, the King of Spain apologized for what they did to them 500 years ago, and the Germans still pay compensation for what Hitler did to the Jews. But the most dangerous topic, according to Islamic journalism, is Jews' and Israel's control of the United

States. Turkey should also be cautious when it comes to Jews, because even today they control Turkey as well. The Turkish economy is under Jewish control and almost all banks work for Israel and the Jews. Israel spies on Turkey and eavesdrops on all phone calls made in Turkey.[76] One of the highlights of using the Christian world's positions against the Jews is the use of blood libels. Blood libels occurred in the Ottoman Empire even by Muslims.[77] Islamic journalism depicted the libel with a modern and anti-Islamic character. For instance, when Israel gave shelter to a group of Muslim Bosnian children during the Yugoslavian War in 1993, *Cuma* blamed Israel for transferring these children to its organ bank in order to sell their organs for money. According to *Zaman* in 1991, slaughter is a Jewish occupation.[78]

In conclusion: The Islamic press in Turkey is hostile toward Israel. This stand is based on two elements: (1) Islamic traditions, which present a negative stance toward Jews and Judaism regardless of Dhimmi. (2) Antisemitic viewpoints, which assisted the media in blurring the political-economic facets and the traditional Islamic stances regarding monotheistic communities, and which widen the hostility to a general anti-Zionist and antisemitic one. Hostile stances toward Israel, sometimes based on Christian antisemitic elements, also exist in political circles that are not Islamic, but these stances are based mostly on political-economic considerations of domestic and foreign policies and less on Islamic religious sentiments as expressed in Islamic circles. In addition, political-economic elements affect anti-Israel stances in Islamic circles and in the Islamic media but their influence is minor compared to the importance given to religious antisemitic sentiments.[79] With regards to antisemitism, the attitude of the Islamist and nationalist intellectuals and publicists is very simple. For them, a Muslim cannot be an anti-Semite. As Ali Bulaç stated in his column in *Zaman*:

> Antisemitism is haram [forbidden] in our religion. One cannot have enmity against the Jew because of his religion/race. The Quran, when speaking of Jews and Christians, states clearly that "not all of them are alike" (3/Al Imran, 113–115) and praises the good ones. As a matter of fact, we have seen in all parts of the world "good Jews" who reacted to the murders [committed by] Israel.[80]

Davut Şahin, a writer in *Yeni Asya*, Said Nursi community's publishing house and journal, agrees on that:

> There is no antisemitism in either the history of Islam or in Turkey. [...] when the media recounts that there is antisemitism in Turkey, it discusses it from perspectives that oppose Islam. Turkey is a Muslim country and this religion [Islam] does not enable antisemitism because this holy religion does not accept any praise or any satire based on people's race or ethnic group.[81]

Entitling his op-ed "A merchant Jew and a Jewish professor," Şahin ridicules Shylock's famous dialogue and compares his behavior to Israel's behavior toward the Palestinians. According to Şahin, Israel humiliates the entire Palestinian nation in front of the world, smiles at its loss, and laughs at its casualties. International treaties pass it by, it alienates its friends through media pressure, and provokes its enemies just because they are Muslims. Şahin suggests replacing Shylock's use of the words "Jews" with "Muslims" in his famous dialogue, so that Israel and/or the Jews would understand the value of Muslims.

> First, I think, their consciousness should be ready for it because the media, which is under Jewish control, continues to be one sided. Everywhere in the world, the media expresses Jewish viewpoints, displays their one sided racist approach. Anyone who criticizes Israel whether it is an academic, author, caricaturist, or producer is immediately labeled an "anti-Semite." Every state is criticized, so why not Israel? Why is Judaism not questioned? Ok, for years we have heard how the Nazis slaughtered the Jews, we know ... hundreds of books, research pieces and articles have been written about it and thousands of films were created in regard ... but has a genuine film, book, or research piece concerning the Palestinian ever been created? If they do exist, they can be counted on the fingers of one hand. God's name "justice" will manifest and we will observe his justice with our own eyes.[82]

According to Kerim Balcı, Islamists can differentiate between "the Jews of Quran" and the current Jews. Balcı gives as an example the ultraradical Islamic thinker and writer Mustafa İslamoğlu, who claims in his book *Yahudileşme Temayülü* (Tendency of Judaization), that the term 'Jew' in the Quran also pertains to a Muslim. Thus, if a Muslim behaves like the Jew described in the Quran, he himself can be considered "a Jew." İslamoğlu makes a separation between Quranic Jews and modern Jews and thus did not become an anti-Semite. According to Balcı, one of the reasons why antisemitism and anti-Israel feelings prevail among the secularists in Turkey is that the secular parts of Turkish society have always had a connection with Israel, but they lacked loyalty and thus no friendships were created.[83] Burak Bekdil, a prolific columnist from *Hürriyet*, who often writes on antisemitism, tried to answer the question of whether antisemitism is necessarily linked with Islamist circles. Bekdil claims that a categorical hatred of Jews exists in the Islamist camp in Turkey, but it can be observed only in the very marginal publications such as the daily *Vakit*. According to Bekdil, even the Islamic media attempts to distinguish between legitimate criticism of Israel and antisemitism:

> there are dozens of columns that appeared in the Islamic/conservative side of the Turkish media in the past few weeks, which, while denouncing Israel's militancy in Gaza, emphasized the need to distinguish between the State of Israel and the Jewish people.[84]

In much more mainstream and popular Islamic/conservative papers, such as *Zaman*, says Bekdil, one can find only condemnations against antisemitism.

Leftists

In the past, leftist newspapers avoided using antisemitic expressions. Although they harshly criticized Israel, they avoided taking a stance against the Jews, perhaps because some radical leftist groups were chaired by Jews.[85] Turkey's leftist intelligentsia tends to see Israel as an imperialist and expansionist state, an extension of American hegemony in the Middle East, and the conflict between Israel and the Palestinian Authority is seen as the imperialists' oppression of the poor and needy. This view has its origins in the political and ideological struggle in the 1970s when leftist advocates of the Marxist ideology often joined the Palestine Liberation Organization (PLO) and were even trained in their camps in Jordan, Lebanon, and Syria. The murderers of the Israeli consul general in Istanbul in 1971 were partly trained at PLO camps and had close relations with the Arabs. For the Turkish left, Zionism is an aggressive ideology that fosters antisemitism. An example of this tendency is the leftist journal *Birikim*, which published a special edition in 2004 that was dedicated to antisemitism and Zionism, which described Zionism and antisemitism as "two sides of the same coin."[86] *Birikim*, it seems, finds it hard to digest that Zionism is nationalism and to find distance between the latter and antisemitism. Muslim and non-Muslim intellectuals signed a petition titled "Zero tolerance for antisemitism" in *Birikim*'s October 2004 issue and even they admitted that the left in Turkey holds double standards when it comes to antisemitism in Turkey:

> what we wish to point out is that a large sector of the Left, including human rights circles in Turkey, fail to include in their agenda antisemitism as a threat in its own right, and when forced to confront it, merely subsume it under the rubric of discrimination, and ignore its vehemence.[87]

Ümit Kıvanç, a publicist, wrote in an article that "the people who actually govern Israel are a band of rogues," and highlighted that "everybody who wants to be a member of humanity must work for the abolition of the State of Israel in its present form because the State of Israel has also captured the Jewish identity."[88] An example of the leftist's strong anti-Israel attitude was the front page announcement published on August 9, 2006 in *Radikal*, titled "We Accuse!" (İtham ediyoruz), a conscious allusion to Emile Zola's famous open letter during the Dreyfus trial (J'accuse). *Radikal*'s statement was directed at the America's President Bush, Britain's Prime Minister Blair, and Israel's Prime Minister Olmert, who were as accused of being responsible for the imperialist, colonialist, and aggressive policies of the three countries during the Second Lebanon War.[89] This announcement was signed by 1,800 people within a short period.

Yet, from a leftist standpoint as well, no leftist can be an anti-Semite since leftists oppose racism and discrimination. Therefore, even the most virulently antisemitic publicist in Turkey, whether Islamist, nationalist, or leftist, will always claim that his criticism should not be interpreted as antisemitism. He will state that he is an anti-Zionist and not an anti-Semite, and that the Zionists always accuse those who make legitimate criticisms of Israel of antisemitism and thus make the State of Israel immune to criticism.[90]

Sometimes, leftist writers express more balanced perspectives toward antisemitism. Şenol Karakaş, for instance, criticized Israel severely during Operation Protective Edge, claiming that Israel needs terror organizations just to show that "it is here." Yet, he says that some writers hide behind Israel's violence and act in an antisemitic manner, such as Faruk Köse from *Yeni Akit*. These people's actions must be blocked. Due to these people, claims Karakaş, radical rightists praise Hitler and believe he should have "finished the job." "Fascism is a sin, *Mein Kampf* is a sin, praising Fascism, turning Jews into an enemy, considering the evil Israel has done as stemming from a religious viewpoint – all these create a basis for human crimes." On one hand, Turks should flock to the streets to demonstrate against Israel's vandalism and support Gaza; on the other hand, Turks must stand against fascism and antisemitism, which helps strengthen fascism in Turkey.[91]

Although leftists and liberals are expected to criticize Islamists for their antisemitism, they don't seem to do so. Rıfat Bali says that the two camps (nationalists and leftists) share a political goal: the democratization of Turkey and reduction of the military influence upon Turkish politics.[92] Because numerous liberal journalists and intellectuals in Turkey were arrested during the military regime after September 1980 and also during the coup of February 1997, they express sympathy toward the Islamists in Turkey who had suffered greatly under the Kemalist order at the hands of the Turkish Armed Forces. Leftists, like Islamists, oppose laws that confine religious freedom (such as the head scarf being banned in state universities) as human rights issues. The absurdity is that the Islamists, who frequently publish antisemitic conspiracy theories, gain the support of the liberals, who believe the Islamists are defending democracy.[93]

Nationalists and ultranationalists

Just like the leftists, nationalists also complain about the illegitimacy of criticizing Israel without being called an "anti-Semite." Ümit Kıvanç writes: "Can't one oppose Israel without being declared an anti-Semite?" Because this debate is conducted between democrats and left-wing people. They consider it a problem to be an anti-Semite or to declare that the nationalists as well as the neo-nationalists' antisemitic perspective has in recent years declared hostility toward the EU, United States, and Israel at the same time. Antisemitism is part of xenophobia. The antisemitism in this camp stems mainly from the popularity that *Mein Kampf* enjoys among its members as an "ideological handbook." The Turkish translation of *Mein Kampf* has indeed become a bestseller in the country and can be purchased in some of the largest supermarket chains and bookstores.

According to Kerim Balcı, the nationalists are against everyone, not only the Jews. According to him they have always been violent. However, the most intimidating popular ideology prevailing in Turkey is the combination of Islamism and ultranationalism. Many of their followers are inspired by Kısakürek's writings and support the MHP.[94] Among those who are influenced by Kısakürek are Erdoğan and Gül. The Turkish daily *Star*, for instance, which is a supporter of the AK Party, distributed in its Saturday edition on March 24, 2012, facsimile prints of Kısakürek's *Büyük Doğu* journal, which was praised by AK Party officials and defined as an "important cultural service."[95] These nationalists refer to Jews as Turks' enemies in particular, and Islam's enemies in general. In the eyes of the nationalists, there is no distinction between world Jewry and Zionism.[96]

In this regard, it is interesting to note Servet Avcı's opinion on nationalism in Turkey. In a continuing op-ed published in two parts, Avcı believes that there is no racism in Turkey because Islam is anti-racist, but that there is discrimination on the basis of culture instead of race. Avcı further states that Turks are inherently nationalistic even if they don't consider themselves nationalists. He criticizes European societies for the rise in racist attitudes without a reason:

> Why does nationalism not rise in Turkey? The question is made meaningless. There is a rising nationalism but it has difficulty expressing itself.... If someone says that the most important political view of himself is as a nationalist, but prefers a politician who says he downgrades nationalism, what are the reasons for this paradox, which is not seen anywhere else in the world.... On this point, The East represents innocence. Racism is not welcome in this land owing to this feature and attitude; both the culture owns our geographic roots and racism is banned by Islam. Even Ziya Gökalp's (the ideologue of Turkish nationalism) points out "Racism" as a subtopic of Zoology and explaining (defining) "nationalism" as culture/cultural stuff, indicates the difference between our nationalism and Europe's (Western) "racism." Nationalism is sensed more during times of danger, when it is threatened. Nations have this sensation/notion (nationalism) against an enemy's increasing threat. In fact, nationalism is not an ideology of "peace periods" and is not for the lazy.[97]

Barry Jacobs, the American Jewish Committee's director of strategic studies in the Office of Government and International Affairs, claimed in an interview with Ruşen Çakır in *Vatan*, on April 4, 2005, that antisemitism is at a serious level in Turkey and that it stems from a rise in nationalism in Turkey.[98]

Another expression of antisemitism among nationalists is the Kuvayı Milliye Derneği (National Forces Society), an organization based in Mersin, Turkey. It was founded on November 11, 2005 by a retired Turkish army colonel, Fikri Karadağ. This organization's members took oaths swearing: "there is no Jewish blood in me; I am ready to kill and be killed for Turkishness."[99] Although this group is quite small and has no influence on Turkish society, its founding alone is problematic.

According to Türkem and Öktem, the last decades' escalation in murders of non-Muslims – such as the Turkish–Armenian author and editor Hrant Dink in Istanbul in 2007, or the murder of three protestant Christian missionaries in Malatya in 2007, or the murder of the Italian Catholic priest in 2006, as well as murders of Turkish Jews, such as the murder of the prominent Turkish-Jewish businessman and a co-founder of Alarko Holdings, Üzeyir Garih, who was murdered in 2001 and was known for having close ties with Erdoğan, and the Jewish dentist Yasef Yahya in 2003 – stems from a new version of radical nationalism that has been on the rise in Turkey until recently. It is not the traditional Turkish nationalism, as the latter was anti-left and pro-Western, in line with Atatürk's Westernization concepts. The new version also involves extreme left factions that were marginalized by globalization, along with having anti-EU and anti-United States sentiments, especially after the American invasion of Iraq in 2003. Their anti-imperialist discourse reflects their fear of losing their Turkish identity. The EU admission process is perceived as a similar threat. Despite this, the two scholars claim that neither diplomatic nor political affairs any longer dictate the Turkish government's attitude toward minorities.[100] The European Council against Racism and Intolerance's (ECRI) report from 2005 seems to support this perspective. According to the report, intolerant remarks are sometimes made in public, including by political leaders and prominent public figures. The targets of these remarks vary according to the circumstances, but recently Armenians, Jews, Greeks, and Kurds have attracted intolerant comments that have not always been sanctioned or even prosecuted by the authorities. Several sources have blamed ultranationalism by some elements for the intolerance among the public at large. These elements perceive anything that is not "Turkish" as posing a threat to the state and the Turkish people.[101]

According to other theorists, antisemitism, apart from some manifestations of right-wing or Christian antisemitism, particularly in Eastern Europe, is to a large extent a thing of the past. Some claim that Jews successfully constructed themselves as 'white' or part of the Judeo-Christian elite, such as in the United States. After the Holocaust, Jews succeeded in putting themselves outside the firing line, but only at the expense of other groups that are considered a threat to Europe, such as Muslims. On the other hand, according to Hirsh, it is very easy to be intertwined within a huge complexity of discourses, ideas, criticism, activism, and unexamined assumptions. Bigoted ways of thinking exist more among people who believe they oppose bigotry. In many cases, people are not even aware of their racist memes, assumptions, and actions, and thus they more easily fall into that trap.[102] In other words, it is easy to call antisemitism other names or to enable it to be part of a broader phenomena, such us ultranationalism or xenophobia.

The Kurdish issue

The Kurdish problem and its relation to antisemitism began long before the AK Party came to rule, but this link was enhanced after the U.S. invasion to Iraq in 2003. Many Turks perceive Israel to be supporting the Kurdish PKK, the terrorist organization because Israel, like some other countries, does not recognize the PKK as a terrorist organization. They see Israel's relations with the northern Iraqi Kurds as linked to support for Turkish Kurds.[103] After the *Mavi Marmara* incident, I approached the Ottoman Archive in its old location in Sultanahmet. One of the visitors there began to converse with me while the workers were on noon break. The day prior to this meeting a Turkish navy base was attacked by the PKK; this man swore that it was not the PKK but Israel, since "Israel helps the PKK otherwise they wouldn't have been so successful." When I looked at him quizzically he explained: "I am a Kurd, I know Kurds. They are incapable of doing what they do. It is only the Israeli brain behind their activities." But the Kurdish problem in Turkey is not related only to Israel as a supportive power to the Kurds in general and PKK in particular, but also supplies firm ground for antisemitic expressions.[104] Over the past few years, the Turkish conservative media more intensively portrayed the outlawed PKK terror organization as "Israeli Spawn." In the bloodiest decade of PKK activity, the PKK was portrayed as collaborating even with the Armenian terrorist organization ASALA[105] and PKK members were often presented as Armenians and not as Kurds. One explanation of this identification of Armenians with PKK terrorism is the desire to avoid recognizing the Kurdish problem. Nuray Mert mentions in *Hürriyet Daily News* that anti-Israeli sentiments serve as a useful tool to hide authoritarian politics. Pro-government writers often hint that any opposition to the AK Party government may be related to the "Israeli lobby" since the new Turkish government policy dares to challenge Israel. The link made between Israel and the PKK aimed at 'killing two birds with one stone' by despising Israel and the PKK at the same time. This is why Turkish society links anti-Israel sentiments and antisemitic implications with the rhetoric of the 'war on terror' aimed against the PKK. Furthermore, antisemitism is not only 'hostility toward Jews' as intellectuals in Turkey think. Antisemitism is also a kind of reaction to modernity, so therefore an essential aspect of almost all authoritarian politics. Thus antisemitism is a threat to democracy and modernity. Therefore, when anti-Kurdish feelings meet antisemitism, democracy is in great danger.[106] The Kurdish issue was also directed at the Turkish Jews themselves. For example, a columnist of *Akşam*, Şakir Süter, wrote on June 24, 2004:

> In Turkey, there are 'sworn enemies' of the Jews. [But] Jews also have some friends, even if they are not 'sworn [friends]' ... quite a few people [in Turkey] are pleased by their friendship with Turkish citizens of Jewish descent. There are some common [shared] historical sorrows and joys. Today, however, we are on the verge of saying 'there WERE' [in the past].
> We will either eliminate this friendship or continue with a 'bad taste.' In Turkey, there is a big 'maybe' hanging in the minds of [even] those who [until now] did not see the Jews as 'enemies.' They [the Turkish Jews] have an obligation to show us that they are distanced from the terror that resulted in the death of thousands in Turkey [due to terrorist activity by the PKK, a separatist Kurdish organization] ... and that the Jews are not 'plotting' against us [the Turks] together with the [Kurdish] elements in northern Iraq, who definitely cannot be our friends.[107]

Hasan Demir from *Yeniçağ* not only links Jews and the PKK, but even presents historical 'evidence' that Barazani, the PKK leader in Iraq, is allegedly of Jewish origin. Demir quotes so-called research proving that Barazani is the descendant of Rabbi Nethanel Barazani Halevi from Mosul, who left his rich library of scriptures to his son, Rabbi Samuel Barazani, in the seventeenth century. Demir claims that the Barazani family is so famous in Israel that a postal stamp was issued after Moshe Barazani, one of the family's famous figures in Israel.[108] The correlation between Jews and militant Kurds or PKK members was also made clear by the *Yeni Akit* newspaper, which dragged criticism from *Birgün* which called this correlation "Islamo-fascist" in Ahmet Meriç Şenyüz's op-ed[109] titled "Her Taşın Altında O Kadın" [Under every stone there is that woman],[110] referring to Professor Büşra Ersanlı, a political science professor at Marmara University who used to be a BDP member (Barış ve Demokrasi Partisi – The Peace and Democracy Party, a Kurdish political party in Turkey which existed between 2008 to 2014). *Yeni Akit* accused her of being a Jew and thus a supporter of the KCK (Koma Civakên Kurdistan). The KCK is the Union of Communities in Kurdistan, an organization founded by the PKK to put into practice Abdullah Öcalan's ideology of "Democratic Confederalism," which is significantly influenced by Communalism.

The KCK Operation (KCK Operasyonu) is an ongoing operation conducted against the Kurds since April 14, 2009 and with greater vigor after the general elections on June 12, 2011. The arrests included Kurdish politicians, NGO members, activists, lawyers, members of trade unions, and students.[111] The KCK is seen as the civil/political wing for the outlawed PKK, and thus also illegal. Professor Büşra Ersanlı was detained by the police on October 28, along with dozens of other party members, in an operation against KCK in Istanbul. Following her arrest, Büşra Ersanlı was detained for five months before being formally charged on March 19, 2012 with "leading an illegal organization" under Article 314 of the Turkish Penal Code and "making propaganda for an illegal organization" under Article 7/2 of the Anti-Terror Law. A few months later, on July 13, 2012, following the first KCK hearing in a court in Silivri prison, Ersanlı was released pending trial in July 2012.[112]

Yeni Akit emphasized the allegedly Jewish origin of Ersanlı as she was married to Professor Cem Behar, a Jewish professor who served as a vice-rector/provost in charge of academic affairs at Boğaziçi University in Istanbul. The newspaper also falsely accused Ersanlı for being one of the founders of George Soros' Helsinki Citizens' Assembly (Helsinki Yurttaşlar Derneği), an NGO working on the notions of fundamental rights and freedoms, peace, democracy, and pluralism.[113] Despite the disinformation and the fact that Ersanlı is not Jewish, *Yeni Akit*'s aim is clear: to link Jews, Israel, and the PKK.[114]

Soros himself was targeted as a "Jew" by *Yeni Akit* once again. In May 2014, Freedom House said it notes with concern some Turkish media outlets resorting to antisemitism in criticizing its report: "Freedom House calls on the government of Turkey to join us in condemning the use of hate speech."[115] Following this declaration, *Star* published on its front page that Freedom House received huge grants from George Soros and Israeli lobby groups, which explains why Freedom House condemned Turkey's antisemitic media manifestations. It also

The rise of the AK Party 93

emphasized that the Freedom House president, David Kramer, is a Jew. *Yeni Akit*, though, tried to link Freedom House to Israel in an attempt to discredit the report.[116]

Another radical example is Figen Aypek's comparison between Israel and the PKK. Again, Israel's image is being stained in Turkey and the narrative that depicts Israel as a terrorist state infiltrates Turks' consciousness. But Aypek believes that Israel is even more bloodthirsty and merciless than the PKK: The Jews who went through the Holocaust exploited their situation, acquired land, and settled down in Palestinian territories. If the Kurds follow the Jews by changing their demand from "the right to live" to "demand for land," they should acknowledge that no such possibility will be given to them in Eastern Turkey.[117]

The Kurdish issue is also related to Israel, as many Turks tend to believe that a Kurdish state will allow the Israeli dream of a "great Israeli state" in the promised territories, as expressed in the Bible, from the Euphrates to the Tigris. As mentioned, this conspiracy theory is very popular in Turkey.[118] This view is depicted in many cartoons, one of which is Murat Yılmaz's cartoon from 2013, in which Israel, depicted as an orthodox Jew, is embraced by the United States, who holds a sign "Welcome to Kurdistan" and says: "you see why you had to apologize [to Turkey]?" whereas under "the gate of peace" Kurds enter and at the same time, a sign saying "great Israeli state" hangs behind the figure that represents Israel.[119]

Figure 3.1 Welcome to Kurdistan.

Notes

1 Ahmet Yükleyen, "Sufism and Islamic groups in contemporary Turkey," in Reşsat Kasaba (ed.), *The Cambridge History of Turkey: Volume 4 Turkey in the Modern World* (Cambridge: Cambridge University Press, 2008), pp. 385–386.
2 Jenny B. White, "Islam and politics in contemporary Turkey," in Reşsat Kasaba (ed.), *The Cambridge History of Turkey: Volume 4 Turkey in the Modern World* (Cambridge: Cambridge University Press, 2008), pp. 374–376.
3 Joshua W. Walker, "Reexamining the U.S–Turkish alliance," *The Washington Quarterly* (winter 2007–2008), p. 94.
4 Joshua W. Walker, "The United States and Turkey in a changing world," in Kerem Öktem, Ayşe Kadıoğlu, and Mehmet Karlı (eds.), *Another Empire: A Decade of Turkey's Foreign Policy Under the Justice and Development Party* (Istanbul: Istanbul Bilgi University Press, 2012), p. 144.
5 See, for example: Michael Rubin, "Mr. Erdoğan's Turkey," *Wall Street Journal*, 19 (October 2006): www.meforum.org/1036/mr-Erdoğans-Turkey, retrieved August 7, 2014.
6 Füsun Türkmen, "Turkish–American relations: a challenging transition," *Turkish Studies*, 10, 1 (2009), p. 119.
7 Walker, "Reexamining the U.S–Turkish Alliance," p. 95.
8 Walker, "The United States and Turkey, p. 148.
9 On the AK Party, see: Ekrem T. Başer, "Shift-of-axis in Turkish foreign policy: Turkish national role conceptions before and during AK Party rule," *Turkish Studies*, 16, 3 (2015), pp. 291–309; Salih Bayram, "Where the AK Party stands: a manifesto-based approach to party competition in Turkey," *New Middle Eastern Studies*, 5 (2015), pp. 1–19; M. Hakan Yavuz (ed.), *The Emergence of a New Turkey: Democracy and the AK Party* (Salt Lake City, UT: University of Utah Press, 2006); Ümit Cizre, *Secular and Islamic Politics in Turkey: The Making of Justice and Development Party* (New York: Routledge, 2007); William Hale and Ergun Özbudun, *Islamism, Democracy and Liberalism in Turkey: The Case of AK Party* (New York: Routledge, 2009); Hasan Turunç, "Islamist or democratic? The AK Party's search for identity in Turkish politics," *Journal of Contemporary European Studies*, 15, 1 (2007), pp. 79–91.
10 Ibrahim Kalın, "US–Turkish relations under Obama: promise, challenge and opportunity in the 21st century," *Journal of Balkan and Near Eastern Studies*, 12, 1 (2010), p. 98.
11 www.tesev.org.tr/assets/publications/file/03122013120651.pdf, retrieved September 2, 2014.
12 Bali, *Antisemitism and Conspiracy Theories*, p. 349.
13 Brink-Danan, *Jewish life in 21st century Turkey*, p. 116.
14 On Zionism and the Ottoman Empire, see: Esther Benbassa, "Zionism in the Ottoman Empire at the end of the 19th and the beginning of the 20th century," *Studies in Zionism*, 11, 2 (1990), pp. 127–140; Mim Kemal Öke, "The Ottoman Empire, Zionism and the question of Palestine 1880–1908," *International Journal of Middle East Studies*, 14, 3 (1982), pp. 329–341; Hasan Kayali, *Arabs and Young Turks: Ottomanism, Arabism, and Islamism in the Ottoman Empire, 1908–1918* (Berkeley, CA: California University Press, 1997).
15 According to Bali this is a common historical conspiracy theory in Turkey; see: Bali, "The banalization of hate," p. 312.
16 Bali, *Antisemitism and Conspiracy Theories*, p. 192.
17 Jacob M. Landau, "Some comments on the Young Turks' attitude toward Zionism," in Gedalya Yogev (ed.), *Anthology to the History of the Zionist Movement and the Jewish Settlement in the Land of Israel* (Tel Aviv: HaKibuts HaMe'uhad and University of Tel Aviv Press, 1984), pp. 195–197. [Hebrew]. On the Young Turks'

attitude toward Zionism, see also: İlber Ortaylı, "Ottomanism and Zionism during the second constitutional period, 1908–1915," in: Avigdor Levy (ed.), *The Jews of the Ottoman Empire* (Princeton, NJ: The Darwin Press, 1994), pp. 527–538; Jacob M. Landau, "Relations between Jews and non-Jews in the late Ottoman Empire: some characteristics," in Avigdor Levy (ed.), *The Jews of the Ottoman Empire* (Princeton, NJ: The Darwin Press, 1994), pp. 539–547.
18 Landau, "Some comments on the Young Turks' attitude," p. 197.
19 Ibid., pp. 198, 200–201.
20 Bali, *Antisemitism and Conspiracy Theories*, p. 53.
21 Ibid., pp. 229, 289.
22 Eldad Beck, "Israel is deliberately ignoring the Turkish antisemitism," *Yediot Ahronot*, June 17, 2011 [Hebrew].
23 Levi expressed solidarity with the Gazans during *Mavi Maramra* and also claimed that there was no antisemitism in Turkey. See: Bali, *Antisemitism and Conspiracy Theories* p. 230.
24 Ersoy Dede, "İsrail Malları," *Yeni Akit*, July 25, 2014.
25 http://maxblumenthal.com/2011/07/being-Jewish-in-Turkey-before-and-after-the-mavi-marmara-part-2-of-2, retrieved 31 July 2013.
26 Interview in Istanbul, July 29, 2013.
27 http://maxblumenthal.com/2011/07/being-Jewish-in-Turkey-before-and-after-the-mavi-marmara-part-1-of-2, retrieved July 31, 2013.
28 www.Israelnationalnews.com/News/News.aspx/163344#.UhpnmvBBRjo, retrieved July 28, 2013.
29 www.memri.org/report/en/print1388.htm, retrieved September 10, 2012.
30 Ibid.
31 Umut Uzer, "Turkish–Israeli relations: their rise and fall," *Middle East Policy*, 20, 1 (2013), p. 102.
32 David Hirsh, "Hostility to Israel and antisemitism: toward a sociological approach," *The Journal for the Study of Antisemitism* 5, 1 (2013), p. 1416.
33 No author, "Turkish PM Erdoğan: Islamophobia, antisemitism same," *Hürriyet Daily News*, February 28, 2013: www.hurriyetdailynews.com/turkish-pm-Erdoğan-islamophobia-anti-semitism-same.aspx?pageID=238&nID=42019&NewsCatID=338, retrieved March 3, 2013.
34 No author, "Başbakan Erdoğan: İslamofobi insanlık suçu görülmeli," *Radikal*, February 27, 2013: www.radikal.com.tr/dunya/basbakan_Erdoğan_islamofobi_insanlik_sucu_gorulmeli-1123152, retrieved April 23, 2013; no author, "Erdoğan'a 'Siyonizm' tepkisi," *Radikal*, March 1, 2013: www.radikal.com.tr/dunya/Erdoğana_siyonizm_tepkisi-1123458; see also: http://yenisafak.com.tr/politika-haber/siyonizm-insanlik-sucudur-20.03.2013-501927; www.dw.de/erdo%C4%9Fana-siyonizm-tepkisi/a-16639265, retrieved April 23, 2013.
35 http://emrehaber.com/2013/03/20/basbakan-Erdoğan-siyonizm-insanlik-sucudur-sozumun-arkasindayim, retrieved April 23, 2013.
36 Interview in Istanbul, February 26, 2015. The Struma commemoration ceremony was celebrated officially for the first time in the history of Turkey in 2015. See: Enver Alas, "Struma faciasına 73 yıl sonra ilk resmi tören," *Hürriyet*, February 24, 2015: www.Hürriyet.com.tr/gundem/28286028.asp, retrieved February 25, 2015. For the meeting of Davutoğlu and minorities' leaders, see: no author, "Davutoğlu, azınlık cemaatlerinin temsilcileriyle yemekte buluştu," *Zaman*, January 3, 2015: www.zaman.com.tr/politika_Davutoğlu-azinlik-cemaatlerinin-temsilcileriyle-yemekte-bulustu_2268290.html, retrieved February 20, 2015.
37 On "new Antisemitism," see: Jeffrey Heff, *Antisemitism and Anti-Zionism in Historical Perspective: Convergence and Divergence* (New York: Routledge, 2007); Phyllis Chesler, *The New Antisemitism: The Current Crisis and What We Must Do About It* (San Francisco, CA: Jossey-Bass, 2003); Paul Iganski and Barry Kosmin

(eds.), *A New Antisemitism?* (London: Profile, 2003); Robert Wistrich, *A Lethal Obsession: Antisemitism – From Antiquity to the Global Jihad* (New York: Random House, 2010).
38 Hirsh, "Hostility to Israel and antisemitism," p. 1405.
39 See, for example: Matti Bunzl, *Antisemitism and Islamophobia: Hatreds Old and New in Europe* (Chicago, IL: Prickly Paradigm Press, 2007).
40 Hirsh, "Hostility to Israel and antisemitism," p. 1403.
41 Kerem Öktem, Ayşe Kadıoğlu, and Mehmet Karlı (eds.), *Another Empire? A Decade of Turkey's Foreign Policy Under the Justice and Development Party* (Istanbul: Istanbul Bilgi University Press, 2012), pp. 1–2. On Turkey and its change in policy, see: Şuhnaz Yılmaz and Ziya Öniş, "Between Europeanization and Euro-Asianism: foreign policy activism in Turkey during the AK Party era," *Turkish Studies*, 10, 1 (2009), pp. 7–24. On Turkey's Middle East policy, see: Bülent Aras, "Turkey's rise in the Greater Middle East: peace-building in the periphery," *Journal of Balkan and Near Eastern Studies*, 11, 1 (2009), pp. 29–41; Şaban Kardaş, "Turkey: redrawing in the Middle East map or building sandcastles?," *Middle East Policy*, 17, 1 (2010), pp. 122–136.
42 Yuval Ben-Bassat, "Israeli lessons from the new Ottoman archive in Istanbul," *Haaretz*, December 7, 2013: http://blogs.haaretz.co.il/sadna/206, retrieved December 10, 2013.
43 Uzer, "Turkish–Israeli Relations," p. 97.
44 Ecevit overtly accused Israel of "applying genocide on Palestinians" following Israeli soldiers besieging Palestinian President Yasser Arafat's headquarters in May 2002. See: no author, "'İsrail soykırım yapıyor,'" *Radikal*, April 5, 2002: www.radikal.com.tr/haber.php?haberno=33996, retrieved November 12, 2012.
45 Uzer, "Turkish–Israeli Relations," p. 98.
46 Ali Balcı and Tuncay Kardaş, "The changing dynamics of Turkey's relations with Israel: an analysis of 'securitization,'" *Insight Turkey*, 14, 2 (2012), p. 113.
47 Hirsh, "Hostility to Israel and antisemitism," p. 1419.
48 Roee Nahmias, "Assad confirms: Olmert said willing to cede Golan," *Ynet News*, April 24, 2008: www.ynetnews.com/articles/0,7340,L-3535361,00.html, retrieved September 18, 2012.
49 Quoted in: Bali, *Antisemitism and Conspiracy Theories*, p. 83.
50 No author, "Benim için Davos bitti," *Hürriyet*, January 30, 2009: www.Hürriyet.com.tr/dunya/10886978.asp, retrieved September 12, 2012.
51 Utku Çakırözer, "Museviler: Panikteyiz," *Cumhuriyet*, August 8, 2014: www.cumhuriyet.com.tr/koseyazisi/103091/Museviler__Panikteyiz.html, retrieved August 13, 2014.
52 Barak Ravid, "Deputy FM Ayalon apologizes to Turkish ambassador," *Haaretz*, January 13, 2010: www.haaretz.com/print-edition/news/deputy-fm-ayalon-apologizes-to-Turkish-Ambassador-1.261346, retrieved September 12, 2012.
53 Hirsh, "Hostility to Israel and antisemitism," p. 1406.
54 Ibid., pp. 1407, 1410.
55 Ibid., pp. 37–38.
56 No author, "Prof. Dr. Talip Küçükcan'dan çarpıcı İsrail analizi," *Stargazete*, August 2, 2014: http://haber.stargazete.com/guncel/turkiye-neden-yahudi-karsiti-olarak-gosterilmeye-calisiliyor/haber-920926, retrieved August 3, 2014. Rıfat N. Bali wrote a book as an attempt to reply to Kıvanç's assertions, and he explains his reasons by saying that the book describes the debate between Umit Kivanç, a *Birikim* writer, and himself. The debate stemmed from an article in *Radikal Iki* of July 4, 2004, and a reply by Bali that objected to the article's translation etiquette and journalistic principles. In response to the second article, Kivanç wrote in an article in *Birikim* in which he explained that "his patience was finally exhausted on this topic which had so long caused him anguish." The subject that Kivanç claimed had caused him such pain was

the charge of antisemitism that he claimed was automatically leveled at those who criticize the political and military actions of the State of Israel and the fact that such charges had for all practical purposes made it impossible to criticize Israel. After implying in his article that the author [Bali] had accused the weekly *Radikal Iki* of antisemitism, Kıvanç first labels him an "antisemitism detector," then as "one of the employed-directed detectors [in the service of] the State of Israel" and indirectly questions his loyalty to Turkey. (Rıfat Bali's internet website is at www.Rıfatbali.com/tr/genel_yazilar/kitaplar/umit_Kivança_cevap_-_birikim_dergisinin_yayinlamayi_reddettigi_makalenin_oykusu.htm.) For the book, see: Rıfat N. Bali, *Ümit Kıvanç'a Cevap: Birikim Dergisinin Yayınlamayı Reddettiği Makalenin Öyküsü* (İstanbul: Kitap Yayıncılık, 2005).

57 Yunus Emre Kocabaşoğlu, "Antisemitizm Korkusu, İsrail'in Eleştirilmesine Engel mi?," *Bianet*, October 3, 2010: www.bianet.org/biamag/azinliklar/119754-antisemitizm-korkusu-israil-in-elestirilmesine-engel-mi, retrieved May 17, 2012.
58 Quoted in: Balcı and Kardaş, "The changing dynamics," p. 111.
59 Yusuf Han Kardeler, "İşte Yahudi kafası," *Milli Gazete*, January 8, 2013: www.milligazete.com.tr/haber/Iste_Yahudi_kafasi/271159#.VQgMeLf9ljo, retrieved January 10, 2013.
60 Israel State Archive, registered 438-351/Ministry of Foreign Affairs/4622/26 CHETZ/Istanbul/July 7, 1971 [in Hebrew].
61 Tezcan Durna and Burak Özçetin, "Mavi Marmara on the news: convergence and divergence in religious conservative newspapers in Turkey," *Middle East Journal of Culture and Communication*, 5 (2012), p. 266.
62 Bali, *Antisemitism and Conspiracy Theories*, p. 104.
63 Mustafa Armağan, "Abdülhamid, Hahambaşı'na nasıl özür diletmişti?," *Zaman*, September 11, 2011: www.zaman.com.tr/mustafa-armagan/abdulhamid-hahambasina-nasil-ozur-diletmisti_1178443.html, retrieved September 1, 2012.
64 Ibid.
65 Ibid.
66 Bali, "The banalization of hate," p. 312.
67 See his book, Marc David Baer, *The Dönme: Jewish Converts, Muslim Revolutionaries, and Secular Turks* (Stanford, CA: Stanford University Press, 2010).
68 Rıfat Bali, "Present-day antisemitism in Turkey," *Jerusalem Center for Public Affairs*, 84, 16 (2009): http://jcpa.org/article/present-day-Antisemitism-in-Turkey, retrieved September 1, 2011.
69 http://vho.org/aaargh/fran/livres8/AntisemTurkish.pdf, retrieved September 2, 2013.
70 Landau, "Tofaot shel Antishemiyut," p. 229.
71 Shmuelevitz, "Emdat HaItonut HaIslamit BeTurkiya," p. 116.
72 Ibid., p. 117.
73 Recai Yahyaoğlu, "Filistin İsrail Esir Değişiminde Psikolojik Üstünlük Kimde?," *Aktüel psikoloji*, October 21, 2010: www.aktuelpsikoloji.com/artikel.php?artikel_id=1324, retrieved April 2, 2012.
74 Shmuelevitz, "Emdat HaItonut HaIslamit BeTurkiya," p. 118.
75 Ibid., p. 119.
76 Ibid., pp. 118–119.
77 Aryeh Shmuelevitz, "Ms Pococke no. 31 as a source for the events in Istanbul in the years 1622–1624," *International Journal of Turkish Studies* 3, 2 (1985–1986), pp. 107–121.
78 Shmuelevitz, "Emdat HaItonut HaIslamit BeTurkiya," p. 120.
79 Ibid., p. 124.
80 Bali, "Present-day antisemitism in Turkey."
81 Quoted in: Yunus Emre Kocabaşoğlu, "Antisemitizm Korkusu."
82 Davut Şahin, "Venedik taciri ve Yahudi bir profesör," *Milli Gazete*, November 22, 2012: www.milligazete.com.tr/koseyazisi/Venedik_taciri_ve_Yahudi_bir_profesor/12372#.U2a6wbCKBYp, retrieved May 2, 2013.

98 Antisemitism under AK Party rule

83 Interview in Istanbul, February 6, 2013.
84 Mustafa Akyol, "Opinion: antisemitism in Turkey: myths and facts (i)," *Hürriyet Daily News*, February 12, 2009: www.Hürriyet.com.tr/english/opinion/10981754_p.asp retrieved October 25, 2013.
85 Landau, "Al Dmuta Shel Haantishemiyut," p. 80.
86 See: *Birikim*, 186 (October) 2004: www.birikimdergisi.com/birikim/bigimage.aspx?dsid=168, retrieved May 2, 2012.
87 http://vho.org/aaargh/fran/livres8/AntisemTurkish.pdf, retrieved January 28, 2014.
88 Quoted in: Bali, "Present-day antisemitism in Turkey."
89 No author, "İtham ediyoruz," *Radikal*, August 9, 2006: www.radikal.com.tr/index.php?tarih=09/08/2006, retrieved August 6, 2011.
90 Bali, "Present-day antisemitism in Turkey."
91 Şenol Karakaş, "İsrail terörü, Faruk Köse ve antisemitizm," *Marksist*, July 24, 2014: http://marksist.org/Israil-teroru-faruk-kose-ve-antisemitizm.html, retrieved July 27, 2014.
92 Eldad Beck, "Israel is deliberately ignoring the Turkish antisemitism," *Yediot Ahronot*, June 17, 2011 [Hebrew].
93 Bali, *Antisemitism and Conspiracy Theories*, pp. 132–133.
94 Ahmet Necip Fāzıl Kısakürek (May 26, 1904–May 25, 1983) was a Turkish prolific poet, novelist, and a playwright. He was noticed by the French philosopher Henri Bergson, who later became his teacher, and Al-Ghazali, a Muslim theologian, jurist, and mystic. He expressed Sufist ideas in his plays and poems. He is also the spiritual father of the Turkish terrorist group IBDA-C (İslami Büyük Doğu Akıncılar Cephesi); he called for a foundation for a new Caliphate in Turkey and encouraged Islam based on pure Islamic values. Kısakürek is known for the ultranationalistic and also antisemitic views expressed in his writings. See, for instance, an anthology of all his articles published in *Büyük Doğu* [The great East] journal: Necip Fāzıl Kısakürek, *Yahudilik-Masonluk-Dönmelik* [Judaism, Freemasonship, Sabbetaism] (Istanbul: Büyük Doğu Yayınları, 2010). On Kisakürek and his antisemitic viewpoints, see: Bali, *Antisemitism and Conspiracy Theories*, pp. 25–26; 140–158.
95 Bali, *Antisemitism and Conspiracy Theories*, p. 127.
96 Interview in Istanbul, February 6, 2013.
97 Servet Avcı, "Türkiye'de milliyetçilik neden yükselmiyor?, "*Yeniçağ*, September 19, 2013: www.yenicaggazetesi.com.tr/turkiyede-milliyetcilik-neden-yukselmiyor-28191yy.htm; Servet Avcı, "Milliyetçiliğin bitmeyen dramı," *Yeniçağ*, September 20, 2013: www.yenicaggazetesi.com.tr/milliyetciligin-bitmeyen-drami-28206yy.htm, retrieved March 12 2014.
98 http://vho.org/aaargh/fran/livres8/AntisemTurkish.pdf, retrieved September 13, 2013.
99 Akyol, "Opinion: antisemitism in Turkey."
100 Türkmen and Öktem, "Foreign policy as a determinant," pp. 13–14.
101 http://hudoc.ecri.coe.int/XMLEcri/ENGLISH/Cycle_03/03_CbC_eng/TUR-CbC-III-2005–5-ENG.pdf, retrieved September 1, 2012, p. 27.
102 Hirsh, "Hostility to Israel and antisemitism," pp. 27–28.
103 Uzer, "Turkish–Israeli relations," p. 106.
104 Israel is often blamed by Turkey for allegedly aiding the Kurds and especially the PKK. See, for example: "Israeli Herons give intelligence to PKK, intelligence officers say," *Today's Zaman*, June 17, 2012: www.todayszaman.com/news-268815-Israeli-herons-give-intelligence-to-pkk-intelligence-officers-say.html, retrieved August 6 2013. Also: Othman Ali, "Possible consequences of PKK–Israeli union," *Today's Zaman*, September 18, 2011: www.todayszaman.com/news-257074-possible-consequences-of-pkk-Israeli-unionby-othman-ali*.html, retrieved August 3, 2013.
105 ASALA (the Armenian Secret Army for the Liberation of Armenia) was an Armenian militant organization that was considered a terrorist organization by some sources, whereas other sources describe it as an armed guerrilla organization.

It operated from 1975 to the early 1990s and assassinated tens of Turkish diplomats. The principal goal of ASALA was to reestablish historical Armenia, which would include eastern Turkey and Soviet Armenia.

106 Nuray Mert, "Relations with Israel and the Kurdish question," *Hürriyet Daily News*, September 11, 2011: www.Hürriyetdailynews.com/default.aspx?pageid=438 &n=relations-with-Israel-and-the-kurdish-question-2011-09-11, retrieved August 5, 2013. Nuray Mert, a Turkish journalist, lost her job in *Milliyet* and was targeted by Prime Minister Erdoğan for criticizing him: http://bianet.org/english/freedom-of-expression/130542-two-female-journalists-attacked, retrieved August 2, 2013.
107 Quoted in: www.memri.org/report/en/print1388.htm#_edn9, retrieved September 1, 2012.
108 Hasan Demir, "Öcalan, Barzani Yahudi ve Kürdistan!," *Yeniçağ*, June 11, 2013: www.yenicaggazetesi.com.tr/ocalan-barzani-yahudi-ve-kurdistan-27082yy.htm, retrieved July 14, 2013.
109 Ahmet Meriç Şenyüz, "Her taşın altından Akit çıkıyor," *Birgün*, November 2, 2011: http://birgunabone.net/actuels_index.php?news_code=1320227639&year=2011& month=11&day=02, retrieved September 2, 2012.
110 www.nefretsoylemi.org/detay.asp?id=303&bolum=bizden, retrieved September 2, 2012.
111 On KCK Operation, see: Kurdistan National Congress's bulletin "'Arrestment storm' against Kurds in Turkey": www.guengl.eu/uploads/_old_cms_files/arrests %20storm%20KCK.pdf; Sait Yılmaz, "PKK Terör Örgütü ve KCK'da Son Durum," http://usam.aydin.edu.tr/analiz/PKK_TEROR_ORGUTUVEKCK_29Mayis2012.pdf, retrieved March 3, 2012.
112 www.englishpen.org/Turkey-focus-2013-busra-ersanli; no author, "KCK davasında tahliyeler," *Radikal*, July 13, 2012: www.radikal.com.tr/turkiye/kck_davasinda_ tahliyeler-1094107; www.bianet.org/english/human-rights/139710-court-rules-to-release-prof-busra-ersanli-after-8-5-months, retrieved March 3, 2012.
113 www.hyd.org.tr.
114 http://kehaber.org/2012/02/01/5467, retrieved March 3, 2012.
115 No author, "Freedom House says Turkish papers resorted to antisemitism," *Today's Zaman*, May 5, 2014: www.todayszaman.com/news-346984-freedom-house-says-Turkish-papers-resorted-to-antisemitism.html, retrieved July 10, 2014.
116 No author, "Finansör İsrail'de basın 'özgür'müş!," *Star*, May 4, 2014: www.stargazete.com/mobil/mobildetay.asp?Newsid=878665, retrieved May 23, 2014.
117 http://kehaber.org/2011/11/05/figen-aypek-israilliler-yerine-yahudiler-dersek-yahudileri-turk-kokenli-kurtlarle-karsilastirmali-miyiz, retrieved September 18, 2011.
118 There are many op-eds regarding this topic; one of them is: Ayşe Karabat, "İsrail'in Kürdistan arayışı," *Al Jazeera*, August 14, 2014: www.aljazeera.com.tr/al-jazeera-ozel/israilin-kurdistan-arayisi, retrieved October 13, 2014.
119 www.kocaeliaydinlarocagi.org.tr/Karikatur.aspx?ID=229, retrieved July 25, 2014.

4 Israeli military operations and their impact on antisemitism

Second Lebanon War 2006

The Second Lebanon War seems to be the turning point in relations between Israel and Turkey. It also shows the media's freedom to publish antisemitic articles. Prior to 2006, Erdoğan seemed to be an advocate of fighting antisemitism. An important example is Turkey's close relations with the ADL. A series of meetings with high-level officials took place between 2004 and 2005 in Istanbul and Ankara. A delegation of leaders from the ADL met with Turkey's prime minister, Erdoğan, who pledged that his country would continue to fight antisemitism and take a leading role in Israeli–Palestinian peace talks. The meetings included talks with the justice minister, members of parliament, representatives of the Jewish community, and Christian, Jewish, and Muslim religious leaders, and were led by Barbara B. Balser, ADL national chair, and Abraham H. Foxman, ADL national director. Foxman told Erdoğan that his clear denunciation of antisemitism and expressions of solidarity with the Jewish community following the bombings of two synagogues in Istanbul in 2003 "will never be forgotten."[1] Erdoğan responded that "antisemitism is a shameful mental illness; it is a perversion. The Holocaust is the heaviest crime against humanity throughout history. Genocide, discrimination, Islamophobia, Christianophobia, ethnic cleansing are all different forms of the same illness."[2] Erdoğan told the ADL leaders that Turkey would send its foreign minister to Israel before the end of the year and that he himself planned to visit Israel in 2005 (Erdoğan did visit Israel in 2005). Foxman emphasized the important role Turkey could play in Israeli–Palestinian negotiations, as well as in re-energizing peace talks between Israel and Syria.[3] On June 10, 2005, at a ceremony attended by various high-level Turkish government ministers, UN diplomats, and leaders of the Turkish and American-Jewish communities, Erdoğan accepted ADL's Courage to Care Award on behalf of diplomats who saved Jews during the Holocaust. At this event, Erdoğan strongly condemned antisemitism and stressed his country's close relationship with the modern State of Israel. Erdoğan reaffirmed his nation's commitment to maintaining strong ties with the United States and the State of Israel. He said that while few Jews still live in Turkey, "They are cherished and prized elements of the Turkish society."[4] This means that Erdoğan himself made the connection between antisemitism and Israel. According to Zali De Toledo, Erdoğan held a positive approach toward Israel in the beginning. She believes that Erdoğan was not always antisemitic. She stressed that she knew him from the days when she worked at the Israeli Consulate in Turkey and that she accompanied him during his visit to Israel: "The Americans thought he would be a great moderate Muslim leader and helped him win elections. I also thought he would be great. He used to be friendly to Israel and Turkish Jews." De Toledo noted that she had lunch with Erdoğan's wife and they discussed fashion, food, and other things: "Everything seemed quite normal and then the change suddenly happened." De Toledo explained that former the Israeli prime minister, Ehud Olmert, got along well with Erdoğan and used to speak about the establishment of peace in the region with him. However, Erdoğan was personally insulted following Operation Cast Lead. She stressed that his reaction to Israel after the outbreak of this was "based on his inflated ego and not politics."[5] When it comes to the crisis with Israel, De Toledo says, apart from the Olmert incident, that ever since Erdoğan became closer to Davutoğlu, who "wrote an imaginative history book claiming that Israel has no right to exist and planted in his mind the establishment of the Neo-Ottoman Empire that will include all of the Turkic countries and the Middle East," he began developing an anti-Israel antisemitic approach. "Since then," said De Toledo, "they believe in it. They both influence each other to reach madness."[6]

On the other hand, it should be noted, he connects Islamophobia, antisemitism, and Zionism, and views all three ideologies as "crimes against humanity." Speaking at the Fifth Alliance of Civilizations Forum in Vienna's Hofburg Palace, Erdoğan underlined the rising trend of fascism across Europe and said: "Just like Zionism, antisemitism, and fascism, it becomes unavoidable that Islamophobia must be regarded as a crime against humanity."[7] At this ceremony, Erdoğan repeated that antisemitism has no place in Turkey and that it is alien to the Turkish culture: "The Turkish nation has been living for centuries with the Jewish people and will continue its close and friendly relations with them in the future, and will struggle together with them against any racism, with determination." Erdoğan said: "It is the task of leaders around the world to join me in condemning the spread of hatred, whether through publications or otherwise. Our consistent policy towards antisemitic diatribes can be nothing short of zero tolerance."[8] Unfortunately, if anyone in Turkey said the same things after the 2006 crisis, he would be labeled a Zionist or a "spy of Israel" by Erdoğan himself or his supporters in and outside the AK Party.

The three ideological wings and a broad sector of Turkish society reacted against Israel after the Second Lebanon War in 2006. These were the accusations:

1 Israel is a non-legitimate state.
2 Israel's treatment of the Palestinian people is no different than Nazi Germany's treatment of the Jews. Israel is an oppressor that conducts genocide and uses terror against the Palestinians.

3   Israel uses the accusation of antisemitism as a shield against its critics. A Muslim can be an anti-Zionist but not antisemitic. Bali quotes Nuray Mert, a professor of political science at Istanbul University and a contributor to *Radikal* who criticized the Turkish Islamist antisemitic responses during the Second Lebanon War. Yet, at the same time he says that "Israel gains its strength through antisemitism."[9]
4   The Jews control the American media and Hollywood and constantly feature the Holocaust to stir up sympathy for Israel. Turkish society believes there is a Jewish lobby in the United States which is involved in undercover international affairs. The terms 'Jewish lobby' appears often in the Turkish media.

During the Second Lebanon War in the summer of 2006, Israeli tourists traveling in south Turkey sometimes encountered hostile reactions from locals. A shop window in Alanya displayed the awkwardly worded placard: "For Children Killers, Israelis No Sale, No Entry."[10] Antisemitism did not even skip on entertainment. Turkish state television broadcaster TRT's decision to drop from its programming schedule the Oscar-winning film *The Pianist*, which deals with the Holocaust, has drawn criticism from those who say the axing was prompted by government pressure. The film, which tells the story of a young Polish Jewish pianist who escapes the mass murder of Jews by the Nazis during World War II, was scheduled to be shown on Wednesday night. But without prior announcement, the American film *Wall Street* was broadcast instead. According to the Islamist-oriented daily *Yeni Şafak*, the decision to show *The Pianist* represented bad timing as the day before Israel murdered 57 people while attacking a refugee camp in Lebanon.

> The movie explains in full detail what the Jews went through during the war, through the point of view of a hopeless pianist which shows that the bitter events and the discrimination the Jews went through years ago, they now inflict on the Muslim Palestinians and Lebanese.[11]

In response, TRT removed the program.[12] Ahmet Hakan, a columnist for the leading daily *Hürriyet* and moderator of a popular debate program at the CNN Türk television channel, criticized TRT's decision. Yet, he claimed the decision, while perhaps necessary, meant "missing the opportunity to show the Turkish people how those who are often 'oppressed' can today become 'the oppressors.'"

On September 13, 2014, the movie *The Pianist*, which was aired on Gün T.V (located in Diyarbakir) a day earlier, was found "not fit to be shown on T.V." by RTÜK (Türkiye Radyo ve Televizyon Üst Kurulu – Radio and Television Supreme Council), a body under the supervision of Yalçın Akdoğan, deputy prime minister of Turkey in that period. RTÜK warned Gün T.V, and actually every other television channel in Turkey, that if they screened this film they would be risking shutdown in a few days or a fiscal penalty. The decision given for prohibiting the airing of *The Pianist* was "violent scenes."[13] The opposition in Turkey strongly opposed this decision, saying "the whole world will laugh at us" and expressed their surprise that RTÜK did not find Seda Sayan's morning show, in which she hosted a murderer, offensive or dangerous in the same way.[14]

The allegations and fierce responses against Israel during the war persisted and manifested in many ways in Turkey: Humanitarian relief organizations operating in member countries of the OIC, the second largest intergovernmental organization after the United Nations) met in Istanbul to discuss aid for Lebanon and Palestine. A Turkish academic and diplomat, Professor Ekmeleddin İhsanoğlu, the 2004–2014 OIC secretary general, and a joint candidate of the two opposition parties in the Turkish parliament (CHP and MHP) for the 2014 presidential election in Turkey qualified Israel's attacks on Lebanon as a "crime against humanity," and stated that they gathered in order to provide a ceasefire.[15] In addition, in response to the Israeli offensive in Lebanon, 263 lawmakers and members of parliament from ruling and opposition parties resigned from the Turkey–Israeli Parliamentary Friendship Group. The head of the group, AK Party MP Vahit Kirişçi, said before considering dissolving the group he would call on Israel to halt its attacks.[16]

However, relations with Israel continued after the war. For instance, Turkey's Prime Minister Erdoğan and Israel's Prime Minister Ehud Olmert met in Ankara on December 22, 2008. Israel's President Shimon Peres toasted with Turkey's President Abdullah Gul and Prime Minister Recep Tayyip Erdoğan at a dinner in his honor at the Cankaya presidential residence in Ankara on November 12, 2007. For these and other meetings he conducted with Israeli politicians, he was called "A Zionist in disguise."[17]

Operation Cast Lead 2008–2009

Operation Cast Lead in 2008–2009 was a direct continuation with regards to Turkish society's reaction toward Israel and antisemitism, but this operation caused the AK Party to discontinue the 'business as usual' approach with Israel in the military and economic sectors.[18] The same assertions that were directed at Israel in the Second Lebanon War were used more extensively during Operation Cast Lead. Prior to the operation, and perhaps the main reason for Erdoğan's harsh criticism of Israel, was Turkey's disappointment at not being able to mediate between Israel and Syria for peace talks, although for a time it looked like the efforts Turkey invested in this mediation were about to succeed. A few days after Olmert's return to Israel from Ankara, where he met with Erdoğan and discussed Syria and other regional challenges, Israel launched Operation Cast Lead in Gaza without giving Turkey advance notice. The operation postponed Syrian–Israeli talks and was viewed by Erdoğan, who saw it as a personal insult, as "an act of disrespect toward Turkey."[19] But it was not only a personal insult of Erdoğan; the Syrian–Israeli talks were a particular source of pride for Turkish statesmanship and diplomacy and Operation Cast Lead put them all on hold and also possibly damaged Erdoğan's prestige as a patron of Hamas.[20] During Operation Cast Lead, Israel's legitimacy was questioned. A few examples follow: Ahmet Turan Alkan, a retired academic and contributor to the daily *Zaman* and the journal *Aksiyon*, described Israel in these terms:

> When Israel emerged as a state after World War II, there was an aspect to it that had the air of a science fiction novel, or a very ancient epic. Israel is the product of a fantasy: a fantasy that is unparalleled, that leaves one speechless and boggles the mind; it's the product of an illusion. Perhaps the most fantastic story of the 20th century is the establishment of an Israeli state in Palestine: Israel reminds one of a sort of Disneyland. An imaginary nation that lived [only] in the minds of Zionist Jews, now resurrected on the territories of Palestine; it's a cartoon.[21]

Some journalists, such as Ayhan Demir from the Islamist *Milli Gazete*, said that the only solution to the "Zionist problem" was the dissolution of the Israeli state. Again, Israel was mentioned in the context of the Holocaust as comparisons between Gaza and Auschwitz were made in some newspapers. A columnist from *Sabah* even demanded creation of a list of children who survived Israel's cruelty and atrocities in Gaza, just like the lists of Jewish survivors that were made after World War II. Ali Bulaç, from *Zaman*, even described Gaza by saying "1.5 million Palestinians live in Gaza under siege for 18 months. In fact, it surpasses the Nazi camps."[22]

Hakan Albayrak wrote these harsh words in *Yeni Şafak*:

> Those who were saved from the remains of Warsaw ghettos that were crushed by the mechanism of the Nazi massacre, carried out what they learned from the Nazis in Palestinian villages like Dir Yassin established the siyo-Nazi occupation regime known as "Israel" over the blood of the Palestinian people. Now also their children do in Gaza what the Nazis did to the Warsaw Ghetto and they try to endure the siyonazi regime, which is fed by Palestinian blood. The Jewish SS at work! and the "people of Israel" who are inside this collective craziness (except for 5%), cheeringly celebrate by crying "zig heil zig heil" their murders of more than 200 kids within 15 days in Gaza as by a professional herd of killers which is proud that comes out of its bosom. May God curse them for a thousand days. Some say that it is not true to compare Nazi deeds to Israel's. There are those who say that there is no comparison to the Nazi's deeds as drawing attention to the difference in quantity and nature between what the Nazis did to the Jews and what the Jews and their Zionism did to the Palestinians ... why wouldn't it be true? Why wouldn't such a comparison be made? The Zionists could not go further with their massacre due to technical problems but their mentality has the same manifestation, doesn't it?[23]

Another example is Evren Gürşen, who said:

> I wonder what Adorno[24] would feel today if he saw that the victims of Auschwitz had become the biggest killer-executioners? As if she [Israel]

proves that the greatest cruelty comes from those victims that did not have their heads cut off, [in the nature of the evidence], Israel, brazenly, continues its ruthless persecution.[25]

The Turkish journalist presents Adorno as the very incarnation of both Jewish intellectualism and denunciation of the Holocaust, and then suggests that, should he still be alive, he would have been appalled, or should have been appalled, by Israel's "Nazi-like" behavior – a classic template of current antisemitism. What probably supports this contention is that the City of Frankfurt created a Theodor W. Adorno Prize in 1977 as a prestigious award for 'ethical' authors; that many of its recipients were Jewish or of Jewish origin; and that some other recipients were Jewish or non-Jewish relatives or absolute anti-Zionists or anti-Semites – from Jean-Luc Godard to Jacques Derrida to Judith Butler.

Under the title: "Not Auschwitz, Gaza" Ahmet Kekeç writes that:

> This saying is attributed to Gündüz Aktan. Israel's attack on Lebanon was used to define the "collective punishment." It's called "diplomatic jargon"; it (diplomatic jargon/speech) always adopts indirect statements. Even this deceased man, who had not concealed that he had been an Israel supporter, [Israel lover] finally lost his temper and indirectly stated that Israel carried out genocide on Israel's occupying lands. For how many days has Gaza been under fire? For how many days have countless children's bodies, bombed houses, mutilated civilians, hunger, thirst, disease, death been shown on our screens? This is not Gaza, it is like Auschwitz. Thousands of novels dealing with genocide, Holocaust history ... thousands of movies, books, music, theater, stage works. Are these the values that the State that complains of suffering from genocide submits to humanity? Thousands of kids' death? Bombed houses?...
>
> What is the difference between Israel's ongoing disgrace to Auschwitz's? What distinguishes between the Holocaust and the method of collective punishment? For years, the Israeli government has been accustomed to the Nazi mindset, the illegal mindset that discriminates against others for being different. The Israeli government believes in the mantra of "he who criticizes me is my enemy," and they've been discriminating against Palestinians, whose lands they occupy ... what Israel is doing is not only illegal, but also inhumane and immoral at the same time.[26]

During the period of Operation Cast Lead, daily life was also affected by antisemitic expressions. As evidence of growing societal antisemitism, they pointed to billboards prominently displayed around Istanbul calling for donations to support the people of Gaza (some, like Solidarity Foundation, clearly sponsored by the AK Party and others bearing the picture of Erdoğan's wife, Emine), as well as some more provocative ones directed toward Jews, saying "Sen Musa'nın çocuğu olamazsın" (You can't be the son of Moses) and featuring a bloody baby shoe.[27]

The former president of the Human Rights Agenda Association (İnsan Hakları Gündemi Derneği), Orhan Kemal Cengiz, told American diplomats on January 21, 2009, with regard to these signs, that the fundamental problem was a Turkish mentality that can be very racist without realizing it. Cengiz said he holds the Turkish press, and in particular the Islamic-leaning press, accountable for inciting antisemitic hatred. But the problem is not related to Erdoğan's remarks as they had been normal political blustering, according to Cengiz. "The real problem is the constant pictures that bring to the fore the Turks' intolerance, foment hatred, and demonstrate Turks' lack of cultural awareness," said Cengiz.[28] But not only pictures appeared. "Killer Israel" was painted on synagogues in Izmir and the Haydarpaşa neighborhood in Istanbul, and even an informal boycott campaign targeting Jewish-owned businesses has been successful, especially among the smaller shops. The Turkish Consumers Union (Tüketiciler Birliği) called for a boycott of Israeli products, a call that repeated itself before and after the Operation. Under the title "Terrorist Israel's ammunition will not be supplied by us" it showed the reader allegedly abusive soldiers and crying Palestinians, as well as a list of Israeli products that should not be purchased. It should be noted that similar lists exist for other countries as well (e.g., United States, Iraq).[29]

On May 27, 2009, there was a press conference aimed at condemning Israel's actions, and also criticizing the "Apologize towards the Armenians" signature campaign started by a group of leftist and liberal intellectuals, apologizing for the 1915 Niyazi Çapa massacres. The chairman of the Eskişehir-based Osmangazi Federation of Cultural Associations declared that "Jews and Armenians are not allowed to enter from this gate" and the "'dogs' entrance is free."[30] A lawsuit against Çapa was filed, demanding one year in prison by the state attorney according to law No. 216 (312 in the older version), second paragraph, which prohibits any discrimination on the basis of social class, language, race, color, sex, political thought, faith, religion, religious sect, and similar reasons. The state attorney asked for 6–12 months' imprisonment, but his request was rejected by the Eskişehir Fourth Magistrates Court. In his defense, Çapa said that before the incident there was a sign saying: "association entrance" and separately "the entrance for dogs is free." These two signs were hung at the same time, but the media interpreted it the same way it was presented to the public. Çapa was eventually fined 3,000 Turkish lira instead of spending five months in jail, as the first decision ruled.[31]

The rampant antisemitism during this period urged Silvyo Ovadya, the president of Turkey's Jewish community, to submit a request to President Gül to add a passage outlawing antisemitism to the Turkish Penal Code Article 216, which contains clear articles prohibiting incitement or discrimination on the basis of language, religion, or race. This attempt, which was rejected, encountered harsh criticism in the Turkish press. In fact, any attempt by the Jewish leadership to confront Turkish society on combating antisemitism is likely to backfire and further exacerbate the problem. For instance, upon reading Ovadya's demand in the Turkish press, radical Islamist writer Nurettin Şirin addressed a message to the community president on the Turkish Islamist website Kudüs Yolu (Jerusalem Way):

Well, since you have demanded that the prosecutors initiate action [against antisemitic publications], please, take your case to one of the prosecutors and let's meet in court. Don't send your attorneys, but come yourself, so that we'll have the opportunity to spit in your ugly face. Let's express it to you in diplomatic terminology: Silvyo Ovadya: persona non grata.[32]

During Operation Cast Lead, Ovadya and vice-president Lina Filiba expressed their concerns to American diplomats. Their greatest concern was that the perceived antisemitism seems to be driven by irresponsible government officials' pre-election rhetoric, a perspective shared by some Turkish intellectuals. They claim that this was the *first time* they had experienced "state-run antisemitism," having previously experienced a very healthy relationship with the goverment even when societal antisemitism peaked during the Israeli invasion of Lebanon in 2006. They pointed to articles that crossed the line into overtly antisemitic language and/or calls for violent action. *Vakit* columnist Hasan Karakaya specifically targeted Ovadya in a recent column and concluded his column with the statement "Jews equal terrorists."[33] Ovadya shrugged off a question about his sense of security, but Filiba said that the Jewish community leadership was extremely concerned for him because of Karakaya's comments.[34]

Mavi Marmara 2010 and the aftermath

It was the death of nine Turkish citizens during the *Mavi Marmara* incident that led to an almost complete degradation of diplomatic relations with Israel and to the suspension of all military ties in September 2011. The *Mavi Marmara* incident, which took place on May 31, 2010, is the name given to the Israeli military raid on a Turkish-led aid flotilla to Gaza that resulted in the death of nine Turks and in the shattering of the once-close ties between Ankara and Jerusalem. The *Mavi Marmara* incident was basically political, but almost immediately after taking place it turned into a great campaign against Jews in general and Turkish Jews in particular. For example, a few days after the incident Erdoğan gave a speech at the Turkish Arab Cooperation Forum (Türk Arab İşbirliği Forumu) and expressed his continuous accusation that Israel dominates the world media: "when the word Media is spoken, Israel and the Israeli administration comes to mind. They have the ability to manipulate it as they wish."[35] The next day, Erdoğan stated again that "the international press is supported by Israel; the press get their instructions from Israel" and then criticized the Turkish press for not prioritizing reports on *Mavi Marmara* over the Turkish government's then overtures to Iran, saying "Turkish newspapers are subcontractors [of Israel]."[36]

Erdoğan's assertions following the *Mavi Marmara* incident were truly antisemitic. Yet, Türkmen and Öktem claim in their article that following *Mavi Marmara*, Israel–Turkey relations had no impact on Turkish Jewry, even though the incident was so rough that it had caused bloodshed for the first time in the history of both countries' long and warm friendship. They say that when

108 Antisemitism under AK Party rule

Erdoğan declared that the Jews of Turkey had nothing to do with the *Mavi Marmara* incident, and moreover he declared that he opposes the Israeli government and not society, the Jews of Turkey, as well as other minorities, were and are no longer affected by diplomatic rows.[37] Unlike this perception, during the incident and afterwards, antisemitic rhetoric grew stronger in Turkey (Figure 4.1). Two interviewees of Jewish origin, who wished to conceal their identities out of fear of upsetting their employers, said the following to blogger Max Blumenthal on their lives as Jews during the *Mavi Marmara* incident:

E: When there were protests at the Israeli Consulate [after the *Mavi Marmara* incident], I felt really scared. I worked right next door and I was sitting at my desk all day thinking, "What if they found out I was Jewish and killed me? Maybe they are angry and ignorant. What will they do to me?" People from the office were joking with me that they would throw me to the protesters – they meant it in a friendly way of course.... After the flotilla things got a lot worse here. The average level of hatred [for the Jewish community] increased. Between 1 and 5, if the level of antisemitism and anti-Israel feeling used to be 2, now it's 4. It was really getting scary for a lot of us here after the Marmara [incident]. People were scared to go out for a few days. Outside the consulate there were fires, the burning of Israeli flags, lots of screaming. But [Recep] Erdoğan made an important statement that the Turkish people are not against Jews; their problem was with the Israeli government. We had another scary time in 2004 when Al Qaida placed bombs outside synagogues around Istanbul. All my friends were inside all day. When we heard the bombs go we actually thought the explosions were the sounds of celebrations at Bar Mitzvah parties. Now people are still afraid, but that doesn't stop them from going to these places. There are several levels of security in our synagogues today beginning with a security check at the beginning and then people come and ask you questions.[38]

B shared a similar experience saying:

B: Everyone was scared to go to malls or synagogues. Not that I ever go to a synagogue but in times of trouble I limit my risks. During the crisis, some protesters blocked the entrance outside the Israeli Consulate and were waving flags and shouting. Even if I wasn't Jewish I would have been scared to go there. This wasn't a peace march. The crowd wanted blood. If it came out that I was a Jew, what would they have done to me?[39]

The same fears are expressed by a Turkish Jew who immigrated to Israel. According to her testimony given to *Milliyet* newspaper, "the day preceding the Mavi Marmara was the scariest day I have ever experienced in Turkey." The fear for her family's future urged her to immigrate to Israel. She also added that following the Mavi Marmara, her old university friend wrote on her Facebook wall: "how can you eat the Israeli bread in peace?"[40] These fears were followed

Figure 4.1 Graffiti in Istanbul shortly after the *Mavi Marmara* incident.
Note
Ozgur Kudus means 'free Jerusalem'.

by enhanced security measures that were taken in Istanbul. The Turkish interior minister and deputy prime minister, Beşir Atalay, said security had been stepped up at 20 different sites alone in Istanbul, which has several synagogues and centers serving 23,000 Jews.[41]

The accusations during the *Mavi Marmara* event were not only directed toward Israel or Israeli policies, but were also directed at Turkish Jews. For instance, some individuals from the community were accused of collaborating with the IDF during the *Mavi Marmara* incident, and the Turkish media demanded from the only Jewish newspaper in Turkey, *Şalom*, a statement about how Turkish Jews felt about the *Mavi Marmara* incident. The chief rabbinate responded mildly, saying that the Turkish Jews felt no differently than the general Turkish society and were saddened by the loss of Turkish citizens' lives.[42] Another example: The Turkish media (mostly of the Islamist wing) reported that Turkish Jews fought on the deck of the *Mavi Marmara* arm in arm with IDF soldiers. The IHH's deputy chairman, Hüseyin Oruç,[43] whose activists fought IDF soldiers on the ship, urged MIT (Millî İstihbarat Teşkilatı – Turkish National Intelligence Organization) to give their personal information to the court and the Ministry of Foreign Affairs, to investigate the participation of these supposed five Turkish Jews from Istanbul and Izmir, dressed as IDF soldiers who took over the ship and then returned to Turkey. Their origin was unveiled when they conversed in Turkish and one was even addressed by the name "Ömer."[44]

Following this libel, Abraham H. Foxman of ADL sent a letter to H.E. Namık Tan, the ambassador of Turkey to the United States. In his letter he stressed that the vague allegations being reported could create a sense of alarm and intimidation among the Turkish-Jewish community. "Throughout Jewish history, similar tactics have fomented antisemitism by publicly raising suspicions of Jewish dual loyalty in the minds of fellow countrymen," said Abraham H. Foxman. "If your government has information about specific individuals under investigation, that should be disclosed immediately in order to relieve any sense of uncertainty about the Turkish-Jewish community in general," Foxman wrote. "If the news reports are unfounded or misleading, an immediate and public clarification is needed."[45] In response, Turkey strongly denied media reports that it had launched a probe into some of the country's Jewish citizens on suspicion that they collaborated with Israel in the 2010 raid on the *Mavi Marmara*.

> There has never been antisemitism in any part of our history and there will never be. Racism does not exist in the culture and tradition of the Turkish nation. Turkey, at its highest levels, has repeatedly said it considers antisemitism and racism crimes against humanity

said Selçuk Ünal, the Turkish Foreign Ministry spokesman, in a statement published on December 22, 2012.[46] Ünal said legal procedures were underway to identify possible perpetrators of the *Mavi Marmara* incident, adding that those procedures have nothing to do with Turkey's Jewish community, who are equal citizens and an integral part of our society. "It is clear that these press reports, which have been picked up by the foreign press, particularly in the US, have been exploited, leading to some misperceptions," said the statement. The statement noted that Turkey is also saddened to see that the way the developments in these legal proceedings are presented has been discomforting and troubling to "our Jewish citizens.... We cannot accept the generalized presentation of allegations regarding possible perpetrators of the incident in a way that targets the Turkish-Jewish community, who are a part of our society and equal citizens of Turkey."[47] We can see that Turks cannot accept the fact that antisemitism exists in Turkey. They always seem to call it something else, but never admit there is antisemitism, perhaps because they hardly ever executed Jews. It is interesting to learn the different understanding of the 'antisemitism' in the eyes of Turks.

The *Mavi Marmara* incident was what Anne-Christine Hoff defined as a manifestation of "normalization of antisemitism" at its highest levels of state.[48] Unlike her, Moshe Kamhi, the Israeli Consul of Israel in Istanbul between 2010 and 2014, marks Operation Cast Lead as the zenith of the skirmish between Israel and Turkey after Davos.[49] According to Hoff, if in the past anti-Israel statements could be diverted to the Turkish Jews, anti-Israel statements are utilized as a political tool that every politician can use to gain popular support and win elections. Semih Idiz from *Hürriyet* blamed Erdoğan for using the *Mavi Marmara* crisis to further his own ambitions for dominance in the region.

In addition to the antisemitic activities of IHH were the demonstrations outside court, as Turkey put four former IDF commanders on trial in absentia for the killing of nine Turks on a Gaza-bound aid ship. The indictment named Israel's former Chief of Staff Gabi Ashkenazi, former Navy Commander Eliezer Marom, former Air Force Commander Amos Yadlin, and former Air Force Intelligence Commander Avishay Levi, sentencing them to prison sentences of more than 18,000 years each. The 144-page indictment sought multiple life sentences totaling over 18,000 for each of the defendants. It lists "inciting murder through cruelty or torture" and "inciting injuries with firearms" among the charges.[50] IHH took advantage of this trial and made it an anti-Israel, anti-Zionist campaign by comparing Zionism to Hitler and the Nazi regime.[51] As we have seen, comparisons between Israel and Hitler have often been made in Turkey, but this comparison was also made with other parts, such as the United States, whose operations for the recapture of the city of Fallujah in November 2004 were followed by the publication of official statements in which U.S. operations were called genocide and compared to the Holocaust.[52] It seems the Turks use the words 'Hitler,' 'genocide,' 'Holocaust' and such whenever they disagree with military and other operations of 'unfriendly regimes.' The uniqueness of the term 'Holocaust' has been long lost, if it ever existed within the Turkish mindset.

Though the Israeli activity was met with universal condemnation, Fethullah Gülen, one of Turkey's most influential religious-spiritual leaders, criticized in the *Wall Street Journal* the pro-Islamic humanitarian organization's attempt to lift the siege of Gaza,[53] and the confrontation on the high seas with Israeli forces, for being provocative and unproductive. Many Islamist as well as secular groups in Turkey accused Gülen of "appeasement" as well as being a supporter of Israel and the CIA. He was even accused of helping the unbelievers and losing his Muslim identity as a result.[54] Yet, some claim that Gülen declared it as part of a continuous struggle between his movement and the AK Party.[55]

As for the Jews' official responses during this time, here again we find an apologetic response that expresses mainly fear. For instance, Rabbi Ishak Haleva, the chief rabbi of the Jewish community in Turkey slammed Israel over the deadly results of the flotilla, accusing Israel of engaging in unnecessary provocation and behavior. At the same time, Haleva praised Turkish Prime Minister Erdoğan three times during this interview, saying he was making a clear distinction between the State of Israel and the Jews of his country, and ensuring their safety: "Israel's security comes first, but it must act more cautiously and do things wisely," Haleva said on an ultraorthodox radio station named 'Kol BaRama,' noting that "Israel must act in an appropriate manner," "[Israel's response] was nothing but a provocation ... Israel should not have drawn the entire world's negative voices ... I believe it acted inappropriately." Later on in this interview, Haleva said: "there is no rioting against the Jews, God forbid. There is nothing, no worries. There was a protest just like in France, and that's all." Haleva denied the fact that relations between Israel and Turkey deteriorated under Erdoğan's term, and praised him.[56] Magnezi, *Ynet*'s journalist, mentions that Haleva's statements are lip service and that they are not a true expression of Haleva's opinions, since in 2003, after his own son Yitzhak was injured in the terror attack on the Istanbul synagogue, he declared: "no one will succeed in breaking my Jewish pride and my connection with Israel."[57] It is hard to expect another response when you are expected to condemn Israel. On August 26, 2004, for example, long before the *Mavi Marmara* incident, Haleva was fiercely attacked by some Turkish newspapers for not condemning Israeli Prime Minister Sharon for his "cruelty" but at the same token they condemned *Vakit*'s columnist Abdürrahim Karakoç, who praised Hitler in his August 17, 2004 column by saying:

> It is impossible not to admire the foresight of Adolph Hitler, who is presented to public opinion as 'racist, sadistic, and monstrous.' Way back then, Hitler foresaw what would happen these [present] days. He cleansed off these swindler Jews, who believe in racism for a religion and take pleasure in bathing the world in blood, because he knew that they would become [this] big curse on the world.

> Hitler indeed was a man of foresight [...] So Hitler did the job, yet Israel is presented to the world public opinion as the innocent victim.

> The second man with foresight is evidently Osama bin Laden. If a stone hits a dog's leg somewhere in the world, Osama bin Laden gets blamed. [...] Bin Laden had foreseen what would happen in Iraq, in Palestine, and in the prisons of Guantanamo.[58]

In addition to the raids and protests following *Mavi Marmara*, Turkish Jews said that some Muslim merchants collected what was called "Gaza tax" from their Jewish counterparts. According to the Jewish merchants, they started collecting payments from businessmen with whom they work. The claim is that the Turkish businessmen pay only a small amount from the payments owed to the Jews; the Muslim businessmen declare that the rest of the money was just given to the "injured Gazan." Alberto Patrini for instance, a Jewish textile merchant who lives in Istanbul, said:

> in the last year, at least five times Turkish merchants who I sold merchandise to have not paid me my money. They claimed that they deducted a "tax for Gaza" from the debt, because Israel killed innocent people on the Marmara and because Israel puts a curfew on Gaza.[59]

Testimonies of the Jewish merchants reached MK Danny Danon, who wrote a letter to Erdoğan saying: "the Turkish regime should be ashamed of itself; these racist behaviors are reminiscent of dark times in the history of Europe."[60] I must note that the Jews I spoke to, including merchants, were not familiar with this "tax," which probably means that the incidents were isolated. This hostile atmosphere continued during and after Operation Pillar of Defense, which was an eight-day IDF operation in the Hamas-governed Gaza Strip, officially launched on November 14, 2012 with the killing of Ahmed Jabari, chief of the Gaza military wing of Hamas. During this time, it seemed like the traditional tendency according to which the liberals in Turkey oppose antisemitism has also changed. According to Ege Berk Korkut, who published in *Die Welt* his impressions of Izmir, known to be the most secular city of Turkey, Jew-hatred has become an everyday phenomenon in Turkey:

> Although I live in Izmir, the most democratic city in Turkey, [even here there is] growing antisemitism. Everywhere I meet Jew-haters and enemies of Israel, listen to their prejudices on the daily bus trip or during a visit to a popular fast-food restaurant. Many of them admired Hitler, wish he would have accomplished his "mission," and not stop at six million murdered Jews.... I visit the twelfth grade of an [exclusive] high school. During a lesson the religious teachers talk about Operation Pillar of Defense in Gaza. Some students began to complain about Israel. They became more and more violent, and the teacher, an official of the Turkish state, said, "Do not worry, Israel will be destroyed one day, and the day is near that all Jews will pay for it." After the teacher had incited the students some students began to praise Hitler, while others expressed their readiness to drive the Israelis into the sea.
>
> I was surprised. I did not expect that a teacher, a Turkish government official, would incite students to kill people just because they are different, especially in Izmir, where the people are known for their tolerance.[61]

114 Antisemitism under AK Party rule

According to Korkut, antisemitism is rampant in Turkey and even in more moderate, secular, modern places. It seems like antisemitism is not limited to radical leftists, nationalists, or Islamists anymore. In that regard, says Korkut, "Turkey's future is not rosy."

The operation was preceded by a period with a number of mutual Israeli and Palestinian attacks. According to the Israeli government, the operation began in response to the launch of over 100 rockets at Israel during a 24-hour period, and an attack by Gazan militants on an Israeli military patrol jeep within Israeli borders.

But it seems that not only Turkish Jews have been intimidated ever since; the perilous atmosphere for Jews went beyond local Jews and risked also Israelis. For instance, an Israeli woman, Ariel Relli Kalderon, who lives alternately in Israel and Panama, spent a few days on vacation on Kos Island, in Greece. They took a ferry to Bodrum and while spending time on the main tourist road of Bodrum they entered a bag shop. After peacefully conversing in Spanish with the shopkeeper, who first insisted knowing where she was from, her sister called her in Hebrew. As the shopkeeper heard Hebrew he started yelling and humiliating her, demanding she leave, and even cursing her: "stinky Jew, trashy Jew, why did you lie to me ... I hate Jews, go out may you all die."[62]

Operation Protective Edge 2014

A cartoon from *Leman*, a famous Turkish comics journal is shown in Figure 4.2. The title says "Israeli Soldiers Greeted the Gaza Massacre by Dancing." The man, who brings his child and wife a bloody gift box, says: "Look, I brought you a puzzle. If you collect all parts together you will get a Palestinian child."

Figure 4.3 shows a further cartoon which declares "Israel invented the 2014 Gaza Games in its inventions contest, AK Turkey watches! Many kids ripped to shreds, dead."

It is very clear that under AK Party rule, antisemitism has escalated in Turkey, peaking during Operation Protective Edge for two main reasons.

1 Political and politician stratum

Unlike the past, when antisemitism was mainly expressed by AK Party members and supporters, the denouncement of Israel echoed throughout all parts of Turkish politics during Operation Protective Edge, where members of the Kemalist opposition party, CHP, applied to the Turkish Ministry of Foreign Affairs to establish a group of CHP members to be convoyed to Gaza in support of the Palestinian people. Vice-chairperson of CHP, Veli Ağbaba, said on the television program *Siyaset Vitrini* [Window to Politics]:

> our work is not done by explaining, we want to present our help in an open and sincere way. This is how we will express our solidarity with the Palestinian people who are under constant bombardment ... whatever the risk, we

Figure 4.2 Gaza massacre.
Source: Behiç Pek, *Leman*, July 29, 2014.

will go to Gaza, we will give the people of Gaza moral support, and we will visit the injured in the hospitals. We will show the entire world that we support them.[63]

Also CHP chairperson Kemal Kılıçdaroğlu stated that if the incidents in Gaza continued, Turkey would be obligated to cease its relations with Israel.[64] It should be noted that the responses of the CHP leaders and its candidate to the Turkish presidency, Ekmeleddin İhsanoğlu, were intended to speak out against Israel in order to win votes. This is why Ekmeleddin İhsanoğlu stated that Turkey would not be neutral and remain silent regarding the Israeli aggression in Gaza, after stating the opposite a while before that.[65] It should also be noted that CHP members participated even in the virulently anti-Israel protest in front of the Israeli Embassy, in which AK Party members of parliament also participated. Mahmut Tanal, Istanbul representative, said that Israel is a criminal state that should learn a lesson: "We stand with the Palestinian people."[66] Following this protest, and as the situation became increasingly more violent, Israel recalled its diplomats' families from Turkey. In response, the Israeli

116 *Antisemitism under AK Party rule*

Figure 4.3 Gaza games.
Source: Behiç Pek, *Leman*, July 23, 2014.

Foreign Ministry said that the Turkish police had failed to provide adequate protection for Israel's Embassy and its Consulate in Istanbul in a "blatant breach of diplomatic regulations."[67] In other words, the Turkish authorities took sides in favor of the Palestinians at the expense of Israeli diplomats' lives.

The reaction to Operation Protective Edge was also unique in its expression of antisemitism because this was the first time in Turkish history when Turkey declared three days of national mourning for Palestinians. Deputy Prime Minister Bülent Arınç told reporters in Ankara in televised comments as the Palestinian death toll topped 500: "We curse the merciless massacre committed by Israel against the Palestinian people, which has turned into a collective punishment. Our Cabinet has decided to declare three days of mourning" (starting from July 22, 2014).[68] Yet, this decision was met with some criticism because declaring mourning was not even suggested when 52 Turks were killed in Reyhanlı in Hatay by a Syrian bomb.[69]

Many other AK Party members denounced Israel using antisemitic rhetoric. A few examples: AK Party's Diyarbakır member of the Grand National Assembly, Cuma İçten, posted Turkey's flag alongside the Palestinian flag on a sign saying: "Israel is Terrorist" on the podium while he was speaking.[70] On July 18, some AK Party members left the parliament and protested against Israel in front of the Israeli Embassy in Ankara. According to Tweet from the AK Party's representative to the Grand National Assembly from Gaziantep, Ali Şahin, this was the first time in Turkish history that parliament members shut down the parliament and protested in front of the Israeli Embassy.

AK Party's Çorum member of the Grand National Assembly, Murat Yıldırım, said:

> For 15 days, the occupying Israel has been carrying out terrorism, turning Palestinian soil into a lake of blood by bombing it. We are here now as parliament members; parliament has a day off, tomorrow will also be a day off.[71]

Şamil Tayyar, a former journalist of *Star* and the AK Party's representative to the Grand National Assembly from Gaziantep, posted the following antisemitic tweet soon after the operation began on July 18: "May your race be extinct and may you never miss your Hitler [may you always have a Hitler]."[72] These words were like the opening of floodgates regarding antisemitic expressions in Turkey. On July 19, during the presidential campaign tour in Ordu, a city on the Black Sea, Erdoğan said: "Those who condemn Hitler day and night have surpassed Hitler in barbarism."[73] The same declaration was tweeted on Erdoğan's Twitter account, including the words: "The terrorist state Israel struck and hit innocent children who were playing on the beach. With these barbaric acts, they have even surpassed Hitler."[74]

As in the past, Erdoğan accused Israel of perpetrating a "systematic genocide" against Palestinians. "Since 1948, we have been witnessing this attempt at systematic genocide every day and every month," he said in his speech at the AK Party's meeting, wearing a keffiyeh. "But above all we are witnessing this attempt at systematic genocide every Ramadan."[75] Erdoğan implies that Israel conducts its battles deliberately during Ramadan.

Erdoğan has long presented himself as a champion of the Palestinian cause and leader of the entire Sunni Muslim world, but his anti-Israel rhetoric reached new heights during Operation Protective Edge, with comments aimed at causing the maximum offense to the Jewish state by comparing its strategy in Gaza to the actions of Nazi Germany. This time, as in the past, Erdoğan accused Israel of being a "terrorist state that commits 'genocide' in Gaza," but unlike before, this time Erdoğan stated that not only does he stand behind his comparison between Israel and Hitler, but he added that "Israel has 'surpassed what Hitler did' in Gaza," and has also compared the mentality of some elements in Israeli society to that of Adolf Hitler.[76] Erdoğan stepped up his verbal attacks on Israel on July 30, 2014, comparing the Jewish State to the Third Reich. Erdoğan declared that it makes some uncomfortable when the Holocaust is brought up in reference to the non-humanitarian and treacherous actions of the State of Israel and the government of Israel; he went on further to say:

> When one explains the similarity between what Israel does and what Hitler and the Nazis did, it makes some uncomfortable.... What is the difference between what the government of Israel does and what Hitler and the Nazis did? How can you explain what the State of Israel does in Gaza, in Palestine, if not as a holocaust? This is racism. This is fascism. This resurrects the soul of Hitler. Hitler said: "We can be unmerciful, but when we save Germany the world will be a merciful place. We can be unjust, but when we save Germany justice will come to the world. We can be immoral, but when we save our people the path towards a moral world will be paved." Hitler adhered to these very perverted thoughts. He caused the death of millions. He carried out a merciless holocaust on the Jews. Israel is currently saying the same as what Hitler said. The State of Israel is doing the same as what Hitler did. Israel is trying to fool the world saying self-defense for what is exhibited as mercilessness, injustice, immorality.... When we speak out, they immediately try to silence us by calling us anti-Semites. According to the Westerners, it is legal to murder a Muslim. But when it comes to a Jew, it is not. We say that antisemitism is a crime against humanity. Islamophobia is also a crime against humanity. You will behave in an inhumane way anyhow; you will kill the children in the hospitals and babies in their cradles. You will randomly bomb everything from the air, killing indiscriminately, even when you are told to stop, you will immorally accuse us of being antisemitic. No one is swallowing it anymore.[77]

Turkish Prime Minister[78] Erdoğan charged Israel with willfully killing Palestinian mothers and cautioned that it would "drown in the blood it sheds." The statement came as Turkey entered the final week of its presidential race. Speaking in front of thousands of supporters at an election rally, Erdoğan compared Israeli actions to those of Hitler, *Reuters* reported. "Just like Hitler, who sought to establish a race free of all faults, Israel is chasing after the same target," he said before a cheering crowd in Istanbul. "They kill women so that they will not give birth to Palestinians; they kill babies so that they won't grow up; they kill men so they can't defend their country.... They will drown in the blood they

Israeli operations and their impact 119

shed."[79] The political situation between Israel and Turkey was so problematic during the Operation that it even resulted in calls for a second *Mavi Marmara* flotilla, this time with a possible escort by the Turkish navy.[80] It is important to note that the clash between Israel and Turkey leading to antisemitic sentiments was created in the wake of the first *Mavi Marmara* flotilla. This time, the political situation created the possible arrival of the second *Mavi Marmara*. Even Erdoğan's eldest daughter, Esra Albayrak, participated in a demonstration conducted by the Association for Women and Democracy [Kadın ve Demokrasi Derneği (KADEM)] against Israel, and criticized Israel.[81]

2 Grassroots actions by Turkish society

There were clear calls for violence against Jews. Some tweets called for burning down synagogues and even mentioned the fact that the Jews of Istanbul live on the islands (islands in the Marmara sea, the largest being Büyükada, "the great island," where many Jews spend their summer vacations). The tweets also suggested burning down all factories owned by Jews. Identifying Jews' location is significant, as it is virtually a call to attack them in their own protected residences.

The open calls to harm Jews were not disseminated solely through social networks;[82] they also appeared in newspapers, such as Faruk Köse's call published in *Yeni Akit*, that clearly intimidated Jews by saying: "1955 Incidents" against the Jewish community in Turkey can result.[83] This call was later mentioned in Abraham H. Foxman's letter to Erdoğan, asking him to "publicly reject all expressions of antisemitism including the scapegoating of Turkish Jews for the actions of Israel,"[84] and giving examples of antisemitic expressions such as Faruk Köse's letter.[85] Köse also suggested that the Turkish-Jewish businessmen of Turkey pay a special tax for the rehabilitation of Gaza.[86] Bülent Yıldırım, head of the IHH, the NGO behind the *Mavi Marmara* flotilla, said: "this Turkish-Jewish community must immediately stop Israel's rotten behavior, otherwise, the people who live here will witness unwanted outcomes."[87] If a non-Zionist Jew could previously be accepted and considered 'a Turk' in the eyes of Turkish society, this time, every Jew seemed to be a target as the journalist Fatih Tezcan tweeted, "every Jew must send money to Israel and enlist in its army."[88]

Synagogues also became a target for the Turkish mob's protests. The first target was the Ashkenazi synagogue in Istanbul. Following a headline in the *Yeni Akit* newspaper saying "Istanbul'daki sinagog görevlilerinden küstah sözler" [The rude utterances of the workers from the synagogue in Istanbul], the newspaper called for an organized rally against synagogues. The newspaper expressed some angry responses as some of the Ashkenazi synagogue officials in Istanbul justified the IDF's operation in Gaza. According to the newspaper, the officials compared the IDF to the Turkish army when it combats PKK terrorism. The officials are quoted as saying that the Palestinians provoke Israel and instigate this violence.[89] Following this incident, social media networks announced an "egg attack" protest, and such attacks were realized. The first

120 *Antisemitism under AK Party rule*

"egg protest" took place on July 22. One group gathered in front of Ortaköy Synagogue carrying anti-Israel posters and then threw eggs at the synagogue. They were dispersed by Turkish security forces.

But attacks on synagogues were only part of larger attacks on Jews. The most shocking manifestation of antisemitism in Turkey during the Operation was an antisemitic rally in Istanbul, where participants called "Jew, don't forget, your turn will come,"[90] resembling 1930s Germany. This is probably the first rally of this kind to take place in Turkey over the last decade. The violent atmosphere in Turkey gave rise to cartoons resembling those of Nazi Germany. One example is the cartoon published on Twitter on August 2, 2014 through the popular cartoon series "Van Minüte" (Figure 4.4).[91] The cartoon says: "The world should see this selfie." It makes one wonder whether this is what Mümtazer Türköne referred to when he wrote in his article:

> Still, though, it does not appear that the tendency towards antisemitism in Turkey has risen. Turkish society is filled with rightful anger against what is happening in Gaza at the hands of Israel. But within this anger there is no anti-Jewishness; most Turkish people instead stand in the same place as the pacifist Jewish protesters demonstrating in Tel Aviv.[92]

The tense situation in Turkey during Operation Protective Edge led to initiatives not only against the Jewish community as a whole but also against individuals, such as the social media campaign to boycott the works of Mario Levi, which have been included on a list of "Israeli products to boycott" circulated on social media in response to the conflict in Gaza. This boycott was widely denounced. The Turkish minister of culture and tourism, Ömer Çelik, said on Twitter:

> The provocative reactions against Turkey's prominent author Mario Levi are ultimately wrong. It is a hate crime. Our Jewish citizens, their culture and synagogues, are an inseparable part of this country. They are not "guests" who live on this soil. We all live in our country; we all are its landlords.[93]

Yet, this is the first time an individual Jew has been targeted as part of a general public campaign against Israel.

It was not only individual Jews that suffered, but the entire Jewish community that served as a scapegoat. Another aspect that made the situation worse for Turkish Jews and which also proved the irrefutable connection between Turkish Jews and Zionism or the connection that is being made within Turkish society, is the call to revoke the citizenship of Turkish Jews who have served in the IDF. The staunch pro-government daily, *Milat*, targeted Turkish nationals from the Jewish community who also hold Israeli passports by arguing that since Israeli citizens are required to serve in the national army, they have blood on their hands and are responsible for killing Gazan civilians during an Israeli offensive that led to over 2,000 deaths since July 2014. *Milat*, which uses political Islamist

Figure 4.4 "The world should see this selfie."

rhetoric, used English in its headline, stating "Go home killers" in reference to Turkish Jews who allegedly served in the Israeli army. The article stated that after Israel announced its recent military campaign, Turkish Jews holding dual citizenship rushed to "massacre" Palestinians. The paper also commented that Turkish-Jewish citizens involved in fighting against innocent Palestinians come back to Turkey and "resume their lives as if nothing happened."

Milat based its report on a social media campaign launched by a number of journalists and activists with the hashtag #israilaskeriistemiyoruz (We do not want Israeli soldiers). A website carrying the same name urged citizens to sign a petition and send it to parliament with the aim of revoking the Turkish citizenship of anyone fighting in the Israeli army on the grounds that they have committed premeditated murder. The petition also requests that the Ministry of Defense abolish an existing legal exemption regarding military service for people who carry dual citizenship and have served in the Israeli army. According to a 1993 law, citizens with more than one nationality are exempt from military service in Turkey if they have served in the military of a country that Turkey recognizes.[94] Another example targeting the Turkish-Jewish community is what Bülent Yıldırım of the IHH said in a television interview on *TVNET* on July 17. According to him,

> [t]here is one vulnerable point where Israel will stop its self-indulgent behavior, which is the Jewish community. Most of Israel's money comes from Turkish Jews. A tax has continuously been paid to the Mossad from here [Turkey]. Soldiers are constantly going to Israel from here. The Turkish community must act and stop Israel's self-indulgence immediately. Otherwise, the people living here will experience unwanted consequences.... I am saying openly, they tell people of this age that they cannot enter the Al Aqsa Mosque [Yıldırım refers to the occasional prohibition for men under the age of 40 to enter the mosque for security reasons]. Shall we also gather the people in front of synagogues? Shall we also tell Jews of this age that they cannot enter? What do they want by doing this? Jewish tourists, what are you looking for in Turkey? The Zionists are putting the future of the Jews in danger. We cannot hold back our youngsters any longer.[95]

These exceptions were accompanied by the 'usual' feelings of intimidation expressed during previous military operations as well, including considering making Aliyah in larger numbers. Requesting to remain anonymous, an Istanbul Jewish resident said:

> It gets worse from day to day – in the press, in the streets, and in general. I do not reveal the fact that I am a Jew and I would deny it if asked. It is a spine chilling thing.[96]

When Israeli journalists tried to converse with officials from one of the synagogues in Turkey, they warned the journalists, saying: "we are not allowed to

Israeli operations and their impact 123

discuss this topic. It is dangerous, very dangerous." A member of the community who spoke with the same journalists in the past was afraid to speak this time, explaining: "the situation is too delicate right now I don't want to take the risk."[97] Jewish community representatives responded to the situation by saying that the community is "in a panic":

> Turkey has become a haven for the most strained society in the world. There is no war in our country but we are stressed as if we are at war. We are fearful. There is a wave of xenophobia and above that antisemitism is rife. It is very stifling for those who live under this continuous problem.[98]

The Jewish writer and lawyer Rita Ender reports that

> Turks come in front of our synagogues, shouting in a threatening way. They hang around the neighborhood where we live, staring straight into the eyes of the Jewish children in a threatening way, wearing T-shirts printed with a picture of Hitler and swastikas.[99]

Utku Çakırözer from *Cumhuriyet* quoted the community's representatives, saying: "wherever the community members go these days we are told that we will pay the price for Israel murdering Gazan children."[100] The source, who remains anonymous, also tells how the stressful situation is exploited to collect protection money: "Very odd things happen. They have threatened a very good famous friend of ours who owns a clothing brand: 'if you don't give us this money, we will protest in front of your shop.'"[101] Again, as happened in the past, shops posted signs on its front windows announcing that "Jew dogs" are banned from entering. A mobile phone accessory shop located in Tahtakalede Hasırcılar İş Merkezi in Istanbul, an area where many Jewish businesses are situated, posted a sign in its front window in August 2014 banning "dog Jews" from entering (Dog Jews cannot enter here; Figure 4.5).[102]

The same happened in a bazaar in Konya, where many shops put up signs saying: "Jewish goods are not sold here" (Figure 4.6). This sign was hung after the Operation and as a protest against Israel's attacks in Gaza, especially what the owner called "the murder of the innocent Palestinian children playing on the beach." The blur between "Israeli goods" and "Jewish goods" should be carefully noted.[103]

Again, as in the past and especially after the *Mavi Marmara* incident, Jews are being accused of being Mossad agents, and abetting Israel against Turkey. A few days after the presidential elections in Turkey, which took place on August 10, 2014, an article was published claiming that five Mossad agents who crossed the border from Syria to Turkey in order to sabotage the election process were killed by Turkish security forces. Subsequent to this article, the Turkish press reported that a young Jewish woman from Izmir, named Yasmin A., was recruited by Mossad a year earlier and "as she was a patriot and was trained by the special units" in Turkey, served as a double agent and informed the Turkish

Figure 4.5 "Jews and dogs not allowed here."

Figure 4.6 "Jewish goods not sold here."

authorities of Mossad's plan.[104] Although this time the Turkish Jew is mentioned as loyal to Turkey, the connection between Mossad and Turkish Jews still exists and undermines the relations between Turkish society and its Jewish constituents.

On August 22, 2014, Georgia and Jak Karako, a prominent and affluent Jewish couple, were found stabbed to death. This murder was committed due to antisemitism or greed, Burak Bekdil from *Hürriyet Daily News* claimed. He also mentioned that the antisemitic atmosphere in Turkey encouraged this murder. He noted a few recent antisemitic statements made by prominent Turks:

> Amid president-elect Recep Tayyip Erdoğan's thundering speeches that, "Israel was worse than Hitler," and regular attacks on Israel's diplomatic missions in Ankara and Istanbul, including rocks thrown at – and hundreds of angry Turks trying to break into – the diplomatic compounds. The mayor of Ankara, Melih Gökcek, was quoted as saying: "We will conquer the consulate of the despicable murderers." The Jewish couple had already been slain. But fortunately, this was not a crime motivated by antisemitism. The police quickly caught the suspects, an Uzbek couple who worked for the Karakos. They confessed to the killing. It was a simple criminal act like hundreds of others committed in Turkey every day. All the same, the poor couple's funeral service at the Ulus Ashkenazi Jewish cemetery was revealing. In fear of an attack, tight security scanned every guest. If you are a Jew in Turkey, not even a funeral is peaceful. All synagogues in Turkey – as well as Jewish (and some other non-Muslim) schools – are heavily guarded. In April, a Turkish judge shared the following *magnum opus* on his Facebook account: "We love you Recep Tayyip Erdoğan. We love you because those who do not love you, do not love this nation; Because Zionist Israel and its conspirators do not love you; Because the world's oppressed and Muslims love you; Because you are one of us, one of your nation; May God save you and make you victorious, for us.
>
> Upon Erdoğan's election victory on March 30, 2014, he wrote that, "The losers [at the ballot box] are Zionists and their conspirators." Just imagine a Turkish Jew having a legal dispute with a Muslim Turk and facing this judge in the courtroom...[105]

Takvim mocked the murder by using a word game: the famous thread company that the Karako couple owned in the past was called "Ören Bayan" (literally means: the knitting lady), but the newspaper deliberately used the words "Ölen Bayan" (lady who died), which enraged many in Turkey and was followed by furious responses on social networks.[106]

Bekdil mentions other examples as well, but his bottom line should be reason for serious concern. According to Bekdil, the Jews of Turkey should leave Turkey as soon as possible, or in his own words, "leave while you can before the second Holocaust happens."

Operation Protective Edge is so far the point at which antisemitism in Turkey peaked, as it involves actions and statements of 'the new antisemitism.'

Comparing Israel to the Nazis (Figure 4.7) has become one of Erdoğan's most common attacks, but during this Operation Erdoğan claimed that Israel is even worse than the Nazis. The anti-Israel sentiments expressed by other parties' members in the past were more resentful this time and included the enthusiastic participation of some members of CHP, a party that is not known for its antisemitic ideas. The chain reaction following the prime minister's accusations of Israel were also harmful and included an antisemitic raid against Jews. Boycotting Israel easily became boycotting Jewish products or products sold at Jewish businesses. The dangerous part of the most recent antisemitic wave in Turkey is that it was manifested in acts against Jews and also that it was led by Erdoğan, and thus through its perceived legitimacy to Turkish society antisemitic manifestations were condoned and even encouraged.

İhsan Dağı, a METU professor in Ankara, in an article published in *Zaman*,[107] reckons that the reason for rising antisemitism in Turkey is not a consequence of Israel's attacks on Gaza (the article was written in 2009). Instead, Dağı suggests that the recent rise of antisemitism is in fact related to the activities and ideology of neo-nationalist (Ulusalcı) groups, some of which are associated with the Ergenekon case.[108] Dağı mentions the writings of three prominent Turkish authors and journalists – Ergün Poyraz, Soner Yalçın, and Yalçın Küçük (on these authors see the section 'Books' in Chapter 5) – as the reason for the Jew

Figure 4.7 God save the Turks.

Note
"God save the Turks" with swastika, Beykoz, Istanbul, February 26, 2015. Efrat Aviv.

hunt in Turkey. According to Dağı, these publications have created a mental climate in which being a Jew or having a Jewish background is something to be ashamed of, and is enough to be considered anti-Turkish. The books raise the assumption that Turkey has always been and is still influenced and controlled by the Jews. The books also claim that ever since the establishment of modern Turkey, the Sabbateans have been playing an influential role in Turkish political, economic, and cultural life. As Dağı puts it, "the Turkish Republic was a Jewish project." The ideas expressed in these books were not new in Turkey, but the problem is that antisemitic sentiments were introduced to new segments of society; people who were urban, educated, professional, and secular. The perspective, which had been a popular theme amid radical Islamists up to that point, penetrated new social-political circles via these books. As Turkey is controlled by Jews, a new struggle for national independence is required. This kind of writing was an attempt to create a siege mentality, provoking antisemitism and justifying a neo-nationalist popular uprising. These books, as well as media discourse, in fact normalize antisemitism, using the code word of "Sabbatean"; by lending it an analytic, research, or academic legitimacy, it gains more adherents and popularity. This new antisemitism is part of an attempt to spread the neo-nationalist position into the grassroots, where the neo-nationalists have tried to forge alliances with conservatives. Dağı believes that antisemitism has been utilized to scare a diverse range of populations, such as leftists, rightists, Islamists, and socialists, and bring them together under a militarist ideology. The antisemitism that began emerging in 2004 and since has been part of an attempt to create a support foundation in society for a nationalist/militarist march to power, whether legally or illegally.[109] Mamoun Fandy seems to agree with the above viewpoint, but stresses a different angle: For Fandy, Israel's past strategy has been to narrow the scope of the conflict and downscale it from an Arab–Israeli conflict to a Palestinian–Israeli conflict. The strategy looked like it was working until Operation Protective Edge in 2014. Israel managed not only to make it a Palestinian–Israeli conflict, but also a war against only one faction of the Palestinian movement, Hamas, on the narrowest piece of Palestinian territory, Gaza. But the involvement of both Turkey and Iran has had the opposite effect. The conflict has been widened and regionalized rather than reduced as Israel intended. The conflict is now regionalized at the geopolitical level, with Iran and Turkey directly involved through their backing of Hizbullah and Hamas, respectively. The conflict has also become religious in nature rather than ethnic, especially after the Israeli government insisted on the Jewish identity of their state.[110] This is another reason that Erdoğan's antisemitic rhetoric is definitely aimed at Jews and not at Israelis.

Hate speeches and their impact: Jews and other minorities

Hrant Dink, who was the editor in chief of *Agos* and who sought to promote Turkish–Armenian reconciliation and fought against many kinds of discrimination in his native Turkey, was murdered by three gun shots to the back of the head on January 19, 2007.[111] The International Hrant Dink Foundation, which was created in his memory, was created to promote equal opportunities and encourage cultural diversity and cultural relations among all the peoples of Turkey. It revealed in its bi-annual report on discrimination in Turkish publications that Jews and Armenians are the top targets of hate speech in Turkey, with Jews edging out the Armenians as the number-one target of hate. Attempting to understand whether antisemitism is a unique phenomenon in Turkey or part of xenophobia or a resistance against all non-Muslim minorities in Turkey, Corry Guttstadt, who has been researching antisemitism and anti-Armenianism in Turkey, claims that antisemitism is a hidden ideology in Turkey whereas Armenians are perceived as the real enemy of the Turks. Furthermore, the Jews are abstract but Armenians are a concrete threat.[112]

For *Agos* journalist Fatih Gökhan Diler, the hatred toward Jews is stronger among Islamic circles in Turkey, whereas the Armenians seem to be the greatest target of nationalist-militant circles.

> For the Muslim Turks, the main point against the Armenians is the Armenian genocide and the Armenian lobby in the US. The Jews, on the other hand, are targeted due to the Jewish lobby in the US, which is considered much stronger than the Armenian one. Yet, it should be noted that the hatred towards Armenians resulted in the genocide, and not vice versa.

According to Güler, the Jews in Turkey suffer even more than other minorities. The security of Jewish institutions in Istanbul is much tighter than the security for their Armenian counterparts. The Jewish school in Ulus, for instance, is secured almost as much as a synagogue, whereas the Armenian schools have no security at all. Güler also adds that currently in Turkey it is much better to be an Armenian than a Jew, as the AK Party government is Islamist and thus targets Jews, but in the past, under the regime of nationalistic governments, it was much worse to be an Armenian. Regarding the relations between Turkish Jews and Israel compared to Armenians' ties with Armenia, Diler explains that Turks generally do not give much attention to Armenia despite its conflict with Turkey's regional ally, Azerbaijan. Thus many Armenians migrate from Armenia to Turkey for work. Israel, on the other hand, has been constantly and harshly criticized and linked to local Jews;[113] İvo Molinas tells in an interview with *Agos* that Turkish Jews' relations with Israel are so overestimated by the Turks that one of his Muslim Turkish friends asked him to request that Prime Minister Netanyahu stop the war with Palestine.[114]

Rıfat Bali raises another reason for the better 'public relations' the Armenian issue gains in Turkey; for the past four decades, Turkey's communal leadership has allied itself to successive Turkish governments who oppose the recognition of the Armenian genocide, whereas the liberals, who support the notion of recognizing the genocide, became patrons of the Armenians. Therefore, when the Islamic-oriented AK Party government came to power, the Jewish community followed their traditional support of the government and the Jews were left with no 'patron' in Turkey.[115]

Israeli operations and their impact 129

The Hrant Foundation publishes a quarterly report titled *Hate Speech in the Media and Discriminatory Discourse*. This report is a periodical review that includes all nationwide news publications in Turkey in order to determine whether certain groups are the targets of hate speech.[116] According to the foundation's website, the project's aims are to combat racism and discrimination based on ethnic and religious grounds through monitoring the newspapers and exposing "problematic" articles in the media. Since Turkey is a country with virtually never-ending internal tensions among different sectors of society, mostly due to the attitude of mass media outlets, which increasingly use a nationalist and biased tone, especially on controversial issues like minority rights, there is an immense need for monitoring. Although there is a general code of ethics for journalists, and even some media outlets have their own guidelines, most journalistic work does not comply with these.[117] The section "Speech in print media" extensively covers content targeting religious and ethnic groups as well as women, LGBT, and other disadvantaged groups. The second section, "Discriminatory discourse in print media," extensively covers the BDP and HDK's (Halkların Demokratik Kongresi; People's Democratic Congress) Black Sea region through four national and two local newspapers.[118] The report also examines four main manifestations of discrimination and hate speech:

1 *Exaggeration/charge/distortion*: including negative generalization of a community or a society due to one person's deed or event.
2 *Swear words/insults/humiliation*: swear words or humiliation directed at a specific community (such as traitor, dog, undignified).
3 *Animosity/war speeches*: hostility toward a community, manifestations calling for war on a certain community (such as Gavur Zulmü, meaning the cruelty of the infidel, the non-Muslim, but this is a very humiliating term for them).
4 *Using natural identity as an element/symbolization of hate and humiliation*: for instance: "your mother is Armenian as it is," or "is your surname Davutoğlu mu Davutyan?" (implies having an Armenian name)[119]

The Armenian genocide, according to Jikeli and Allouche-Benayoun, is also an obstacle for the Jews as the Turkish society automatically associates the Holocaust with the Armenian genocide, and as the Armenian genocide is seen as a total lie so is the Holocaust.[120]

Begüm Burak from *Today's Zaman* admits that all media actors in Turkey use discriminatory and biased language from time to time. "We all have our 'constitutive others' and so do the media … these biased attitudes erode the chance for a liberal media environment."[121] Burak adds that there is no monolithic media structure or monolithic hate speech in Turkey's media because media actors have various ideological orientations and financial backers, but generally speaking, says Burak, the media discourse in Turkey can be characterized as liberal monist and biased at the same time.[122] However, when exploring the report, it is quite obvious that most of the antisemitic and discriminatory expressions are generally popular in the Islamist media and not the liberal leftist and secular right media; hate speech was mostly observed in the following national newspapers: *Milli Gazete* (21 publications, 20.19 percent), *Ortadoğu* (19 publications, 18.26 percent), *Yeni Akit* (13 publications, 12.5 percent), *Yeni Mesaj* (11 publications, 10.57 percent), *Yeni Çağ* (11 publications, 10.57 percent), and *Anayurt* (5 publications, 4.8 percent).[123]

Burak finds the Hrant Dink report very important in a number of ways. First of all, it reveals the fact that under the guise of freedom of speech and freedom of the press, the media can easily vilify certain segments of society by employing stereotyping linguistic devices and negative-other representation techniques. Monitoring such media representations can serve the interests of democracy by undermining polarizing and stigmatizing language that ultimately leads to some elements of society, such as non-Muslims or Alevis, for example, being treated as second-class citizens. Second, the report indirectly increases the awareness about current media–politics relations in Turkey, and how this relationship leads to the establishment of provocative and polarizing language among media actors as well. It is obvious that print media outlets fail to adopt a more inclusive language, attacking each other in the 'sacred' task of deifying their own identity and/or demonizing the identities of others based on their ideology and economic situation instead. In this sense, the report indirectly shows that these kinds of attacks ultimately produce racist, prejudiced, and exclusionary media discourse.[124]

From the report:

- Compared to the same period in 2012, there was a slight rise in the amount of hate speech. According to the report, the hate speech cases in 2012 were distributed as follows: First quarter (114), second quarter (101), and third quarter (97). The first quarter of 2013 exhibited 104 hate speech cases.
- Similar to previous terms, it seems that most hate speech cases were observed in opinion columns. The distribution of different types of material with hate speech included: opinion columns (74), news articles (27), book reviews (1). Two publications were cited under the 'media archive' category.
- The groups that attracted the most hate speech included Armenians, Jews, and Christians. As a primary or secondary figure, Greeks and Kurds were also subjected to hate speech.[125]

The first graph of the report presents the number of hate speech cases as they appear in the Turkish newspapers according to their publication year (Figure 4.8). We can see that despite the decrease from the first third of 2012, the incidence of hate speech increases in the first third of 2013.[126]

In the period between September and December 2012, for instance, Jews were the most frequent targets of hate speech in Turkey, followed closely by Armenians, then Christians, and then there was a sharp drop to fourth place for Greeks living in Turkey (Figure 4.9). Westerners in general and then Greeks

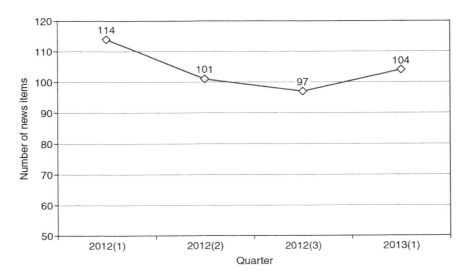

Figure 4.8 Hate speech content per quarter.

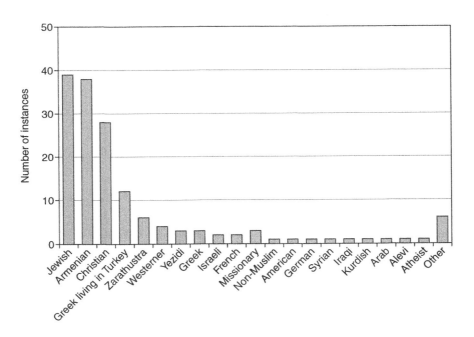

Figure 4.9 Hate speech content by target groups.

132 Antisemitism under AK Party rule

make up the bulk of the remaining victims of Turkish hate speech, according to the Dink Foundation report.

It is extremely important to look at the fourth graph in this report,[127] which illustrates that the greatest number of hate speech cases appears in the opinion columns, meaning that hate speeches mostly reflect individuals' opinions; but it also shows how much influence opinion column writers in Turkey have when it comes to the topic of antisemitism.

Being one of the top three groups that were subjected to hate speech, the Jewish population, just like the Armenian, Christian, and in greater numbers the Kurdish and Greek ones, was mostly targeted within the category of enmity/war discourse (Figure 4.11). Six of the items detected fell under the blasphemy/insult/degradation category, five items under the exaggeration/attribution/distortion category and one under symbolization.[128]

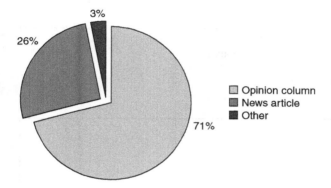

Figure 4.10 Hate speech by genre.

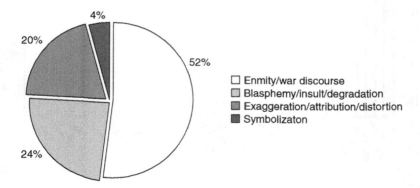

Figure 4.11 Hate speech toward Jews.

Notes

1. On November 15, 2003, two trucks carrying bombs slammed into the Bet Israel and Neve Shalom synagogues in Istanbul and exploded. The explosions devastated the synagogues and killed 27 people, most of them Turkish citizens, and injured more than 300 others. Five days later, on November 20, as U.S. President George W. Bush was in the United Kingdom meeting with Prime Minister Tony Blair, two more truck bombs exploded. Suicide bombers detonated the vehicles at the headquarters of HSBC Bank AS and the British Consulate, killing 30 people and wounding 400 others. An Islamic militant group, BDA-C (Great Eastern Islamic Raiders' Front), claimed responsibility for the blasts, but Turkish government officials dismissed these claims, pointing out that this minor group did not have enough resources to carry out such an intricately planned and expensive attack. Turkish governmental representatives have participated in the annual commemoration ceremony conducted by the Jewish community ever since the event. On the bombing, see: http://arsiv.ntvmsnbc.com/news/243967.asp, retrieved March 16, 2012. On Erdoğan's response and his strong condemnation of the terror attack, see: http://dosyalar.Hürriyet.com.tr/almanak2003/news_detail.asp?nid=196&sid=2, retrieved March 16, 2012.
2. Murat Yetkin, "Antisemitism is a perversion," *Hürriyet Daily News*, May 22, 2014: www.Hürriyetdailynews.com/Antisemitism-is-a-perversion.aspx?PageID=238&NID=66785&NewsCatID=409, retrieved May 24, 2014.
3. http://archive.adl.org/presrele/mise_00/4604_00.html#.UzrGimeKBjq, retrieved March 16, 2012.
4. http://archive.adl.org/presrele/asint_13/4730_13.html#.UzrHMGeKBjq, retrieved March 16, 2012.
5. Rachel Avraham, "Turkish Jewish leader condemns recent antisemitic incitement within her country," *Jerusalem Online*, January 25, 2015: www.jerusalemonline.com/news/middle-east/Israel-and-the-middle-east/Turkish-Jewish-leader-condemns-recent-antisemitic-incitement-within-her-country-11003, retrieved January 26, 2015.
6. Ibid.
7. JTA, "Turkish prime minister to U.N: antisemitism is a crime against humanity," *The Jewish Daily Forward*, February 28, 2013: http://forward.com/articles/172036/Turkish-prime-minister-to-un-Antisemitism-is-a-c; Anatolia News Agency, "Turkish PM Erdoğan: Islamophobia, antisemitism same," *Hürriyet Daily News*, February 28, 2013: www.Hürriyetdailynews.com/Turkish-pm-Erdoğan-islamophobia-Antisemitism-same.aspx?pageID=238&nID=42019&NewsCatID=338, retrieved March 27, 2013.
8. http://archive.adl.org/presrele/asint_13/4730_13.html#.UzrHMGeKBjq, retrieved March 16, 2012.
9. Quoted in: Bali, "Present-day antisemitism in Turkey."
10. Miri Hasson, "Turkey: entrance for murderer Israeli is prohibited," *YNET*, August 15, 2008: www.ynet.co.il/articles/0,7340,L-3291258,00.html, retrieved July 10, 2010.
11. https://yenisafak.com.tr/arsiv.2006/temmuz/31/televizyon.html, retrieved May 3, 2010.
12. See, for example: no author, "TRT Yeni Şafak'ı mı dinledi?," *Radikal*, August 3, 2006: www.radikal.com.tr/haber.php?haberno=194672; no author, "İsrail Tepkisi Ödülü Filmi Yayından Kaldırdı," *Medya Radar*, August 2, 2006: www.medyaradar.com/israil-tepkisi-odullu-filmi-yayindan-kaldirdi-haberi-15238, retrieved August 14, 2010.
13. Meltem Özgenç, "RTÜK, Piyanist'i şiddetli buldu," *Hürriyet*, September 13, 2014: www.Hürriyet.com.tr/gundem/27199827.asp, retrieved September 15, 2014.
14. No author, "RTÜK, Piyaniste ceza kesti," *Bir Gün*, September 15, 2014: www.birgun.net/news/view/rtuk-piyaniste-ceza-kesti/5444, retrieved September 15, 2014.
15. www.scoop.co.nz/stories/WL0608/S00210/cablegate-ankara-media-reaction-report.htm, retrieved September 4, 2013. In 2014, during Operation Protective Edge,

İhsanoğlu, who was considered much more of a moderate than the other candidate, Erdoğan, labeled Israel as a country which "violates international law and ethics" and conducts massacres. He urged Palestinians to turn to the International Criminal Court (ICC). No author, "Ekmeleddin İhsanoğlu: İsrailin bu Alçakça saldırısını kiniyorum," *Hürriyet*, August 18, 2014: www.Hürriyet.com.tr/gundem/26837513.asp, retrieved September 12, 2014.

16 No author, "Türkiye-İsrail Dostluk Grubu'nun 25 üyesi daha istifa etti," *Zaman*, August 1, 2006: www.zaman.com.tr/gundem_turkiye-israil-dostluk-grubunun-25-uyesi-daha-istifa-etti_320368.html.

17 Cem Ertür, "A Zionist in disguise: Turkey's prime minister Erdoğan's phony anti-Israel rhetoric," *Global Research*, November 30, 2012: www.globalresearch.ca/a-zionist-in-disguise-Turkeys-prime-minister-Erdoğans-phony-anti-Israel-rhetoric/z531 3589, retrieved September 15, 2006. This newspaper was shut down by the government almost a year ago and their webpage has disappeared

18 Dan Arbell, "The U.S–Turkey–Israel triangle," *Brookings: Center for Middle East Policy*, 24 (2014), p. 11. www.brookings.edu/~/media/research/files/papers/2014/10/09%20Turkey%20us%20Israel%20arbell/usTurkeyIsrael%20trianglefinal.pdf, retrieved November 1, 2014.

19 Ibid.

20 Ibid.

21 Bali, "Present-day antisemitism in Turkey."

22 Ali Bulaç, "İsrail!," *Zaman*, Decemeber 29, 2008: www.zaman.com.tr/ali-bulac/israil_789396.html, retrieved September 4, 2013.

23 Hakan Albayrak, "Nazi benzetmesi niye rahatsız etti?," *Yeni Şafak*, January 10, 2009: http://yenisafak.com.tr/yazarlar/?t=10.01.2009&y=HakanAlbayrak, retrieved September 3, 2012.

24 Theodor W. Adorno (1903–1969) was a German Jewish sociologist, philosopher, and musicologist known for his critical theory of society. Adorno's work emphasized the horror and irrationality of the Shoah and the inability to incorporate it into philosophies of history (Hegel, Marx, etc.), and this amounted to an emphasis on the particular over the universal. However, he also universalized the conditions that gave rise to the Shoah (commodification, monopoly capitalism) and this amounted to an emphasis on the universal over the particular. Essentially, Adorno is famous for his remark that "poetry after Auschwitz is immoral."

25 Kocabaşoğlu, "Antisemitizm Korkusu."

26 Ahmet Kekeç, "Gazze değil Auschwitz," *Timetürk*, December 12, 2008: www.Timetürk.com/tr/makale/ahmet-kekec/gazze-degil-auschwitz.html#.U6vvdLdZpjo, retrieved September 10, 2010.

27 No author, "Sen Musa'nın çocuğu olamazsın," *Haber Vaktim*, January 8, 2009: www.habervaktim.com/haber/50896/sen-musanin-cocugu-olamazsin.html, retrieved May 12, 2012.

28 http://cables.mrkva.eu/cable.php?id=188079, retrieved September 23, 2011.

29 www.tuketiciler.org/?com=news.read&ID=3409, retrieved June 15, 2013; Bali, *Antisemitism and Conspiracy Theories*, pp. 233–234.

30 Bali, "Present-day antisemitism in Turkey."

31 Kemal Atlan, "'Ermeni, Yahudi Giremez' yazısına ceza davası," *Milliyet*, February 16, 2009: www.milliyet.com.tr/default.aspx?aType=SonDakika&ArticleID=1060416; No author, "'Yahudiler ve Ermeniler giremez"e hapis," *CNN Turk*, May 27, 2009: www.CNNTürk.com/2009/turkiye/05/27/yahudiler.ve.ermeniler.giremeze.hapis/528351.0, retrieved July 20, 2012.

32 Bali, "Present-day antisemitism in Turkey."

33 Hasan Karakaya, "Hey Dünya gör artık Yahudi eşitti terörist!?" *Vakit*, January 6, 2009: www.Timetürk.com/tr/makale/hasan-karakaya/hey-dunya-gor-artik-yahudi-esittir-terorist.html, retrieved July 10, 2012.

Israeli operations and their impact 135

34 A joint Embassy Ankara/Consulate General Istanbul report, dated January 21, 2009: http://cables.mrkva.eu/cable.php?id=188079, retrieved March 15, 2013.
35 Quoted in: Bali, *Antisemitism and Conspiracy Theories*, p. 84.
36 Bali, *Antisemitism and Conspiracy Theories*, p. 84.
37 Türkmen and Öktem, "Foreign policy as a determinant," p. 14.
38 http://maxblumenthal.com/2011/07/being-Jewish-in-Turkey-before-and-after-the-mavi-marmara-part-1-of-2, retrieved July 31, 2013.
39 http://maxblumenthal.com/2011/07/being-Jewish-in-Turkey-before-and-after-the-mavi-marmara-part-2-of-2, retrieved July 27, 2012.
40 No author, "Kapının dışı İsrail evimizin içi İstanbul," *Milliyet*, July 28, 2012: http://dunya.milliyet.com.tr/kapinin-disi-israil-evimizin-ici-istanbul/dunya/dunyadetay/28.07.2012/1572975/default.htm, retrieved August 28, 2013.
41 www.jpost.com/Jewish-World/Jewish-News/Turkey-boosts-security-for-Jews, retrieved September 1, 2012.
42 Anne-Cristine Hoff, "Normalizing antisemitism in Turkey," *The Journal for the Study of Antisemitism*, 5, 1 (2013), pp. 185, 191.
43 Oruç is known for his antisemitic rhetoric: www.terrorism-info.org.il/Data/articles/Art_20456/H_273_12_784420210.pdf, retrieved April 10, 2013.
44 Arpacik Cihat, "Mavi Marmara katilleri aramızda," *Yeni Şafak*, December 13, 2012: http://yenisafak.com.tr/gundem-haber/mavi-marmara-katilleri-aramizda-14.12.2012-435777; in this source the IHH chairperson is not mentioned as the source of the information on Turkish Jews' participation in the *Mavi Marmara* incident: http://m.haber5.com/haber/224182, retrieved August 28, 2013.
45 www.Israelnationalnews.com/News/News.aspx/163344#.UhpnmvBBRjo, retrieved 28 August 2013.
46 www.haberler.com/tarihimizde-yahudi-karsitligi-yok-4192108-haberi, retrieved December 25, 2012.
47 Ibid.
48 Hoff, "Normalizing antisemitism in Turkey," p. 186.
49 Lecture at Bar Ilan University, January 7, 2014.
50 Ayşegül Usta, "Mavi Marmara iddianamesi kabul edildi," *Hürriyet*, May 29, 2012: www.Hürriyet.com.tr/planet/20646153.asp, retrieved August 25, 2013.
51 www.haksozhaber.net/caglayanda-katil-israil-katil-esed-sloganlari-foto-33446h.htm, retrieved December 12, 2013.
52 Ioannis N. Grigoriadis, "Friends no more? The rise of anti-American nationalism in Turkey," *Middle East Journal*, 64, 1 (2010), p. 60.
53 Joe Lauria, "Reclusive Turkish imam criticizes Gaza flotilla," *Wall Street Journal*, June 4, 2010: http://online.wsj.com/article/SB10001424052748704025304575284721280274694.html, retrieved October 25, 2012. See also: Umut Uzer, "Turkish–Israeli relations," p. 101.
54 M. Hakan Yavuz, *Toward an Islamic Enlightenment: The Gülen Movement* (New York: Oxford University Press, 2013), p. 238.
55 On the linkage and relations between the Gülen Movement and AK Party, see: Gareth Jenkins, "AK Party forming closer links with the Gülen Movement," *Eurasia Daily Monitor*: 4, 217: www.jamestown.org/single/?no_cache=1&tx_ttnews[tt_news]=33187, retrieved August 6, 2013; Ahmet Kuru, "Changing perspectives on Islamism and secularism in Turkey: the Gülen Movement and the AK Party," in: Ihsan Yilmaz (ed.), *Muslim World in Transition: Contributions of the Gülen Movement* (London: Leeds Metropolitan University Press, 2007), pp. 140–151; Ahmet Kuru, "Fethullah Gülen's Search for a Middle Way between Modernity and Muslim Tradition," in: M. Hakan Yavuz and John L. Esposito (eds.), *Turkish Islam and the Secular State: The Gülen Movement* (Syracuse, NY: Syracuse University Press, 2003), pp. 115–130; Yavuz, *Toward an Islamic Enlightenment*, pp. 198–220.

On Gülen's attitude toward Jews and Israel, see: Efrat E. Aviv, "Fethullah Gülen's 'Jewish Dialogue,'" *Turkish Policy Quarterly*, 9, 3 (2010), pp. 101–115.
56 Kobi Nahshoni, "Turkey's chief rabbi: navy raid a provocation," *Ynet*, June 2, 2010: www.ynetnews.com/articles/0,7340,L-3898025,00.html, retrieved October 9, 2011.
57 Aviel Magnezi, "How will Turkey's Jews vote?," *Ynet*, June 10, 2011: www.ynetnews.com/articles/0,7340,L-4080382,00.html, retrieved October 9, 2012.
58 Quoted in: www.memri.org/report/en/0/0/0/0/0/0/1365.htm#_edn7, retrieved December 12, 2012. In February 2005, publication of this newspaper was banned in Germany for antisemitic incitement and its denial of the Holocaust.
59 Arik Bendar, "Jews in Turkey: we pay 'Marmara tax,'" *NRG*, September 28, 2011.
60 Ibid.
61 Ege Berg Korkut, "Judenhass hat türkischen Schulunterricht erreicht," *Die Welt*, December 20, 2012: www.welt.de/debatte/kommentare/article112151074/Judenhass-hat-tuerkischen-Schulunterricht-erreicht.html, retrieved August 3, 2013.
62 Shimon Ifarghan, "Turkia: ba'al Chanut Kina Tayeret Israelit 'yehudiya masricha,'" [Turkey: a shop keeper called an Israeli tourist: "a stinky Jew"], *Globes*, September 29, 2013: www.globes.co.il/news/article.aspx?did=1000880793#fromelement=hp_morearticles, retrieved August 23, 2014.
63 Mikail Pelit, "CHP'den Gazze'ye Gitme Kararı," *Hürriyet*, July 20, 2014: www.Hürriyet.com.tr/gundem/26850899.asp, retrieved July 22, 2014.
64 Ali Kemal Akan-Mustafa Güngör, "İsrail'le İlişkilerimizi Askıya Almak Zorundayız," *Anadolu Ajansı*, July 23, 2014: www.aa.com.tr/tr/haberler/363539-israille-iliskilerimizi-askiya-almak-zorundayiz, retrieved July 24, 2014.
65 No author, "Ekmeleddin İhsanoğlu'ndan Tarafsızlık Açıklaması," *TRT Haber*, July 25, 2014: www.trthaber.com/haber/gundem/ekmeleddin-ihsanoglundan-tarafsizlik-aciklamasi-136251.html, retrieved July 21, 2014.
66 No author, "Milletvekilleri İsrail Büyükelçiliğine Yürüdü," *Haber7*, July 18, 2014: www.haber7.com/siyaset/haber/1181679-Milletvekilleri-israil-buyukelciligine-yurudu, retrieved August 4, 2014.
67 *Ynet* reports: "Israel recalls diplomats' families from Turkey after protests grow violent," *Ynet*, July 18, 2014: www.ynetnews.com/articles/0,7340,L-4545774,00.html, retrieved July 20, 2014; Abe Katsman, "Turkish anti-Israel protests grow violent, threats made to Jewish community," *Breitbart*, July 18, 2014.
68 No author, "İsrail'le Ticari İlişkilerimiz Sürüyor!," *Sözcü*, July 21, 2014: http://sozcu.com.tr/2014/gundem/uc-gunluk-yas-ilan-edildi-561122, retrieved July 24, 2014.
69 Ibid.
70 http://m.ensonhaber.com/haber.php?id=313783, retrieved September 10, 2014.
71 No author, "Milletvekilleri İsrail Büyükelçiliğine yürüdü," *Haber7*, July 18, 2014: www.haber7.com/siyaset/haber/1181679-Milletvekilleri-israil-buyukelciligine-yurudu, retrieved August 4, 2014.
72 https://twitter.com/samiltayyar27/status/489904703963406336, retrieved July 30, 2014.
73 Mehmet Ali Berber, "'Barbarlıkta Hitler'i Geçtiler,'" *Sabah*, July 20, 2014: www.sabah.com.tr/Gundem/2014/07/20/barbarlikta-hitleri-gectiler retrieved July 21, 2014.
74 https://twitter.com/RT_Erdoğan/status/490532074173243393, retrieved July 22, 2014.
75 No author, "Erdoğan, o Görüntüleri İzletti," *Milliyet*, July 22, 2014: www.milliyet.com.tr/Erdoğan-o-goruntuleri-izletti/siyaset/detay/1915432/default.htm, retrieved July 24, 2014.
76 No author, "İsrail'in Gazze'de Yaptığı Hitler'i Aştı," *Taraf*, July 25, 2014: www.taraf.com.tr/haber-israilin-gazzede-yaptigi-hitleri-asti-160014; no author, "Erdoğan: İsrail bir Terör Devleti," *Sabah*, July 26, 2014: www.sabah.com.tr/Dunya/2014/07/26/Erdoğan-israil-bir-teror-devleti, retrieved July 26, 2014.
77 Hacı Yılmaz and Cihad Coşar, "Erdoğan Van'da Halka Hitabetti," *Hursedahaber*, July 31, 2014: http://hurseda.net/Haber/121918-Erdoğan-Vanda-Halka-Hitabetti.html, retrieved August 2, 2014.

78 All titles refer to before the presidential election in June 2014.
79 No author, "Köşk Yolunda Dev Buluşma," *Akşam*, August 3, 2014: www.aksam.com.tr/siyaset/kosk-yolunda-dev-bulusma/haber-329250, retrieved August 5, 2014.
80 No author, "Gazze'ye İkinci Mavi Marmara Gidecek" İddiası," *CNNTürk*, July 27, 2014: www.CNNTürk.com/haber/dunya/gazzeye-ikinci-mavi-marmara-gidecek-iddiasi, retrieved July 29, 2014.
81 No author, "Başbakan Erdoğan'ın Kızı Esra Albayrak Gazze Eyleminde," *Hürriyet*, July 15, 2014: www.Hürriyet.com.tr/gundem/26813597.asp, retrieved July 20, 2014.
82 On antisemitism in social networks, see: Turkay Salim Nefes, *Online Antisemitism in Turkey* (London: Palgrave Macmillan, 2015).
83 *Köse*, "Hahambaşı'na Çağrı."
84 www.adl.org/Israel-international/Israel-middle-east/content/l/letters-adl-Erdoğan.html, retrieved September 10, 2014.
85 No author, "Akit Yazarına İsrail'den Davet," *T24*, September 10, 2014: http://t24.com.tr/haber/akit-yazarina-israilden-davet,270330, retrieved September 10, 2014.
86 Faruk Köse, "Gazze'yi Yahudi İşadamları İmar Etsin," *Yeni Akit*, September 7, 2014: www.yeniakit.com.tr/yazarlar/faruk-kose/gazzeyi-yahudi-isadamlari-imar-etsin-7578.html, retrieved September 10, 2014.
87 No author, "İHH Başkanından Türk Yahudileri'ne Tehdit," *Odatv*, July 18, 2014: www.odatv.com/n.php?n=ihh-baskanindan-turk-yahudilerine-tehdit-1807141200, retrieved July 20, 2014.
88 https://twitter.com/fatihtezcan/status/491678528199753728/photo/1, retrieved July 24, 2014.
89 No author, "Istanbul'daki Sinagog Görevlilerinden Küstah Sözler," *Yeni Akit*, July 11, 2014: www.yeniakit.com.tr/haber/istanbuldaki-sinagog-gorevlilerinden-kustah-sozler-23704.html, retrieved July 20, 2014.
90 No author, "Türkiye'deki Yahudiler'e Tehdit," *OdaTV*, July 30, 2014: www.odatv.com/n.php?n=turkiyedeki-yahudilere-tehdit-3007141200; the rally can be seen at www.odatv.com/vid_video.php?id=8D315, retrieved July 20, 2014.
91 https://twitter.com/Batman_dark_/status/495523627472027648/photo/1, retrieved August 3, 2014.
92 Mümtazer Türköne, "Israel's attack on Gaza and antisemitism in Turkey," *Today's Zaman*, July 19, 2014: www.todayszaman.com/columnist/mumtazer-turkone_353 475_Israels-attack-on-gaza-and-Antisemitism-in-Turkey.html, retrieved July 22, 2014.
93 No author, "Kültür Bakanı Levi'ye Yapılan Nefret Şüçüdü," *Durustv*, July 25, 2014: www.durustv.com/haber/5743/kultur-bakani-leviye-yapilan-nefret-sucudur, retrieved July 26, 2014.
94 No author, "Daily targets Turkish Jews in headline," *Today's Zaman*, August 14, 2014: www.todayszaman.com/national_daily-targets-Turkish-Jews-in-headline_355659.html; www.butungazetemansetleri.com/milat-gazetesi-14.08.2014, retrieved August 15, 2014.
95 M. Serdar Korucu, "Ortaköy Sinagogu'na Yumurtalı Saldırı," *CNN Türk*, July 24, 2014: www.cnnturk.com/haber/turkiye/ortakoy-sinagoguna-yumurtali-saldiri; http://yenisafak.com.tr/video-galeri/ihh-baskani-bulent-yildirim-israil-dunyaya-rezil-olacak/18751, retrieved July 24, 2014.
96 Globes Service: "First samples: Erdoğan won the presidential elections," *Globes*, August 10, 2014: www.globes.co.il/news/article.aspx?did=1000962044, retrieved August 10, 2014 [Hebrew].
97 Ibid.
98 No author, "Hitler tişörtü kişiler sinagogların önünde dolaşıp işyerlerini tehdit ediyor," *T24*, August 8, 2014: http://t24.com.tr/haber/hitler-tisortu-kisiler-sinagoglarin-onunde-dolasip-isyerlerini-tehdit-ediyor,266978, retrieved August 9, 2014.
99 Rita Ender, "Farz Edelim Ki Biz Yahudiler Türkiye'den Gittik!," *Bianet*, August 2, 2014: www.bianet.org/biamag/toplum/157482-farz-edelim-ki-biz-yahudiler-turkiye-den-gittik, retrieved August 6, 2014.

100 Çakırözer, "Museviler: Panikteyiz."
101 Ibid.
102 No author, "Eminönü Tahtakale'de Yahudi düşmanlığı," *Şalom*, September 4, 2014: www.salom.com.tr/haber-92271-eminonu_tahtakalede_yahudi_dusmanligi.html?rev =1, retrieved September 1, 2014.
103 Kevser Kızılkaya, "Burada Yahudi Malı Satılmaz," *Anadolu Bugün*, August 21, 2014: www.anadoludabugun.com.tr/burada-yahudi-mali-satilmaz-51490h.htm, retrieved August 20, 2014.
104 No author, "Netanyahu Çıldırdı, Tel Aviv Panikte," *Beyazgazete*, August 19, 2014: www.beyazgazete.com/haber/2014/8/19/netenyahu-cildirdi-tel-aviv-panikte-2338440.html, retrieved August 19, 2014.
105 Quoted in: Burak Bekdil, "To all Jews in Turkey: there is an enormous red dragon coming after you. Leave while you can before the second holocaust happens," *Shoebat Foundation*, September 7, 2014: http://shoebat.com/2014/09/07/Jews-Turkey-red-dragon-two-horns-leave-now, retrieved September 11, 2014.
106 No author, "Takvim'in 'Ölen bayan' başlığına tepki yağdı," *T24*, August 23, 2014: http://t24.com.tr/haber/takvimin-olen-bayan-basligina-tepki,268533, retrieved August 27, 2014.
107 İhsan Dağı, "Yeni anti-Semitler kimler?," *Zaman*, February 6, 2009.
108 Ergenekon group was named after a mythical Central Asian valley of the Altay Mountains, connected to Turkish nationalist lore, and was described as consisting of members of the armed forces and civilians in the media, academia, and opposition political parties. The group was accused of being part of a secret "deep state" and were said to view themselves as the protectors of Turkey's national identity and the secular values of the country's founder, Mustafa Kemal Atatürk.
109 Dağı, "Yeni anti-Semitler kimler?"
110 Mamoun Fandy, "Opinion: no longer an Arab–Israeli conflict," *Asharq al-Awsat*, August 11, 2014: www.aawsat.net/2014/08/article55335312, retrieved August 11, 2014.
111 On the murder of Hrant Dink, see: Maureen Freely, "Why they killed Hrant Dink," *Index on Censorship*, 36, 2 (2007), pp. 15–29.
112 Jerusalem, February 3, 2015.
113 Interview in Istanbul, February 22, 2015.
114 Fatih Gökhan Diler, "No moz karışayamoz a la eços del hükümet," *Agos*, February 2, 2015: www.agos.com.tr/tr/yazi/10577/no-moz-karisayamoz-a-la-ecos-del-hukumet, retrieved February 28, 2015.
115 Bali, *Antisemitism and Conspiracy Theories*, p. 133.
116 Lori Lowenthal Marcus, "Jews are number one target of hate speech in Turkey," *The Jewish Press*, March 4, 2013: www.Jewishpress.com/news/Jews-are-number-one-target-of-hate-speech-in-Turkey/2013/03/04, retrieved August 10, 2013.
117 http://nefretsoylemi.org/en/amac_hedefler.asp, retrieved August 10, 2003.
118 The report for the months January and April 2013 appears here: http://nefretsoylemi.org/rapor/Ocak-Nisan-2013-NS-Rapor-Final.pdf, retrieved August 10, 2013.
119 http://nefretsoylemi.org/rapor/Ocak-Nisan-2013-NS-Rapor-Final.pdf, p. 7, retrieved August 23, 2013.
120 Rıfat N. Bali, "Perceptions of the Holocaust in Turkey," in: Günther Jikeli and Joëlle Allouche-Benayoun (eds.), *Perceptions of the Holocaust in Muslim Societies: Sources, Comparisons and Educational Challenges* (Dordrecht: Springer, 2013), p. 68.
121 Begüm Burak, "Hate speech in 'our media,'" *Today's Zaman*, August 23, 2013: www.todayszaman.com/blog-324418-hate-speech-in-our-media.html, retrieved August 26, 2013.
122 Ibid.
123 No author, "Nefret Söylemini En Çok Köşe Yazarları Üretiyor," *Bianet*, August 23, 2013: www.bianet.org/bianet/medya/149353-nefret-soylemini-en-cok-kose-yazarlari-uretiyor, retrieved August 25, 2013.

124 Burak, "Hate speech in 'our media.'"
125 No author, "Nefret Söylemini En Çok Köşe."
126 http://nefretsoylemi.org/rapor/HSR-January-April-2013.pdf, retrieved August 10, 2013.
127 Ibid.
128 Ibid.

5 Antisemitism in the Turkish media

Before discussing the Turkish media's role in spreading and provoking antisemitism, the Turkish media and its relation with the government should be noted. The AK Party has strong control over the media in Turkey. It's reach extends beyond the conservative Islamist press. Many Turkish newspaper editors and journalists respond to signals from their government and alter their tone accordingly – much more so than in the loosely regulated American market, significant players in the Turkish media have business interests that depend on good relations with the ruling party.[1]

Antisemitic articles are occasionally published in the Turkish press, mostly in Islamist or nationalist right-wing newspapers (such as *Yeni Şafak*, *Yeniçağ*, *Milli Gazete*, *Bugün*, and *Vakit*). These articles use antisemitic motifs such as Holocaust denial, incitement against Israel or the United States, and a comparison between Nazi crimes and Israel's crimes against the PA. There is an overwhelming use of the word "Zionism" for every negative colonial act or thought, especially in the spirit of the Elders of Zion, depicting the Zionist Jews as attempting to take over the world. The media often accuse Jews of crying over Hitler's crimes but committing even worse crimes against Palestinians, while concurrently dehumanizing Israel. In other cases, Jews are condemned for their so-called cooperation with the Freemasons. The rising antisemitism in the Turkish media in the last decade is a complex phenomenon that manifests itself in several forms:[2]

1 Animosity toward Jews, Judaism, and 'Jewish lobbies.' Jews are targeted as individuals, a community, people, and a race, and as a sinister political entity seeking Jewish dominance of world affairs, businesses, and the media. Jews are demonized in many conspiracy theories, including causing earthquakes and globalization. In fact, as Hirsh says, there is no single historical antisemitism; instead, there are distinct types of antisemitism at different times and in different places. Nevertheless, it is not surprising that Jews occasionally tend to experience each new incident of hostility as just another manifestation of "the oldest hatred." It is still less surprising given that each new incident of antisemitism tends to draw upon mythology and imagery created by previous hostilities toward the Jews. For example, Nazi

antisemitism was radically different from medieval Christian antisemitism but still made use of some of the same imagery and stereotypes. Each type of antisemitism creates something enduring that remains in the cultural reservoir, ready to be drawn upon and reinvigorated. There are two prominent recurring motifs within this cultural reservoir: blood libel, which charges Jews with ethnically motivated crimes of cruelty, often against children, involving the consumption or use of blood or body parts; and conspiracy theory, which depicts Jews, who are very few in number, as being hugely, selfishly, and secretly influential on a global scale.[3] On June 18, 2013, Erdoğan claimed that the protests raging in Turkey are part of an effort by the American Jewish lobby to undermine Turkey's government. This assertion was no surprise for Faik Tunay, a member of parliament of CHP, who believes that conspiracy theories are so well established in Turkey that they even precede religion.[4]

2   A hostile approach toward the Jewish citizens of Turkey, questioning their loyalty.
3   Antisemitism directed at Israel and Zionism. The word 'Zionists' often replaces the word 'Jews' in the press, with derogatory adjectives; inciting the public by citing Quran verses hostile to Jews and creating an atmosphere conducive to violence.
4   Depicting Jews as linked with 'other' world-control groups or 'evil' organizations, such as Freemasons, intelligence organizations, globalization forces, etc.

Newspapers

A common feature in the Turkish media is that it depicts 'the Jews' as playing a central role in everything that is wrong with the world. As portrayed by anti-Semites, Jews are deemed to have a universal importance for humankind. The same is true regarding Israel and Zionism; Israel or Zionism, as used by anti-Zionists, are deemed to be globally important as well. Israel is the keystone of the whole edifice of imperialism; Israel is the main obstruction to peace and democracy throughout the Middle East; the Israel lobby is responsible for wars; Israel is a sign of things to come because 'American power' may be undergoing a process of 'Israelization'; Jews are depicted as not only controlling the world, but also striving to control Turkey. This is something Turkish journalism frequently raises. In an article titled "Mein Kampf and the protocols of Zion," Ayşe Hür wrote in the left-of-center liberal daily *Radikal*:

> Recently there are two interesting books on the bestseller lists: Adolf Hitler's *Mein Kampf* and *The Protocols of Zion*.... In the same newspaper [*Akşam*] we read about sociologist Prof. Mustafa Erkal who said: "Reading Hitler is a reaction. Israel's policies and goals cause a reaction. Naturally, people get curious about Hitler's antisemitism and want to learn more about what he did and wanted to do." What our academician failed to say is the

fact that in Turkey, as in the rest of the world, animosity toward the Jews, that disgusting form of racism called antisemitism, is fast growing and causing the increased interest for *Mein Kampf.* We know that publishing this book in Europe is banned; and in Germany even its possession is a crime.... Having *Mein Kampf* and the *Protocols* on our bestseller list today must make us think twice before we claim there is no antisemitism here.[5]

Some journalists took further step regarding *Mein Kampf*: One of them is the columnist Arslan Tekin of the nationalist-Islamic daily *Yeniçağ*, who wrote in an article titled "Yes, *Mein Kampf* should be taught in schools" ... "Everybody should read it, and should learn the reasons why Hitler came about."[6]

If this were not enough, another columnist from *Vakit*, Hüseyin Üzmez, wrote that even the persecution of Jews by Hitler was much exaggerated:

> It is true that persecution [of Jews] by Hitler is much exaggerated. We are sick and tired of [listening to] stories of the inhumane persecution and torture he committed against the Jews. It is said that Hitler himself was a Jew ... that he committed cruelty only to force the Jews to migrate from Europe to Palestine ... and that it was the Israeli Zionists who dictated these acts upon him, at the time they were founding Israel. Two great powers (money and media) are in Jewish hands. The 'treacherous local collaborators' and some international organizations are also in their command. All humanity knows the fact that they [the Jews] are unequalled in [their] lobbying [skills]. With all this power and the tools, they can make or break anyone.... Who can oppose them? We saw the best example of this in what the German Interior Minister did to our newspaper *Vakit*. Against all the European human rights agreements, German police put pressure on our paper. We were in the midst of a judicial process. Our paper was illegally shut down.... Then the German Interior Minister interfered. He banned our paper.... This was a [perfect] example of execution without a trial.... It is obvious that he [the interior minister] was directed [by someone high above] into making such a decision.... This is how powerful the Zionists are. And this is the supposedly 'civilized and modern' West.[7]

Another motif that is being repeated is one claiming that respect for Christians and Jews harms Turkey. This perspective is also used for religious justification for hating non-Muslims, and often involves historical accounts. Burhan Bozgeyik, for example, wrote:

> Some people in this country are mistaken in how they treat Christians and Jews. Such mistakes harm not only the perpetrators, but also all the young Muslims of this land, and directly or indirectly, this country. At the top of these mistakes is the respect and reverence shown to Christians and Jews.... It is a mistake to include them in the protocol of meetings, to let them speak, to applaud them, to quote their words in the newspapers.... It is not just

wrong, it is a frighteningly grave mistake.... It is a mistake for so-called professors, writers, thinkers, and famous intellectuals to make 'sympathetic' statements about Christians and Jews. Particularly, to say that 'they too will go to heaven' is an even bigger mistake.... Christians and Jews, who have rejected our Prophet and refuse to recite 'Mohammed is the Messenger of God' belong in Hell for eternity. In the eyes of God, there is only one religion, and that is Islam.... There is only one book, and that is the Quran ... for so-called 'dignitaries' to present Christianity and Judaism as 'godly religions' is terribly wrong.

Terrorist organizations also contribute to antisemitism. *Aylık* is a monthly magazine published in Turkey by the IBDA-C (İslami Büyükdoğu Akıncılar Cephesi – The Great Eastern Islamic Raiders' Front), which is the terrorist organization that claimed responsibility for November 2003.[8] Turkish authorities have stated that this organization is linked to al-Qaeda. The April 2005 edition of *Aylık* includes 18 pages of antisemitic propaganda. The first article concerning the Jews, titled "The internal and external enemy: Jew," was written by Salih Izzet Erdiş, also known as Salih Mirzabeyoğlu, leader of the organization. He was sentenced to life imprisonment but was released in 2014 due to "new evidences."[9] He wrote:

The race that bred in evil and treachery, creating the real Jew, and the one that has become a curse to the world, is the Jew.... The one who blamed the Prophet Jesus [for blasphemy], who came from their own [kind], and whom they sold to the Romans ... that lowly treacherous one, is [Judah], the Jew.... The one who later distorted the belief of Jesus and made up the lie and the insult that he is the son of God is [St. Paul] the Jew.... The ones who, through planning and plotting, brought to Turkey adultery, immorality, and destruction, who built Israel right in the heart of Islam and next to the oil and other natural resources ... as a tiny model of their secret [world] empire.... Like an octopus hiding its tentacles under its belly, watching [for opportunities] to grab Iraq with one arm, Syria with another arm, and with others Kuwait, Hijaz [Saudi Arabia], Egypt, and Libya; they who need a world tragedy in order to carry out their aims.... In short, those who stir the witches' cauldron to melt all civilizations within it are Jews.... It is only the Jew, always the Jew.... Yahudi the thief!... These few examples provide a glimpse of the 'Jewish ideology.' ... If the Talmud says all these things, then we say: 'Nobody should shed tears and mucus, or mourn when a Jew dies. The best Jew is a dead Jew!'[10]

The next article in the magazine, "Why antisemitism?" by Cumali Dalkılıç, declares Jews the enemy of the Turks, of Islam, and of the entire world. Jews are alleged to have a disgusting nature and are defined as the people eternally cursed by God and His prophets, who are not wanted by anyone and are thrown out of every place. The article quotes many pages from Hitler's *Mein Kampf* and shows admiration for Hitler, calling him "a hero," "a rare mind" that grasped the ["real"] meaning of the Jew and the Jewish problem, "a true statesman to whom no other can stand up." The article, which also includes excerpts from the notorious *Protocols of the Elders of Zion*, ends with Holocaust denial, cuts down the number of Jewish victims from millions to 130,000–150,000, and calls on its readers to read and understand Hitler through his own writings instead of believing the "historic fraud" of the Jews that "prostitute" the conscience.[11]

Historical-setting accounts were given by the Islamist columnist Fahri Güven from *Milli Gazete:*

> The Ottomans saved the Jews from the hands of Christians, who murdered them along with the Muslims in Endulus [Muslim Spain]. When Russia and Hungary persecuted the Jews, again the Ottomans saved them. The Muslim Turks rescued Jews yet again, from the hands of Hitler, who was himself a hidden Jew.... From the beginning, the Ottomans showed hospitality, seemingly even by allotting the *best homes* to the Jews – along the Bosphorus, in Istanbul's most luxurious area. And, characteristic of their savage, treacherous [nature], in return they [the Jews] first overthrew Sultan Abdülhamid and destroyed the Ottomans;[12] [then], like insects, they ate away at the Ottoman [Empire]; and as if this were not enough, they stabbed the Muslim Turkish soldiers in Palestine in the back.... 'Judaism' is synonymous with 'treason.' ... They [the Jews] even betrayed God.... When God told them to bow their heads while entering Al-Quds [Jerusalem], they entered with their heads up. The prophets sent to them, such as Zachariah and Isaiah, were murdered by the Jews.... In fact, no amount of pages or lines would be sufficient to explain the Quranic chapters and our Lord Prophet's [Muhammad's] words that tell us of the betrayals of the Jews.[13]

In some cases, the accusations and conspiracy theories set against Israel are so harsh that they are rendered utterly illogical. An example is Fatih Tezcan's theory, which claims that the State of Israel murdered Atatürk because he opposed the establishment of the Israeli state. According to Tezcan, Britain proposed that the State of Israel be established in 1936 and Atatürk subsequently opposed it. Tezcan also requested a biopsy of Atatürk's body so the alleged poisoning by Israel could be proved.[14]

Unfortunately, even when a prominent writer speaks against antisemitism, he simultaneously ends up believing in antisemitic ideas, perhaps without even being aware of his antisemitic tone. Murathan Mungan is a good example. In an interview given to *Radikal* in 2014 on the publication of his book *Merhaba Asker*,[15] Mungan, a Turkish writer and poet, raises various topics ranging from discrimination in Turkey to the indifference and silence of Turkish society. He also does not hesitate to express that he is concerned on behalf of the Jewish community. In his book, which he claims to be "unique for Turkey," Mungan claims that:

You're alienating civilian life, you underestimate the enemy, you are making a confrontation by gathering the identities who you know as enemies into the same military facilities. No trigger is a one night deed, there are centuries behind the trigger [which killed] Hrant Dink.[16]

There are centuries behind Hrant's gun trigger. My interest for this topic is not to sharpen people's hatred, to refresh their memory, or to discuss the extensions of this topic. One of the topics I am uncomfortable with is antisemitism. Coming out against Israel is one thing and antisemitism is another thing. I feel uncomfortable about the name of the Jews in Turkey. You are "othering" the Armenians, the Kurds, the Alevis ... it is necessary to work cooperatively in order to have a society not marked according to people's language, religion, faith, sexuality and gender. The only thing we need in order to have a culture of living together is basic universal values. This is something both left and right should learn. I'd say minimum common democracy. How out of fashion it sounds, I think that is why I still use these words at my age. Unfortunately, Turkey is a country that makes its people feel old."[17]

Despite this call to oppose antisemitism, Mungan said in a lecture he gave at the Political Academy of BDP that "the world is not a fair place; for that reason those who are oppressed must be more equipped, more knowledgeable, and conscious." Mungan specified that America uses cinema as a propaganda tool, and explained that Jews that had been alienated began producing films dealing with genocide after they "*took over*" the American cinema.[18]

Books

During the first decade under AK Party rule, antisemitic publications have flourished in Turkey and quite a few of the books published became bestsellers in the country. Several examples appear at the Intelligence and Terrorism Information Center on the Israel Intelligence Heritage & Commemoration Center's (IICC) website.[19] The books are divided into two themes: politics and Zionism.

(1) As discussed earlier, 'classical' antisemitic literature translated into Turkish, such as *The Protocols of the Elders of Zion*,[20] *Mein Kampf* by Adolf Hitler, and *The International Jew* by Henry Ford.[21] Already in 1943 there was a Turkish translation of *The Protocols of the Elders of Zion* titled *Jewish History and the Protocols of the Elders of Zion*,[22] translated by Sami Sabit Karaman, an officer in the Turkish army. Karaman added false information on Jewish history and included incitement against the Jews because of a relatively major part in various occupations. Afterwards, *The Protocols* was translated again and again. For example, in 1971 Kemal Yaman called his translation: *Treachery Plans of the Nation's Enemies* where he adds the "Jewish betrayal" with the Communists' and Greek Patriarchy's plots.[23] *Kavgam* was first published in Turkey in 1939, although throughout the years it has been translated several times. For example, in 1963 it was translated under the title *The Communists and the International*

Jew,[24] and was sold until 2005, when the Bavaria State of Germany went to court. Apparently they have the intellectual property rights to this book.

In 2007 it was banned. However, the book has six volumes and some of the volumes are still being sold. *Mein Kampf*, which is the 'handbook' for the ultranationalists of Turkey, was translated into Turkish and published about 45 times between 1940 and 2005. In early 2005, a Turkish translation of *Mein Kampf* was published by several small publishers and sold at discount prices at newsstands, supermarkets, and bookstores in Turkey. An international uproar ensued, prompting the Turkish government to ban the publication of the book on technical grounds that the publishers had not been granted publication rights by the government of Bavaria, the book's copyright holder.[25] *The Protocols of Zion*, which inspired *Mein Kampf*, was published in full or in digest form, in book form or as a series of newspaper articles 102 times between 1923 and 2008. Seventy-two percent of these publications were published by Islamist newspapers and publishing houses, 8 percent by ultranationalist and Islamist publishers, and 20 percent by ultranationalists.

The Protocols is popular among Islamists, *Mein Kampf* is popular among ultranationalists. Mein Kampf was translated and published 30 times between 1940 and 2000. The number and frequency of *The Protocols* publications runs almost coincidentally with the growth and ascendance of the Islamist movement, while the increase in the *Mein Kampf* translations has been directly related to domestic political turmoil. Most *Mein Kampf* publications appeared in the 1960s and 1970s, a period in which Turkey went through a type of low-level civil war between ultranational rightists and militant leftists, a war that was believed by ultranationalists and Islamists to be a Zionist plot to destroy Turkey.[26] According to Bali, at least one generation was influenced by antisemitic ideology nurtured by these books.

Mein Kampf, thought to sell about 1,000 copies per year, is now being marketed by 11 publishers. In 2005, when new editions of *Mein Kampf* reappeared on the shelves of every mainstream bookstore, up to 100,000 copies, a huge number for the Turkish readership, were sold within a few months.[27] According to 2005 bestseller lists of the two most popular bookstores in Turkey, D&R and Remzi's, *Kavgam* is among the top ten most sold books (Figure 5.1). According to Serkan Öznur, from Ada Kitapevi, in one of the most popular bookstores in Ankara, *Kavgam* was their fifth most sold book. The number of printing houses that published *Kavgam*, as far as its circulation can be tracked in Turkey, increased to 13 in 2005. According to Mefisto bookstore, *Kavgam* appeared on the same shelf with two other books dealing with Hitler: *Hitler'in Sekreteri* (Hitler's Secretary) and *Bilinmeyen Hitler* (The Unknown Hitler),[28] which were sold together at a discount. It made the book's circulation as high as 50,000. It was also revealed that most of the book's buyers are young people between 18 and 30 years of age.[29]

Kavgam was not bought exclusively by Islamists or ultranationalists. It was considered a bestseller in 2009 as well. In her article, Ayşe Hür mentions that the cheap price of the book (almost 6 lire at that time) is appealing. She quotes

Figure 5.1 Picture of bookstore selling *Kavgam*.

Note
Kavgam (full text) in a bookstore in Ortaköy, Istanbul, not far from the "Etz Hachayim" Synagogue. Since the old edition is rare, the price of Kavgam is 70 Lira. Efrat Aviv, February 25th, 2015.

the owner of Emre Press, which sold 31,000 copies of the book, who said the following to the *Akşam* newspaper:

> According to the research and observation we have conducted, the book *Mein Kampf* is "readable" nowadays. We thought it was something that society wants. Social events also determine the course of the book sales. *Mein Kampf* was affected by these developments, and sales exploded. The book seems to be popular amongst police academy students.[30]

Mein Kampf can still be found easily in Turkey. The early version costs 70 lire in second-hand bookstores. Regarding the availability of *Kavgam*, while we believe the book should not be published or sold, it is interesting to note that Serkan Öznur from Ada Kitapevi says that if the book were widely read: "those who read the book, would realize what a psychopath Hitler was, had more people read this book, WWII would never have begun."[31]

But it's not only about *Mein Kampf*. Over the years, various antisemitic books were translated into Turkish, usually including supplements written by the translator and his intellectual circles.[32] Every political wing aligned in blaming the Jews: the Right blamed communists and Jews, the Left blamed nationalists and Jews. For instance, pan-Turkists, such as Reha Oğuz Türkan, in his book *Leftists and Red Ones*, thought the danger for Turkey was embodied by Jews, Freemasons, and Communists. Mustafa Hakki Akansel, a physician 'father' of race theory in Turkey, wrote in his book *Of the Turk: Researchers Regarding the Turkic Race*, a pseudo-scientific analysis explaining the superiority of the Turkic race by blaming other races, particularly the Jews, who he believed to be the most inferior race and who were responsible for the collapse of the Empire.[33]

These books have been very influential in Turkey. Shay Cohen, Israel consul general to Istanbul since summer 2014, said that the perception of the Jew in Turkey is greatly dictated by *The Protocols of the Elders of Zion*:

> I feel like I cannot avoid this feeling of discomfort when I hear the stereotypes attributed to Jews, and not only toward the Turkish Jews. There is an inherent problem; stereotypes like "Jews control the diamond market," "Jews control the jewelry market." The concept of the Jews falls under the *Protocols of the Elders of Zion* concept and unfortunately it is not something I have heard once or twice here, and not from ignorant people. Not too long ago I had a meeting with someone who told me that "the Jews in the US are so strong that they can influence Obama." I corrected him but the concept was so rooted that he could not even imagine that his mindset was not right.[34]

(2) Antisemitic books originally written in Turkish, such as Dr. Recai Yayaoğlu's (MD) *Yahudi Psikolojisi* (Jewish Psychology),[35] published in 2010, allegedly followed Israel's attacks on Gaza between 2008 and 2009. According to the author, the atrocities Israel caused and the blockade of ships carrying humanitarian aid to Gazans require a discourse regarding Jews' psychology. In order to understand how cruel Israelis can be, the "Jewish psychology" must be deeply understood. A partial expression of the Jewish psychology is their self-perception as "the chosen nation" and "superior race."

(3) Antisemitic books that explicitly involve current politics and/or utilize antisemitism as a gage to manifest dissatisfaction with specific political Turkish parties or leaders. Such books strongly criticize the current Islamic government, including the Turkish president, the prime minister, and the ruling party, describing them as pawns in the Jewish scheme to take over Turkey and the world. The books are written by radical Islamic elements in Turkey, which believe that the current Islamic government is not conformist enough. These types of books were also written by AK Party opponents, some of whom belong to MHP or even CHP. One example the book of Soner Yalçın, who is a leftist author and journalist that writes for *Hürriyet Daily News*: *Efendi: Beyaz Türklerin Büyük Sırrı* (The Great Secret of the White Turks).[36]

Yalçın began working in 1987 for the center-left periodical called *2000'e Doğru* (Toward 2000) as a permanent political correspondent in Ankara. Since then he worked for *Aydınlık* and *Siyah – Beyaz*. He started a new career in television in 1996 for a TV show and worked for several other channels. From February 4, 2007, he worked as a columnist for the Sunday editions of the daily *Hürriyet*. At the end of 2007 he launched his own online news website, *OdaTV*. Yalçın probably served as an adviser for the film *Valley of the Wolves: Iraq* and as a conceptual adviser to the television series *Valley of the Wolves*, where his book is even shown in one of the scenes.[37] He was arrested in February 2011 along with other OdaTV journalists and charged with links to the Ergenekon organization. He was released pending trial in December 2012. He published his book *Efendi: Beyaz Türklerin Büyük Sırrı* in 2004. In this book he claimed that the Turkish Republic was in the hands of the secular Dönmes who held key positions in Turkish society and the political establishment. He also wrote *Efendi 2 – Beyaz Müslümanların Büyük Sırrı* (The Great Secret of the White Turks) in 2006, published by Doğan, which belongs to Turkey's largest media group, Doğan Holdings, known for its opposition to the AK Party. This book, categorized as "research," sold almost 150,000 copies, breaking sales records, and was reprinted 82 times since April 2008.[38] In this book he claimed that most of the key figures and Islamist leaders also had Dönme roots. It questions the legitimacy of the founders of modern Turkey, including Atatürk, because they are depicted as Dönme who actually strived to make Turkey a Jewish state.[39] Yalçın Küçük followed Soner Yalçın. Yalçın Küçük is an academic socialist writer, philosopher, economist, and historian with a Marxist background who was arrested for being part of the Ergenekon gang. He bases his arguments on a study of onomastics. He allegedly reveals the names of those who were Dönme in the Turkish establishment and constantly claims that the Dönme control Turkey.[40]

Another famous example of this sort of writing is Ergün Poyraz's books.[41] Poyraz wrote a series of books on the so-called link between the ruling party's members and Israel. He is best known for his 2007 book, *Musa'nın Çocukları* (Children of Moses), which accused Prime Minister Recep Tayyip Erdoğan and his wife of being secret Jews and of cooperating with Israeli intelligence to undermine Turkish secularism; it was number two on the 2007 bestseller list.[42] Poyraz was arrested in 2007 and was a defendant in the Ergenekon trials; on August 5, 2013, he was sentenced to 29 years in prison.[43] Interesting to note is what a website named 'Internethaber' mentioned after Poyraz's sentence was announced. It says: "29 years in prison for calling Erdoğan a Jew," meaning that the problem in Poyraz's writings was not the fact that he criticized the government, but that he called Erdoğan and other AK Party members Jews.[44] His books were bestsellers in Turkey, and it is said that each unit of the gendarmerie bought about 5,000 copies of Poyraz's books. They were sold to all gendarmerie units throughout the country.[45] In fact, receipts were found and according to them, between 2002 and 2004, the gendarmerie spent 7.5 million Turkish lire for the books *Musa'nın Çocukları* and *Musa'nın Gülü* (Moses' Rose). Both books sold over 150,000 copies in 2007 alone. Other books were sold to the general secretary of the General Command of Gendarmerie and Afyon Airport Command.[46]

The problem with Poyraz is that he does not present evidence to support his baffling claims, which are not documented, footnoted, or backed up with credible facts. In his book *Musa'nın Gülü*,[47] he describes the life story of the Turkish foreign minister and presidential candidate (the former president of Turkey), starting from his childhood. The book claims to reveal Gül's association with the British, his connections with the Jewish lobby, the secret conversations he holds with the United States, his interest in obtaining American citizenship, and more. In the foreword, Gül is accused of betraying his Turkish nationality by being a Jew. The author goes on to describe Gül's life story, emphasizing his relations with Jews, Americans, and the British. The author attempts to delegitimize the two current political leaders of Turkey, Prime Minister Recep Tayyip Erdoğan and President Abdullah Gül, linking them to an insidious Jewish plot to take over Turkey.[48]

Another famous book of Poyraz's is *Musa'nın Mücahiti* (The Warrior of Moses).[49] In the foreword, the author claims that Jews who were exiled from Spain and came to the Ottoman Empire were responsible for its downfall, and that they have been doing the same since the establishment of the Turkish Republic while hiding their Jewish identity. The book includes sections about friendly messages sent by Bülent Arınç to the Jews, his visit to the United States, and his association with Freemasonry. It also accuses him of being an imposter Jew – Dönme, that is, a Jew who has converted to Islam but continues to serve "world Jewry."[50]

The book *Musa'nın AKP'si* (Moses' AK Party),[51] also written by Poyraz, covers the issues he believes are most concerning to Turkey's Islamic population, such as the ban on women wearing headscarves, and others. The author claims that during the current administration, unemployment has increased and Turkish money has been transferred to Jewish hands. He accuses Israeli businessman Sami Ofer of attempting to buy Istanbul's harbors for a bowl of soup, claiming that the result was a lot of money siphoned abroad. He goes on to note the names of the companies that he claims are owned by the Freemasons, and blames the Israeli Mossad for the attack organized by the special Turkish forces that operated in northern Iraq against the Kurds. The book also claims that Erdoğan is of Jewish descent, which supposedly drives him to conspire against Turkey.[52] It should be mentioned here that Poyraz, Yalçın, and Küçük were mentioned by İhsan Dağı, in an article published in *Zaman*,[53] as those who promote the perception that Jews control Turkey and that in order to break these "Jewish chains" Turkey must declare a war for its national independence.

Another significant example is Hasan Demir's book *Ankarada'da Gizli İsrail Devleti mi var?* (Is there a Hidden State of Israel in Ankara?), which deals with an allegedly secret alliance between Christians and Zionists aimed at ensuring the safety of Israel and allowing it to appropriate natural resources such as oil, gas, gold, and water. The author claims that Erdoğan is the engineer of this anti-Islam campaign.[54] The book, which belongs to a "study and research" series (Araştırma-İnceleme Dizisi), was published in 2007. The book binds the Mossad, CIA, Millî İstihbarat Teşkilatı (MIT, the Turkish government intelligence agency), Milli Güvenlik Kurulu (MGK, Turkey's National Security Council), Turkish politicians such as Erdoğan, the PKK, Freemasons, and prominent Turkish Jews such as Ishak Alaton into one conspiracy theory that places Turkey and its religion at risk.

What is certain is that these books (as well as the accompanying public relations work, such as interviews in the press) are an effective and efficient tool to spread and normalize antisemitism in Turkey. The books prove that Turkish society can seemingly unite around its solidarity with the Palestinian side of the conflict and the inhumane nature of Israel.[55]

Yet, Mustafa Akyol, a prominent journalist in Turkey, published an article titled "The Protocols of the Elders of Turkey" on October 7, 2007 in the *Washington Post*. The article also appears at the end of the Intelligence and Terrorism Information Center in the IICC's report regarding antisemitism in Turkey.[56] Akyol claims that unlike the general accusations that the AK Party is an antisemitic party that incites against Israel, many of the antisemitic books depict Erdoğan and other AK Party members as allies of Israel and as crypto-Zionist conspirators. For instance, Akyol claims that Poyraz argues that Zionism has decided to steer Turkey away from its secularity and turn it into a "moderate Islamic republic."[57] Akyol attempts to prove that it is the secularists who are more open-minded than others within Turkish society who support antisemitism. According to Akyol, the so-called Islamists are generally on the liberal pro-Western side, while secularists are often on the other side, which motivates them to be more antisemitic and anti-Israeli. Akyol quotes Ziya Onis, a political economist from Koç University in Istanbul, who says that the power struggle in Turkey is actually between "conservative globalists" and "defensive nationalists," including the ultra-secular Kemalists.[58] In other words, antisemitism is a tool or another factor or element that manifests the breach between secularist and religious parts in Turkey. The books, which contain antisemitic content, are a tool for secularists who hope that vilifying the AK Party leadership as Jews or Jewish agents will help reduce the party's popularity and stave off EU membership, as well as limit Turkey's exposure to European ideas. According to Akyol, Turkey, unlike its European allies, failed to criticize itself. This allowed ultranationalist themes to persist as legitimate ideas, even though the EU admission process pushed Turkey to liberalize itself; at this point the nationalists and secularists should have confronted the EU accession process so their resistance toward self-criticism would not be evident.

Entertainment

Antisemitism in Turkey did not skip the entertainment world either. One example is the controversial Hitler shampoo commercial. On March 26, 2012, Turkey's Jewish community protested against a Turkish commercial that used old film footage of Adolf Hitler to sell shampoo. Biota Laboratories, the company that makes Biomen, is responsible for the commercial. The Jewish community and the chief rabbi's office called Hitler "the most striking example of cruelty and savagery" and said using his image in a commercial was unacceptable. The statement also demanded a public apology from the advertising company "to repair the damage this commercial has caused to society's conscience."[59]

The Biomen commercial lasts 12 seconds and shows black and white archival footage of Hitler at a political rally. Hitler shouts in a dubbed-over Turkish voice: "If you don't wear women's dresses, you shouldn't be using women's shampoo either!"[60] The ADL said on its website that it was "repulsed" by the company's attempt to sell shampoo using images of the Nazi leader.[61] Abraham H. Foxman said: "The use of images of the violently antisemitic dictator who was responsible for the mass murder of 6 million Jews and millions of others in the Holocaust to sell shampoo is a disgusting and deplorable marketing ploy."[62] Jewish community leader Silvyo Ovadya quoted Biomen as saying they would not get rid of the commercial because the idea is humorous. Ovadya added that they are pursuing legal avenues to get it off the air, but did not specify how they intended to do so. Cefi Joseph Kamhi called on the courts to punish M.A.R.K.A İletişim tanıtım Yayıncılık Hizmetleri Ltd., who were responsible for the advertisement, for violating Turkish penal code Articles 130/1 and 216/2, claiming they had

> represented a broad insult to the memory of the six million Jews who were murdered during WWII, had in the advertisement praised a person who had perpetrated the crime of genocide and incites the population to enmity and hatred and insulted and disparaged [the Jews]

and that "except for the implication of making soaps out of Jews, Biomen's 'upper race' advertisement has no significance."[63]

A criminal investigation was indeed opened, but the prosecutor ultimately decided that there were insufficient grounds to open a case against the offending parties.[64] Criticism against the commercial included the chairperson of RTÜK, Professor Davut Dursun, who appealed for the removal of the commercial. Others, such as *Milliyet* journalist Ali Eyüpoğlu, expressed their dismay at this commercial. Eyüpoğlu was overwhelmed, saying: "I couldn't believe what I heard."[65] The fact is that Hitler stars in a commercial for shampoo when he produced soap out of Jews. He also mentioned the fact that the commercial was made in black and white and contained German subtitles, which added to the dismay he felt. It seems Hitler, and especially his writings, have always been popular in Turkey, but in the last decade it seems like his popularity has soared. Another example that might prove it is the crossword puzzle run by *Yeni Akit*, which shows the final answer displayed under a photo of Hitler as "we miss you."[66]

Valley of the Wolves: Iraq is a blockbuster film produced in Turkey in early 2006, with an estimated four million viewers. The movie is about U.S. activity in Iraq, portraying the United States as a perpetrator of atrocities against Iraqi civilians and representing American soldiers as being particularly brutal. The film, directed by Serdar Akar and written by Bahadır Özdener, contains antisemitic motifs. For example, one of the characters in the movie is a Jewish doctor played by American actor Gary Busey. The Jewish doctor, who is portrayed as corrupt, greedy, and barbarous, removes kidneys from Iraqi soldiers killed in the war and ships them to Tel Aviv, New York, and London to implant them in Jewish patients. In one of the scenes, a man dressed like a Hassidic Jew eats dinner in an expensive American hotel in northern Iraq and leaves the building only a few minutes before a bomb destroys the hotel. This scene implies that the Jews were warned beforehand about the destruction of the World Trade Center and thus only a few Jews died during 9/11.[67] The movie was screened around the world and was particularly successful among the Turkish community in Germany. However, due to its anti-American and antisemitic slant, the movie was pulled from theaters in the United States and triggered harsh criticism in Germany (but was not pulled from theaters). The movie was screened at the Alexandria Film Festival in September 2007 and is based on a successful television series that ran for three consecutive seasons on Turkish television. The film's website is still online and scenes from the movie can be viewed from anywhere in the world.[68] The movie made $27.9 million at the box office: $25.1 million in Turkey and $2.8 million in Europe. The film was watched by 1.2 million people within the first three days of its release in February 2006. The film's popularity should not be the only issue raised, but also the support it gained. For instance, the film's premiere in Ankara was attended by the country's most powerful politicians, including Emine Erdoğan, Prime Minister Erdoğan's wife, the Istanbul ,mayor, Kadir Topbaş, and the Deputy Prime Minister Bülent Arınç, who described the film as "absolutely magnificent."[69]

This film was even followed by two sequels; one called *Kurtlar Vadisi: Gladio* (Valley of the Wolves: Gladio) in 2008, and the other called *Kurtlar Vadisi-Filistin* (Valley of the Wolves – Palestine), which was screened in November 2011 and was number three in the admissions charts with 2,028,057 admissions.[70] The story revolves around a Turkish commando team which go to Israel to track down the Israeli military commander responsible for the Gaza flotilla raid. Pana Film had already settled on the Palestinian territories as the setting of the film and was about to start shooting when the Gaza flotilla raid occurred on May 31, 2010. The existing script was subsequently rewritten to feature the raid as the centerpiece of the plot. "This is not about taking revenge for Mavi Marmara," stated producer Zübeyr Şaşmaz.

> The goal of the film is to show what the Palestinians are going through. The announcement of the film's release came just days after Israel's attack on the Gaza flotilla. The movie aims to take revenge on Israel for the deadly raid that led to an international outcry, with the film costing over $10 million, making it one of the most expensive Turkish films ever. According to the script, the hero of the series, Polat Alemdar, a gun-toting agent, and his men go to Palestine in the wake of Israel's attack on the aid flotilla. After much effort, Polat and his men capture the Israeli commander named Moshe Ben Eliezer, who planned and managed the raid.[71]

Prior to the release of *Kurtlar Vadisi-Filistin*, an intensive marketing campaign was launched in Turkey to advertise the film. The campaign included a series of promotional film posters that showed hands holding stones, people holding guns, or the lead actor who plays the Turkish agent aiming his weapon. Several trailers with anti-Israel messages were screened and, according to Turkish media, were seen by millions of people. The trailers show, among other things, a battle aboard a ship (the *Mavi Marmara*), Israeli tanks (possibly on the streets of Gaza) confronting stone-throwing Palestinians, and Israeli soldiers being killed by the Turkish agent and his team.[72] In one of the trailers, an Israeli (probably a senior official) is heard saying that the Arab population will grow faster than the Jewish population, and that it cannot be permitted to happen. The film was screened in about 100 movie theaters in Germany and attracted a large number of moviegoers, particularly among the Turkish immigrants residing there. The film premiered on January 27, the same day as International Holocaust Remembrance Day. The release of the film, and particularly the timing chosen for its premiere, were strongly criticized by many in Germany. For example, Christian Democratic Union spokesman Philipp Missfelder said that the timing of the film's release showed disrespect and disregard for the feelings of Holocaust victims. Kerstin Griese, a member of parliament for the Social Democratic Party of Germany, said that the movie was problematic because it is anti-Israel and "incites antisemitic sentiments." Green Party representative Jerzy Montag claimed that the decision to release the film on January 27 was irresponsible and took it out of its historic context. In response, a spokesman for Pana Film, which produced *Kurtlar Vadisi-Filistin*, said the company was unaware of the sensitivity of the release date.[73] The movie script writer, Bahadır Özdener, mentioned in *Zaman* during an interview given while the film was still being shot that if "Israel continues with its deadly activities, another film like it will be made." He also mentioned that the accusations that connect film makers to the AK Party government are all wrong.[74]

Another example is the popular television series *Ayrılık: Aşkta ve Savaşta Filistin* (Separation: Palestine in Love and War), which was broadcast on TRT – Turkish State Television – during prime time in October 2009. The film was produced with the assistance of the Islamist newspaper *Yeni Şafak*'s columnist Hakan Albayrak, who was one of the journalists on the *Mavi Marmara*. *Ayrılık* depicted IDF soldiers murdering Arab civilians and newborn babies in cold blood and depicted Israeli soldiers as sex-crazed, treating Gaza as a sex-tourism destination where they plan rape or to seduce Palestinian women. This series increased the demonization of Israel and Zionists in Turkey.[75] The series resulted in angry protests from politicians and the media in Israel. The Simon Wiesenthal Center even sent a notice on the series to Erdoğan.[76] Dr. Lütfü Şahsuvaroglu was the series' consultant. In an interview with *Haaretz*, he said that the Turkish government was not involved in making the series and the fact that the series was screened parallel to the deterioration of relations between Israel and Turkey was coincidental.[77] Due to growing concerns, Israeli Foreign Minister Avigdor Lieberman summoned the Turkish ambassador and complained about the

Antisemitism in the Turkish media 155

antisemitic content of *Ayrılık*. Turkish Foreign Minister Ahmet Davutoğlu concluded that the Turkish government is not liable for the series' content.

Another example is the election of Can Bonomo, the young Turkish pop star of Jewish origin who was elected to represent Turkey in 2012 in the Eurovision Song Contest. Having a Jew represent Turkey was met with much skepticism in Turkey regarding how a Jew could represent a Muslim country. The selection provoked a range of reactions and a controversy. Although the Jewish community was very satisfied with Bonomo's election, others were less so.

One argument is whether being a Muslim is necessary for Turkish identity – can you be Turkish and not be a Muslim? On one hand, it is claimed that Bonomo was selected simply to mend the rift between Turkey and Israel and that this is Turkey's response to the Zionists' antisemitic claims in Turkey. Many have wondered how a Jew can represent Muslim Turkey or, even worse, how a Jew can be a 'Turk.' Others raised the discourse regarding Turkish Jewry's identity and called for there to be no difference between them, and also between other minorities in Turkey (e.g., Circassians, Kurds), and the Muslim citizens of Turkey. Bonomo was directly asked by a young reporter: "Are you a Jew?" Hincal Uluç from Sabah considered the question itself "discriminatory."[78] The chairperson of the Parliamentary Assembly of the Council of Europe and AK Party's Antalya representative in 2012, Mevlüt Çavuşoğlu, strongly defended Bonomo and the Jews in general, saying that:

> Our brother of Jewish origin will represent us.... We may have problems with Israel, but we shouldn't be racists. What is our legacy from our ancestors? When Mehmed II conquered Istanbul, he gave rights and protected the people of other religions. This Jewish citizen served his country (Turkey), paid his taxes, he has talent, and TRT chose him because of that. He is a citizen of Turkey and you can't complain "how can a Jew represent us." We are ashamed of such comments, and we condemn people who say such things.[79]

In other words, the dispute over Bonomo representing Turkey elicited antisemitic viewpoints but also served those opposed to antisemitism in their struggle against hate speech and antisemitism in Turkey. As Burak Bekdil put it: "government overture" and more like a "correction from the government's partners across the Atlantic."[80] Bonomo himself replied to allegations by half apologizing and half explaining that:

> I am a Turk, Judaism is a religion. Music has no language, religion, race. Thirty six different ethnic groups live in Turkey, we have been here for 540 years there is no connection to Israel. We settled here 540 years ago from Spain. I am Turkish, I will represent Turkey.[81]

Not only the entertainment sphere was influenced, but also art. The well-known curator and the founding director of Platform Garanti Contemporary Art Center in Istanbul, Vasıf Kortun, resigned from his advisory position at the Israel

Museum in protest of the war, and refused a similar offer from the Bezalel Academy of Fine Arts and Design in Jerusalem in 2009. Kortun called for boycotting Israel after he was greeted by the Israeli cultural attache in a New-Year email; he wrote in response to the greeting email:

> Since the occupation of Lebanon I haven't entered Israel. I resigned from my consulting job at the Israel Museum, I turned down the Bezalel Fine Arts Academy's offer to serve as their consultant.... What a pity that if even Avi Mograbi [an extreme left-wing Israeli artist and film director] comes with funding from the State of Israel, he is better not coming. I will write to Turkish organizations in order to request the cancellation of their projects that are to be carried out in Turkey in cooperation with Israel. I boycott! I welcome you to also boycott.[82]

The Pera Museum in Istanbul postponed the opening of an exhibition of works by Marc Chagall, on loan from the Israel Museum in Jerusalem, due to the war in Israel.[83] The famous female vocalist Yıldız Tilbe invoked curses on Israel during a television program, saying, "May God bring down one disaster after another upon Israel." The studio audience answered, "Amen."[84] Yıldız Tilbe expressed an antisemitic message during Operation Protective Edge on July 10, 2014 when she tweeted:

> God bless Hitler. What he did was not even enough, he was so right. Not much time left until the demise/end of Israel. Neither your walls nor the trees you planted will be able to save you. There will be no death for you. The sons of evil, America and Israel. The Muslims will bring the end of the Jews, God willing. Not much time left. Just as there is little time left for Iftar [fast-breaking meal], so little time left for your end.[85]

However, these declarations were quite widely denounced in Turkey and included a published condemnation by the Israeli consul general, Moshe Kamhi, who said:

> These words coming from this so-called low grade singer are too low to be taken seriously; they are nonetheless very grave and should be condemned. This incident has shown that lawmakers are obligated to make hate crimes punishable by law. In recent years, Turkey has started to conduct educational activities on the Holocaust. Also this year a commemoration meeting on the International Commemoration Day of Jewish Holocaust is being held on January 26th in Istanbul with the participation of Deputy Minister of Foreign Affairs Naci Koru. These words have shown that these activities need to be considerably increased in both qualitative and quantitative forms.[86]

Although the singer did not apologize, she declared that she was no anti-Semite and that she had no problem with the Jews or Christians of Turkey, proving it by saying that her best clothes are bought at shops owned by Jews. She said: "Likewise, one person cannot represent a nation; a nation cannot represent some of its members. Good is good everywhere, bad is bad everywhere, whoever he is or wherever he is."[87]

Sometimes antisemitism is not directly involved in the content of films or commercials, but with the actors themselves. Such is the case with the famous Turkish actor Kıvanç Tatlıtuğ, who was reported to be playing the role of a Jew in an American movie. News of this made his fans "very sad" and they called on him to "give up the role."[88]

Education

In 2012, Turkish schoolchildren in Istanbul's Maltepe received a series of books denouncing scientific figures, including one denying the theory of evolution and describing Charles Darwin as a big-nosed Jew. These books, whose author is not listed, aimed at children aged 11–15, were distributed to 1,000 pupils after the government-affiliated local education authority approved their content. The book on Darwin reportedly states that he had two problems: "first he was a Jew and he should have kept it a secret; second, he hated his prominent forehead, big nose, and misshapen teeth," which are images that very often characterize Jews in antisemitic publications. Freud is defined as the "father of the weirdoes." Also, "especially Communists and Zionists protect Freud's ideas."[89] Additionally, Maltepe's director of education, Faik Kaptan, confirmed that he was unaware the books contained antisemitic references, adding:

> when you look at the book's cover, it looks like it contains a moderate message. I don't know its style, I haven't read it. Using slang against people is not nice. It has no meaning. It is incorrect. It is impossible to check all the books distributed in the district.[90]

Daily life

Manifestations of antisemitism in daily life in Turkey are quite common. One of the most recent examples is the story of two Turkish-Jewish businessmen who stopped for lunch at a fish restaurant during a business trip to Edirne in the Babaeski region. After placing their order, the restaurant owner figured out that they were Jews. Once he did, he claimed he wouldn't serve Jews, and began cursing them and the Torah. He then took a kitchen utensil off the counter and threatened to kill them. The men ran for their lives. The story was first posted on one of the Turkish-Jewish community mailing lists on February 7, 2014. One of the two businessmen described it like this:

> Yesterday my friend and I went on a 2 day business trip in the Trakya region. We stopped for lunch in Babaeski on our way back from Edirne. We ordered but once the owner of the restaurant understood that we were Jews,

158 *Antisemitism under AK Party rule*

he said he wouldn't serve us and he cursed our Torah uncontrollably. Due to his fury he took some sort of utensil and planned to assault us. We couldn't defend ourselves so we had to run away from this anti-Semite, we barely saved our souls.

This incident was reported outside Turkey but, as in other cases, the two victims asked not to be named to prevent any further threats.[91] Yet, antisemitic incidents do not include only physical assaults but also psychological ones. What seems to be popular among anti-Semites recently is hanging posters containing antisemitic content on their cars. Figure 5.2 is an example seen in March 2014.

It says: "We are not 3–5 million Jewish bastards. We are Muslims who govern the Jewish bastards who make the world vomit blood. Live your life. Lives may be sacrificed for you."[92] Another poster hung on a car was captured in Mecidiyeköy, in front of Quasar, on February 26, 2014 at 11:00 (Figure 5.3).[93]

But it is not only about violence or clear antisemitism; it is mostly about how Jews are seen within Turkish society and how this external view influences how they see themselves. Turkish Jews usually change their names to Turkish ones. Sometimes they add a Turkish name to their Jewish one and in other cases they use the Turkish version of their Jewish name, such as Shlomo becoming Süleyman, David becoming Davut, and so on.

Sometimes Jews feel obliged to use Turkish names. The following story proves that: An Istanbul Jew who asked to remain anonymous testified that

Figure 5.2 "Jewish bastards."

Antisemitism in the Turkish media 159

Figure 5.3 This Jewish bastard will not be able to slaughter a Muslim.

during Operation Protective Edge his sister was looking for a rental apartment. In one of the apartments she liked, she was asked for her name. Her name is a Jewish name; the landlord said: "We do not do business with non-Muslims." Yet, Aron Bünyel, an actor in the Turkish film and TV industry of Jewish origin, claims that thanks to Erdoğan, the situation for minorities in Turkey has improved in this regard: "In the past, you could not use your Jewish name but now you can freely express your Jewish name. Look at me, I have a Turkish name (Erol), but I use my Jewish name Aron everywhere I go."[94] Another Turkish actor of Jewish origin claims that using both Turkish and Jewish names (whether they are surnames or given names) is an act signifying modernization, cultural survival, and assimilation.[95] It is important not only for Jewish 'survival' but also for Turkish Jews' 'Turkish' identity. It's interesting to note that having a Turkish name is mandatory for becoming a bureaucrat or a minister.[96]

The identity factor surfaced also during the Soma crisis – an explosion that took place on May 13, 2014 in the Soma mine in western Turkey and caused an underground fire. This was the worst mine disaster in Turkish history, leaving 301 men dead. Prior to 2005, the Soma mine was state-owned. In 2007 it was taken over by a private company, Soma Holdings, owned by Alp Gürkan. CHP submitted a motion in October 2013 calling for an independent commission to investigate a series of accidents that previously occurred in the Soma mine. A few weeks prior to the accident the AK Party voted against the commission, with Erdoğan declaring disparagingly that the opposition should not be hampering the political system with such trivialities.[97] This created much tension and criticism against Erdoğan in Turkey. Furthermore, in a protest conducted following these events, the prime minister's aide, Yusuf Yerkel, appeared to kick a protester in Soma.[98] On May 20, Erdoğan said in the Turkish parliament that he did not know and had never met the owner of the company. Immediately afterwards, *Yeni Akit* allegedly found the culprit for the rising criticism against Erdoğan. It appeared that Alp Gürkan's son-in-law was Jewish; his original name was Mario Asafrana, which he had changed to the Turkish name Mahir.

Yeni Akit deciphered the reason why Zionism-manipulated domestic and foreign media attacked Erdoğan by taking advantage of Soma. It also compares Gürkan's son-in-law with one of the mafia members of the series *Kurtlar Vadisi*, İplikçi Nedim, whose origin is also Jewish and who also, as the newspaper claims, hides his real "business."[99] Thus instead of questioning the failures of the company and the government in not taking the necessary safety measures in advance, *Yeni Akit* sought the 'real' reason for the mine crisis.[100] On the same day that *Yeni Akit* published the aforementioned article, Erdoğan thanked Israel for canceling its National Day reception in respect of the three days of mourning in Turkey because of Soma. But Yaşın Aktay, the AK Party's deputy chairman assistant in charge of foreign relations, told *A-Haber*: "some things might be done on purpose. The possibility of sabotage is even mentioned. But I don't want to focus on this."[101]

AK Party's head of parliament's Constitutional Commission, Burhan Kuzu, a professor of law, tweeted: "Jewish lobbies from abroad assigned too much guilt and pressure to Erdoğan in the aftermath of the Soma incident. However, the son-in-law of Soma's owner is a Jew. Don't you think something is weird here?"[102]

This incident led to another one in which Erdoğan's allegedly antisemitic remark was expressed against a demonstrator who protested following the Soma disaster. On May 17, Erdoğan was ostensibly heard yelling at a protester in video footage circulated by the opposition *Sözcü* newspaper, using an expression considered a curse in Turkish: "Why are you running away, Israeli spawn?" In the video,[103] Erdoğan is seen surrounded by angry protesters in the market, shouting at him as he visited the tragedy-hit town of Soma a day after the blast. Some local media claimed Erdoğan hit the protester in the commotion, but this is not clearly visible on the video, and was denied by the deputy chairman of the party, Hüseyin Çelik. Whether this video is authentic or not, whether Erdoğan said these words or not, the most important thing is that many Turkish people believe that their prime minister may well have done so.[104] The fact that this incident and these words were accepted quite serenely in Turkey indicates much more than the words themselves or the authenticity of this video.

The Jews are 'known' for their 'bad Turkish' as well as for their speaking loudly and using non-Turkish words. Because the Turkish Jews knew little Turkish during the first years of the Republic, this impression has followed them until today:

> Last year my son won an academic award. The university dean congratulated him on speaking "such excellent Turkish – for a foreigner!"... He is interested in politics and studied political science in one of the best universities in Turkey. Nonetheless, he can't be a politician in Turkey with our family name. He feels very frustrated by this as he has no interest in living abroad.[105]

The most bothersome thing is that this stereotype has infiltrated some Jews' self-identity and awareness to the degree that they adopted it as a characteristic of their own behavior. Marcy Brink-Danan mentions in her book a response that was conveyed to her after expressing her desire to travel to Büyük Ada for vacation: "What kind of vacation is that? With all those Jews around it will be so crowded and everyone will be yelling!"[106]

A said his fear of being conceived as "the foreigner" was one of the reasons to create loyalty to the Turkish regime and nationalistic values. A 28-year-old male described this as follows:

> My girlfriend wishes the community were more open ... less like the stereotypical 'korkak yahudi' [cowardly Jew, a very popular derogatory name for Jews]. But she is very naïve, she doesn't know that if you are a Jew, Muslims will never see you as a person. When my girlfriend and I go out with friends, she fits in perfectly, she doesn't have a foreign name or a Jewish accent and can pass for a Turkish girl. But because I speak Ladino with my parents at home I have an accent. As a Jew you might be stereotyped as being good at business or they might hate you for it. Think about Neve Şalom – they killed them just for being Jewish.[107]

N, a 65-year-old Jewish businessman living in Istanbul, said that antisemitism is mainly sensed in business life:

I have been working in the same place for the last 25 years. In my environment the people are very good and we feel happy with them, we are friends. Yet, I have Arab customers who informed me that the owner of the business next to me had warned them not to buy from me, "the Jew." Sometimes my neighbors refer customers to other places some distance away where the quality of goods is lower than mine just because I am Jewish. Some cannot buy from Jewish businesses because they are related to the AK Party or to businesses that do business with AK Party sympathizers only. Their antisemitism is expressed when they are angry with you. When you are friends it's ok but when they get angry with you, they are capable of telling you: "Hitler did well by prosecuting you." Today, for instance, I went in a taxi. The driver was listening to a religious program and said: "there is only Islam. Jews and others are irreligious." Of course he was not aware of my Jewishness. Even if you don't hear it, you feel it in their looks and behavior indirectly.[108]

C, a Jewish housewife in her sixties, from Istanbul, partially disagrees with him. She said:

I do not sense any antisemitism because I don't do business. Most of the residents living in my environment are Jews and there is no difference between them and the Muslim inhabitants. I often hear: "Jews are rich" but I say there are poor Jews as well but you don't see them because they are not sensed. I feel united with non-Jews, for example, with my hair dresser whose customers are mostly Jewish. Same with our neighbors who even understand Ladino to some extent. I think that in trade you can sense antisemitism but not so much in daily social life."

A, a 44-year-old business administrator, says the same:

I grew up in a 42-apartment building inhabited by Muslims and two apartments of Jews and we have never experienced any problems. I think it is not against the Jews but something more general related to the Turks' mentality; for example when something happens with France, there are immediate calls to boycott French products. The government always says that the problem is with the Israeli government but I think this is not their true approach. Yet, I do not feel antisemitism in any direct way.[109]

These examples of daily life are accompanied by Turkish identification and cultural national background. An example is Orhan Seyfi Orhon (1890–1972), a popular and renowned Turkish poet who dedicated a chapter in his famous book *Dün Bugün Yarın* (Today Yesterday Tomorrow) to describe how Jews profiteered in Turkey during World War II.[110] Orhon mentions that the Jews took over many of the occupations in Turkey and in general they take over everything including housing in Büyük ada (the largest of the nine so-called Princes' Islands in the Sea of Marmara, near Istanbul, known for its great Jewish population,

Antisemitism in the Turkish media 163

especially in the summertime), coal, wool, and others. Even if you want to breathe fresh air in Boğaziçi says Orhon, you can't as the Jews have already settled there before you arrive.[111]

In order to elucidate Turkish society's approach toward Jews, I took an independent poll in Turkey in 2012. But already in 2009, the Jewish community in Turkey conducted a research study that was part of the Project Presenting Turkish Jewry and Jewish Culture funded by the European Union. The purpose of the study was to understand the outlook of the general population toward 'the other' in general while measuring the perception and image of Turkish Jews. In 2012 I conducted a poll aimed at examining the Israeli–Palestinian conflict and its impact on antisemitism inside Turkey. Furthermore, the poll aimed to examine AK Party voters' viewpoint toward the Jews of Turkey. Before comparing the polls, it is important to note that Jews seem to be the least known minority in Turkey; according to the 2012 poll, only 15 percent declared having a Jew in their close environment (such as educational institution, neighborhood, business, etc.), whereas 21 percent declared knowing an atheist and 23 percent declared knowing a Christian. Among AK Party's voters, only 9 percent declared having a Jew in their close environment, whereas 24 percent of CHP voters and 10 percent of MHP voters declared being acquainted with Jews.

According to the 2009 poll, 42 percent of Turks wouldn't want Jews as neighbors. This increases to 61 percent among those who identify themselves as Muslims; 57 percent among those who do not have any different people around them; 52 percent among those with low education levels, those who live in rural areas, and women. Forty-nine percent of AK Party voters, and 47 percent of MHP voters are against Jewish neighbors. The 19 percent who said no to Jewish neighbors have the lowest ratio and are among the university educated. According to the 2012 poll, a positive change appeared as the number of those who opposed neighboring Jews (and others) decreased. According to the new poll, only 34 percent of Turks wouldn't want Jews as their neighbors (and 14 percent answered "maybe"). Only 44 percent of AK Party voters and 37 percent of MHP voters were against Jewish neighbors. It is interesting to note that the numbers referring to Christian neighbors decreased as well, from 32 percent in 2009 to 27 percent in 2012 (Figure 5.4).

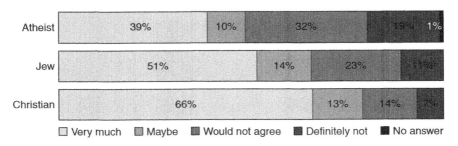

Figure 5.4 Would you agree to have a ... as a neighbor?[112]

164 Antisemitism under AK Party rule

According to the 2009 poll, 48 percent of the interviewees believe that Jews are not loyal to the Republic of Turkey, which is 1 percent more than for Armenians and Greeks (47 percent each). However, in the 2012 poll, only 18 percent of the respondents believed that "Jews cannot be trusted." Other perceived characteristics of Jews in Turkey are: "Turkish Jews have a lot of money" (37 percent), "the Turkish Jews are more talented and successful than non-Jews" (19 percent), "the Turkish Jews are conceited, keep to themselves and are disrespectful" (12 percent), and "noisy and impolite" (4 percent) (Figure 5.5). The first two characteristics are somewhat 'positive' in the eyes of many Turks; thus when a Turk says "Jews are rich" he is not always aware of the antisemitic tone this assertion includes and refers to it as a compliment.

According to the poll, AK Party voters are those who highly believe that "Jews cannot be trusted" (23%) (Table 5.1).

Generally speaking, trust of the other is very low.[113] It seems that the response to this question is given based on memorized stereotypes and teachings. As the level of trust increases, acceptance of the other increases as well. The older aged, university graduates, urban, higher income have a generally higher level of trust

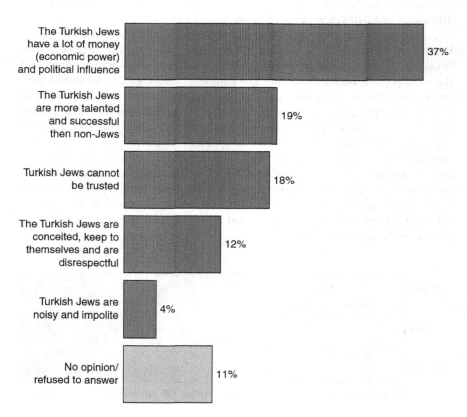

Figure 5.5 Which sentences best represent Jews?

Table 5.1 Can Jews be trusted?

		The Turkish Jews have a lot of money (economic power) and political influence (%)	The Turkish Jews are more talented and successful than non-Jews (%)	The Turkish Jews are noisy and impolite (%)	The Turkish Jews are conceited, keep to themselves and are disrespectful (%)	Turkish Jews cannot be trusted (%)	No opinion/ refused (%)	Total (%)
Sex	Male	38	19	4	12	16	11	100
	Female	36	19	3	12	19	12	100
Age	18–35 ages	38	16	4	13	18	11	100
	36–50 ages	35	19	4	10	21	12	100
	51+ ages	37	22	3	13	14	11	100
Education	Primary school or less	29	19	4	14	23	11	100
	High school	40	18	5	10	17	10	100
	University	50	20	1	10	6	14	100
Settlement	Urban	38	18	4	12	16	12	100
	Rural	29	21	1	14	24	11	100
HH_income	Less than 1000 TL	29	18	3	14	20	16	100
	1001–2000 TL	39	19	4	10	18	10	100
	2001+ TL	43	19	4	14	15	4	100
	No answer	39	22	0	4	9	26	100
Self expression	Low income	34	18	2	11	20	14	100
	Medium or high	39	19	5	13	16	9	100
Party preferences	AKP	33	16	5	12	23	11	100
	CHP	49	21	2	8	11	10	100
	MHP	57	3	3	13	17	7	100
	Other	21	43	0	7	14	14	100
	Undecided/no response	33	22	3	15	15	13	100

vis-a-vis the other. The lowest trust level is perceived in those who define themselves as Muslims. Comparing the results of international surveys, Turkey is among the countries with the lowest level of trust.[114]

Replying to the question of whether expressions against Israel and against Jews are antisemitic, 37 percent replied "yes" in almost all cases or in most cases; 38 percent said only in a few cases; and 21 percent denied anti-Israel or anti-Jewish expressions are antisemitic. Compared to other parties' voters, 23 percent of those who denied any affinity between anti-Israel or anti-Jewish expressions and antisemitic ones were AK Party voters, and those who replied; "in most cases," were equally AK Party and CHP voters at 23 percent. As for the perception of Turkish Jewry in the eyes of Turks in light of the Israeli–Palestinian conflict, the 2009 poll makes it evident that 51 percent of respondents hold a negative or a very negative perception of Jews.

When asked in 2012 whether the existence of the State of Israel increased or reduced antisemitism in Turkey, 46 percent replied that it greatly increased or just increased, 46 percent of AK Party voters replied that it increased, whereas 50 percent and 60 percent of CHP and MHP voters, respectively, replied the same. Fifty-one percent of Turkish society believes that the Israeli government's policy regarding the Israeli–Palestinian conflict reinforced antisemitism in Turkey (54 percent of AK Party voters). But 17 percent of AK Party voters and 23 percent of CHP voters thought that Israeli policies did not reinforce antisemitism in Turkey at all, while 56 percent of CHP voters thought that Israel's policies create and even strengthen antisemitism in Turkey. This is not the first poll that indicates animosity toward Jews in Turkey. In a 2011 Pew poll observing Muslim–Western relations, titled "Muslim–Western tensions persist amid common concerns about Islamic extremism," it seems that only 4 percent of Turkish citizens are favorable toward Jews, 2 percent less than are favorable toward Christians.[115]

A Hrant Dink Foundation study conducted in 2014 that tracked derogatory coverage of over 30 different groups in media reports between May and August 2014 found that Jews (and Armenians) were the subject of over half of the recorded incidents in a media landscape filled with "biased and discriminatory language use." Jews led the pack with 130 incidents, followed by Armenians (60), Christians (25), Greeks (21), Kurds (18), and Syrian refugees (10). According to a poll that the ADL released in the latter half of 2014, 69 percent of Turks harbor antisemitic attitudes. Asked if Jews were more loyal to Israel than to the countries in which they lived, 69 percent of respondents replied affirmatively, and 70 percent of those surveyed agreed that Jews only cared about "their own kind." Over half agreed that Jews were responsible for "most of the world's wars," and 61 percent said that people hated Jews due to their behavior.[116] The poll results lead to the inevitable question of whether the AK Party enhances antisemitism in Turkey or whether antisemitism would have grown stronger regardless of the AK Party government.

The discourse of Erdoğan as reflected in the Turkish media

"Is Erdoğan an anti-Semite?" is a hard question to answer. As seen in Chapter 1, antisemitism has always prevailed in Turkey, so Erdoğan was not the first to lead such an ideology. But Erdoğan's history is something that will accompany him for the rest of his term, whether as prime minister or president. In 1974, Erdoğan was chief of a youth branch of the National Salvation Party's (Milli Selamet Partisi, MSP) Beyoğlu district, and he wrote and directed a play entitled *Mas-Kom-Yah*, the acronym of Mason (Freemasons), Komünist (Communists), and Yahudi (Jew), the three main groups on the MSP's agenda.

Further evidence of Erdoğan's early antisemitism is found in the memoirs of Professor Mehmet Erdaş, while living in Berlin, in the form of a reply to Ruşan Çakır's article published in 2009 after the Davos incident claiming that Erdoğan is not an anti-Semite. Erdaş describes Erdoğan's attitude toward the Jews by recounting his encounter with Erdoğan in March 1994, when Erdoğan was elected mayor of Istanbul. Erdaş recalls his encounter with Üzeyir Garih, in front of Erdoğan's office, waiting to greet the latter for his election. As Erdaş knew Garih very well, they both hugged and spoke to each other warmly. When Erdoğan saw this gesture he immediately

> took me to his office and in the same angry tone that he displayed at Davos, his hands in the air, yelled at me as if I made a big mistake: "how can you hug this Jew in front of my office? Are you not ashamed? What sort of hypocrisy is this? Are you not a Muslim?" My answer was this: "Tayyip Bey, this man is the third largest businessman of Turkey, I know him from the State Planning Organization [Devlet Planlama Teşkilatı, DPT]. It was he who hugged me, did I have to reject him? What sort of Islam can accept such an attitude?[117]

As Turkey's prime minister, a representative of Bursa in the opposition Republican People's Party until 2014, Aykan Erdemir said in an interview given to *The Times of Israel*, Erdoğan is very much responsible for the ongoing antisemitism in Turkey:

> But after 12 years of Erdoğan's rule, we are at a more dangerous place. The anti-Israel and antisemitic feelings are deeper and stronger. And to be frank, even after Erdoğan and the AK Party are gone, even if CHP comes to power, it will take us quite some time to mend inter-social relations through dialogue, awareness raising, and sensitivity training.[118]

Zali De Toledo agrees with Erdemir; according to De Toledo, Erdoğan is behind these antisemitic comments:

> Because Erdoğan is playing the tune of the music by being antisemitic, everyone wants to imitate him in order to get more respect from the smallest mayor to Ankara's mayor to anybody with a microphone. It is incredible

what kind of imagination they have. As one Turkish-Jewish person told me, "If the leaf of a tree falls, they will blame Israel." It is a hysterical attitude and because everyone wants to please Erdoğan, there is no end because he is the main personality in this antisemitic activity.[119]

Turkish society is ambivalent about Israel and Jews, according to Aydemir, who insisted that

> positive attitudes toward Jews can coexist alongside antisemitic feelings. The problem cannot be reduced to negative feelings about interstate relations – it is deeper than that. Erdoğan is a very skillful master who manipulates public sentiments and capitalizes on them. So in that respect, as long as Erdoğan is in power there will always be the possibility of a new and prolonged crisis.... Erdoğan is "Janus-faced" in that he has two seemingly opposing approaches to relations with Israel,

Aydemir continued. "He can be quite pragmatic toward Israel while also capitalizing on the existing anti-Israel sentiment in Turkey," he said.

> We have to accept that some of that sentiment is not just anti-Israel but antisemitic.... He is not only capitalizing on the existing sentiments but he is in a way fueling some of that anti-Israel and antisemitic feeling. How? With his rhetoric, conspiracy theories, campaign slogans, and actions.[120]

Even if Erdoğan has no influence on Turkish politics, and even if the relations between Israel and Turkey improve, the damage of spreading antisemitic seeds within Turkish society has already been done. As Aydemir puts it: "Diplomatic relations between Ankara and Jerusalem could improve very quickly, but deep-seated animosity toward Jews is more problematic."[121]

> At the policy level you can take concrete steps, you can initiate joint projects and increase volume of trade. But as an anthropologist who has researched prejudice, discrimination, and hate crimes, I'm very concerned about the long-term repercussions of hate and prejudice. When you provoke prejudice and hatred, it's not that easy to reverse it. It will take a lot of time and effort. Turkish society will have to live with these problems for years to come.[122]

In a different interview Erdemir indicates that antisemitism in Turkey is increasing but the AK Party government that is responsible for its escalation and which discusses it in private conversations does not publish the data, in order to prevent public pressure. In other words, although the common assertion is that the AK Party in general and Erdoğan in particular exploits the Turkish public by his fierce antisemitic rhetoric against Israel, here Erdemir claims that the government is afraid to express the rise in antisemitism due to possible negative public opinion, once the public is aware of this fact. Erdemir opposes this alleged concealment, saying that if the Turkish political route follows public opinion, Turkey will never be able to rid itself of discrimination and hate. Erdemir agrees that for many years CHP had an anti-Jewish viewpoint, especially during the first decades of the Turkish Republic (Varlık Vergisi, Trakya Incidents, Turkification efforts, etc.). "In the Israel–Palestine conflict, I have witnessed that the newer generations are biased against Israel." Erdemir also said that he was upset that CHP did not confront Erdoğan when he called the terrorist organization Hamas "my brothers." In addition, during Operation Protective Edge, neither the AK Party nor CHP condemned the 4,500 rockets launched at Israel. Even when Erdoğan called a demonstrator, following the tragedy in Soma, "Israil Dölü" (spawn of Israel), no one protested:

> I wrote several CHP members including the chairperson Kılıçdaroğlu but none have responded. Unless major portions of the population react and the judiciary does not do what it needs to do, CHP's reactions and protests will have no effect.[123]

According to the journalist Caroline Glick, the fact that Erdoğan cannot reconcile with Israel is not because he hates Jews; Erdoğan's antisemitism is part of his general authoritarian outlook, informed by a paranoid mindset. Even if Turkish antisemitism does not necessitate a rejection of Jews and Israel, when antisemitism is tied to several other political and economic pathologies, as it is in the case of Turkey, there is a problem with Erdoğan's views of the Jews. Furthermore, says Glick, Erdoğan sees a Jewish conspiracy behind every independent power base in Turkey;[124] the fact that even the Jews outside Turkey are often seen as a destructive element for Turkey by Erdoğan can help us shape the picture.

On July 1, 2013, Deputy Prime Minister Beşir Atalay blamed "the Jewish Diaspora" for inciting unrest in Turkey in what is known as the Gezi Park Protest. The Jewish community, in response, expressed its concern that all Jews around the world, including Turkish Jews, may become the target of such generalization.[125] Atalay also reportedly repeated government claims that the international media had played a big role in "the conspiracy" and had led the unrest as well. "The ones trying to block the way of Great Turkey will not succeed," he said.

> There are some circles that are jealous of Turkey's growth. They are all uniting, on one side the Jewish Diaspora. You saw the foreign media's attitude during the Gezi Park incidents; they brought it and started broadcasting immediately, without evaluating the [situation][126]

Atalay is heard in a video that appears on several websites. The deputy prime minister immediately denied that he made the comments, but it is clear from the video that he said the things he was accused of saying.[127]

Ankara mayor, İbrahim Melih Gökçek, a member of the AK Party, has been vocal about his distaste for the protesters in Istanbul's Gezi Park, having both mocked and criticized them through a series of tweets on his personal Twitter account. But his rhetoric became more sinister as he posted on Twitter that Turkish intelligence has learned that the protests are a result of a February meeting of the American Enterprise Institute, which the note further asserts is a branch of the America Israel Public Affairs Committee. The note claims that it was suggested at the meeting to have Turkish youth spill out into the streets to protest.[128] It seems they all repeat Erdoğan's accusation, dated about a month earlier, when the latter said that an "interest rate lobby" was responsible for orchestrating the protests, which some interpreted as a thinly veiled attack on Jews.[129] Erdoğan mentioned the "interest rate lobby" during his speech outside the Atatürk airport upon his arrival from his North African Rainbow Tour on June 7, 2013. "The interest rate lobby believes it can threaten Turkey with stock market speculation,"[130] Erdoğan said, and called them "çapulcu," meaning plunderers, looters. He also blamed the "interest rate lobbies" for the recent losses at the stock exchange, saying these "lobbies think that they could threaten the government by making speculations in the stock exchange" and vowed not to "waste the efforts of the people on interest rate lobbies."[131]

These statements aligned with his reference to "domestic extremists" and "foreign powers" which were behind the Gezi Park demonstration. Erdoğan did not specify who the members of this lobby were, but according to articles in a daily owned by the conglomerate where the prime minister's son-in-law is CEO, the lobby is a coalition of Jewish financiers associated with both Opus Dei and the Illuminati. It seems the two sworn enemies have put aside their differences to ruin Turkey.[132] The Jewish community of Turkey published their response on the community's website, saying:

> we are trying to obtain more information about the remarks with regard to the details, meaning, and content. But in any case, we would like to express our concern and sorrow that all Jews around the world, including Turkish Jews, may become the target because of this sort of generalization in almost every situation.[133]

This scores good electoral points for Erdoğan. A pro-Israel or pro-Jewish approach would never benefit a politician who still tries to portray himself as the leader of the Sunni world. Faik Tunay agrees, in an interview during which he emphasized that he represented himself only. Tunay's mindset, as he testifies, is more AK Party oriented than CHP, but still Tunay openly spoke about Erdoğan and antisemitism. He claims that compared to Europe, antisemitism in Turkey is much less evident and even when it emerges it is usually aimed at Israel's policies regarding the conflict with the Palestinians, and is not clear antisemitism. Tunay asserts that what Erdoğan did was simply exploit antisemitism along with sympathy toward the Palestinians in order to gain more votes and popularity within Turkish public opinion. Erdoğan was no different from the earlier Turkish political leaders, but he was the first to use it in public. Ahmet Muharrem Atlığ, general secretary of the Journalists and Writers Association (belonging to the Gülen Movement) seems to agree on this viewpoint, but he adds that the AK Party creates the link between Jews and Israel in an antisemitic way as part of its constant use of "Turkey's three external enemies" – the United States, Gülen Movement, and Israel – in order to distract the masses from the AK Party's corruption and to find a specific target to agitate the masses against.[134]

As Tunay says, the anti-Israel sentiments have always been a latent secret. When asked if Erdoğan is an anti-Semite, Tunay's knee-jerk reply was yes but then he said that Erdoğan is not an anti-Semite but he "does not like Jews." Tunay is convinced that Erdoğan's fierce rhetoric against Israel affects the rise of antisemitism in Turkey, since many AK Party supporters did not hate Jews or Israel before his era but "thanks to" Erdoğan they have developed negative feelings toward Jews. The more Erdoğan speaks negatively against Jews, the more the Turkish public sees Jews as the ones to blame.[135] Salih Bıçakçı from Kadir Has University in Istanbul claims that Erdoğan follows Erbakan's footsteps. In his opinion, even if Erdoğan does not mean to be antisemitic or even when he speaks of Israel, his sayings create "a mentality of antisemitism."[136] Maybe Mario Levi's suggestion is more applicable in reference to Erdoğan. Levi claims that in many states, including Turkey, no one feels comfortable declaring himself an anti-Semite. Even Erdoğan, while harshly condemning Israel during Operation Pillar of Defense, said that antisemitism is a crime that must be eradicated. Yet, as hard as it is to say "I am an anti-Semite" it was pretty easy to condemn Israel, and the antisemitism in Turkey is tightly interwoven in Turks' attitudes toward Israel.[137] According to Balcı, their lack of acquaintance with Jews is the reason for antisemitism. There is only one type of a "good Jew" and that would be their neighbor. Balcı gives Trabzon inhabitants as an example: The most antisemitic province in Turkey is Trabzon and that is because they have never had any experience of living near Jews. This claim is very common in Turkey. C, a Jewish housewife in her sixties from Istanbul, says the same: "the ignorant masses who do not know us, the Jews, don't like us but those who knows us – love us."[138]

On the other hand, it is hard to say that Erdoğan's hatred toward Jews is unique to Jews. It seems that Erdoğan is struggling with the question of who is a Turk and so his understanding of who is a Turk or the supremacy of the Muslim Turks is not exposed in regard to Turkish minorities only; in one of Erdoğan's interviews on TV during the presidential campaign, Erdoğan said:

> In Turkey someone who wants to say he/she is Turkish, let them say! Someone who wants to say he/she is Kurdish let them say! What haven't they said about me? I've been called Georgian and even Armenian. But I am a Turk.[139]

In an interview with Utku Çakırözer for *Cumhuriyet*, one of the Jewish community representatives said similar things:

in the past I did not think this way but now I think that the Prime Minister is an anti-Semite. The Alevi, the Sunni, the Turks, the Kurds, the Laz, all of them are his brothers but words such as I am a brother with the Greeks, the Jews, the Armenians, and the Asyrians have never come out of his mouth.[140]

It seems like Erdoğan confronts only the non-Muslims in Turkey. This aligned with Fandy's opinion, expressed on page 127, according to which the Israeli–Palestinian conflict is not an ethnic or national one, but a religious one.

Antisemitic expressions from Erdoğan seem like they are expressed unintentionally sometimes. It feels as if Erdoğan does not even pay attention to what slips out of his mouth. A good example is his speech at the opening of the 2009–2010 academic year at Yıldız Teknik University in Istanbul. At this ceremony, Erdoğan mentioned the prominent Turkish-Jewish businessman and co-founder of Alarko Holdings, the Jewish tycoon Üzeyir Garih. In this speech, Erdoğan stressed Jews' success in trade.

> We worked together and we have decided two things: first, that we would administer knowledge, second, that we would administer money well. In fact, if you look at it, Jews are very good at discoveries and inventions, thanks to which they print money while sitting around.[141]

One of Erdoğan's typical characteristics is the attempt to defend Turkish Jews immediately after slamming Israel or mentioning Hitler. This behavior has repeated itself during the years of Erdoğan's regime. One example is Erdoğan's victory speech after being elected as Turkey's president in August 2014. Erdoğan's fierce rhetoric against Israel during the presidential elections was followed by antisemitic incidents, but once he was elected a different tone was expressed:

> We are 77 million people marching toward the future under the shadow of the same flag. We are one nation with one flag, one motherland, and one state. We come from the same ancestors, same culture, same civilization, and same history. We may have different political views and life styles. We may believe in different religions, sects and have different values, ethnic origins, and mother tongues; yet at the end of the day, we are all people of this country. This country belongs to all of us. Being a citizen of Turkey comes before being Muslim, Christian, Jewish, Assyrian, Yezidi, Alawite, or Sunni. Being a citizen of Turkey comes before being Turkish, Kurdish, Arab, Laz, Georgian, Bosnian, Circassian, Roman, Pomak, Greek, or Armenian.[142]

Another example of Erdoğan's change of rhetoric toward the Jews is his speech given on August 14, 2014, where he said there was no other country in the world as sensitive toward its minorities as Turkey. The outgoing prime minister and president-elect, Recep Tayyip Erdoğan, said at a gathering of the ruling AK Party, "We have enacted historical reforms for everyone within the borders of the

Republic of Turkey to freely express their faith, culture and identity especially to protect their lifestyle and to freely express their thoughts." He said:

> All minorities in Turkey are at peace. So many incidents are taking place in Gaza. We said, the Jews of Turkey are our citizens, nobody can show any negative behavior toward them, they are under our guarantee. Our problem is with the Israeli government, not with the Israeli people. We will act with commonsense, not with emotion.[143]

Erdoğan attempts to calm the agitation he himself created. His defense of the Turkish Jews appears to reflect a somewhat tardy and meager reaction. This way, Erdoğan depicts himself as an enlightened leader on one hand but on the other hand he gains popularity among the masses and so obtains the political advantage he wants to achieve. This double standard is one of Erdoğan's main tactics when it comes to antisemitism.

Aykan Erdemir also claims that Erdoğan's pragmatism is the main reason for the criticism he receives from his Islamist opposition, because they claim that if Erdoğan is so anti-Israel he should not maintain any ties with Israel. Thus, as mentioned before, Islamists and nationalists treat Erdoğan as if he were the gage of Israel and the United States.[144] Erol Aron Bünyel, a famous Turkish actor of Jewish origin, believes that Turkey has never been democratic and secular in the way it is under Erdoğan's leadership. According to Bünyel, Erdoğan is not antisemitic, although a Muslim antisemitic community exists in Turkey: "Erdoğan pretends to be antisemitic in order to change this community's mindset. He knows how to talk to them, how to open their mind." For Bünyel, the fact that Erdoğan closed factories or other institutions that were in Jewish hands does not make him antisemitic. "Erdoğan attempts to create equality between members of all religions and if there is a need to create that on the account of the Jews – it does not mean the motivation was antisemitic."[145]

For Talip Küçükcan, none of the above is true regarding Erdoğan; for him, Erdoğan is far from being an anti-Semite, he simply reacts to the alleged Israeli atrocities. As a devoted Muslim, he is strongly in favor of the Abrahamic religions:

> Erdoğan is a strong critic of Israeli policies towards Palestinians. In his remarks he makes a distinction between the people of Israel and the state/government of Israel. Moreover, his remarks after the Mavi Marmara incident became much more critical because Israeli security forces killed a number of Turkish citizens. If you take the context in which he speaks about Israel, you should see that his tone and emphasis in on current politics. Therefore I cannot consider him an anti-Semite. In my opinion many have a misguided opinion about Mr. Erdoğan and the AK Party. Those who look at their political statements against the Israeli government's policies confuse these statements with antisemitic views simply because they think that Islamist parties and political figures are directly or indirectly antisemitic.

Erdoğan always underlines the fact that historically and currently Turkey has been open to Jews. It is his government that sits with non-Muslim communities around the same table to listen to their concerns. If you look at the records of the Directorate of Foundations, you would see that the AK Party returned many Jewish and Christian properties back to their historical owners. These policies are supported by Erdoğan. Finally, in his understanding of Islam, Abrahamic religions come from the same source and therefore Muslims cannot categorically oppose or deny the rights and presence of Jews and Christians.[146]

Explaining antisemitism by blaming Israeli policies is not new in Turkey; it is actually an explanation that AK Party supporters repeat. On January 15, 2009, for example, Deputy Chief of Staff Yunus Emre Karaosmanoğlu told American diplomats that the widespread national sentiment and Erdoğan's reactions to Operation Cast Lead were solely a reaction to "the massacre." AK Party Foreign Affairs Committee Chairman Murat Mercan spoke along similar lines during a January 16 roundtable. Erdoğan's harsh statements against Israel, he said, were the result of Erdoğan reacting to the deaths of Palestinian children "as a father, not as a politician."[147]

Hüseyin Çelik, former deputy chairman in charge of publicity and media for the AK Party, agrees with Küçükcan, and says that not only is Erdoğan not an anti-Semite, but he also prevents antisemitism from occurring:

> the fact is, if there were any other party in power today other than the AK Party and such incidents [*Mavi Marmara*] were to take place, if this had not been the AK Party's attitude and there wasn't this effective and influential foreign policy, believe me, antisemitism would have increased much more.[148]

N., a 57-year-old Jewish businessman from Istanbul who is very much involved in the community management, stresses the same, but from a Jewish point of view. For him, Erdoğan is not an anti-Semite but a good politician. He only benefits from antisemitism after becoming aware of the political benefits he can gain from antisemitic statements. Thus Erdoğan encourages antisemitism, knowing that Turkish society is easily agitated, but he is not an anti-Semite. He is not a real democrat but also not a real anti-Semite, says N. In addition, he testifies that the best ever period for the Turkish-Jewish community took place under the AK Party regime:

> The cooperation between the AK Party government and the Jewish community during the AK Party's term climaxed. If Erdoğan was a real anti-Semite, he could have done much worse things to the Jewish community and he has many tools and ways to do it.[149]

Yet, with all due respect to Erdoğan's character, it is more important to deal with his deeds and their effect on Turkish society. Erdoğan, a popular leader, the only one to be elected three times in a row to the premiership of Turkey and then, in June 2014, as Turkey's first president to be elected by the people and not by the parliament, has been using extreme accusations against the State of Israel. Over the years, his assertions have become more and more extreme, with the peak being Operation Protective Edge. Unfortunately, it seems that Erdoğan's influence runs parallel to the growing antisemitism in Turkey. The poll I conducted in 2012 proved it unequivocally. Asked whether Erdoğan's assertions against Israel increase antisemitism in Turkey, 43 percent of respondents replied positively, 38 percent said they neither reduced nor increased, and only 16 percent said they reduced antisemitism in Turkey. Forty-three percent of AK Party voters admitted that Erdoğan's assertions increased antisemitism in Turkey. That means that Erdoğan's capability to direct the people's viewpoint is strong and certain. Talip Küçükcan vehemently opposes this assertion, saying that Erdoğan cannot be responsible for Israel's deeds, which are the real reason for increasing antisemitism, if it does increase at all:

> In my view, antisemitism is not on the increase under this government. If it is on the increase one should look at the origins and reasons for such an increase? Is it related to Israeli policies, Israel's attack on the Mavi Marmara, Israel's bombing of Gaza, etc.? Or is it because of what Erdoğan says. One should also mention that this year this government officially held an event to commemorate the Holocaust. It should finally be noted here that there is an awareness of the consequences of antisemitism in Europe among the Turkish public opinion. Especially Erdoğan and the AK Party even liken Islamophobia to antisemitism and ask European governments to take measures to prevent it as they did to prevent antisemitism.[150]

Whether Erdoğan is an anti-Semite or not, one thing is clear: Antisemitism appeared in Turkey long before Erdoğan appeared on Turkey's historical landscape. According to Corry Guttstadt, the link between Islamists and the Muslim Brotherhood in Turkey began after World War II.[151] Later on, in the 1950s, Holocaust denial was common in Turkey when it was a taboo topic in Europe. Later on, in the 1960s and 1970s, rising antisemitism was pushed aside due to the left–right dispute in Turkey.

Guttstadt claims that although antisemitism in Turkey long preceded Erdoğan, the latter is definitely an anti-Semite. Since he could not reveal it during the first years of his term he had to hide it. One of the main reasons for the dissemination of antisemitism was the criticism of Kemalism in the 1990s; this criticism meant the baby was thrown out with the bathwater, because the critics let Islamists enter the discourse of Turkish liberalism. Liberals wanted to cooperate with Islamists so they could, for the first time, target the joint enemy that was Kemalism.[152] This is the reason why, Aykan Erdemir explicitly says, antisemitism will not disappear from the Turkish agenda with the disappearance of the AK Party. The progressive new government would not agitate the people, it will not eliminate antisemitism from Turkey since antisemitism is not just a political issue in

Turkey. For that, claims Erdemir, there is an urgent need on three planes: political, academic, and using NGOs. These bodies should inculcate liberal values and protect weak communities.

Yet, claims Erdemir, Erdoğan is an anti-Semite and there is no question about that. The fact that his antisemitic beliefs appeared after 2006 is explained as follows. Erdoğan revealed three forms of himself: until 2001, Erdoğan adopted the Milli Görüş mindset and was clearly antisemitic, anti-Western, and Islamist. From 2001 to 2006, after the AK Party split from the Felicity Party (Saadet Partisi), he played a neoconservative, moderate, Islamic, pro-Western leader. But from 2006 onwards, Erdoğan returned to his original antisemitic identity. Generally, his career rests on antisemitic values. Erdoğan does not hate Israel as a state, but does as a Jewish state. Thus, he is very pragmatic and nurtures the trade and tourism between Israel and Turkey, but this pragmatism is always at risk due to his antisemitism. The main problem with Erdoğan, claims Erdemir, is that the government enables hatred. Hatred receives legitimacy in Turkey. Despite Erdemir's supportive approach and dynamic fight against antisemitism, for Erdemir antisemitism has no special place in the current political social agenda in Turkey; antisemitism is only one color in a rainbow of racism and discrimination in Turkey. Erdemir counts antisemitism as part of attacks against LGBT communities, women, Alevis, etc.[153]

As for the question of whether Turkey is an "antisemitic state," Consul General Shy Cohen says: "Turkey is a country where antisemitism exists but it is not an antisemitic country."[154]

Jews' responses

The peaceful harmonious existence of Turkey's Jewish community is a primary basic and repetitive theme used by the Rabbinate and also the community's secular representatives, and of course Turkish politicians and leaders. Turkey's welcoming of the refugees from Spain in 1492 is mentioned even in political speeches. Even during Operation Protective Edge, Faruk Köse wrote on July 15, trying to make the Jewish community in Turkey, including their chief rabbi, apologize for Israel's "atrocities" in Gaza: "You have lived comfortably among us for 500 years and have gotten rich at our expense. Is this your gratitude – killing Muslims? Erdoğan, demand that the community leader apologize!" This argument is usually followed by two other reminders of Turkish history, whether true or false: Several Turkish diplomats rescued "hundreds" of Turkish Jews from Nazi death camps in World War II; and Turkey saved Jewish scientists from Nazi Germany by recruiting them to its newly established higher education system.[155] Although in the 1940s Turkey permitted Yishuv officials to operate in Istanbul and assisted the safe passage of European Jewish immigrants to Palestine, it is hard to claim that the Turkish Republic's attitude toward the Jewish refugees wishing to immigrate to Palestine through Turkey was welcoming and helpful, as it is portrayed in Turkey.[156]

In response to that, says Leyla Navaro, a Turkish academic of Jewish origin: "Am I still indebted because my ancestors were accepted by the Ottoman Sultan? Am I still a guest in this land where I grew up, fulfill my duties as a citizen, and actively contribute to its development?"[157] Yet, most Jews do not express this viewpoint. Throughout the history of the Jews in Turkey, the latter have responded by declaring their loyalty to the Turkish Republic and by counting the Jews' debts to the Turks throughout their joint history. The Jews have demonstrated their great loyalty to the Turkish authorities. For instance, during every religious event a prayer for the sake of the Turkish state has been said. The Jews usually avoid identifying with any political party and avoid passing judgment on the authorities, fearing their criticism would be taken as disloyalty. Depicted as very wealthy, the Jews have been donating to non-Jewish institutions but to no avail.[158] Of all the other minorities in Turkey, the Jews are the ones who have given up their culture; they were the first to give their children Turkish names, and they killed Ladino, unlike the Greeks and Armenians who preserve their culture and language.[159] This apologetic stance has characterized Jews' responses and is still relevant today.[160] This sort of behavior includes a dedicated campaign of self-representation reflected among Turkish Jews for years: "the good Jew."

Brink-Danan mentions the Quincentennial Foundation (QF) organization as "responsible" for building representations of the Turkish Jews as "the good minority." The QF claims that Turkey's national spirit infused with a cosmopolitan regard for the 'other' set the agenda for a public awareness campaign to improve Turkey's international image. But even from the Jewish side, the campaign was built around the notion of Jewish 'gratitude' for Ottoman and Turkish hospitality and through emphasizing the warm relations between Turkey and Israel and the United States.[161] Bali also claims that what stands behind the will of Turkish Jews to keep discussions on antisemitism away from the public eye is unwillingness to damage Turkey's image in the eyes of the world.[162] Prominent Turkish Jews challenged the decision of the ADL, which supported a US congressional resolution (House Resolution 106) calling the Armenian tragedies "genocide." They claimed that such an announcement would risk the Turkish Jewish community and would also damage the Israeli–Turkish–American diplomatic relations. Support of this call by the Armenians was declared as "endangering" the Turkish-Jewish community and risking relations with Israel. Thus, being the "good minority" helped Turkey display a history of cosmopolitanism and to refute the bad press it gains in regard to the Armenian tragedy.[163]

Yet, prior to discussing Jews' responses, we have to look at Turkish Jewry's take on antisemitism. Some clearly state that "no antisemitism exists in Turkey" whereas others definitively say antisemitism exists, and others claim that as long as antisemitism is not embodied in action it has no importance; for example, a 67-year-old housewife, a university graduate, said the following to Şule Toktaş:

> Antisemitism is believed to be non-existent but it does exist. There is a hidden antisemitism. But it is not important. I want to kill you too, but I don't kill you and keep talking to you. You have to ignore what is inside a human. If you

investigate what's inside the human what you find will not be that nice. Therefore you have to look at the style of things. The content may be different than style. You have to care for what is seen on the outside, the visible part, in Turkey, the style is not antisemitism and this is what I consider.[164]

Yet, even those who claim that antisemitism is not encountered in Turkey or that it could be dismissed as trivial or exceptional as there are only isolated cases, pointed out that there were stereotypes of Jews that are dominant in Turkish society. Common stereotypes are that Jews are rich (but also stingy), and a powerful nation who control the world. Another perspective applicable within the Jewish community is that a law that prohibits Jews from becoming deputies in Parliament or president or prime minister does not exist. Jews hardly serve in the security forces, such as the police or as high-ranked military officers, and in the history of Turkey no Jew has ever been a court judge. According to İvo Molinas, the reason is that Turkish Jews usually continue their ancestors' professions. The textile industry, for instance, is a traditional Jewish occupation, although in recent years it has been disappearing as 'big players' take control of this industry. Young Jews no longer feel obligated to continue their fathers' work. Jews, says Molinas, prefer to be their own bosses; professional management has never been very attractive.[165]

Looking at the Jewish community poll conducted in 2009 under the auspices of the EU, this discrimination can be easily seen: 57 percent of the respondents said they would disapprove of, or feel uncomfortable if, non-Muslim minorities worked in the State Intelligence Agency; 55 percent opposed non-Muslim's serving in the judiciary; 55 percent opposed their work in the police corps and army; 51 percent opposed them being in senior position in political parties; 46 percent in municipalities; and 44 percent even opposed them working in healthcare services.[166] This has turned into a lack of faith in the Jewish capacity to serve in higher ranks. This perspective penetrated their consciousness. As a 77-year-old housewife, high-school graduate, told Şule Toktaş:

> I wouldn't favor Jews holding high state positions, because there are very talented and competent people among the Muslims for these positions. I don't think Jews or other non-Muslims would be proficient to serve the state, because they've never done so in the past. They don't know how to administer a state. I would prefer a Turk to administer the state. I also think that in terms of identity, it wouldn't be proper for a Jew to hold a high position. The majority is Muslim and a Muslim should represent this majority. Society wouldn't accept a non-Muslim representing it. They may see a Jew as being different from themselves. There is democracy in Turkey, and it's a real democracy. But democracy means that the majority rules society. This is normal.[167]

This feeling of self-accusation is expressed by other members of the community as well. N, a 65-year-old Jewish businessman living in Istanbul referred to antisemitism as "our fault," saying:

antisemitism is also our fault because we like to be seen, we like to flaunt our wealth unnecessarily ... there is a stereotype in Turkey that the Jews are noisy [see poll] so sometimes when one of us is shouting we tell him "do not behave like a Jew."[168]

When antisemitic incidents took place and especially after antisemitic campaigns in newspapers, the authorities express a balanced, fair, and tolerant stance, but never make an effort to halt the campaign, especially when there is no physical attack. The more the pressure rises, the more apologetic Jews become, attempting to prove their guiltlessness and deposit their fate in the hands of the Turkish authorities.[169] The traditional response of Turkey's Jewish leaders is to make a clear distinction between Turkish Jewry and the State of Israel, and to repeatedly declare that they are "Turks," while carefully refraining from expressing any view on the conflict. Nevertheless, during Operation Cast Lead the Islamist press exerted constant pressure on the chief rabbi and the community president, including frequent calls on them to condemn Israel, accusing Turkish Jews of being "Zionists" if they did not do so, and implying that failure to condemn Israeli actions indicated support for "Jewish terror." Such sentiments were not limited to the Islamist press. At one point, Serdar Turgut, a writer for the mainstream *Akşam*, issued a similar call.[170]

There are several characteristic responses to antisemitism from the Jewish side.

(1) Kayadez: The 'historical' response of Turkish Jewry is indicated in the Ladino word Kayadez (meaning keeping silent) by Rıfat Bali. This is not even a viewpoint, but a way of life. Kayadez means that Jews should keep a low profile. The Kayadez stemmed from a primeval fear that often led to the low-profile policy and even caused a need to be 'hidden' from the public, invisible. İvo Molinas uses the famous Ladino saying that expresses the Kayadez differently: "no mos karisayamoz a la echos del hukumet" (We do not intervene in the government's matters). This phrase means that Jews must not create any problems with the government and must always be good citizens.[171] The Kayadez policy was well expressed by Efraim Elrom during the Turkish civil war between radical leftists and nationalists in 1971; he wrote:

> a nervous and insecure feeling prevails amongst non-Jews as well as amongst Jews but the non-Jews hold a feeling of a citizen in his country who would not hesitate to activate the police and voice out his complaint whereas the Jew ... has always tended not 'to cause problems,' not to complain and not need the authorities' interference in his matters. The insecurity that fear and panic stem from.[172]

This was also engaged as self-censorship as a way of protecting themselves from social discrimination and physical harm. Thus, Jews have found ways to discuss sensitive topics in public. This is why Turkish Jews will never say "Israel" in public; they will rather use the Hebrew word for "the state," "Hamedina."

I was once conversing with a Turkish Jew in Istanbul and at the beginning the word "Israel" was brought up fearlessly, but after a while my interlocutor said "I don't want to mention this word too much, we should use a different word." Similarly, while speaking of their origin they will not use the word "Jew" (Yahudi/musevi) in Turkish but rather use the Ladino term Judio or Cudio.[173]

A Jewish editor once revealed her 'secret' of how to publish stories in a way that only intimates would recognize. She mentions neighborhood names instead of cities, foreign terms. As antisemitic journals rely on Jewish newspaper publications to allegedly prove their Jewish pseudo-conspiracies, the editor must publish stories where both their topic and their writing style would not endanger the Jewish community.[174] This idea is well manifested by a cartoon published in the pages of the Turkish press after the 2003 bombings of Neve Şalom synagogue. In this cartoon, two Jewish men discuss the terror attack. One of the men says that due to the terror attack the public "has gotten to know us better. For example, how big a population we are, how long we have been in this territory ... etc." whereas the second man says worriedly "Do you think they found out my home address?"[175]

But the Kayadez is not only avoiding protest, it is also partly related to a distinction that the Turkish Jews attempt to create between themselves and the State of Israel. *Jerusalem Post* reporter Sam Sokol described his own experience with the Kayadez policy of the Jewish community in Turkey, saying that after he visited an Istanbul synagogue in 2013 and published an article on the local community's preparations for celebrating Israel's Independence Day, the community requested through an intermediary that the article be taken offline in an apparent bid to avoid being linked to Israel in the media. "The Turkish-Jewish community will prefer to keep their mouths shut because of their public safety, and they are right to do this," one émigré explained to the *Post* afterward.[176]

It is quite easy and convenient to keep a low profile, if you are a Jewish trader or businessman, but for famous Jews such as Mario Levi keeping a low profile cannot be a solution, as he said in an interview. According to Levi, whenever he lectures on creative writing in academia he enjoys the immunity of a "Turkish writer" but "when news from Gaza comes, I immediately receive invective responses. No one would call me 'a stinky Jew' but they would call me 'Palestinians' murderer.'"[177] In other words, keeping a low profile is possible only for specific sectors, but it proves one more thing: Despite being 'quiet,' antisemitism will always find you.

Fatih Gökhan Diler, from *Agos*, agrees that although the Jewish community keeps a low profile just as much as the Armenian community does, the Armenian daily *Agos* is much more brazen than the Jewish magazine *Şalom*. The voices raised in *Agos* are stronger than those emerging from *Şalom*.[178] Diler bases his statement on an interview he conducted with İvo Molinas from *Şalom*. In this interview, Molinas admits that although the newspaper has changed in recent years, it still uses a constructive, positive language. The goal is always to get along "so you can never get any viewpoint from our society. At most, you would be able to find good wishes aimed at our government."[179]

Regardless of the reasons that might ease one's criticism of the Jewish community's responses, Rıfat Bali differentiates between the community's formal representatives and its public figures who, in many cases, represent the Jewish community in the eyes of the average Turk. In his opinion, until recently, both types of leaders have preferred expressing their concerns regarding antisemitism privately to Ankara in a sort of "quiet diplomacy," and at the same time express their gratitude to Turkey for its allegedly tolerant attitude toward its minorities instead of going public and demanding that the antisemitic publications in Turkey be abolished. When they began going public, says Bali, it was too late and not only was it not met with encouragement from the media, which had been expected to offer support, it was also met with harsh responses from the Islamist and nationalist sectors in Turkey. This made the Jewish leadership return to their communal invisibility and quiet diplomacy.[180]

In other words, the Jewish community's official approach follows the Kayadez in several aspects.

(2) Active response: After the two businessmen were attacked in Edirne (see earlier), one of the immediate responses should have been to report to the police station. The writer says that as nothing would change the mind of the attacker, there were two options: To leave Turkey and settle somewhere else or to fight in the framework of the law as much as possible. "It was a mistake not to inform the authorities," says D. "It should not be forgotten that Kayadez hasn't been and still isn't helpful." A similar response called for an immediate call to the district attorney. "Even if complaining won't be effective, there is still a need to complain," say others.

In one of the discussions following the antisemitic car posters, a question asking where to complain about the incident, to IHRA (International Holocaust Remembrance Alliance), ECRI, or ADL is raised. The involvement of international institutions and organizations is one of the common options to fight antisemitism in Turkey, or at least to report it. When the famous Turkish singer Yıldız Tilbe tweeted an antisemitic message starting with the words "God bless Hitler," the Jewish community's reaction was very strict and prompt. Except for wide media coverage, it initiated a petition that called for Tilbe's apology.[181] The demand for 'active response' is well expressed by an elderly Turkish Jew who said: "You have to please everyone; the government, the rabbis, the community members. The community still operates as if we were tolerated subjects in the Ottoman Empire, not as if we were equal citizens. They aren't brave like the Armenians."[182]

Unlike the Islamists, Armenians, and Kurds, who challenged Kemalist nationality, Jews have supported the classical Turkish national identity, which might be one of the reasons why Erdoğan's expressions toward the Jews were so harsh. It should be noted that even today these aforementioned communities run 'self-defense' campaigns in order to stand up for their rights to be treated equally. For instance, when Erdoğan said "Someone who wants to say he\she is Kurdish, let them say! What haven't they said about me? They've called me Georgian and even uglier things – Armenian. But I am a Turk,"[183] the Armenian community condemned it publicly, drawing Turkish society's attention to these words and beginning a campaign against them. It should also be noted that "Nefret Söylemi" (hate speech organization) follows and targets hate speeches in the Turkish media.[184]

But it's very obvious that despite Turkey's minorities sharing a similar fate and often being lumped together, there are major differences in their levels of integration from both sides: their own and Turkish society's. İvo Molinas' writings published in Şalom, the Jewish newspaper, often express an active confrontational response. During Operation Protective Edge, for instance, he raised the question of why Israel is the only country in the region whose actions are questioned, while in many other places in the region much suffering is caused. Molinas confronts the generalization of the Jews and strictly opposes the attribution of world evil to them.[185] In order to fight antisemitism, to explain what it means and to distinguish between antisemitism and hate in general, a website entitled "antisemitizm.Info" was founded in late 2014. This is an important attempt to fight antisemitism by examining its historical roots and the ideology behind it. The website is accompanied by a YouTube channel and Facebook page.[186]

For some Jews, 'an active response' might be 'a cultural reply.' As a museum director says in a 2007 interview: "the Jews here have been very careful in showing their culture in public. We want to show ourselves in public, not to be hidden anymore, we like sharing our culture."[187] Being seen in cultural venues seems like a decent response that contributes to the visibility of the Jewish community by some of its members.

Another example is the manifest of Leyla Navaro, a Turkish-Jewish academic from Istanbul, published in *Radikal* shortly after Operation Cast Lead ended. Navaro expressed her concern not only in regard to antisemitism in Turkey, but also for the future of Turkey itself, and she said: "I feel worried, sad, and scared for myself and for my country's future, which is leaning toward racism."[188] In her manifest, Navaro finds it difficult to understand why the Jews are seen as 'different' when they share the same values, culture, and history with the Muslim Turks. She concludes by saying: "if there is no conscious and responsible end, I'm afraid Turkey will be doomed to isolation. Dark isolation."[189]

(3) Distrust of authorities and desperation: F says:

> If it were for the past, I would have said there is no need to fear, but today I cannot say so because security men are being scolded due to daily propaganda that there is no chance that they would take it seriously. I don't remember exactly but in the synagogue in Caddebostan [Asian side of Istanbul] I heard the policeman who was on duty and stood in the entrance saying: "in order to enable them to pray, we cannot commit our Namaz" ... we must already see the facts in Turkey. In my opinion this is not the first incident and won't be the last.

This sort of response is often accompanied by despair from Turkey, as D. says after being exposed to a car poster containing antisemitic text in 2014:

"This country is finished, friends, just finished." This view leads to either remaining in Turkey without any expectation of the Turkish authorities, or making Aliya. It is very clear to Jews that anti-Israel propaganda has released secretive old antisemitic feelings, making Aliya to Israel seems the only solution for some. B says: "I know many of you don't like to hear it but making Aliya is the only solution."[190]

(4) Denial: Some Jews deny the fact that there is antisemitism in Turkey. Some claim that antisemitism exists everywhere and Turkey is no exception.

(5) Taking a pro-government or pro-Muslim stance: This response includes two sub-responses: (i) Ideological support of the Turkish authority or criticism toward Israel (and sometime even an anti-Israel viewpoint). Following Operation Protective Edge, a group of Turkish-Jewish intellectuals condemned being targeted over Israel's recent operations in Gaza, describing attempts to hold them responsible for Israel's policies as "racist." Prominent figures, such as scholar and columnist Soli Özel, leftist writer Roni Margulies, economist Cem Behar, and former radio host and activist Avi Haligua, stressed their opposition to Israel's actions in a letter published on August 29. However, they also added that no one should expect unity of opinion in a community of 20,000 people, and stated that they did not want their opinion to be interpreted based on their identity.[191] The full letter says:

> Israel's latest attack on Gaza led, once again, to cries of "Why does the Jewish community remain silent?" A campaign was even launched that claimed that the Jews of Turkey bear responsibility for what Israel does in Gaza. No citizen of this country is under any obligation to account for, interpret, or comment on any event that takes place elsewhere in the world, and in which he/she has no involvement. There is no onus on the Jewish community of Turkey, therefore, to declare an opinion on any matter at all.... No human community can be monolithic and the Jewish community is not. Its members include people of all kinds, with a great variety of opinions. In the same way the people of Turkey cannot be held responsible for the barbarity of what the ISIS does because a number of Turks are among its fighters, the Jewish community of Turkey cannot be held responsible for what the State of Israel does. It is racism to hold a whole people responsible for the actions of a state and we wish to declare that we are opposed to this. We, the undersigned, are children of Jewish families in Turkey. It is incumbent upon us to express an opinion on the attack on Gaza precisely to the same degree that it is on any other citizen of Turkey, no less, and certainly no more. Nonetheless, we wish to declare that we are opposed to the Israeli state's policies on Gaza, not because we are of Jewish origin, but because we are human. We may not agree on all matters, some of us oppose all of Israel's policies, some of us oppose some of them. But all of us are opposed to Israel's aggression, militarism, expansionism, and the violence it brings upon the Palestinian people.[192]

Erol Aron Bünyel, a Turkish-Jewish actor, agrees with this perception because

> Turkey is a Muslim country and it is clear that people like those who are close to them. I do not expect the Turks to understand or to support Israel and of course this has nothing to do with my Jewishness ... when political discussions of this type arise on the set, I always tell my fellow actors that I have nothing to do with Israel as my family and I have been living here for more than 500 years and Jews have been living here even before some Muslims.[193]

A pragmatic view, such as what one of the community leaders called "quiet diplomacy, not contestation," has worked to the community's advantage compared to the treatment of other minorities. In this way, according to the community leader, the Jewish community has achieved the permission to construct new synagogues and other benefits.[194] Such is the case with Erdoğan's Courage Award, given to him in 2004 for Turkey ensuring protection against all forms of malice against the Jewish community in the past, by the American Jewish Congress (AJ Congress), which demanded that Erdoğan return this award following his harsh criticism of Israel during Operation Protective Edge in 2014. The Turkish-Jewish community condemned the AJ Congress for sending an open letter to Erdoğan demanding that he return the courage award. The Jewish community sent a fierce letter to the American Jewish Congress and Jack Rosen, who is the chairman of the American Jewish Congress.[195] They denounced the congress' demands from Erdogan to return the Prize he received in 2004, due to what they called Erdogan's anti-Semitic assertions. Later, a senior figure of the Turkish Jewish community admitted that the letter was dictated to the community.[196]

Rabbi Haleva expressed this viewpoint very well in an interview on the Israeli website *NRG*, on January 4, 2015. According to Haleva, there is no "governmental antisemitism" in Turkey. Haleva claims he has warm relations with the Turkish prime minister and president and that he and Erdoğan are "good friends" and that Erdoğan even calls him "Haleva." For Haleva, politics "destroys everything." Haleva quotes Erdoğan's "constant sayings" that the Jews of Turkey are under his protection. As long as politics are ignored, the Turkish Jews live in peace in Turkey, he said. The war is between Israel and Palestine, and this war is equivalent to a war between England and France. It does not affect the relations between Judaism and Islam. Israelis and Palestinians can live peacefully when politics are not involved. Furthermore, says Haleva, "I mention and mention again we have no political affinity to the State of Israel. There is our joint religion and love of course but a political relationship does not exist. Israel is Israel and Turkey is Turkey."

Haleva also said that unlike the aforementioned belief, he is not afraid of anyone and thus it is ridiculous to think that anyone imposes on them this supportive viewpoint of the Turkish regime: "everyone who visits Turkey can see that there are no problems. Some people like to fish in troubled water." Haleva admits, though, that antisemitism exists in Turkey "like everywhere in Europe. It was not like that in the past, the Turks love us but with all the unrest they started loving the Muslims."[197]

Shay Cohen, consul general of Israel in Istanbul tends to understand this position:

> the legislation system in Turkey is very different than the ones in Europe and the US: it is prohibited in Turkey to officially establish any organization such as Bney Brith, The Bond, or even AIPAC, which are affiliated with a country other than Turkey. No open transparent community life regarding Israel is possible according to the law. This is why the Rabbinate and the community's chairpersons are afraid of identifying with Israel. They are afraid that this identification would affect the authorities' positive attitudes toward the Jewish community.[198]

Shy Cohen says that the Jews' responses are driven less by fear and more by protecting their interests. "The Jews," he says,

> are threatened physically so they receive official aid from the government, full cooperation between the minorities and the state exists. The government also returns millions of dollars worth of properties to the minorities in Turkey. The Jewish community is afraid to lose all this and that is why they keep quiet. They tell me, "you [Israeli diplomats] come and go but we stay here and we must take care of our interests."[199]

Pragmatism has another manifestation: protecting Turkish Jews by asserting that they are assimilated enough not to pose a threat to the moral and national unity of the Turkish Muslim community. For example, Jefi Kamhi's statement following the *Mavi Marmara* incident: "My father's second wife is the cousin of Egypt's Princess Feride. My sister is a Muslim. My wife is the granddaughter of Sinan Erdebili. My daughters are also Muslim."[200]

Yet, according to Rıfat Bali, the Jews in Turkey have only two possibilities: To continue living in Turkey without complaining about antisemitism as it only exacerbates the situation, or to emigrate.[201]

Sometimes it looks as if the Turkish Jews are just a bargaining chip within Turkish politics. This is what Bilal Macit wrote in *Daily Sabah* regarding the Law of Foundations; an outburst by a former CHP parliamentarian toward AK Party members is still remembered: "You keep defending Agop's possessions, please at least once defend Mehmet's possessions." It should also be remembered that the Law of Foundations issued by the AK Party government in 2006 was partially vetoed by then President Sezer on the grounds that it was against national interests. Furthermore, this year a member of parliament from the MHP, in reaction to the restitution of foundation assets, said: "We will take them all back."[202] Attempting to prove that the AK Party is better for the Turkish Jews,

Macit claims that the CHP, which is a secular party considered "friendly to Jews," is not really like that and the party that really assists the Jews in protecting their rights is the AK Party.

Reflections of awareness

Throughout the years there have been positive voices that have spoken out against antisemitism and called for tolerance. One such voice is journalist Ayşe Önal, who wrote an article protesting the Turkish media's accusation of the Jews for every disaster in the world:

> 335 children and teachers were murdered in Beslan by the Jews. The barbarism of 9/11 was a Jewish plot. Turkish society and family values are being destroyed by the Jews. It is the Jews who are cutting off heads in Iraq. They [the Jews] are so blinded [with hatred] that in order to conceal the Jewish finger [role] in all of that, they sometimes butcher [their fellow] Jews as well. It was them [the Jews] who bombed their own synagogues. And when their own families died, they shed false tears. The Jews are like a punching bag. Hit [them] and hit [them], as much as you can.... Punch [them] as much as you want, with no fear, shame, respect, or sense of boundaries.... In any event, only about 15,000 Jews remain [in Turkey], and they have no voice to be heard. The Jews are a convenient, living shield for all immorality, all murders, savagery, and lies.... If you place a Jew where there is barbarism or fraud, you have solved the problem.... And knowing too well what would await them, nobody has the possibility, or the courage, to ask, "Where are the human rights and freedoms, values of equality, principles of non-discrimination with regard to religion, race, and ethnicity?" If the honor [of the citizens] is indeed under the protection of the [Turkish] constitution, this means that according to the State, Jews are either not human, or not citizens.[203]

Some journalists utilize the same terminology that anti-Semites use in order to reflect the absurdity of their statements. Antisemitic writers often claim that tolerance toward Jews is a crime against Turkey. The Islamist writer Burhan Bozgeyik, for instance, wrote in *Milli Gazete*, on April 13, 2005, that treating the Jews badly harms Turkey:

> Some people in this country are mistaken in how they treat Christians and Jews. Such mistakes harm not only the perpetrators, but also all the young Muslims of this land, and directly or indirectly, this country.[204]

Columnist Mehmet Barlas from *Sabah* says that being 'European' implies that all the people and the 'media' accept a particular philosophy:

> Three days ago, the European Council against Racism and Intolerance (ECRI) published a report on Turkey which included the following criticism of the

Turkish media:[205] Antisemitic propaganda continues to be published by some Turkish media organs. Identifying the Turkish-Jewish community ... with the policies of the State of Israel is frequent in the Turkish media. All those who follow world developments know what this statement means. Publication of materials that incite and generate hatred and hostility against a race or an ethnic group is now considered a 'crime against humanity.' The concept of crime is not only valid for bureaucrats and politicians. For example, Nigerian journalists who engaged in similar practice against their country's minorities were convicted last year by the international court. It is becoming dangerous for the members of the Turkish media to engage in racism as they hide behind the assertion, 'I'm commenting on Middle East politics.' Those who make remarks such as 'anyway, he's a Sabbatean, we know his [real] identity' may cause serious harm to their country and their profession and bring serious problems upon themselves. Those who aspire to be patriots, nationalists, or Arab sympathizers can [easily] turn into Neo-Nazis ... we in the media should refrain from using expressions which do not fit the European pattern. This kind of behavior is 'shameful,' even when not 'criminal.'[206]

Barlas is part of a phenomenon that characterizes the Turkish media in recent years: Whenever there is an antisemitic article, there is almost always a journalist or columnist to respond to these antisemitic publications and defend the Jewish community on one hand and Turkish morals on the other. Yet, the *Mavi Marmara* affair reflected an attempt to deliberately emphasize a distinction between the Israeli people/Jews and the Israeli state/government in most of the Turkish religious-conservative newspapers (except for *Anadolu'da Vakit*). These newspapers condemned antisemitism as a crime against humanity. *Zaman*, for example, called on its readership to evaluate the issue calmly and gave moderate messages; in order to achieve this, the newspaper frequently quoted well-known figures from the Turkish-Jewish community and Jews who are respected worldwide, such as Holocaust survivors or Jewish academics. Other newspapers such as *Yeni Asya* tried to move away from antisemitism by reporting that "the Jews also responded to the Mavi Marmara Attack" (June 3, 2010) and the "rabbis visited the injured activists."[207]

Muslim and non-Muslim intellectuals signed three petitions that were organized throughout the years following the Islamic and Nationalist press' antisemitic publications. These petitions were organized by Ayşe Günaysu and Defne Sandalcı. The first petition was signed by 117 intellectuals and was titled "Zero tolerance for antisemitism," and was published in *Birikim*'s October 2004 issue. The second and third signature campaigns followed Operation Cast Lead in 2009. The second petition was signed by 61 prominent Turks and was titled "Using war as a pretext, there's antisemitism everywhere." It was published in 2009. The third was signed by 250 people and was titled "Antisemitism at every opportunity." Yelda Özcan joined Günaysu and Sandalcı. These petitions were a brave step as the organizers were accused by both leftist and Islamist circles of being pro-Israel and for displaying "hostility to Islam."[208]

The first petition said:

> We, the undersigned, wish to draw attention to the ever present and steadily increasing antisemitism in Turkey, and to share our observations. The various historical examples of racist violence and discrimination against non-Turkish, non-Muslim non-Sunni citizens of the Turkish Republic have, albeit to a limited extent, pointed out and criticized, whereas antisemitism remains, with few exceptions, a subject which is met with silence, underestimation or outright denial ... publications have become vehicles for promoting confusion regarding concepts such as Nazism, fascism, Zionism, the Holocaust, genocide, etc., emptying these of their [true] content and blurring their differences.... The situation illustrates the fact that antisemitism is not limited to saluting Hitler but emerges in many different guises.... Antisemitism today is most actively perpetrated by the Islamist press, a large segment of which has gone so far as to recklessly praise Hitler for his "foresight." Concurrently, there has been an unprecedented array of publications and campaigns against so-called "Sabbataists" whose Jewish roots are traced and emphasized in a manner reminiscent of the Nazi obsession with creating a "pure race," targeting them as the evil-intentioned members of a secret sect which is integral to the "Jewish plot to dominate the world." The rising tide of antisemitism has been allowed to flow unhindered in the channels of the Islamist as well as the mainstream media, and to settle into Turkish daily life and discourse. It is now second nature to find "a Jewish finger" under every stone, and to invent conspiracy theories with "the Jew" as the villain. We hereby proclaim our opposition to this unquestioned and pervasive pattern of antisemitic assumptions and our determination to attain zero tolerance of antisemitism to become informed, to object, to write, to draw, to raise our voice and to maintain solidarity with all who deal and think likewise.[209]

According to Kressel, this petition was not useful. The struggle against antisemitism in the Muslim world cannot begin with *Birikim*'s petition, with a circulation of around 1,000, and of which one-fifth of its signatories were Jews; in Kressel's opinion this sort of petition should be signed by "thousands, tens of thousands, hundreds of thousands, and even millions" in order to be effective.[210] Furthermore, it should not be ignored by the mainstream media and should have an impact. I would argue that the deed itself has great importance since if antisemitism does exist in Turkey, then the intellectuals who signed this petition might have risked themselves by doing so. Another point is that a similar petition in any Western country would yield no different reaction or impact. These actions should be highly encouraged instead of discouraged and they definitely express that Turkey is not lost in the battle against antisemitism.

The AK Party's policies toward non-Muslim communities are a reflection of its adoption of passive secularism. It seems like the AK Party, due to its religious orientation, is active on matters related to non-Muslim minorities in

Turkey, unlike the assertive secularists, such as CHP, which have hardly been active on this issue at all. As the assertive secularists have focused on the exclusion of religion from the public sphere, regardless of which religion, they have quite ignored non-Muslim communities' problems and needs. Moreover, they have been concerned about non-Muslims' rights of association because if the Christians and Jews were free to have legal entities, foundations, and open private temples, then independent Muslim communities in Turkey would want these freedoms too. Furthermore, non-Muslim communities in Turkey have faced several official restrictions since the founding of the Republic, such as the "absence of legal personality, education and training of ecclesiastic personnel as well as full enjoyment of property rights." The AK Party initiated certain reforms to alleviate such conditions. In 2003, the AK Party in the parliament led the legal reform concerning religious places, replacing the word "mosque" in the law with "place of worship." This allowed all religions to open temples in Turkey. In 2004, the AK Party government canceled state surveillance on non-Muslim citizens by abolishing the Subcommittee for Minorities, which had been monitoring non-Muslim citizens for 42 years. Moreover, Erdoğan has made several visits to Jewish synagogues and Christian churches in Turkey, a gesture that has been appreciated by these communities.[211]

Some nationalist laws in Turkey aimed at minorities, including the Jews, began long before the AK Party came to power, but that does not absolve the AK Party of responsibility to change these laws. For instance, on August 1, 2013, *Agos* revealed an official document penned by the Istanbul Provincial Education Directorate, revealing that Turkey's population administration system has been recording citizens who have Armenian, Jewish, or Anatolian Greek (Rum) origins with secret "race codes." According to the *Agos* report, the document, sent from the Istanbul Provincial Education Directorate to the Şişli District National Education office, stated that "since 1923, the secret code of Armenians is '2' on identity registration certificates."[212] As part of the practice, Greeks were coded 1, Armenians were coded 2, Jews were coded 3, Asyrians were coded 4, and "others" (such as Hindus, Buddhists, etc.), were coded 5. These secret "race codes" have been valid since 1923. An official from the population administration in the Turkish Ministry of Interior told the daily *Radikal* newspaper that, first of all, the responsibility of this matter lies with the Ministry of Education and not the Ministry of Interior (as the case began when an Armenian mother tried to register her daughter in an Armenian school and therefore was required to prove that she belongs to code number 2).[213] Second, he mentioned that the practice was conducted during the Ottoman era and that it was conducted in order "to allow minority groups to use their rights stemming from the Lausanne Treaty" signed between Turkey and Western countries, which led to the establishment of the modern Turkish Republic. According to paragraphs 38 and 52 of the Lausanne Treaty, every minority is in charge of its own school children and only they are allowed to register at a community's school.[214]

Another change in the understanding of the Turkish-Jewish community in Turkey is the new program implemented by the Ministries of Education and

Foreign Affairs. In 2008 Turkey became an observer to the Holocaust Task Force (ITF – the Task Force for International Cooperation on Holocaust Education, Remembrance and Research, which decided to change its name to IHRA in 2012), an intergovernmental organization aiming to commemorate and teach the lessons of the Holocaust to the new generations.

Turkey accepted the Stockholm declaration adopted in 2000, defining the aims of the organization and expressing its will to become a member of the ITF. Consequently, the Holocaust has been commemorated every year since 2012, on January 27, the date set by the UN as the International Day of Commemoration in memory of the victims of the Holocaust.[215] In 2015 the ceremony took place for the first time in Turkish history in Ankara. As a result, Turkey invited prominent global experts of Holocaust studies to Ankara to assist in formulating study programs and preparing textbooks, videos, and articles to be taught at schools and universities. Three main institutions participated in an educational gathering, held in Istanbul during the first week of December 2013: the U.S. Holocaust Memorial Museum, Anne Frank House, and the Association for Social Change. Thirty teachers and educational staff were selected to participate in the gathering out of 300 who applied.[216]

The awareness of the Holocaust has been manifested in different ways as well. On January 6, 2012, for instance, the French director Claude Lanzmann's 9.5-hour film *Shoa* (Holocaust), was shown on TRT for the first time in any Muslim country. The screening of *Shoah* was part of the France-based Project Aladdin, which is dedicated to disseminating information about the Holocaust in Arab and Muslim countries through the translation of Holocaust literature into Arabic and Persian, and which seeks to build greater understanding between Muslims and Jews through culture.[217]

Shoah was screened upon a request from the Ministry of Foreign Affairs. It was also screened on January 26 in the ceremony commemorating International Holocaust Day, which took place in Neve Shalom synagogue in Istanbul. It should also be noted here that the ceremony commemorating International Holocaust Day has been attended in recent years by an increasing number of Turkish officials who wish to honor this day in general and the Jewish community in Turkey in particular. For instance, the 2012 ceremony was attended by the governor of Istanbul, Hüseyin Avni Mutlu, Ambassador Ertan Tezgör who represented the Ministry of Foreign Affairs but who is also the Turkish representative on the Task Force, and Beyoğlu's mayor, Ahmet Misbah. Cemil Çiçek, spokesperson of the parliament, Minister of Foreign Affairs Ahmet Davutoğlu, and Head of the Presidency of Religious Affairs Mehmet Görmez sent a message. The former head of the Jewish community, Silvyo Ovadya, said that "this could be the proof that there is no discrimination in Turkey ... we should really congratulate this."[218]

On January 27, 2013, the ceremony took place in the Ortaköy Synagogue Etz HaChayim in Istanbul and was attended by Greek Orthodox Patriarch Bartholomeos, Ambassador Ertan Tezgör, foreign diplomats, academics, and Aykan Erdemir, a member of parliament from the opposition Republican People's

Party. Speaker of the Parliament Cemil Çiçek, Deputy Prime Minister Bülent Arinç, Foreign Minister Davutoğlu, and Minister for European Affairs Egemen Bagis all sent messages to the ceremony. In 2013, for the first time, the ceremony was conducted at Kadir Has University and not at a Jewish institution.[219]

For İvo Molinas from *Şalom* newspaper, in a country where "antisemitism increases every passing day," it is even more meaningful than usual.[220] In addition to the film screening, Aladdin Project also organized a conference in April at Bahçeşehir University in Istanbul, on the immigration of Jewish scientists to Turkey during World War II, and their contribution to the modernization and reform of universities there. In June, despite the tensions between the two countries resulting from the 2010 flotilla affair, Turkish representatives arrived in Israel to participate in a conference at Yad VaShem on teaching the Holocaust.[221] In addition, the Aladdin Project, along with the IHRA and the ICHEIC (International Commission on Holocaust Era Insurance Claims) held at the Yad Vashem International School in June 2014 a seminar about teaching the Holocaust, where 15 Turkish academics participated. The seminar was a continuation of an international conference that took place in Ankara in 2013.[222] According to Uzer, this interest in the Holocaust might be a tactical tool, an opening to Israel in light of the crisis of the past few years. Whatever the motive, the fact that the issue is discussed in a Muslim-majority country is significant. It disproves the allegation that there is radical Islamist hegemony in the AK Party's thinking.

Another significant development was the Anne Frank exhibition at Kadir Has University in Istanbul in March 2012, attended by Ertan Tezgör, head of the Turkish ITF delegation. More events dealing with the Holocaust are to be expected. These events are promoted by the AK Party government.[223] On the other hand, according to Burak Bekdil, Western observers concluded that the screening of *Shoah* was a key part of Turkey's observance of the International Holocaust Remembrance Day; that it was part of Turkey's policy to separate its differences with the Israeli government from the Jewish people; that it was a shrewd diplomatic move by the government. According to Bekdil, this description can only fit into the rhetoric and work of another group – the Gülenists. The Gülenists have put their signature on something that is completely consistent with their declared philosophy regarding interfaith dialogue:

> But I know Turkish politics enough to guess that "Shoah" cannot be a must-see documentary for any member of the Cabinet, its cherry-picked civil servants, and a majority of Turks who do not hide their hatred for Israel/Zionism/Jewry. The surprise smells less like a "government overture" and more like a "correction from the government's partners across the Atlantic.... The Turks have not become Zionists because their state TV screened Shoah."[224]

Aykan Erdemir also suspects the agenda behind the AK Party's rising tide of interest in the Holocaust, but he believes all these efforts have been made in order to gain access to the European Union. This strategy also stands behind the officials' participation in Holocaust Day ceremonies and other "symbolic gestures," as Erdemir says, aimed at deluding the public. "Even when they speak at these ceremonies," says Erdemir, they always refer to the Jews as 'they' or 'you' but never as 'us' and that fits well into the AK Party's neo-Ottomanist agenda."[225]

Though stressing the meaningfulness of Holocaust Day ceremonies, İvo Molinas from *Şalom* also criticized them by saying that there is no logical explanation to the fact that, on the one hand, the Holocaust Day ceremonies take place in Turkey, but on the other hand, Jews are exposed to hate speech. According to Molinas, ceremonies are meaningful but useless in fighting prejudice that can only be combated with education and law.[226] Corry Guttstadt agrees. She claims that Turkish politicians from the AK Party participate in the Holocaust Remembrance Day simply in order to deny the existence of antisemitism, as well as racism and discrimination in general in Turkey, and also to "celebrate the myth of Turkey's 'rescue of the Jews' and to deny Armenian genocide."[227]

Unlike them, Taner Aydın, who served as chief of Anadolu Agency's Jerusalem Bureau between 2012 and 2015 (Anadolu Ajansı, state-run news agency), claims that

> the commemoration of the Holocaust as well as the property return to non-Muslim communities is a "historical justice" which could not be conducted in the Kemalist era. Indeed this is one of the Copenhagen criteria but it is just as well a manifestation of the civilization code process that Turkey has been going through.[228]

In fact, the Holocaust commemoration and return of property are just another proof for Turkish society that the rule of the AK Party is just and fair and corrects a historical injustice in contrast to the Kemalist rule/CHP which caused this injustice. Again, the Jewish community can be seen as part of a bigger political rivalry.

The Holocaust memorial ceremony was followed on February 24, 2015 by the first official ceremony to commemorate the *Struma* sinking after 73 years.[229] Since the *Struma* was drowned in Turkey's nautical territory, the ceremony is conducted on the Black Sea coast (in Sarayburnu, nearby Atatürk Monument) in Istanbul. The official ceremony was preceded by non-official ceremonies in previous years, where Jews and non-Jews participated.[230] In the official ceremony, Ömer Çelik, the minister of culture and tourism, represented the government for the first time in Turkish history. Also in attendance were Istanbul's mayor, Kadir Topbaş, Vasip Şahin, a Turkish civil servant, currently serving as the governor of Istanbul Province (Istanbul Valisi), and several bureaucrats from the Ministry of Foreign Affairs, along with other Muslim and non-Muslim participants. It was widely reported in the Turkish media.[231]

On March 30, 2012, *Radikal* published an article describing how İnsan Hakları İnceleme Komisyonu (Turkish Parliament Human Rights Investigation Committee's Subcommittee for Terrorism) member Mehmet Metiner of the AK

Party approached every representative of the Jewish community who was invited to this committee the day before, and apologized to each and every one of them for the terrorism and violent incidents perpetrated by al-Qaeda on November 15, 2003, in which the Neve Shalom and Beth Israel synagogues were bombed. The apology was followed by statements made by representatives of the Jewish community, such as Sami Herman, chairperson of the Jewish community, and his vice-chairperson, İshak İbrahimzade, expressing their fear of entering synagogues after the bombing, as well as similar events held against Turkish Jews such as the 1986 bombing of the Neve Shalom and Bet Israel synagogues, and the murder of the Jewish dentist Yasef Yahya in August 2003. According to the police, the murderers of Yahya were Islamic fundamentalists and they murdered Yahya simply because he was Jewish. They chose him when they saw his name in a dentistry advertisement on the street, but Jack Moreno, who is also a member of the Turkish Dental Association (Türk Dişhekimleri Birliği) and who was also sent death threats at the same time, insists that the murder did not have an antisemitic motive but a financial one. The murderers wanted money and they chose Yahya because he was both rich and socially active.[232]

The question of protection and security in the synaogues in Turkey is problematic and complicated because, on the one hand, this is the right way to defend the Turkish Jews, but on the other hand it enhances hostility toward them and creates more walls between them and the non-Jews in Turkey. Burak Bekdil from *Hürriyet Daily News* mentioned that unlike what some think, security for Jewish buildings is justified and not a sign of paranoia.[233] The Jewish community in Turkey, although anxious, did not take collective action demanding public attention to this murder.[234] That same year Herman said: "for the last 26 years we have been entering our synagogues with a guilt complex ... it is much easier to enter an airport," meaning Jews enter their highly protected synagogue as if they have to feel guilty for something they have done wrong. In his apology, Metiner said: "as a matter of fact, we were the killers. As Turks we owe you an apology. We separated you from us. We did not protect you. There is no significance to hide behind any other words."[235]

This terror attack was indeed a reason for concern; according to the ECRI report it was this incident that began a fearful atmosphere amid Turkish Jewry. Until 2003, the Turkish-Jewish community enjoyed a relatively peaceful existence in Turkey, aside from a few isolated antisemitic incidents. In the opinion of representatives of the Jewish community, the climate changed suddenly, mainly in the wake of a series of international terrorist attacks in November 2003, of which two synagogues in Istanbul were targets. There is now a feeling of insecurity in the Jewish community because of these and other incidents, such as physical assaults on individuals purely because they are Jewish, at least one of which proved fatal. Antisemitic propaganda continues to appear in certain sections of the media and it is apparently not unusual to come across sweeping statements in the press in which Turkey's Jewish community is equated with the policies of the State of Israel. It also appears that legal proceedings are not always instituted under Article 216 (312 in the older version) in order to punish those who make antisemitic remarks in public, although this article prohibits incitement to racial hatred. However, the ECRI notes with satisfaction that the police are working with the Jewish community to improve security and that antisemitic remarks made by the son of one of the perpetrators of the aforementioned attacks have been condemned by the government and that legal proceedings were instituted against him by the judicial authorities.[236]

Much of the changes in favor of the non-Muslim minorities, as well as ethnic Muslim minorities, are a result of the Turkish campaign to access the EU. According to EU requirements, the government has to enable minorities to promote their identities through allowing the use of their mother tongue in political communication, education, and radio and TV broadcasting. In doing this, Turkey takes measures to adhere to EU standards regarding minority protection as laid down in the post-Cold War era in the different European institutions, such as the Council of Europe. The first reform package, dated February 2002, amended Article 216 (312 in the older version) of the Turkish penal code with an aim to further expand the scope of freedom of expression relating to ethnocultural diversity. Later, in an effort to solve problems related to the property rights of the non-Muslim foundations, the third reform package introduced a modification to the Law of Foundations introduced in 2008. As a result of the law, property worth $2.5 billion was returned to minority foundations. The minister of culture and tourism, Ömer Çelik, stated "you can go back to your country," referring to the Jews and Christians, due to some mistakes in the past.[237] Community foundations were given the right to acquire and possess any kind of property at their disposal. Religious foundations can purchase property provided that they are registered, and a procedure has been introduced for recovering property that has been lost.

The law has also helped to rectify various inequalities by granting places of worship belonging to minority religious groups the same status as mosques, including the payment of electricity bills, for example. Before, the Directorate of Religious Foundations paid for electricity only in the case of mosques. The law on construction, furthermore, now covers places of worship and not just mosques. In addition, the Mufti's permission to build a non-Muslim place of worship is no longer required.[238] As long as the minorities can prove ownership and present this proof to the authorities within six month's time, they can register their existing property as their own. To make it even easier, they were given an 18-month extension by the sixth reform package in 2003.

Foundation property issue was also dealt with on August 27, 2011. İvo Molinas said:

> The view of AK Party governments toward non-Muslims and their foundations is in line with contemporary democratic norms which is a silent revolution and should be acknowledged as the starting point to ending the everlasting discrimination and alienation experienced on our soil. The restitution of the rights of non-Muslim foundations thanks to the laws adopted in 2003 and 2008 has been a very significant historic milestone.[239]

Since then, according to Türkmen and Öktem, many properties have been returned to the foundations. Hatemi, a long-term advocate of non-Muslim minority rights in Turkey, has called it "a revolution."[240] Yet, non-Muslim minorities continue to have problems, particularly due to the lack of legal recognition for foundations and lasting restrictions on religious education.[241] For instance, clerics of any religion other than Islam cannot register and obtain legal status for the non-Muslim religious communities. Instead, they have to operate indirectly through foundations or associations.[242] An ECRI report supports this claim by saying that minority religious groups still experience problems in practice. The above-mentioned laws, some of which were enacted over a year ago, have not really come into force in the opinion of representatives of the religious communities concerned. According to these representatives, they encounter major resistance whenever they call for the laws to be applied, including notably from the Directorate of Religious Foundations, which is affiliated with the Prime Minister's Office. The Directorate is said to be unduly restrictive in how it implements the legislative changes, rendering them virtually useless.[243] For İvo Molinas, the fact that the government supports minority schools, opens churches, restores synagogues, and returns minorities' properties, without applying legal sanctions on antisemitism, is pretty confusing. Moreover, Molinas is not too optimistic regarding the steps taken by the government; as he says, "we will have to wait and see what the cost of this transition will be."[244]

According to Türkmen and Öktem, the Turkish government's attitude toward minorities was not in order to satisfy the EU and match its standards, but was a genuine turning point in traditional Turkish policy. It was the first time in contemporary Turkey that foreign policy had a positive effect on the fate of the minorities, especially due to the transformation of the state/political system via the adoption of the reforms and the transformation of minority groups from objects of top-down state policy into sub-national actors involved in Turkey's democratization process.[245] The reason for the change in Turkey is also an inner process that Turkey is undergoing; in other words, the democratization process led by the AK Party. After the long-running public debates over the implementation of a "democracy package," an initiative to extend rights to Turkey's disadvantaged minorities, hate crime entered the Turkish statute books for the first time in December 2013. Hate and prejudice crimes are defined as "crimes committed against someone or some group based on their language, race, nationality, skin color, gender, disability, political views, philosophical beliefs or religion." Yet, unlike the preferred definition of the Organization for Security and Cooperation in Europe (OSCE), it lacks criteria based on ethnicity and sexual orientation. In addition, the largest ethnic minority in Turkey, Kurds, are not specifically included in the regulation. The Parliamentary Assembly of the Council of Europe (PACE) issued a public declaration in January 2014 to draw attention to these gaps in Turkey's hate crime legislation.[246] The punishment set for hate crimes would be up to three years' imprisonment.

The democratization package also aims to reduce hate crimes, bringing harsher punishment for these types of crimes. Erdoğan said sentences for crimes related to racist, hate, or discriminatory speech or attacks would increase. He also said that the amendments will make it easier for groups and particularly individuals to freely perform their religious duties. A council tasked with fighting discrimination and for equality is also being established. The punishments for hate crime are as follows: The punishment for first degree murder based on hatred was increased to life imprisonment; the punishment for injuring someone based on hate was increased to six years in prison instead of two years; the punishment for torturing due to prejudice or hate crime conducted by a public employee increased from eight to fifteen years. Those who try by force or by threat to change someone's thoughts or to prevent religious, social, political, or philosophical beliefs could be punished with between one and three years in jail. Whoever prevents by force or by threat someone from praying or committing a religious ritual as an individual or as a group could be punished with between one and three years in jail.[247]

On March 2, 2014, a draft of a law also known as "democratization package," which reinforces basic rights and liberties, was accepted by the Turkish Grand Assembly. A person or group who prevents another's engagement in common economic activity may be punished by 1–3 years' imprisonment. The punishment for the prevention of public activity or prevention of someone benefiting from a service given by a public authority is 2–5 years of imprisonment. According to the law, the use of the term "çengene" (gypsy) is prohibited. The following are all statements that will exacerbate the penalty: Kızılbaş, filthy Turk, gypsy thief, filthy infidel, Armenian progeny, Yazid, bigot, Negro, atheist.[248]

Whether the democratization process in Turkey was made to coincide with EU demands, or whether it fulfills the AK Party's interests, Aykan Erdemir says what many seem to think: "I don't attribute much importance to the latent agenda behind the AK Party's 'good deeds.' I keep on praising the AK Party every time they come up with a positive move toward reducing hatred in Turkey."[249] Fatih Gökhan Diler from *Agos* agrees that the motives behind the government's agenda are not important, although he does believe that the government returning property to the non-Muslim communities is insincere as it reflects an alleged change in the government's discourse but not in the practice.[250]

In addition, despite whatever interests it might serve, the AK Party's positive move toward reducing hatred in Turkey resulted in harsh criticism even from AK Party supporters. An example is Servet Avcı's criticism published in *Yeniçağ* (this Turkish daily newspaper is a synthesis of radical Islam and MHP) on October 17, 2013. According to Avcı, it is important to understand who stands behind the law against hate crimes. A law against those who commit any hate crime or disturb the public peace, or provoke an individual or a group on the basis of race, religion, or school, or committed against regional groups who hold different characteristics, already exists in Turkey (Turkish penalty law nos. 125, 126, and 216) – why should a new law be created? The hate crime is even worse if it is committed by any media organization, according to Turkish law no. 218. This law, says Avcı:

In fact, it [this law] CAN be a boomerang and will hit, strike one day those who prepared it [the law] ... the definition, except for what is mentioned above, whatever the need of whoever it was, was, it would serve the influence of rate power of tomorrow's governments/regimes and would damage the opposition. We are moving toward a concept/an order from calling a gavur-gavur [Gavur is a derogatory name for a non-muslim] to almost not calling evil evil, if he is from a different ethnic background. [In other words, he says that if the hate crime law is cast, people would not be able to call evil evil if the evil person is not a Muslim because it will be considered hate speech.] Corruption or disorder caused by an ethnic group or person will not be explained, understood by their "national" background. The history would have to carefully told according to this [meaning, the history would not be able to mention the ethnicity or nationality of one who did wrong]. It is obvious that this law will be used for narrowing the activity fields of those who are not under media control. The law is unclear and it leaves a wide area of interpretation to the judges. Even those who belong to the conservative press and support the AK Party were surprised and curious as to where this law came from. The blame [for this law] is on the Zionists, sexual freedom advocates, and especially to the minority lobbies in Istanbul.[251]

But some did see the AK Party's move as a positive one. Even the ECRI praised Turkey for their reforms regarding human rights and tolerance: Major changes have taken place in Turkey with regards to human rights, with various repercussions for the fight against racism and racial discrimination. The ECRI notes that Turkey now has numerous entities tasked with reviewing human rights compliance, whether from a general point of view or by monitoring individual applications. These include the Petitions Committee and the Human Rights Committee of the Grand National Assembly. On the governmental side, Act No. 4643 from April 12, 2001 created a series of human rights bodies, all of which come under the wing of the prime minister: the Human Rights Presidency, human rights councils operating at the provincial and district level, the Human Rights Advisory Committee, the High Council for Human Rights, the Human Rights Inquiries Committee, and the National Committee on the Decade for Human Rights Education. However, the ECRI notes that there is still no national independent specialized body in Turkey for combating racism and racial discrimination, and believes that one should be set up as soon as possible. Such a body should be able to play a role in raising awareness of the problems of racism and racial discrimination in Turkey.[252]

As for Erdoğan, he made Israel–Nazi comparisons during Operation Protective Edge, but Erdoğan also called for the country's Jews to be left alone. "I don't approve of any [bad] attitude towards our Jewish citizens in Turkey, despite all this. Why? They are citizens of this country."[253] During the same operation, Ahmet Hakan from *Hürriyet* created a list of "7 things you shouldn't do when you curse Israel" and although this column is not ideal, it distinguishes, at least, between the Turkish Jews and Israelis; the recommendations say:

give up on annoying the Jews living in Turkey ... they are not Israelis, they are your citizens. Second recommendation: don't point at the Turkish Jews don't target these people who are not responsible for Israel's designated politics. Third: don't hide behind the man who caused the greatest atrocities in history while saying "there is a need in a new Hitler" ... fifth: don't state that "Israel put Turkish Jewry in this difficult situation with its actions." A Turkish Jew is a citizen of Turkey.... You will be shocked when he says "why should I be in a difficult position because of what other countries are doing" ... sixth: do not threaten Israel using the Turkish Jews. Threatening a handful of Jews here is not a manly behavior to challenge Israel. Seventh: don't be as merciless and unjust as Israel. Make sure you separate the words "Jew" and "Israel" in every sentence.[254]

Another overture to the Jewish community of Turkey under AK Party rule is adding the Turkish-Jewish community's newspaper, *Şalom*, to the library of the Turkish Grand National Assembly for the first time.[255]

Another point of sanity within the Turkish political discourse is the fact that even during Operation Protective Edge, calls for a differentiation between Israelis and Jews were heard. Such is the campaign published on the www.change.org website and all over social networks. The campaign, which gathered several hundred signatures, declares:

We don't want to seem as if we did not hear the voice of antisemitism which is hiding behind the increasing anti-Israel sentiment. On July 15th in *Yeni Akit* Faruk Köse's article and many similar ones, even beyond well known antisemitic language, they openly threaten Turkish Jews and invite aggression. In articles throughout the history of the state, government and non-salaried officials of government in newspaper and magazine articles, it is repeated that native potential guilty people, Jews, are invited to prove their loyalty. The ones who can't prove their loyalty are declared that their lives are in danger. Humiliation and threats reached the point of inviting Jews to leave the country. While several opposition groups claim they are in solidarity with Palestine, they don't see that Islamists cannot create a different language than antisemitism. To be silent to the calls of "death to Jews" you have to forget the 1934 Trakya events, 6–7 September Maraş, Çorum, Madımak Hotel, Hırant Dink, in short the history of this nation is full of genocide. We remember. In the name of solidarity with Palestine we actively defy aggression towards Jews and antisemitic actions and rhetoric.[256]

Again, although antisemitism reached its peak during Operation Protective Edge, the diatribe against antisemitism and the attempts to differentiate between the Turkish Jews and Israel, just like the aforementioned campaign, are more evident than in previous years. The chair of the Turkish Grand Assembly, Cemil Çiçek, said in a TV interview:

This is Turkey's attitude, which carries out politics, this distinction must be conveyed well ... it is not a special attitude against the Jews. Especially from the viewpoint of our citizens, this distinction must be made well. To the best of my knowledge, we have 30,000 Jewish citizens. They are dear people of this country. Exactly like you and like me, they are legal and rightful citizens of this country, there are people [Jews] showing their efforts to contribute to the prosperity of the country. I know it due to some of my previous positions. I, myself, am a witness to their efforts made in Turkey's favor.[257]

The AK Party's vice-chairperson, Yalçın Akdoğan, said:

A stalk and straw must not be confused. We criticize the State of Israel. The criticism is not directed at a Jew living anywhere in the world nor to Israeli society. There is a need to act according to common sense. No one should attribute Israel's injustice to them [Jews]. No Jew will be tested according to his origin.[258]

The calls against antisemitism came from religious figures as well, like Sunni Imam Ahmet Taşkıran, who said that those who attack the Jewish citizens of Turkey actually damage the brotherhood message of the Quran:

Their only aim is to provoke society. There is no such tendency of hatred in Islam.... I invite all Muslim people in Turkey to use their common sense against those who want to place hatred among brothers and sisters who have been living side-by-side for hundreds of years in this country. What keeps us together is the brotherhood dynamic of Islam, and those who want to terrorize Jewish citizens in Turkey only aim to connect Islam to such sort of bad behavior.[259]

The minister of culture, Ömer Çelik, also rejected calls for a boycott, saying:

The reaction shown against those who murder victims in Gaza is a right. However, trying to turn this rightful reaction into a reaction against Jewish people in general, and Turkish citizens of Jewish descent in particular and to synagogues, has nothing to do with right.[260]

Bülent Şenay, a professor of philosophy and religious studies at Uludağ University in Bursa, and a human rights adviser for the OSCE, said it is not fair to turn criticism against Israel's state policies into an antisemitism discourse. There is no antisemitism in the cultural genetics of Turkish-Islam tradition. In every culture there can be some discourses and prejudices aimed at stereotyping and sometimes humiliating some segments deemed as 'others.' But, that line of thought cannot be generalized to society as a whole.[261] He also mentioned that Islamic culture has been and will continue to be a guarantee against antisemitic rhetoric in Turkey. In addition, he said that antisemitism is, just like Islamophobia, a hate speech and a hate crime. Şenay added that those who engage in anti-Israel debates should make their opinions clear without falling into the trap of antisemitism. Regarding the use of the Quran, he said:

> Islam and the Quran are not antisemitic. The criticism of Jews in the Quran is of a theological nature. In addition, in the famous constitution of Medina, penned by the Prophet Muhammad, Arabs, Jews and all other segments of society were described as one community with religious freedoms.[262]

Talip Küçükcan agreed that raising criticism against Israel should not be confused with antisemitism, which means being against Jews because of their identity.

> With the deepening of nation-state ideologies and identity politics, an effort to establish homogeneous nations rather than multicultural structures has emerged, leading to some discrimination and infringements of rights of ethnic and religious minorities. Islam is a religion that predicates itself on tolerance against other beliefs and cultures as well as religious freedoms. It is not fair to generalize some conjectural developments with the essence of the religion. Islam rejects categorical hatred against Jews and a language of violence. Antisemitism is not a by-product of Islamic culture and does not take root among Muslims. For sure, Muslims have the right to criticize, condemn, and protest Israel's state policies, and cannot be considered as antisemitic when using this right. However, when benefitting from that right, they should pay attention to the language used and should not focus their anger against Jews or Jewish institutions.[263]

But more important than individual opinions are the actions of the leftist organization "Say Stop to Racism and Nationalism" (Irkçılığa ve Milliyetçiliğe DurDe, or "DurDE"), founded in February 2007 to combat racism and nationalism and which has grown rapidly since then. DurDe is a grassroots organization and has local groups in the main cities in Turkey. DurDe has carried out three major campaigns and organized various events since its foundation. It is engaged in several major campaigns, including the "Apologizing to our Armenian brothers and sisters" campaign. DurDe initiated a campaign against the growing antisemitism in Turkey. In August 2014, DurDe initiated a campaign titled "Say stop to racist attacks against the Jewish citizens of the Republic of Turkey."[264]

> Recently we have been following with concern the racist-hatred propaganda that is being systematically spread by some parties against our Jewish citizens. In this context, we want to draw attention to the hateful statements against the Jews of Turkey and the racist attacks that can be purportedly justified by those saying it is a reason or excuse for the bloody attacks which the State of Israel is doing in Gaza. The media, state officials, and

politicians bear a large responsibility on this issue. From this point of view, including members of parliament of the governing party as well, the antisemitic-fed-declarations of politicians in recent days have reached a concerning extent.[265]

"Say stop to racism" is part of numerous groups and organizations devoted to combating hate speech and racism (which have begun to include antisemitism under the umbrella of "hate speech" in recent years). Among them is the "Legal campaign against hate crimes" (Nefret Suçları Yasa Kampanyası; nefretme.net) and the Association of Social Change (Sosyal Değişim Derneğş; www.sosyaldegisim.org), established in 2009.[266]

For this and the aforementioned reasons, Fatih Gökhan Diler from *Agos* is convinced that Turkish society is undergoing a social transformation, because minorities' lives are much better now than in the past. They feel much more comfortable in the streets or in public spaces and institutions.[267]

Notes

1 Soner Cağaptay, "Where goes the U.S. –Turkish relationship?," *Middle East Quarterly*, 1, 4 (2004): www.meforum.org/657/where-goes-the-us-Turkish-relationship, retrieved July 4, 2011.
2 www.vho.org/aaargh/fran/livres8/AntisemTurkish.pdf, retrieved September 2, 2013.
3 Hirsh, "Hostility to Israel and antisemitism," p. 1419.
4 Interview in Istanbul, July 29, 2013.
5 www.vho.org/aaargh/fran/livres8/AntisemTurkish.pdf; the entire article appears here: Ayşe Hür, "Kavgam ve Siyon Protokolleri," *Radikal*, March 13, 2005: www.radikal.com.tr/radikal2/kavgam_ve_siyon_protokolleri-872397#, retrieved October 10, 2013. For comparing the number of antisemitic books and the effect of the political situation in Turkey on their publication by ideological groups throughout the years in Turkey, see Rıfat Bali's tables: Bali, *Antisemitism and Conspiracy Theories*, pp. 254–255.
6 www.vho.org/aaargh/fran/livres8/AntisemTurkish.pdf, retrieved September 2, 2013.
7 www.memri.org/report/en/print1388.htm, retrieved October 10, 2013.
8 In Istanbul, Turkey, on November 15, 2003, two car-bomb attacks were carried out simultaneously at the Beth Israel and Neve Shalom synagogues. The synagogues were full of Sabbath congregants when the blasts went off; 29 people were killed, and hundreds were wounded. A local organization influenced by, and under the aegis of, Al-Qaeda carried out the attacks.
9 No author, "Salih Mirzabeyoğulu'na tahliye," *Cumhuriyet*, July 28, 2014: www.cumhuriyet.com.tr/haber/turkiye/97709/Salih_Mirzabeyoglu_na_tahliye.html, retrieved October 23, 2014.
10 All quoted in: www.memri.org/report/en/print1388.htm, retrieved October 10, 2013.
11 Ibid.
12 Ottoman Sultan Abdülhamid II (1842–1918) was dethroned in 1909 by the Young Turks revolution.
13 Quoted in: www.memri.org/report/en/print1388.htm, retrieved October 10, 2013.
14 No author, "Atatürk'ü İsrail öldürmüş!," *Rota Haber*, June 21, 2013: http://haber.rotahaber.com/Ataturku-israil-oldurmus_378081.html. Tezcan was much interviewed in the Turkish media on this topic: www.youtube.com/watch?v=kY_kDIRslnU, retrieved October 15, 2013.

15 Murathan Mungan, *Merhaba Asker (Murathan Mungan'ın Seçtikleriyle)* (Istanbul: Metis, 2014).
16 Pınar Öğüç, "'Her şeyin normalleşmesi Türkiye'yi açık tımarhaneye çevirdi' *Radikal*, March 3, 2014: www.radikal.com.tr/yazarlar/pinar_ogunc/her_seyin_normallesmesi_turkiyeyi_acik_timarhaneye_cevirdi-1179216, retrieved March 10, 2014.
17 Ibid.
18 No author, "Murathan Mungan, BDP Siyaset Akademisi'nde ders Verdi," *Radikal*, January 28, 2012: www.radikal.com.tr/turkiye/murathan_mungan_bdp_siyaset_akademisinde_ders_verdi-1077036, retrieved March 10, 2014.
19 www.vho.org/aaargh/fran/livres8/antisemTur.pdf, retrieved August 14, 2012.
20 Sergius Nilus, *Siyon Liderlerinin Protokolleri: ikinci basım*, second edition (Istanbul: Nokta Kitap, 2005). The book is available on many internet bookstores such as ideafix and others.
21 Ford, *Beynelmilel Yahudi*.
22 Sami Sabit Karman, *Yahudi Tarihi ve Siyon Önderlerinin Protokolleri* (Ankara: Yeni Cezaevi Matbaası, 1943).
23 Kemal Yaman (ed.), *Millet Düşmanlarının İhanet Planları*, (İstanbul: Otağ Yayınları, 1971).
24 Adolf Hitler, *Komünistler ve Beynelmılel Yahudi* (İstanbul: Abdullah Işıklar Kitabevi, 1963).
25 www.vho.org/aaargh/fran/livres8/antisemTur.pdf, retrieved October 15, 2013. *Kavgam* was published by many book publishers such as: Adolf Hitler, *Kavgam* (Konya: Mola Kitap, 2010). Most of them, on ideafix website for instance, are sold out: www.idefix.com/kitap/kavgam-adolf-hitler/tanim.asp?sid=G45MUQN4HM1M4ILBTSNT, retrieved December 1, 2013. In 2010 Kavgam also appeared as a manga comic book; see: Adolf Hitler, *Kavgam* (Istanbul: Karşı Yayınları/Çizgi Roman Dizisi, 2010).
26 Bali, *Antisemitism and Conspiracy Theories*, p. 256.
27 Bali, "The banalization of hate," p. 311.
28 Traudl Junge, *Hitler'in Sekreteri* (Istanbul: Alkım Yayınevi, 2004); Aytunç Altındal, *Bilinmeyen Hitler* (Istanbul: Alfa Yayıncılık, 2004).
29 www.byegm.gov.tr/turkce/haber/trkyede-ndrmdek-kavgam-ktabi-y-satarken-endeler-artiriyor/22387, retrieved January 13, 2012.
30 Hür, "Kavgam ve Siyon Protokolleri."
31 www.byegm.gov.tr/turkce/haber/trkyede-ndrmdek-kavgam-ktabi-y-satarken-endeler-artiriyor/22387, retrieved January 13, 2012.
32 For more examples, see: Landau, "Tofaot shel Antishemiyut," pp. 226–227.
33 Reha Oğuz Türkan, *Solcular ve Kızıllar* (İstanbul: Bozkurtçu Yayını, 1943); Mustafa Hakki Akansel, *Türkün Kitabı: Türl ırkı hakkında tetkiler* (İstanbul: Kenan Matbaası, 1943). See in: Landau, "Tofaot shel Antishemiyut," pp. 227–228.
34 Interview in Istanbul, February 26, 2015.
35 Recai Yayaoğlu, *Yahudi Psikolojisi* (Istanbul: Nesil Yayınları), 2010.
36 Among Yalçın's works are: *Hangi Erbakan* (Ankara: Öteki Yayınevi, 1999); *Bay Pipo, Bir MİT Görevlisinin Sıra Dışı Yaşamı: Hiram Abbas* (Istanbul: Doğan Kitapçılık, 2000); *Behçet Cantürk'ün Anıları* (Istanbul: Doğan Kitapçılık, 2003); *Binbaşı Ersever'in İtirafları* (Istanbul: Kaynak Yayınları, 1996); *Reis Gladio'nun Türk Tetikçisi* (Istanbul: Doğan Kitapçılık, 2003); *Teşkilat'ın İki Silahşörü* (Istanbul: Doğan Kitapçılık, 2001). On Yalçın, see Rıfat Bali's piece: www.rifatbali.com/images/stories/dokumanlar/what_is_efendi_telling_us.pdf, retrieved November 3, 2013.
37 Hoff, "Normalizing antisemitism in Turkey," pp. 185, 190.
38 Dağı, "Yeni anti-Semitler kimler?"
39 www.vho.org/aaargh/fran/livres8/antisemTur.pdf, retrieved October 10, 2013. The book is: Soner Yalçın, *Efendi: Beyaz Türklerin Büyük Sırrı* (Istanbul: Doğan Kıtap, 2004).

40 Yalçın Küçük is referred to in Turkey as 'Hoca' (learned respectful teacher). He was given this title by *Hürriyet* editor in chief Enis Berberoğlu in a poll conducted by the paper of the "10 most influential Turks." He was arrested in connection with the Ergenekon trial investigation in 2009 and was released in 2014. See: Bali, *Antisemitism and Conspiracy Theories*, p. 45. Some of his books include: Yalçın Küçük, *İsimlerin İbranileştirilmesi Tekelistan* (İstanbul Salyangöz: Yayınları, 2008); Yalçın Küçük, *Şebeke "Network" 1* (İstanbul: İthaki Yayınları, 2004). Bali notes a few more cases of anti-Semites who are considered intellectuals and gain appreciation and respect in Turkey. See: Bali, *Antisemitism and Conspiracy Theories*, pp. 86–89.
41 Among his bestseller books.
42 Ergün Poyraz, *Musa'nın Çocukları Tayyip ve Emine* (Istanbul: Togan Yayıncılık, 2007). The list can be found here: www.uslanmam.com/edebiyat/244268-2007-yili-icersinde-turkiye-hangi-kitaplari-okudu.html, retrieved Februry 23, 2011.
43 www.aktifhaber.com/ergun-poyraza-verilen-ceza-833960h.htm, retrieved October 14, 2013.
44 www.internethaber.com/ergun-poyraza-da-agir-ceza-geldi-568066h.htm#, retrieved 23 December 2013.
45 No author, "Eruygur blamed for siphoning money through fake firm," *Today's Zaman*, October 16, 2010, retrieved November 25, 2013.
46 No author, "Jandarma ödeneğinde Ergün Poyraz'ın da kitapları çıktı," *T24*, October 16, 2013: http://t24.com.tr/haber/jandarma-odeneginde-ergun-poyrazin-da-kitapari-cikti/105677, retrieved November 25, 2013.
47 Ergün Poyraz, *Musa'nın Gülü 8 baskı* (Istanbul: Togan Yayıncılık 2007).
48 www.vho.org/aaargh/fran/livres8/antisemTur.pdf, retrieved October 15, 2013.
49 Ergün Poyraz, *Musa'nın Mücahiti* (Istanbul: Togan Yayıncılık, 2007).
50 www.vho.org/aaargh/fran/livres8/antisemTur.pdf, retrieved October 15, 2013.
51 Ergün Poyraz, *Musa'nın AKP'si* (Istanbul: Gökbörü Yayıncılık, 2007).
52 www.vho.org/aaargh/fran/livres8/antisemTur.pdf, retrieved October 15, 2013.
53 İhsan Dağı, "Yeni anti-Semitler kimler?," *Zaman*, February 6, 2009.
54 Hasan Demir, *Ankarada'da gizli Israil Devleti mi var?* (Ankara: Akasya Kitap, 2007).
55 Hoff, "Normalizing antisemitism in Turkey," pp. 185, 192.
56 www.vho.org/aaargh/fran/livres8/antisemTur.pdf. For the original article, see: www.washingtonpost.com/wp-dyn/content/article/2007/10/04/AR2007100401357.html, retrieved August 13, 2013.
57 www.washingtonpost.com/wp-dyn/content/article/2007/10/04/AR2007100401357.html, retrieved August 13, 2013.
58 Ibid.
59 No author, "Türk Musevi Cemaati'nin reklam tepkisi," *IHA*, March 24, 2012: www.iha.com.tr/haber-turk-musevi-cemaatinin-reklam-tepkisi-220498, retrieved September 10, 2013.
60 www.youtube.com/watch?v=SIsp8v-_9bM, retrieved November 15, 2014.
61 www.adl.org/press-center/press-releases/holocaust-nazis/adl-repulsed-by-use-of-hitler.html, retrieved September 18, 2011.
62 Ibid.
63 Murat Kazancı, "Biomen 'yüce ırk' demek," *Hürriyet*, March 31, 2012: www.hurriyet.com.tr/gundem/20243450.asp, retrieved August 6, 2013.
64 Bali, *Antisemitism and Conspiracy*, p. 21.
65 Ali Eyüboğlu, "Hitler'le şampuan reklami!," *Milliyet*, March 21, 2012: http://cadde.milliyet.com.tr/2012/03/21/YazarDetay/1517860/hitler-le-sampuan-reklami, retrieved October 28, 2012.
66 No author, "Akit'in 'Hitler'li bulmacası: Seni arıyoruz," *Gözcü*, July 19, 2014: www.gozcu.org/medya-haberleri-akitin-hitlerli-bulmacasi-seni-ariyoruz-936.html, retrieved July 20, 2014.

67 Hoff, "Normalizing antisemitism in Turkey," pp. 185, 187.
68 www.vho.org/aaargh/fran/livres8/antisemTur.pdf, retrieved August 2013. For more on the TV series, see also: Kurtlar Vadisi Fenomeni, "bu bir mafia kitabıdır": http://istihbaratsahasi.files.wordpress.com/2013/10/kurtlar-vads-fenomen.pdf, retrieved October 10, 2013.
69 Hoff, "Normalizing antisemitism in Turkey," pp. 187–188.
70 Gönül Dönmez-Colin, *The Routledge Dictionary of Turkish Cinema* (New York: Routledge, 2014), p. 9.
71 www.todayszaman.com/national_valley-of-the-wolves-palestine_219062.html, retrieved June 13, 2012.
72 See, for example: www.youtube.com/watch?v=ltCETIlSCkk, retrieved January 27, 2014.
73 The Meir Amit Intelligence and Terrorism Information Center: www.terrorism-info.org.il/en/article/17964, retrieved January 3, 2012.
74 Bünyamin Köseli, "Kurtlar Vadisi Filistin'in setine girdi; işte ilk fotoğraflar," *Zaman*, August 14, 2010, retrieved July 18, 2012.
75 Bali, "The banalization of hate," p. 316.
76 No author, "Nazi avcısı örgütten Erdoğan'a mektup," *Hürriyet*, November 13, 2009: http://arama.Hürriyet.com.tr/arsivnews.aspx?id=12935671, retrieved October 27, 2012.
77 www.haaretz.co.il/misc/1.1288877, retrieved February 27, 2011.
78 Hincal Uluç, "Can Bonomo'nun Yahudiliği!," *Sabah*, January 22, 2012: www.sabah.com.tr/Yazarlar/uluc/2012/01/22/can-bonomonun-yahudiligi, retrieved August 12, 2013.
79 Emre Baylan, "'Askere giderken iyi de Eurovision'a giderken mi kötü,'" *Radikal*, January 13, 2012: www.radikal.com.tr/turkiye/askere_giderken_iyi_de_eurovisiona_giderken_mi_kotu-1075509, retrieved September 12, 2013.
80 Burak Bekdil, "'Jewish, Turkish, Israeli,'" *Hürriyet Daily News*, February 1, 2014: www.Hürriyetdailynews.com/Jewish-Turkish-Israeli-.aspx?pageID=449&nID=12723&NewsCatID=398, retrieved September 2, 2014.
81 No author, "Can Bonomo'dan 'Yahudi misin' sorusuna yanıt," *Milliyet*, January 12, 2012: www.milliyet.com.tr/can-bonomo-dan-yahudi-misin-sorusuna-yanit/gundem/gundemdetay/12.01.2012/1487857/default.htm, retrieved August 12, 2013.
82 www.Hürriyet.com.tr/pazar/10795577.asp, retrieved May 25, 2013.
83 Ibid.
84 Bali, "Present-day antisemitism in Turkey."
85 No author, "Yıldız Tilbe'nin 'ırkçı' mesajları tepki çekti," *Hürriyet*, July 11, 2014: www.Hürriyet.com.tr/kelebek/paparazzi/26783541.asp; no author, "Allah Hitler'den razı olsun," *Odatv*, July 10, 2014: www.odatv.com/n.php?n=allah-hitlerden-razi-olsun-1007141200, retrieved July 11, 2014.
86 No author, "İsrailli konsolostan Tilbe'ye tepki: Aşağılık," *Türkiye*, July 12, 2014: www.turkiyegazetesi.com.tr/magazin/170483.aspx; no author, "İsrailli konsolostan Yıldız Tilbe'ye tepki," *Ensonhaber*, July 12, 2014: www.ensonhaber.com/israilli-konsolostan-yildiz-tilbeye-tepki-2014-07-12.html, retrieved July 13, 2014.
87 No author, "İsrailli konsolostan Tilbe'ye tepki: Aşağılık….," *Türkiye*, July 12, 2014: www.turkiyegazetesi.com.tr/magazin/170483.aspx, retrieved July 12, 2014.
88 No author, "Kıvanç Tatlıtuğ Yahudi oluyor!," *İlkben*, February 22, 2015: www.ilkben.com/yahudi-olan-Kıvanç-tatlitug-sevenleri-cok-uzdu-kararindan-vazgec-138681-haberi.html, retrieved February 22, 2015. The full article was removed shortly after it appeared online.
89 Umay Aktaş Salman, "Çocuklara daha 'enfes' kitaplar bulamadınız mı?," *Radikal*, October 19, 2012: www.radikal.com.tr/turkiye/cocuklara_daha_enfes_kitaplar_bulamadiniz_mi-1104570, retrieved July 30, 2013.

90 Ibid. See also: Daniel Dombey and Funja Guler, "Turkish book on Darwin sparks outrage," *Financial Times*, October 19, 2012: www.ft.com/cms/s/0/f27adba8-1a01-11e2-a179-00144feabdc0.html#axzz2aXts5TyH, retrieved July 30, 2013.
91 See, for instance: http://jpupdates.com/2014/02/10/antisemitic-attack-2-Jewish-businessmen-restaurant-Turkey; http://antisemitism.org.il/article/85064/Jews-attacked-%E2%80%98dangerous-tool%E2%80%99-restaurant; www.algemeiner.com/2014/02/09/Jews-attacked-with-dangerous-tool-at-restaurant-in-Turkey, retrieved March 1, 2014.
92 https://twitter.com/sayinugurunsoy/status/441522222398963712/photo/1, retrieved March 27, 2014.
93 https://twitter.com/sayinugurunsoy/status/441522461394628608/photo/1, retrieved March 27, 2014.
94 Interview in Istanbul, February 26, 2015.
95 Brink-Danan, *Jewish Life in 21st Century Turkey*, p. 64.
96 Toktaş, "Perceptions of antisemitism," p. 217.
97 On the crisis, see: www.CNNTürk.com/haber/turkiye/somada-maden-faciasiş www.bbc.com/news/world-europe-27415822, retrieved June 1, 2014.
98 www.bbc.com/news/world-europe-27415822, retrieved June 1, 2014.
99 No author, "Soma patronunun damadı Yahudi," *Yeni Akit*, May 20, 2014: www.yeniakit.com.tr/haber/soma-patronunun-damadi-yahudi-18448.html, retrieved May 22, 2014.
100 Yetkin, "Antisemitism is a perversion."
101 No author, "Erdoğan: Yahudi Düşmanlığı Sapıklıktır," *Aktif Haber*, May 22, 2014: www.aktifhaber.com/Erdoğan-yahudi-dusmanligi-sapikliktir-987848h.htm, retrieved July 10, 2014.
102 Ibid.
103 Retrieved May 20, 2014.
104 Yetkin, "Antisemitism is a perversion."
105 Brink-Danan, *Jewish Life in 21st Century Turkey*, p. 65.
106 Ibid., p. 93.
107 Ibid., pp. 86–87.
108 Interview in Istanbul, February 25, 2012.
109 Interview in Istanbul, February 25, 2012.
110 Orhan Seyfi Orhon, *Dün bugün yarın* (İstanbul: Çınar Yayınevi, 1952). See in: Landau, "Tofaot shel Antishemiyut," p. 228.
111 Orhon, *Dün bugün yarın*, pp. 47–48.
112 All diagrams are from the 2012 poll.
113 In a poll taken in 2011, 69 percent of the population of Turkey had a very unfavorable view of Jews and 14 percent had a somewhat unfavorable view of Jews. See: Jikeli, *European Muslim Antisemitism*, p. 52.
114 According to the World Values Survey from 2007, only 10.2 percent of Turks think that most people can be trusted: www.jdsurvey.net/jds/jdsurveyMaps.jsp?Idioma=I&SeccionTexto=0404&NOID=104, retrieved October 17, 2013.
115 www.pewglobal.org/2011/07/21/muslim-western-tensions-persist/1, retrieved September 1, 2012.
116 http://global100.adl.org/public/ADL-Global-100-Executive-Summary.pdf, retrieved October 16, 2015.
117 Quoted in: Bali, *Antisemitism and Conspiracy Theories*, p. 356.
118 Raphael Ahren, "Turkish MP: Erdoğan's antisemitism difficult to reverse," *The Times of Israel*, February 5, 2014: www.timesofIsrael.com/Turkish-mp-Erdoğans-Antisemitism-difficult-to-reverse, retrieved March 1, 2014. Note: The prime ministers surname was mistakenly written as "AYdemir" in some sources.
119 Avraham, "Turkish Jewish leader."
120 Ahren, "Turkish MP: Erdoğan's antisemitism."

206 Antisemitism under AK Party rule

121 Ibid.
122 Ibid. This interview later appeared in Turkish too: www.Timetürk.com/tr/ 2014/02/06/antisemitizm-halkin-dokusuna-girdi.html#.Uzr2A2eKBjp, retrieved March 3, 2014.
123 Rafael Sadi, "Milletvekili Aykan Erdemir Rafael Sadi'nin sorularini cevaplandirdi," *Hastürk*, October 7, 2014: www.hasturktv.com/arsiv/6907.htm, retrieved November 13, 2014.
124 Caroline Glick, "Why Turkey is gone for good," *Jerusalem Post*, February 4, 2014: http://carolineglick.com/why-Turkey-is-gone-for-good, retrieved March 30, 2014.
125 www.aksam.com.tr/siyaset/atalay-yahudi-diasporasi-karisikliklari-tetikledi/haber-221143, retrieved July 20, 2013.
126 The video was published, among other sources, on Saman Yolu website: www.samanyoluhaber.com/web-tv/besir-atalay-inkar-etti-ama-2844-video-haberi, retrieved July 20, 2013.
127 www.turktime.com/haber/Besir-Atalay-Inkar-Etti-ama-/230715, retrieved July 10, 2013.
128 Zach Pontz, "Erdoğan associate blames American 'Jewish lobby' for Turkey protests," *The Algemeiner*, June 18, 2013: www.algemeiner.com/2013/06/18/Erdoğan-associate-blames-american-Jewish-lobby-for-Turkey-protests, retrieved October 15, 2013.
129 Alana Goodman, "Turkish politician links Jews to unrest in Turkey," *The Washington Free Beacon*, July 3, 2013: http://freebeacon.com/Turkish-politician-links-Jews-to-unrest-in-Turkey, retrieved August 10, 2013; no author, "Turkish deputy prime minister denies remarks on 'Jewish diaspora'" *Hürriyet Daily News*, July 2, 2013: www.Hürriyetdailynews.com/Jewish-diaspora-behind-gezi-protests-Turkish-deputy-prime-minister-says.aspx?pageID=238&nID=49858&NewsCatID=338#.UdK96 Re4HbM.twitter, retrieved July 10, 2013.
130 Emre Deliveli, "The Chapull-Jew (çapulcu) interest rate lobby," *Hürriyet Daily News*, June 10, 2013: www.Hürriyetdailynews.com/the-chapull-jew-capulcu-interest-rate-lobby.aspx?pageID=449&nID=48497&NewsCatID=430, retrieved March 10, 2014. According to Deliveli, these accusations of foreign investors are ridiculous as nearly two-thirds of Turkey's stock market is owned by foreign investors.
131 No author, "Turkish PM Erdoğan calls for 'immediate end' to Gezi Park protests," *Hürriyet Daily News*, June 7, 2013: www.Hürriyetdailynews.com/Turkish-pm-Erdoğan-calls-for-immediate-end-to-gezi-park-protests-.aspx?pageID=238&nID=48 381&NewsCatID=338, retrieved March 10, 2014.
132 Deliveli, "The Chapull-Jew (çapulcu) interest rate lobby."
133 www.turkyahudileri.com/content/view/2595/287/lang,tr; no author, "Musevi Cemaati'nden Atalay'ın iddiasına yanıt," *Radikal*, July 2, 2013: www.radikal.com.tr/politika/musevi_cemaatinden_atalayin_iddiasina_yanit-1140092; no author, "Musevi cemaatinden Atalay'a yanıt," *Hürriyet*, July 2, 2013: www.Hürriyet.com.tr/gundem/23635948.asp, retrieved July 10, 2013.
134 Interview in Istanbul, February 4, 2013.
135 Interview in Istanbul, July 29, 2013.
136 Interview in Istanbul, January 30, 2014.
137 Omer Lachmanovitz, "Lihiyot Yehudi zo Tchusha Tivit Avuri" [Being a Jew is a natural feeling for me], *Israel Hayom*, February 21, 2013: www.Israelhayom.co.il/article/75331, retrieved February 24, 2013 [Hebrew].
138 Interview in Istanbul, February 25, 2012.
139 No author, "'Gürcü daha çirkini Ermeni dediler,'" *Sözcü*, August 5, 2014: http://sozcu.com.tr/2014/gundem/Erdoğandan-aciklamalar-571592, retrieved August 5, 2014.
140 Utku Çakırözer, "Museviler: Panikteyiz," *Cumhuriyet*, August 8, 2014: www.cumhuriyet.com.tr/koseyazisi/103091/Museviler__Panikteyiz.html, retrieved August 13, 2014.

141 No author, "Yahudiler bilgiyi ve parayı iyi yönetiyor," *Milliyet*, October 10, 2009: www.milliyet.com.tr/Siyaset/HaberDetay.aspx?aType=HaberDetay&ArticleID=114 7787&Date=08.10.2009&b=Yahudiler%20bilgiyi%20ve%20parayi%20iyi%20 yonetiyor&KategoriID=4, retrieved May 12, 2012.
142 www.byegm.gov.tr/english/agenda/presidential-victor-Erdoğans-balcony-speech/ 65403, retrieved August 17, 2014.
143 www.AKPartyarti.org.tr/english/haberler/Turkey-is-sensitive-towards-its-minorities-says-pm/66112#1, retrieved August 17, 2014.
144 Interview in Ankara, February 11, 2015.
145 Interview in Istanbul, February 26, 2015.
146 Internet interview, March 17, 2015.
147 http://cables.mrkva.eu/cable.php?id=188079, retrieved May 12, 2012.
148 Quoted in: Bali, *Antisemitism and Conspiracy Theories*, p. 105.
149 Interview in Tel Aviv, September 23, 2014.
150 Internet interview, March 17, 2015.
151 The books of the Muslim Brotherhood founder, Sayyid Qutb, were read in youth organizations of the Islamist National Salvation Party (Millî Selâmet Partisi) in the early 1970s. Qutb's book *Our war Against the Jews* [Yahudi ile Savaşımız] was translated into Turkish and was published in four editions, starting from 1982. According to the journalist Mustafa Akyol, Qutb's writings have been a major influence on the new generation of Islamists who grew up since the 1960s and employ antisemitic speech today. See: Bali, *Antisemitism and Conspiracy Theories*, pp. 35–36. The book can still be easily found in Turkey.
152 Interview in Jerusalem, February 3, 2015.
153 Interview in Ankara, February 11, 2015.
154 Interview in Istanbul, February 26, 2015.
155 Bali, *Antisemitism and Conspiracy Theories*, p. 100. On the salvation of the Turkish consul general in Rhodes, Selahattin Ülkümen, who was also recognized by Yad VaShem as Righteous Among the Nations, see: Selahattin Ülkümen, *Emekli Diplomat Selahattin Ülkümen'in Anıları: Bilinmeyen Yönleriyle Bir Dönemin Dışişleri* [The Memories of Retired Diplomat Selahatin Ulkumen: The Foreign Affairs of a Period with its Unknown Aspects] (Istanbul: Gözlem Yayınları, 1993).
156 Bali, *Antisemitism and Conspiracy Theories*, p. 203.
157 Leyla Navaro, "Kendim ve ülkemin geleceği için tedirginim, üzülüyorum, ürküyorum," *Radikal*, January 1, 2009: www.radikal.com.tr/yorum/kendim_ve_ulkemin_ gelecegi_icin_tedirginim_uzuluyorum_urkuyorum-918064, retrieved July 10, 2013.
158 Achi-Yaakov, "Al Yehudey Turkiya," p. 82.
159 Diler, "No moz karışayamoz."
160 Some responses called for refraining from being prominent in the republic: Moiz Cohen (Munis TekinAlp), called in his book, for instance, to assimilate within the Turkish culture, to use Turkish names instead of Jewish ones, to pray in Turkish and not in Hebrew, etc. The same attitude was manifested by Abraham Galante, who emphasized in his book *The Turks and the Jews* only the good treatment of the Turks in a one-sided way. This attitude was also taken up by Turkish Jews in America who conducted parties and demonstrated for the sake of Turkey. See: Levi, *History of the Jews in the Republic of Turkey*, pp. 52–53. On Tekinalp, see: Jacob M. Landau, *Tekinalp, Turkish patriot, 1883–1961* (Leiden: Nederlands Instituut voor het Nabije Osten, 1984); Rıfat N. Bali, *Bir günah keçisi: Munis Tekinalp*, 3 volumes (Istanbul: Libra, 2012).
161 Brink-Danan, *Jewish Life in 21st Century Turkey*, pp. 34, 36.
162 Bali, *Antisemitism and Conspiracy Theories*, p. 226.
163 Brink-Danan, *Jewish Life in 21st Century Turkey*, p. 56. Bali believes that the QF was founded in order to establish ties with the Jewish lobby in America and to seek support for Turkish positions in the American congress. See: Bali, *Model Citizens of the State*, p. 313.

164 Toktaş, "Perceptions of antisemitism," pp. 211–212.
165 Diler, "No moz karışayamoz."
166 ww.turkyahudileri.com/images/stories/dokumanlar/perception%20of%20different %20identities%20and%20jews%20in%20turkey%202009.pdf, retrieved November 3, 2013.
167 Toktaş, "Perceptions of antisemitism," p. 216.
168 Interview in Istanbul, February 25, 2014.
169 Levi, *History of the Jews in the Republic of Turkey*, p. 42.
170 Bali, "Present-day antisemitism in Turkey."
171 Diler, "No moz karışayamoz."
172 Israel State Archive registered 351.1/Ministry of Foreign Affairs/4631/26 CHETZ/ Istanbul/April 28tht 1971 [in Hebrew].
173 There is no difference in the meaning of the two names Musevi or Yahudi, but in the past there was little use of the latter as Yahudi went together with derogatory names such as "korkak Yahudi" (coward Jew) or "pis yahudi" (dirty Jew). The term Musevi derives from the prophet Moses – Musa – and thus cannot be used while cursing. In recent years, though, the Jews themselves started using 'Yahudi' so the negative tone was removed, although when Jews are cursed even today they are always cursed as 'Yahudi' and not 'Musevi.'
174 Brink-Danan, *Jewish Life in 21st Century Turkey*, p. 159.
175 Ibid. p. 85.
176 Sam Sokol, "Study: antisemitism most common prejudice in Turkish media," *Jerusalem Post*, January 6, 2015: www.jpost.com/Diaspora/Study-Antisemitism-most-common-prejudice-in-Turkish-media-386882, retrieved January 10, 2015.
177 Lachmanovitch, "To be a Jew is a natural feeling."
178 Interview in Istanbul, February 22, 2015.
179 Diler, "No moz karışayamoz."
180 Bali, *Antisemitism and Conspiracy Theories*, pp. 44–45.
181 No author, "Yıldız Tilbe'nin 'ırkçı' mesajları tepki çekti," *Hürriyet*, July 11, 2014: www.Hürriyet.com.tr/kelebek/paparazzi/26783541.asp; retrieved July 11, 2014.
182 Brink-Danan, *Jewish Life in 21st Century Turkey*, p. 56.
183 No author, "'Gürcü daha çirkini Ermeni dediler,'" *Sözcü*, August 5, 2014: http://sozcu.com.tr/2014/gundem/Erdoğandan-aciklamalar-571592, retrieved August 5, 2014.
184 www.nefretsoylemi.org/en, retrieved August 28, 2014.
185 Molinas, "'Yeni Türkiye'de antisemitizm olmasın."
186 http://antisemitizm.info, retrieved February 21, 2015.
187 Brink-Danan, *Jewish Life in 21st Century Turkey*, p. 60.
188 Navaro, "Kendim ve ülkemin geleceği için tedirginim."
189 Ibid.
190 Leshem Shamayim virtual group.
191 No author, "Türkiyeli Yahudilerden sert açıklama," *Cumhuriyet*, August 29, 2014: www.cumhuriyet.com.tr/haber/turkiye/112363/Turkiyeli_Yahudilerden_sert_aciklama. html, retrieved August 30, 2014.
192 No author, "Turkey's Jewish intellectuals denounce being targeted over Israel's Gaza assault," *Hürriyet Daily News*, August 30, 2014, www.hurriyetdailynews.com/turkeys-jewish-intellectuals-denounce-being-targeted-over-israels-gaza-assault.aspx?PageID=238&NID=71095&NewsCatID=341, retrieved August 30, 2014.
193 Interview in Istanbul, February 26, 2015.
194 Brink-Danan, *Jewish Life in 21st Century Turkey*, pp. 58–59.
195 No author, "Turkey replies to American Jewish Congress for demanded award," *Daily Sabah*, July 29, 2014: www.dailysabah.com/politics/2014/07/29/Turkey-replies-to-american-Jewish-congress-for-demanded-award, retrieved September 2, 2014.

196 Boaz Bismuth, "Turkiya ze HaBayit" [Turkey is home], *Israel Hayom*, August 29, 2014, http://news.walla.co.il/?w=//2780662, retrieved September 2, 2014 [Hebrew].
197 Zvika Klein, "Rabah shel Turkiye: en lanu kesher politi im Israel" [Turkey's chief Rabbi: "We have no political relation with Israel"], *NRG*, January 4, 2015: www.nrg.co.il/online/11/ART2/667/548.html, retrieved January 10, 2014 [Hebrew].
198 Interview in Istanbul, February 26, 2015.
199 Interview in Istanbul, February 26, 2015.
200 Durna and Özçetin, "Mavi Marmara on the news," p. 277.
201 Bali, "Present-day antisemitism in Turkey."
202 Bilal Macit, "The AK Party and religious minorities," *Daily Sabah*, July 5, 2014, www.dailysabah.com/opinion/2014/07/05/the-ak-party-and-religious-minorities, retrieved July 20, 2014.
203 www.memri.org/report/en/print1388.htm#_edn, retrieved September 1, 2012.
204 Ibid.
205 Barlas refers to the ECRI third report which can be found at: http://hudoc.ecri.coe.int/XMLEcri/ENGLISH/Cycle_03/03_CbC_eng/TUR-CbC-III-2005-5-ENG.pdf, retrieved September 1, 2012.
206 Quoted in: www.memri.org/report/en/1388.htm, retrieved November 27, 2013.
207 Durna and Özçetin, "Mavi Marmara on the news," pp. 276–277.
208 Bali, *Antisemitism and Conspiracy Theories*, pp. 17–18.
209 http://vho.org/aaargh/fran/livres8/AntisemTurkish.pdf, retrieved January 28, 2014.
210 Neil J. Kressel, *"The Sons of Pigs and Apes": Muslim Antisemitism and the Conspiracy of Silence* (Washington, DC: Potomac Books, 2012), p. 182.
211 Ahmet Kuru, "Changing perspectives on Islamism and secularism in Turkey: the Gülen Movement and the AK Party," in: Ihsan Yilmaz (ed.), *Muslim World in Transition: Contributions of the Gülen Movement* (London: Leeds Metropolitan University Press, 2007), pp. 147–148.
212 Ferda Balancar, "90 yıldır 'soy kodu' ile fişlemişler," *Agos*, August 1, 2013: www.agos.com.tr/haber.php?seo=90-yildir-soy-kodu-ile-fislemisler&haberid=5479, retrieved August 6, 2013.
213 Ismail Saymaz, "Süryaniler 4, diğerleri 5…," *Radikal*, August 3, 2013: www.radikal.com.tr/turkiye/suryaniler_4_digerleri_5-1144690, retrieved August 6, 2013.
214 Uygar Gültekin, "İçişleri Bakanlığı: Soy durumları Milli Eğitim Bakanlığı'na veriliyor," *Agos*, August 2, 2013: www.agos.com.tr/haber.php?seo=icisleri-bakanligi-soy-durumlari-milli-egitim-bakanligina-veriliyor&haberid=5487, retrieved August 6, 2013.
215 Umut Uzer, "Turkish–Israeli relations," p. 107.
216 Bahar Bakır, "Yahudi soykırımı ders kitaplarında anlatılacak," *HaberTürk Gazete*, December 12, 2013: www.haberturk.com/tv/haber/901702-yahudi-soykirimi-ders-kitaplarinda-anlatilacak/0, retrieved December 11, 2013.
217 Dorian Jones, "Turkey marks International Holocaust Remembrance Day," *Voice of America*, January 26, 2012: www.voanews.com/content/turkey-marks-international-holocaust-remembrance-day-138212329/170996.html, retrieved November 2, 2013.
218 Bülent Aydemir, "Bonomo talebi Dışişleri'nden Dışişleri, TRT ile Yahudi açılımı başlattı," HaberTürk Gazetesi, January 28, 2012. www.haberturk.com/gundem/haber/710298-bonomo-talebi-disislerindenö, retrieved March 30, 2012.
219 No author, "Holokost kurbanları anıldı," *Hürriyet*, January 28, 2013: www.Hürriyet.com.tr/gundem/25670641.asp; no author, "Holokost Kurbanlarını Anma Günü," *Mynet*, January 28, 2013: www.mynet.com/haber/guncel/holokost-kurbanlarini-anma-gunu-1003833-1, retrieved January 31, 2013.
220 Diler, "No moz karışayamoz."
221 https://humanities.tau.ac.il/roth/images/General_Anaiyses/general-analysis-12.pdf, retrieved October 1, 2013.
222 www.yadvashem.org/yv/he/pressroom/pressreleases/pr_details.asp?cid=523, retrieved October 2014.

223 Uzer, "Turkish–Israeli relations," p. 107.
224 Bekdil, "'Jewish, Turkish, Israeli'."
225 Interview in Ankara, February 11, 2015.
226 Diler, "No moz karışayamoz."
227 https://azadalik.wordpress.com/2014/09/19/abusing-the-holocaust-commemoration-and-politics-of-denial-in-turkey, retrieved January 29, 2015.
228 Ankara, February 2014.
229 The *Struma* tragedy is a well-known topic which the Turks find interesting. Some popular figures, such as Zülfü Livaneli and Sunay Akın, published romances on this topic. See, for instance: Zülfü Livaneli, *Sernad* (Istanbul: Doğan Kitap, 2011); Sunay Akın, *Önce Çocuklar ve Kadınlar*, first edition (Istanbul: Çınar Yayınları, 1999); Halit Kakınç, *Struma* (Istanbul: Destek Yayınları, 2012).
230 www.efe.net/2012/02/25/struma-katliami-anildi, retrieved April 25, 2012.
231 Alas, "Struma faciasına."; Hasan Ay, "Struma'ya ilk devlet töreni," *Sabah*, February 25, 2015: www.sabah.com.tr/yasam/2015/02/25/strumaya-ilk-devlet-toreni, retrieved February 25, 2015.
232 Interview, Edirne August 23, 2015.
233 Quoted in: Bekdil, "To all Jews in Turkey."
234 Toktaş, "Perceptions of antisemitism," p. 209.
235 Tarik Işık, "Vekillerden Musevi Özrü," *Radikal*, March 30, 2012: www.radikal.com.tr/politika/vekillerden_musevi_ozru-1083338, retrieved April 2, 2012. See also: Evrin Güvendik, "'Mekânlarımıza suçluymuş gibi giriyoruz,'" March 30, 2012: www.sabah.com.tr/Gundem/2012/03/30/26-yildir-meknlarimiza-sucluymus-gibi-giriyoruz, retrieved August 1, 2013.
236 http://hudoc.ecri.coe.int/XMLEcri/ENGLISH/Cycle_03/03_CbC_eng/TUR-CbC-III-2005-5-ENG.pdf, retrieved 1 August 2013, p. 24.
237 Macit, "The AK Party and religious minorities."
238 http://hudoc.ecri.coe.int/XMLEcri/ENGLISH/Cycle_03/03_CbC_eng/TUR-CbC-III-2005-5-ENG.pdf, p. 24, retrieved August 1, 2013.
239 Macit, "The AK Party and religious minorities."
240 Türkmen and Öktem, "Foreign policy as a determinant," p. 11.
241 İçduygu and Soner, "Turkish minority rights regime," pp. 463–464.
242 Türkmen and Öktem, "Foreign policy as a determinant," p. 2.
243 http://hudoc.ecri.coe.int/XMLEcri/ENGLISH/Cycle_03/03_CbC_eng/TUR-CbC-III-2005-5-ENG.pdf, p. 24, retrieved September 7, 2013.
244 Diler, "No moz karışayamoz."
245 Türkmen and Öktem, "Foreign policy as a determinant," p. 2.
246 Meltem Naz Kaşo, "'Minority groups face increasing discrimination in Turkey,'" *Today's Zaman*, March 20, 2014: www.todayszaman.com/news-342607-minority-groups-face-increasinGodiscrimination-in-Turkey.html, retrieved March 24, 2014.
247 No author, "İşte Nefret Cezaları, Taslak Belli Oldu," *Türkiye*, October 10, 2013: www.turkiyegazetesi.com.tr/gundem/87191.aspxç, retrieved October 20, 2013.
248 Ayfer Mallı, "Nefret suçu artık TCK'da," *Yeni Şafak*, March 3, 2014: http://yenisafak.com.tr/gundem-haber/nefret-sucu-artik-tckda-04.03.2014-623194, retrieved March 10, 2014.
249 Interview in Ankara, February 11, 2015.
250 Interview in Istanbul, February 22, 2015.
251 Servet Avcı, "'Nefret yasası' çıkarsa Kur'an-ı Kerimleri ne yapacağız?" *Yeniçağ*, October 17, 2013: www.yg.yenicaggazetesi.com.tr/yazargoster.php?haber=28491, retrieved October 20, 2013.
252 http://hudoc.ecri.coe.int/XMLEcri/ENGLISH/Cycle_03/03_CbC_eng/TUR-CbC-III-2005-5-ENG.pdf, retrieved October 20, 2013.
253 Mehmet Ali Berber, "'Barbarlıkta Hitler'i geçtiler,'" *Sabah*, July 20, 2014: www.sabah.com.tr/Gundem/2014/07/20/barbarlikta-hitleri-gectiler, retrieved July 21, 2014.

254 No author, "Hürriyet yazarı 'İsrail'e lanet ederken yapmaman gereken 7 şey'i yazdı," *Birgün*, July 19, 2014, www.birgun.net/haber-detay/hurriyet-yazari-israil-e-lanet-ederken-yapmaman-gereken-7-sey-i-yazdi-65717.html, retrieved July 20, 2014.
255 No author, "Musevi gazetesi Meclis'e girdi," *Demokrat Haber*, January 3, 2014: www.demokrathaber.net/medya/musevi-gazetesi-meclise-girdi-h26755.html, retrieved May 2, 2014.
256 www.change.org/tr/kampanyalar/t%C3%BCrkiye-toplumu-islamc%C4%B1-%C3%A7evreler-t%C3%BCrkiyeli-yahudileri-a%C3%A7%C4%B1k%C3%A7a-tehdit-ediyor-ve-sald%C4%B1r%C4%B1lara-davetiye-%C3%A7%C4%B1kar%C4%B1yor-filistinlilerle-dayan%C4%B1%C5%9Fma-ad%C4%B1na-t%C3%BCrkiyeli-yahudileri-hedef-g%C3%B6steren-antisemitizmi-reddedin?share_id=cwYdPhJnRX&utm_campaign=share_button_action_box&utm_medium=facebook&utm_source=share_petition.
257 No author, "Türkiye'de antisemitizm tavan yaptı," *Şalom*, July 23, 2014: www.salom.com.tr/haber-91854-turkiyede_antisemitizm_tavan_yapti.html?rev=2, retrieved July 24, 2014.
258 Ibid.
259 Menekşe Tokyay, "Dini kanaat önderleri Yahudi karşıtlığına son verilmesi çağrısında bulunuyor," *Ses Türkiye*, August 12, 2014: http://Turkey.setimes.com/tr/articles/ses/articles/features/departments/world/2014/08/12/feature-01, retrieved August 23, 2014.
260 Ibid.
261 Ibid.
262 Menekşe Tokyay, "Dini kanaat önderleri Yahudi karşıtlığına son verilmesi çağrısında bulunuyor," *Ses Türkiye*, August 12, 2014: http://Turkey.setimes.com/tr/articles/ses/articles/features/departments/world/2014/08/12/feature-01, retrieved August 23, 2014.
263 Menekşe Tokyay, "Dini kanaat önderleri Yahudi karşıtlığına son verilmesi çağrısında bulunuyor," *Ses Türkiye*, August 12, 2014: http://Turkey.setimes.com/tr/articles/ses/articles/features/departments/world/2014/08/12/feature-01, retrieved August 23, 2014.
264 www.durde.org/2014/08/turkiye-cumhuriyeti-vatandasi-yahudilere-yonelik-irkci-saldirilara-dur-diyoruz, retrieved September 2, 2014.
265 Ibid.
266 Bali, *Antisemitism and Conspiracy Theories*, p. 128, fn. 275. Bali claims that despite these and other organizations' fight against racism, the leftist and liberal intellectuals who founded these organizations do not blame Islamists and Kemalists for antisemitism, and do not condemn Islamist terror attacks as an antisemitic acts. Bali gives the murder of the Jewish dentist as well as the synagogue blasts in 2003 by al-Qaeda militants as incidents which were only a little, if at all, mentioned by leftist liberal circles: Bali, *Antisemitism and Conspiracy Theories*, p. 130.
267 Interview in Istanbul, February 22, 2015.

Conclusions

Antisemitism in the past decade is divided into several characteristics: first, the most common antisemitic expressions are embodied by long and detailed op-eds that are usually accompanied by provocative photos. The op-eds replace the public speeches made by politicians during election campaigns and are usually published in the same newspapers – mostly Islamist and neo-nationalistic ones. Second, awareness of antisemitism in Turkey is growing stronger. Maybe the large number of antisemitic op-eds contribute to that, but also due to the more open trends within Turkish society, fighting against antisemitism does not depict the Jew as the 'state enemy.' The term, in its several manifestations, is more familiar than in the past and Jews write op-eds themselves to point out antisemitic phenomena. Awareness is highly important as it enables Jews to respond but also justifies fighting it.

Antisemitism and anti-Zionism in Turkey are often used as a political gage for different parties and ideologies. In other words, the idea of being Jewish is seen as a negative thing, and thus it can characterize opposing sectors or ideological circles. The fact is that accusing someone of being 'a Jew' is considered to be accusing them of something negative which the accused party attempts to refute and reject. One of the first accusations against Erdoğan and the AK Party was that they have Jewish origins – it was a way to prove how dangerous Erdoğan and his counterpart were, how untruthful they were, and how they all cooperate with Western intelligence agencies. In addition, when Turkey declares official commemoration ceremonies as in the case of the *Struma* and Holocaust Day, it is done to some extent to improve Turkey's image in the eyes of the world. Thus, the Jewish community is being exploited for the sake of Turkish interests.

It should also be noted here that, unlike what one might think, antisemitism in Turkey cannot be compared to xenophobia or Turkish nationalism. Turkey's government slammed the Israeli government directly in many cases in ways that cannot be compared to Greece or Armenia, for example. In addition, the image of the Jew as one who controls the world, the world press, the United States, or similar accusations are not found in regard to Armenians or Greeks in Turkey. True, many statements similarly denounce Jews, Greeks, and Armenians, but there are still special characteristics that separate Jews from other non-Muslims.

Attempting to reply to the question of whether there is more antisemitism in Turkey under AK Party rule or not or whether antisemitism has increased in recent years in comparison to the past is irrelevant. Even if the view that antisemitism has increased is untrue, and the escalation seems to be due to the 'visibility' of antisemitic comments, especially in social networks, the important part of the discussion is not the amount of antisemitic or anti-Israeli comments or their growing visibility, but the fact that current antisemitism in Turkey is led by Turkey's government – not mentioning Turkey's president. The fact that even if a Turkish Jew does not feel intimidated in daily life by his colleagues, neighbors, or friends, he still feels insecure, he still feels 'un-Turkish' due to the government that is supposed to represent him but that is in fact a significant and problematic part of current antisemitism in Turkey. Further, even if the number of instances of harassment is low and even if he feels secure right after some antisemitic or anti-Israeli incident takes place, the Turkish Jew knows that the government does not see him as an integral part of Turkish society. Even if the government gives money to the non-Muslim communities and returns assets to their original owners, it will still carry on with its former antisemitic comments. Therefore, even if the Turkish Jew sees himself as Turkish even before being Jewish, he knows that according to the ruling circles he is not.

From this point it is also understandable that when Turkish society mixes anti-Israeli feelings with antisemitism, once antisemitic expressions are made, the distinction between both ideas is not important anymore. In other words, if anti-Zionism or anti-Israeli tendencies are so integrated that the average Turk cannot even distinguish between them, there is no need to differentiate between them in Turkey. Once the average Turk comes up with antisemitic assertions, it does not matter if he is a real anti-Semite or 'just' an anti-Israeli. In the final analysis, he reacts in an antisemitic way.

The Jews themselves seem to be confused sometimes when it comes to Israel; and although they might confront antisemitism, especially in recent years, they will hardly ever defend Israel's rights in public. The community is not homogeneous and thus it is hard to define a specific agenda. Some Jews, like Rıfat Bali, expect the State of Israel to take a much stronger stance against antisemitism in Turkey, and at the same time claim that Israel prefers to maintain good relations with Turkey on account of its Jewish community. What emerges from this research is that some Jews believe they should remain in their homeland and integrate, while some seek to immigrate to Israel, thinking this is the best option, while others declare having no Zionist or Jewish identity. The answer to the question of whether there is growing antisemitism in Turkey or even whether antisemitism actually still exists completely depends on which group one asks. The Israeli Jews as well as Jews outside Turkey are also highly concerned by the ongoing antisemitism. Israeli tourists gave up on the Turkish coasts for what used to be their top sand, sea, and sun vacation destination after the peak in 2008 (560,000 Israeli tourists). One of the main reasons for this drop is a fear of antisemitism.

When it comes to Erdoğan himself, antisemitism perhaps also becomes something personal and not only religious or political, as Jews in Turkey have always been ardent supporters of Kemal Atatürk and thus usually vote for the CHP. Erdoğan probably knows he will never be able to win Jewish affection. Erdoğan, despite his own ideology and religious beliefs, is in a delicate situation. If he holds close ties with Israel he will lose votes from Islamic circles in Turkey, which is his political lifeline. As it is, and as economic relations between Israel and Turkey reach record-breaking levels, criticism for Erdoğan grows. Islamist circles accuse him of maintaining relations with Israel. Thus, Erdoğan himself is in a difficult position from his point of view; his pragmatic approach does not enable him to cease relations with Israel completely, which leads to domestic criticism, but on the other hand his anti-Israel statements incur criticism from the West and especially from America.

Antisemitism was on the rise in the 1990s, when Turkish society began undergoing more liberal processes. Yet, it is only fair to claim that Erdoğan is definitely the main reason for the growing antisemitism in Turkey. Polls showed that very clearly, and the legitimacy that anti-Israel sentiment receives in Turkey as well as the support antisemitic journalists and columnists receive from the current government makes it difficult to point to a different reason for the rise of antisemitism. However, this conception is also a reason for optimism: If antisemitism is not nurtured by the government, society might exhibit a more tolerant approach or at least won't feel legitimized to express antisemitic ideas when the AK Party government is not ruling. Kerim Balcı once said in a television interview that, unlike Europeans who say that they adore all Jews but cannot stand their Jewish neighbor, the Turks claim they cannot stand Jews but they adore their Jewish neighbor. If I were to judge according to Balcı's saying, I could say that the Turks are anti-Semites but under no circumstances do they hate Jews.

Bibliography

Achi-Yaakov, David, "Al Yehudey Turkiya" [On the Jews of Turkey], *Gesher* [Bridge], 4, 61 (1969), pp. 78–84 [Hebrew].
Adler, Frank H., "Jews in contemporary Turkey," *Macalester International*, 15, 1 (2005), pp. 127–134.
Akansel, Mustafa Hakki, *Türkün Kitabı: Türl ırkı hakkında tetkiler* (İstanbul: Kenan Matbaası, 1943).
Akçuraoğlu, Yusuf, *Türk Yılı 1928* (Istanbul: Yeni Matbaa, 1928).
Akın, Sunay, *Önce Çocuklar ve Kadınlar*, first edition (Istanbul: Çınar Yayınları, 1999).
Akturk, Sener, "Persistence of the Islamic *Millet* as an Ottoman legacy: mono-religious and anti-ethnic definition of Turkish nationhood," *Middle Eastern Studies*, 45, 6 (2009), pp. 893–909.
Alev, Çınar, "The Justice and Development Party: Turkey's experience with Islam, democracy, liberalism and secularism," *International Journal of Middle East Studies*, 43 (2011), pp. 529–541.
Ali, Sabahattin, *Kürk Mantolu Madonna* (Istanbul: Yapı Kredi Yayınları, 2013).
Alp, Mustafa, "Yabancıların Çalışma İzinleri Hakkında Kanun," *Ankara Üniversitesi Hukuk Fakültesi Dergisi*, 53, 2 (2004), pp. 33–59.
Altabé, David, Erhan Atay, and Israel Katz (eds.), *Studies on Turkish-Jewish History: Political and Social Relations, Literature, and Linguistics – the Quincentennial Papers* (Brooklyn, NY: Sefer-Hermon Press, 1996).
Altındal, *Aytunç, Bilinmeyen Hitler* (Istanbul: Alfa Yayıncılık, 2004).
Aras, Bülent, "Turkey's rise in the Greater Middle East: peace-building in the periphery," *Journal of Balkan and Near Eastern Studies*, 11, 1 (2009), pp. 29–41.
Arbell, Dan, "The U.S–Turkey–Israel triangle," *Brookings: Center for Middle East Policy*, 24 (2014), p. 11. www.brookings.edu/~/media/research/files/papers/2014/10/09%20Turkey%20us%20Israel%20arbell/usTurkeyIsrael%20trianglefinal.pdf.
Aviv, Efrat E., "The Efraim Elrom affair and Israel–Turkey relations," *Middle Eastern Studies*, 49, 5 (2013), pp. 750–769.
Aviv, Efrat E., "Turkey and Elrom affair: a unique affair or a link in a chain of terrorist events in 1970s Turkey?," *Hamizrah Hehadash – The New East*, 52 (2013), pp. 286–308 [Hebrew].
Aviv, Efrat E., "Fethullah Gülen's 'Jewish dialogue'," *Turkish Policy Quarterly*, 9, 3 (2010), pp. 101–115.
Baer, Marc David, *The Dönme: Jewish Converts, Muslim Revolutionaries, and Secular Turks* (Stanford, CA: Stanford University Press, 2009).

216 Bibliography

Baer, Marc David, "Turkish Jews rethink 500 years of brotherhood and friendship," *Turkish Studies Association Bulletin*, 24, 2 (2000), pp. 63–73.

Baer, Marc David, "Globalization, cosmopolitanism, and the Dönme in Ottoman Salonica and Turkish Istanbul," *Journal of World History*, 18, 2 (1997), pp. 141–170.

Baer, Marc, Ussama Makdisi, and Andrew Shryock, "Tolerance and conversion in the Ottoman Empire: a conversation," *Comparative Studies in Society and History* 51, 4 (2009), pp. 927–940.

Balcı, Ali and Tuncay Kardaş, "The changing dynamics of Turkey's relations with Israel: an analysis of 'securitization,'" *Insight Turkey*, 14, 2 (2012), pp. 99–120.

Bali, Rıfat N. (ed.), *Anti-Greek riots of September 6–7, 1955: documents from the American National Archives* (Istanbul: Libra Kitap, 2015).

Bali, Rıfat N. (ed.), *The Wealth Tax (Varlık Vergisi) affair: documents from the British National Archives* (Istanbul: Libra Kitap, 2015).

Bali, Rıfat N., *The Banalization of Hate: Antisemitism in Contemporary Turkey* (Istanbul: Libra Kitap, 2015).

Bali, Rıfat N., *"Azınlıkları Türkleştirme Meselesi" Ne İdi? Ne Değildi?* (Istanbul: Libra Kitap, 2014).

Bali, Rıfat N. *Antisemitism and Conspiracy Theories in Turkey* (Istanbul: Libra Kitap, 2013).

Bali, Rıfat N., *The Silent Minority in Turkey: Turkish Jews* (Istanbul: Libra Kitap, 2013).

Bali, Rıfat N., "The banalization of hate: antisemitism in contemporary Turkey," in: Alvin H. Rosenfeld (ed.), *Resurgent Antisemitism: Global Perspectives* (Bloomington, IN: Indiana University Press, 2013), pp. 308–336.

Bali, Rıfat N., *1934 Trakya Olayları* (Istanbul: Libra Kitap, 2012).

Bali, Rıfat N., *Bir Günah Keçisi: Munis Tekinalp*, 3 volumes (Istanbul: Libra, 2012).

Bali, Rıfat N., *Model Citizens of the State: The Jews of Turkey during the Multi-Party Period* (Princeton, NJ: Fairleigh Dickinson University Press, 2012).

Bali, Rıfat N. (ed.), *6–7 Eylül 1955 Olayları: Tanıklar – Hatiralar* (Istanbul: Libra Kitap, 2010).

Bali, Rıfat N., "Küçuk Türkiye Kozmopolit Mi?," *Memlekent, Ülkeler Ve Kentler Dergisi*, 4 (2010), pp. 82–85.

Bali, Rıfat N., "Present-day anti-Semitism in Turkey," *Bulletin of the Stephen Roth Institute for the Study of Contemporary Antisemitism and Racism*, 84 (2009): http://jcpa.org/article/present-day-anti-semitism-in-turkey.

Bali, Rıfat N., *A Scapegoat for all Seasons: The Dönmes or Crypto-Jews of Turkey* (Istanbul: ISIS, 2008).

Bali, Rıfat N., *Sarayın ve Cumhuriyetin Dişçibaşısı Sami Günzberg* (İstanbul: Kitabevi, 2007).

Bali, Rıfat N., *The "Varlık Vergisi" Affair: A Study On Its Legacy-Selected Documents* (Istanbul: Isis, 2005).

Bali, Rıfat N., *Ümit Kıvanç'a Cevap: Birikim Dergisinin Yayınlamayı Reddettiği Makalenin Öyküsü* (İstanbul: Kitap Yayıncılık, 2005).

Bali, Rıfat N., "Bir Dönmenin Hikayesi: Nazıf Özge kimdir?" *Tarih ve Toplum* 38, 223 (2002), pp. 15–22.

Bali, Rıfat N., *Les Relations Entre Turcs et Juifs Dans la Turquie Moderne* (Istanbul: Isis, 2001).

Bali, Rıfat N., *Musa'nin Evlâtlari Cumhuriyet'in Yurttaşları* (Istanbul: İletişim Yayınları, 2001).

Bibliography 217

Bali, Rıfat N., *Cumhuriyet Yıllarında Türkiye Yahudileri: Bir Türkleştirme Serüveni (1923–1945)* (Istanbul Iletişim Yayınları, 1999).
Bali, Rıfat N., "Cevat Rıfat Atilhan-I," *Tarih ve Toplum*, 30, 175 (1998), pp. 15–24.
Bali, Rıfat N., "Irkçı Bir Dernek: Türkiye Siyonizmle Mücadele Derneği" [A racist association: Turkish Association for Fighting Zionism], *Toplumsal Tarih*, 29 (1996), pp. 32–36.
Barkey, Karen, *Empire of Difference: The Ottomans in Comparative Perspective* (New York: Cambridge University Press, 2008).
Barnai, Jacob, "Messianism and leadership: the Sabbatean movement and the leadership of the Jewish communities in the Ottoman Empire," in: Aron Rodrique (ed.), *Ottoman and Turkish Jewry: Community and Leadership* (Bloomington, IN: Indiana University Press, 1992), pp. 167–182.
Barnai, Jacob, "On the history of the Jews in the Ottoman Empire," in: Esther Juhasz (ed.), *Sephardi Jews in the Ottoman Empire* (Jerusalem: The Israel Museum, 1990), pp. 19–36.
Başer, Ekrem T., "Shift-of-axis in Turkish foreign policy: Turkish national role conceptions before and during AK Party rule," *Turkish Studies*, 16, 3 (2015), pp. 291–309.
Bayram, Salih, "Where the AK Party stands: a manifesto-based approach to party competition in Turkey," *New Middle Eastern Studies*, 5 (2015), pp. 1–19.
Behar, Izzet, *Turkey and the Rescue of European Jews* (New York: Routledge, 2014).
Benbassa, Esther (ed.), *Itinéraires sépharades: Complexité et diversité des identities* (Paris: Presses de l'Université Paris-Sorbonne, 2010).
Benbassa, Esther and Aron Rodrigue, *Sephardi Jewry: A History of the Judeo-Spanish Community, 14th–20th Centuries*, second edition. (Berkeley, CA: University of California Press, 2000).
Benbassa, Esther (ed.), *Haim Nahum: A Sephardic Chief Rabbi in Politics, 1892–1923* (Tuscaloosa, AL: University Alabama Press, 1995).
Benbassa, Esther, "Zionism in the Ottoman Empire at the end of 19th century and the beginning of 20th century," *Studies in Zionism*, 11, 2 (1990), pp. 127–140.
Ben-Bassat, Yuval and Eyal Ginio (eds.), *Late Ottoman Palestine: The Period of Young Turk Rule* (London: I.B. Tauris, 2011).
Bengio, Ofra, *The Turkish–Israeli Relationship: Changing Ties of Middle Eastern Outsiders* (London: Palgrave, 2009).
Ben-Naeh, Yaron, *Jews in the Realm of the Sultans* (Jerusalem: Magness Press, 2007).
Bessemer, Paul, "Who is a crypto-Jew? A historical survey of the Sabbatean debate in Turkey," *Kabbalah: Journal for the Study of Jewish Mystical Texts*, 9 (2003), pp. 121–122.
Bilici, Mucahit, "The Fethullah Gülen Movement and its politics of representation in Turkey," *The Muslim World*, 96 (2006), pp. 1–20.
Birtek, Faruk, "From affiliation to affinity: citizenship in the transition from empire to the nation-state," in Seyla Benhabib, Ian Shapiro, and Danilo Petranovic (eds.), *Identities, Affiliations, and Allegiances* (New York: Cambridge University Press, 2007), pp. 17–44.
Bornstein-Makovetsky, Leah, "Jewish lay leadership and Ottoman authorities during the sixteenth and seventeenth centuries," in: Aron Rodrigue (ed.), *Ottoman and Turkish Jewry: Community and Leadership* (Bloomington, IN: Indiana University Press, 1992), pp. 87–121.
Bozkurt, Celil, *Yahudilik ve Masonluğa karşı Cevat Rıfat Atilhan* (Istanbul: Doğu Kütüphanesi, 2012).

Bibliography

Braude, Benjamin, and Bernard Lewis (eds.), *Christians and Jews in the Ottoman Empire: The Functioning of a Plural Society* (New York: Holmes and Meier, 1982).

Brink-Danan, Marcy, *Jewish Life in 21st Century Turkey: The Other Side of Tolerance* (Bloomington, IN: Indiana University Press, 2012).

Bunzl, Matti, *Antisemitism and Islamophobia: Hatreds Old and New in Europe* (Chicago, IL: Prickly Paradigm Press, 2007).

Çağaptay, Soner, "Race, assimilation, and Kemalism: Turkish nationalism and the minorities in the 1930s," *Middle Eastern Studies*, 40, 3 (2004), pp. 86–101.

Çağaptay, Soner, "Where goes the U.S. –Turkish relationship?," *Middle East Quarterly*, 1, 4 (2004): www.meforum.org/657/where-goes-the-us-Turkish-relationship.

Çağaptay, Soner, "Citizenship policies in interwar Turkey," *Nations and Nationalism*, 9, 4 (2003), pp. 601–620.

Campos, Michelle, *Ottoman Brothers: Muslims, Christians, and Jews in Early Twentieth-Century Palestine* (Stanford, CA: Stanford University Press, 2011).

Çay, Mustafa Murat, "Cevat Rıfat Atilhan-Askerî, siyasî ve fikrî yönleriyle," unpublished dissertation submitted to Selçuk University, Konya, 2013: http://acikerisim.selcuk.edu.tr:8080/xmlui/handle/123456789/1205?show=full.

Chesler, Phyllis, *The New Antisemitism: The Current Crisis and What We Must Do About It* (San Francisco, CA: Jossey-Bass, 2003).

Cizre, Ümit, *Secular and Islamic Politics in Turkey: The Making of Justice and Development Party* (New York: Routledge, 2007).

Cohen, Mark, *Jews Under Crescent and Cross* (Princeton, NJ: Princeton University Press, 1994).

Demir, Hasan, *Ankarada'da gizli Israil Devleti mi var?* (Ankara: Akasya Kitap, 2007).

Deshen, Shlomo A., and Walter P. Zenner, *Jews Among Muslims: Communities in the Precolonial Middle East* (New York: New York University Press, 1996).

Dinçşahin, Şakir and Stephen R. Goodwin, "Towards an encompassing perspective on nationalism: the case of Jews in Turkey during the Second World War, 1939–1945," *Nations and Nationalism*, 17, 4 (2011), pp. 843–862.

Dönmez-Colin, Gönül, *The Routledge Dictionary of Turkish Cinema* (New York: Routledge, 2014).

Durna, Tezcan and Burak Özçetin, "Mavi Marmara on the news: convergence and divergence in religious conservative newspapers in Turkey," *Middle East Journal of Culture and Communication*, 5 (2012), pp. 261–281.

Düzgün, Mücahit, "Cumhuriyetin İlanından İsrail'in Kuruluşuna Kadar Türkiye'deki Yahudiler," *Çağdaş Türkiye Tarihi Araştırmaları Dergisi*, 3, (1999–2000), 9–10.

Faroqhi, Suraiya, *The Ottoman Empire and the World Around It* (London: Tauris & Co, 2004).

Florence, Ronald, *Blood Libel: The Damascus Affair of 1840* (Madison, WI: University of Wisconsin Press, 2004).

Ford, Henry, *Beynelmilel Yahudi* (Ankara: Serdengeçti Neşriyatı, 1961).

Frankel, Jonathan, *The Damascus Affair: "Ritual Murder," Politics, and the Jews in 1840* (Cambridge: Cambridge University Press, 1997).

Freely, Maureen, "Why they killed Hrant Dink," *Index on Censorship*, 36, 2 (2007), pp. 15–29.

Friling, Tuvia, "Nazi-Jewish negotiations in Istanbul in mid-1944," *Holocaust and Genocide Studies*, 13, 3 (1999), pp. 405–436.

Galanté, Abraham, *Histoire des Juifs de Turquie*, 9 volumes (Istanbul: Isis, 1985).

Galanté, Abraham, "HaYehudim BeMishley Ha'amim (Yavan, Turkia, Sfard)" [The Jews in Folk Proverbs (Greece, Turkey, Spain), *Reshumot*, 4 (1924), pp. 163–166 [Hebrew].
Gibb, H.A.R and H. Bowen, *Islamic Society and the West: A Study of the Impact of Western Civilization on Moslem Culture in the Near East, Vol. 1, Islamic Society in the Eighteenth Century* (London: Oxford University Press, 1950).
Goffman, Daniel, "The Quincentennial of 1492 and Ottoman-Jewish studies: a review essay," *Shofar*, 11, 4 (1993), pp. 57–67.
Goldberg, Harvey (ed.) *Sephardi and Middle Eastern Jewries: History and Culture in the Modern Era* (Bloomington, IN: Indiana University Press, 1996).
Grigoriadis, Ioannis N., "Friends no more? The rise of anti-American nationalism in Turkey," *Middle East Journal*, 64, 1 (2010), pp. 51–66.
Gülen, Fethullah, *İnsanın Özündeki Sevgi* (İstanbul: Da Yayıncılık, 2003).
Guttstadt, Corry, *Die Türkei, die Juden und der Holocaust* (Hamburg: Assoziation A, 2008).
Güven, Erdem and Mehmet Yılmazata, "Milli İnkilap and the Thrace Incidents of 1934," *Modern Jewish Studies*, 13, 2 (2014), pp. 190–212.
Haberlein, Mark, "A 16th century German traveller's perspective on discrimination and tolerance in the Ottoman Empire," in: Guðmundur Halfdanarson (ed.), *Discrimination and Tolerance in Historical Perspective* (Pisa: Pisa University Press, 2008), pp. 71–84.
Hacker, Joseph R., "Ottoman policy toward the Jews and Jewish attitudes toward the Ottomans during fifteenth century," in: B. Braude and B. Lewis (eds.), *Christians and Jews in the Ottoman Empire* (New York : Holmes & Meier Publisher, 1982), pp. 117–126.
Hale, William and Ergun Özbudun, *Islamism, Democracy and Liberalism in Turkey: The Case of AK Party* (New York: Routledge, 2009).
Hanioğlu, M. Şükrü, *Preparation for a Revolution: The Young Turks, 1902–1908* (New York: Oxford University Press, 2001).
Heff, Jeffrey, *Antisemitism and Anti-Zionism in Historical Perspective: Convergence and Divergence* (New York: Routledge, 2007).
Hirsh, David, "Hostility to Israel and antisemitism: toward a sociological approach," *The Journal for the Study antisemitism* 5, 1 (2013), pp. 1401–1422.
Hoff, Anne-Cristine, "Normalizing antisemitism in Turkey," *The Journal for the Study of Antisemitism*, 5, 1 (2013), pp. 185–195.
İçduygu, Ahmet and B.A Soner, "Turkish minority rights regime: between difference and equality," *Middle Eastern Studies*, 42, 3 (2006), pp. 447–468.
Iganski, Paul and Barry Kosmin (eds.), *A New Antisemitism?* (London: Profile, 2003).
İnalcık, Halil, "The status of the Greek Orthodox Patriarch under the Ottomans," *Turcica*, 21–23 (1991), pp. 407–435.
İnceoğlu, Efecan, "Türkiye' de Siyasal İslamcılığın Evrimi," MA thesis submitted to Ankara University, 2009.
Jacobson, Avigail, *From Empire to Empire: Jerusalem between Ottoman and British Rule – Space, Place, and Society* (Syracuse, NY: Syracuse University Press. 2011).
Jenkins, Gareth H., "Occasional allies, enduring rivals: Turkey's relations with Iran," Central Asia-Caucasus Institute, Silk Road Studies Program, Johns Hopkins University, May 2012, p. 20: www.silkroadstudies.org/new/docs/silkroadpapers/1205Jenkins.pdf21.
Jikeli, Günther, *European Muslim Antisemitism: Why Young Urban Males Say they Don't Like Jews* (Bloomington, IN: Indiana University Press, 2015).
Junge, Traudl, *Hitler'in Sekreteri* (Istanbul: Alkım Yayınevi, 2004).
Kakınç, Halit, *Struma* (Istanbul: Destek Yayınları, 2012).

Kalın, Ibrahim, "US–Turkish relations under Obama: promise, challenge and opportunity in the 21st century," *Journal of Balkan and Near Eastern Studies*, 12, 1 (2010), pp. 93–108.

Karaca, Özen, "The theme of Jewish conspiracy in Turkish nationalism: the case of Cevat Rıfat Atilhan," unpublished thesis submitted to the Graduate School of Social Sciences of Middle East Technical University, Ankara, 2008: http://etd.lib.metu.edu.tr/upload/12609505/index.pdf.

Karbell, Zachary, *Peace be Upon You: The story of Muslim, Christian and Jewish Coexistence* (New York: Alfred A. Knopf, 2007).

Kardaş, Şaban, "Turkey: redrawing in the Middle East map or building sandcastles?," *Middle East Policy*, 17, 1 (2010), pp. 122–136.

Karman, Sami Sabit, *Yahudi Tarihi ve Siyon Önderlerinin Protokolleri* (Ankara: Yeni Cezaevi Matbaası, 1943).

Karpat Kemal and Yetkin yildirim, *The Ottoman Mosaic: Exploring Models for Peace by Re-exploring the Past* (Seattle, WA: Cune Press, 2010).

Kayali, Hasan, *Arabs and Young Turks: Ottomanism, Arabism, and Islamism in the Ottoman Empire, 1908–1918* (Berkeley, CA: California University Press, 1997).

Khalidi, Rashid, *Palestinian Identity: The Construction of Modern National Consciousness* (New York: Columbia University Press, 1997).

Kirişçi, Kemal, "Disaggregating Turkish citizenship and immigration practices," *Middle Eastern Studies*, 36, 3 (2000), pp. 1–22.

Kısakürek, Necip Fâzıl, *Yahudilik-Masonluk-Dönmelik* [Judaism, Freemasonship, sabbetaism] (Istanbul: Büyük Doğu Yayınları, 2010).

Kressel, Neil J., *"The Sons of Pigs and Apes": Muslim Antisemitism and the Conspiracy of Silence* (Washington, DC: Potomac Books, 2012).

Küçük, Yalçın, *İsimlerin İbranileştirilmesi Tekelistan* (İstanbul Salyangöz: Yayınları, 2008).

Küçük, Yalçın, *Şebeke "Network" 1* (İstanbul: İthaki Yayınları, 2004).

Kuru, Ahmet, "Changing perspectives on Islamism and secularism in Turkey: The Gülen Movement and the AK Party," in: Ihsan Yilmaz (ed.), *Muslim World in Transition: Contributions of the Gülen Movement* (London: Leeds Metropolitan University Press, 2007), pp. 140–151.

Kuru, Ahmet, "Fethullah Gülen's search for a middle way between modernity and Muslim tradition," in: M. Hakan Yavuz and John L. Esposito (eds.), *Turkish Islam and the Secular State: The Gülen Movement* (Syracuse, NY: Syracuse University Press, 2003), pp. 115–130.

Kushner, David, *The Rise of Turkish Nationalism: 1876–1908* (London: Frank Cass, 1977).

Landau, Jacob M., *Exploring Ottoman and Turkish History* (London: C. Hurst & Co., 2004).

Landau, Jacob M., "Relations between Jews and non-Jews in the late Ottoman Empire: some characteristics," in: Avigdor Levy (ed.), *The Jews of the Ottoman Empire* (Princeton, NJ: The Darwin Press, 1994), pp. 539–547.

Landau, Jacob M., *Pan-Turkism: From Irredentism to Cooperation* (Bloomington, IN: Indiana University Press, 1992).

Landau, Jacob M., "Al Dmuta Shel Haantishemiyut BaRapublika Haturkit" [On the form of antisemitism in the Turkish Republic], *Ninth World Congress of Jewish Studies, Division B, Vol. II, The History of the Jewish People* (Jerusalem: World Union of Jewish Studies, 1986), pp. 77–82 [Hebrew].

Landau, Jacob M., *Tekinalp: Turkish Patriot 1883–1961* (Istanbul: Nederlands Historisch-Archaeologisch Instituut, 1984).
Landau, Jacob M., "Some comments on the Young Turks' attitude toward Zionism," in: Gedalya Yogev (ed.), *Anthology to the History of the Zionist Movement and the Jewish Settlement in the Land of Israel* (Tel-Aviv: HaKibuts HaMe'uhad and University of Tel Aviv Press, 1984), pp. 195–205 [Hebrew].
Landau, Jacob M., *Radical Politics in Modern Turkey* (Leiden: Brill, 1974).
Levi, Avner, "Yahas HaShiltonot ve HaChevra HaTurkim Klapey HaYehudim Agav Parashat Aliza Niego" [The attitude of the Turkish authorities and society towards Jews in the aftermath of the Aliza Niego Incident], in: Avraham Hayim (ed.), *Chevra VeKehilla: MiDivrey Hakongress HaBenleumi HaSheni LeCheker Moreshet Yahadut Sfarad ve HaMizrach 1985* [Society and Community: Proceedings of the Second (International) Congress on Sephardi and Oriental Jewish Heritage] (Jerusalem: Misgav Yerushalayim, 1991), pp. 237–246 [Hebrew].
Levi, Avner, *Toldot HaYehudim Barapublika HaTurkit* [History of the Jews in the Republic of Turkey] (Jerusalem: Lafir Press, 1992) [Hebrew].
Levi, Avner, "Hapra'ot BeYehudeyTrakaya, 1942" [The pogroms against the Jews of Thrace, 1942], *Pe'amim*, 20 (1984), pp. 11–132 [Hebrew].
Levy, Avigdor, "Ottoman attitudes to the modernization of Jewish education: nineteenth and twentieth centuries," in Michael Laskier and Yaacov Lev (eds.), *The Divergence of Judaism and Islam: Interdependence, Modernity, and Political Turmoil* (Gainesville, FL: University Press of Florida, 2011), pp. 17–28.
Levy, Avigdor, (ed.), *Jews, Turks, Ottomans: A Shared History, Fifteenth through the Twentieth Century* (New York: Syracuse University Press, 2002).
Levy, Avigdor, "Togarmah: Jewish life in the Ottoman Empire," *Le'Ela*, 39 (1995), pp. 25–29.
Levy, Avigdor, (ed.), *The Jews of the Ottoman Empire* (Princeton, NJ: The Darwin Press, 1994).
Levy, Avigdor, "The establishment and development of the institution of Haham Bashi in the Ottoman Empire (1835–1865)," *Pe'amim*, 55 (1993), pp. 38–56 [Hebrew].
Livaneli, Zülfü, *Serenad* (Istanbul: Doğan Kitap, 2011).
Mallet, Laurent-Olivier, *La Turquie, les Turcs et les Juifs: histoire, Représentations, Discours et Strategies* (Istanbul: Isis Press, 2008).
Mickolous, Edward and Susan L Simmons, *Terrorism 1992–1995: A Chronology of Events and a Selectively Annotated Bibliography* (Westport, CT: Greenwood Press, 1997).
Mungan, Murathan, *Merhaba Asker (Murathan Mungan'ın Seçtikleriyle)* (Istanbul: Metis, 2014).
Nefes, Turkay Selim, "The history of the social constructions about Dönmes," *The Journal of Historical Sociology*, 25, 3 (2013), pp. 413–439.
Neyzi, Leyla, "Strong as steel, fragile as a rose: A Turkish Jewish witness to the twentieth century," *Jewish Social Studies* 12, 1 (2005), pp. 167–189.
Nilus, Sergius, *Siyon Liderlerinin Protokolleri: ikinci basım*, second edition (Istanbul: Nokta Kitap, 2005).
Ofer, Dalia, *Escaping the Holocaust: Illegal Immigration to the Land of Israel 1939–1944* (New York: Oxford University Press, 1990).
Oğuzlu, Tarik, "The changing dynamics of Turkey–Israel relations: a structural realist account," *Mediterranean Politics*, 15, 2 (2010), pp. 273–288.
Öke, Mim Kemal, "The Ottoman Empire, Zionism and the question of Palestine," *International Journal of Middle East Studies*, 14, 3 (1982), pp. 329–341.

Bibliography

Öktem, Kerem, Ayşe Kadıoğlu, and Mehmet Karlı (eds.), *Another Empire? A Decade of Turkey's Foreign Policy Under the Justice and Development Party* (Istanbul: Istanbul Bilgi University Press, 2012).

Orhon, Orhan Seyfi, *Dün bugün yarın* (İstanbul: Çınar Yayınevi, 1952).

Ortaylı, İlber, "Osmanlı'da Tolerans ve Tesamuh," in: İlber Ortaylı, *Osmanlı Barışı* (İstanbul: Timaş, 2007), pp. 53–60.

Ortaylı, İlber, "Ottomanism and Zionism during the second constitutional period, 1908–1915," in: Avigdor Levy (ed.), *The Jews of the Ottoman Empire* (Princeton, NJ: The Darwin Press, 1994), pp. 527–538.

Pekesen, Berna, *Nationalismus, Türkisierung und das Ende der jüdischen Gemeinden in Thrakien, 1918–1942* (München: R. Oldenbourg Verlang, 2012); Hatice Bayraktar, *"Zweideutige Individuen in schlechter Absicht," Die antisemitischen Ausschreitungen in Thrakien 1934 und ihre Hintergründe* (Berlin: Klaus Schwarz, 2011).

Pirzade, İ.H, *Türkiye ve Yahudileri* (Istanbul: Ark Matbaacılık, 1968).

Porat, Dina and Roni Stauber (eds.), *Antisemitism Worldwide 2000/2001* (Lincoln, NE: Nebraska University Press, 2002).

Poyraz, Ergün, *Musa'nın AKP'si* (Istanbul: Gökbörü Yayıncılık, 2007).

Poyraz, Ergün, *Musa'nın Çocukları Tayyip ve Emine* (Istanbul: Togan Yayıncılık, 2007).

Poyraz, Ergün, *Musa'nın Gülü 8 baskı* (Istanbul: Togan Yayıncılık 2007).

Poyraz, Ergün, *Musa'nın Mücahiti* (Istanbul: Togan Yayıncılık 2007).

Reisman, Arnold, *Turkey's Modernization: Refugees from Nazism and Atatürk's Vision* (Washington, DC: New Academia Publishers, 2006).

Rıfat, Cevat, *Suzi Liberman* (İstanbul: Türkiye Matbaası, 1935).

Rodrigue, A. and Nancy Reynolds, "Difference and tolerance in the Ottoman Empire," *Stanford Humanities Review*, 5 (1995), pp. 81–92.

Rozen, Minna, *A History of the Jewish Community in Istanbul: The Formative Years, 1453–1566* (Leiden: Brill, 2002).

Rozen, Minna, *Yeme Ha-Sahar: Perakim be-Toldot Ha-Yehudim Ba-Imperyah ha-'Otomanit* (Tel-Aviv: ha-Katedrah le-heker Yahadut Saloniki ve-Yavan: ha-Makhon le-heker ha-tefutsot, Universitat Tel-Aviv Press, 1996). [Hebrew].

Rubin, Michael, "Mr. Erdoğan's Turkey," *Wall Street Journal*, 19 (2006). www.meforum.org/1036/mr-Erdoğans-Turkey.

Rumford, Chris, "Resisting globalization? Turkey–EU relations and human and political rights in the context of cosmopolitan democratization," *International Sociology*, 18, 2 (2003), pp. 379–394.

Şaul, Mahir, "The mother tongue of the polyglot: cosmopolitianism and nationalism among the Sepharadim of Istanbul," in: Mehmet Tütüncü (ed.), *Turkish–Jewish Encounters* (Haarlem: SOTA 2001), pp. 129–168.

Scholem, Gershom, *Sabbatai Sevi: The Mystical Messiah* (Princeton, NJ: Princeton University Press, 1973).

Shaw, Stanford J., *Jews of the Ottoman Empire and the Turkish Republic* (New York: New York University Press, 1991).

Shmuelevitz, Aryeh, "Emdat HaItonut HaIslamit BeTurkiya Klapey Israel" [The attitude of the Turkish Islamic press towards Israel], *HaMizrah HeHadas* [The New East], 39 (1997–1998), pp. 114–124 [Hebrew].

Shmuelevitz, Aryeh, "Ms Pococke no. 31 as a source for the events in Istanbul in the years 1622–1624," *International Journal of Turkish Studies* 3, 2 (1985–1986), pp. 121–107.

Sisman, Cengiz, *The Burden of Silence: Sabbatai Sevi and the Evolution of the Ottoman-Turkish Dönmes* (New York: Oxford University Press, 2015).

Bibliography 223

Sisman, Cengiz, *Sabatay Sevi ve Sabataycılar: Mitler ve Gerçekler* (İstanbul: Aşina Kitaplari, 2008).
Solberg, Anne Ross, *The Mahdi Wears Armani: An Analysis of the Harun Yahya Enterprise* (Stockholm: Södertörn University, 2013).
Sonyel, Salahi R., *Minorities and the Destruction of the Ottoman Empire* (Ankara: Turkish Historical Society Printing House, 1993).
Tamari, Salim, *Mountains Against the Sea: Essays on Palestinian Society and Culture* (Berkeley, CA: University of California Press, 2009).
Tanyu, Hikmet, *Tarih Boyunca Yahudiler ve Türkler I–II* [Jews and Turks throughout History] (Istanbul: Yağmur Yayınları, 1976).
Tibi, Bassam, *Islamism and Islam* (New Haven, CT: Yale University Press, 2012).
Toktaş, Şule, "Perceptions of antisemitism among Turkish Jews," *Turkish Studies*, 7, 2 (2006), pp. 203–223.
Toktaş, Şule, "The conduct of citizenship in the case of Turkey's Jewish minority: legal status, identity and civic virtue aspects," *Comparative Studies of South Asia, Africa and the Middle East*, 26, 1 (2006), pp. 121–133.
Türesay, Özgür, "Antisionisme et antisémitisme dans la presse ottomane d'Istanbul à l'époque jeune turque (1909–1912): L'exemple d'Ebüzziya Tevfik," *Turcica*, 41 (2009), pp. 147–178.
Türkan, Reha Oğuz, *Solcular ve Kızıllar* (İstanbul: Bozkurtçu Yayını, 1943).
Türkeş, Alparslan, *Dava* (İstanbul: Kamer Yayınları, 2013).
Türkeş, Alparslan, *Savunma* (İstanbul: Kamer Yayınları, 2013).
Türkmen, Füsun, "Turkish–American relations: a challenging transition," *Turkish Studies*, 10, 1 (2009), pp. 109–129.
Türkmen, Füsun and Emre Öktem, "Foreign policy as a determinant in the fate of Turkey's non-Muslim minorities: a dialectical analysis," *Turkish Studies*, 14, 3 (2013), pp. 463–482.
Turunç, Hasan, "Islamist or Democratic? The AK Party's search for identity in Turkish politics," *Journal of Contemporary European Studies*, 15, 1 (2007), pp. 79–91.
Tuval, Shaul, *HaKehilah haYehudit be-Istanbul, 1948–1992* [The Jewish community in Istanbul 1948–1992] (Jerusalem: World Zionist Organization, 2004) [Hebrew].
Ülken, Hilmi Ziya, *Yahudi Meselesi* (Istanbul: Üniversite Kitabevi, 1944).
Ülker, Erol, "Assimilation, security and geographical nationalization in interwar Turkey: the Settlement Law of 1934," *European Journal of Turkish Studies, Thematic issue: Demographic Engineering*, 1, 7 (2008): http://ejts.revues.org/index2123.html.
Ülkümen, Selahattin, *Emekli Diplomat Selahattin Ülkümen'in Anıları: Bilinmeyen Yönleriyle Bir Dönemin Dışişleri* [The memories of retired diplomat Selahatin Ulkumen: the foreign affairs of a period with its unknown aspects] (Istanbul: Gözlem Yayınları, 1993).
Ünal, İsmail, *Fethullah Gülen'le Amerika'da Bir Ay* (İstanbul: Işık Yayınları, 2001).
Uzer, Umut, "Turkish–Israeli relations: their rise and fall," *Middle East Policy*, 20, 1 (2013), pp. 97–110.
Uzer, Umut, "Racism in Turkey: the case of Nihal Atsız," *Journal of Muslim Minority Affairs*, 22, 1 (2002), pp. 119–130.
Walker, Joshua W., "The United States and Turkey in a changing world," in: Kerem Öktem, Ayşe Kadıoğlu, and Mehmet Karli (eds.), *Another Empire: A decade of Turkey's Foreign Policy Under the Justice and Development Party* (Istanbul: Istanbul Bilgi University Press, 2012).
Walker, Joshua W., "Reexamining the U.S.–Turkish alliance," *The Washington Quarterly* (2007–2008), p. 94.

Weiker, Walter F., *Ottomans, Turks and the Jewish Polity: A History of the Jews of Turkey* (Lanham, MD: University Press of America, 1992).
Weiss, Adina, "Yehudey Turkia: Misgeret Datit BeMishtar Stagrani [The Jews of Turkey: religious framework in closed regime]," *Tfutzot Israel* [Israel diaspora], 12, Choveret [booklet] Bet (1974), pp. 93–120 [Hebrew].
White, Jenny B., "Islam and politics in contemporary Turkey," in Reşsat Kasaba (ed.), *The Cambridge History of Turkey: Volume 4 Turkey in the Modern World* (Cambridge: Cambridge University Press, 2008), pp. 357–380.
Wistrich, Robert, *A Lethal Obsession: Antisemitism – From Antiquity to the Global Jihad* (New York: Random House, 2010).
Yahya, Harun, *Soykırım Vahşeti* (Istanbul:Araştırma Yayıncılık, 2003).
Yahya, Harun, *Soykırım Yalani* (Istanbul: Alem, 1995).
Yahya, Harun, *Yahudilik ve Masonluk* (Istanbul: Sezgin Neşriyat, 1992).
Yalçın, Soner, *Efendi: Beyaz Türklerin Büyük Sırrı* (Istanbul: Doğan Kıtap, 2004).
Yalçın, Soner, *Behçet Cantürk'ün Anıları* (Istanbul: Doğan Kitapçılık, 2003).
Yalçın, Soner, *Reis Gladio'nun Türk Tetikçisi* (Istanbul: Doğan Kitapçılık, 2003).
Yalçın, Soner, *Teşkilat'ın İki Silahşörü* (Istanbul: Doğan Kitapçılık, 2001).
Yalçın, Soner, *Bay Pipo, Bir MİT Görevlisinin Sıra Dışı Yaşamı: Hiram Abbas* (Istanbul: Doğan Kitapçılık, 2000).
Yalçın, Soner, *Hangi Erbakan* (Ankara: Öteki Yayınevi, 1999).
Yalçın, Soner, *Binbaşı Ersever'in İtirafları* (Istanbul: Kaynak Yayınları, 1996).
Yaman, Kemal (ed.), *Millet Düşmanlarının İhanet Planları* (İstanbul: Otağ Yayınları, 1971).
Yavuz, M. Hakan, *Toward an Islamic Enlightenment: The Gülen Movement* (New York: Oxford University Press, 2013).
Yavuz, M. Hakan (ed.), *The Emergence of a New Turkey: Democracy and the AK Party* (Salt Lake City, UT: University of Utah Press, 2006).
Yavuz, M. Hakan, *Modernleşen müslümanlar: Nurcular, Nakşiler, Milli Görüş ve AK Parti* (İstanbul: Kitapyayınevi, 2003).
Yavuz, M. Hakan, "Search for a new contract in Turkey: Fethullah Gülen, the Virtue Party and the Kurds," *Sais Review*, 19, 1 (1999), pp. 114–143.
Yayaoğlu, Recai, *Yahudi Psikolojisi* (Istanbul: Nesil Yayınları), 2010.
Yılanlıoğlu, Ismail Hakki, *Üç büyük tehlike Siyonizm-komünizm-farmasonluk* (İstanbul: Güven Basımevi, 1968).
Yılmaz, Şuhnaz and Ziya Öniş, "Between Europeanization and Euro-Asianism: foreign policy activism in Turkey during the AK Party era," *Turkish Studies*, 10, 1 (2009), pp. 7–24.
Yükleyen, Ahmet, "Sufism and Islamic groups in contemporary Turkey," in: Reşsat Kasaba (ed.), *The Cambridge History of Turkey: Volume 4 Turkey in the Modern World* (Cambridge: Cambridge University Press, 2008), pp. 381–387.

Archives

AJJDC
US NARA
Israel State Archive

Newspapers and media

Hebrew

Globes
Israel Hayom
Maariv
NRG
Yediot Ahronot

English

The Algemeiner
Asharq al-Awsat
Breitbart
Daily Sabah
Der Spiegel
Eurasia Daily Monitor
Financial Times
Haaretz
Hürriyet Daily News
Jerusalem Online
Jerusalem Post
The Jewish Daily Forward
The Jewish Press
MEMRI
New York Times
Shoebat Foundation
The Times of Israel
Today's Zaman
Voice of America
Wall Street Journal
The Washington Free Beacon
YNET

Turkish

Agos
Akbaba
Akşam
Aktif Haber
Aktüel psikoloji
Al Gazeera
Anadolu Ajansı
Anadolu Bugün

Beyaz Gazete
Bir Gün
Birikim
CNN Türk
Cumhuriyet
Demokrat Haber
Die Welt
Durustv
Ensonhaber
Gözcü
Haber Vaktim
Haber7
HaberTürk Gazete
Hastürk
Hursedahaber
İlkben
Marksist
Medya Radar
Milli Gazete
Milliyet
OdaTV
Radikal
Rota Haber
Sabah
Şalom
Sendika.org
Ses Türkiye
Sözcü
Star
T24
Tercüman
Timetürk
TRT Haber
Türkiye
Yeni Akit
Yeni Şafak
Yeniçağ
Zaman

Index

Page numbers in *italics* denote tables, those in **bold** denote figures.

1936 Declaration 37

Abdülhamid II, Sultan 23, 72, 81–2
adalet (justice) 9, 13
ADL 100
Adorno, Theodor W. 104–5, 134n24
Ağbaba, Veli 114–15
Agos 180, 189
AK Party 69–99, 117, 151, 170–1; adoption of passive secularism 188–9; control of the media 140; criticism of Israel 78–80, 87–8; democratization package 195–6; foreign policy 70–1, 76–7; Holocaust commemoration 191–2; and Islamic philosophy 69–70; Islamists 81–6; Israel and Zionism, relations with 72–8; Kurdish issues 90–3; leftists 87–8; nationalists and ultranationalists 88–90
Akansel, Mustafa Hakki 148
Akdoğan, Yalçın 199
Akyol, Mustafa 151
Albayrak, Hakan 104
Ali, Sabahattin 3
Aliyah 44–5, 122, 183
Aliza Niego Affair 35–6
Alkan, Ahmet Turan 104
Altabev, Isak 47–8
American Jewish Congress 184
Ankara'da gizli Israil Devleti mi var? (Demir) 150–1
anti-Zionism 2, 212, 213; anti-Zionist writings 52; and antisemitism 75–6
antisemitism 85, 86; and anti-Zionism 75–6; categories of 55–6; characteristics of 212; continuing existence of, in Turkey 213; and criticism of Israel 78–80; definition 2, 79; and the Kurdish issue 90–3; leftist view of 87–8; and nationalism 88–90; op-eds 212; posters **53**, 158, **158**, **159**, 181; public life examples of 1–2; publications 29, 38, 38–40, **39**, **40**, **41**, 42–3, 44, 45, 46, 48–51, 51–2, 54, 56–7, 58–60, 126–7, 141–5, 145–51, **147**, 157; theoretical aspects of 76; threatening letters 55, **55**; *see also* media and antisemitism; military operations and antisemitism
antisemitizm.Info (website) 182
Armağan, Mustafa 81–2
Armenians 10, 11, 20, 21, 24, 27, 29, 128, 129, 177, 181–2
Atalay, Beşir 169
Atatürk *see* Kemal, Mustafa (Atatürk)
Atilhan, Cevat Rıfat 42–3, 45, 72
atrocities 21
Atsız, Nihal 38, 43
Avcı, Servet 89, 196–7
Ayalon, Danny 78
Aydemir, Bülent 168
Aydın, Taner 192
Aylık 143
Aypek, Figen 93
Ayrılık: Aşkta ve Savaşta Filistin (TV series) 154–5

Balcı, Kerim 52, 86, 88, 214
Bali, Rıfat N. 4, 30, 42, 59, 73, 88, 102, 128–9, 171, 177, 179, 181, 185, 213
Barkey, Karen 10, 14–15, 21
Barlas, Mehmet 186–7
BAV 59
Behar, Cem 183

228　Index

Bekdil, Burak 86, 125, 193
Birikim 87
blood libels 2, 20, 21, 22, 78, 85, 141
B'nai Brith 83
Bonomo, Can 155
books 145–51, **147**, 157
Bozgeyik, Burhan 142–3, 186
Braude, Benjamin 13
Brink-Danan, Marcy 161, 177
Bugün 51–2, 54, 84
Bulaç, Ali 85
Bülent, Şenay 199–200
Bünyel, Erol Aron 173, 184
Burak, Begüm 129, 130

Çapa, Niyazi 106
cartoons 38–40, **39**, **40**, **41**, 50, **93**, 114, **115**, **116**, 120, **121**, 180
Çavuşoğlu, Mevlüt 155
Çelik, Hüseyin 81, 174
Çelik, Ömer 120, 192, 194, 199
Çelikkol, Ahmet Oğuz 78
Cengiz, Orhan Kemal 106
CHP 71, 114–15, 126, 160, 169
Christianity and Christians 10, 11, 13, 17, 20–2; hostility to Jews 19
Çiçek, Cemil 198–9
citizenship 12, 23, 25, 27–8
Civil Code 28
Cohen, Shay 75, 148, 176, 185
commercials 151–2
Committee of Union and Progress 72
communism 49, 54, 57–8
conspiracy theories 141, 144
constitutions 4, 23, 28, 44, 48
criminal acts 2
Cyprus 46

Dağı, İhsan 83, 126–7, 150
Dalkılıç, Cumali 143–4
Danon, Danny 113
death threats 51
Dede, Ersoy 73
Demir, Ayhan 104
Demir, Hasan 91–2, 150–1
Democrat Party 45
Dhimmis 9–10, 11, 13; and contemptuous language 15; preference of Jews over Christians 17; status of and restrictions on 9–11, 13, 15–16, 18–19
Diler, Fatih Gökhan 4, 128, 180, 196
Dink, Hrant 127–8
Directorate General of Foundations (DGF) 37

Directorate of Religious Foundations 194, 195
Doğan, Erdal 28
Dönme 82–3, 149
Dün Bugün Yarın (Orhon) 162–3
DurDe *see* Say Stop to Racism and Nationalism (DurDe)
Düzgün, Mücahit 44

education 157, 189–90
Efendi 2: Beyaz Müslümanların Büyük Sırrı (Yalçın) 149
Efendi: Beyaz Türklerin Büyük Sırrı (Yalçın) 148–9
Elrom, Efraim 3, 51, 179
Ender, Rita 123
entertainment 151–7
Erbakan, Necmettin 52, 63–4n97, 69
Erdaş, Mehmet 167
Erdemir, Aykan 167, 168–9, 173, 175–6, 191–2, 196
Erdiş, Salih İzzet 143
Erdoğan, Recep Tayyip 3, 75, 77–8, 103, 107–8, 126, 141, 149, 181; comments on Operation Protective Edge 117–19; Courage Award 184; discourse of Erdogan as reflected in the Turkish media 167–76; personal aspects of antisemitism 213–14; Soma crisis 160–1; views on antisemitism 100–1, 197
Ersanlı, Büşra 92
European Council Against Racism and Intolerance (ECRI) 90, 193–4, 195, 197
European Union (EU) 70, 194, 195

Fandy, Mamoun 127
fascism 75, 88
Felicity Party 70
Filiba, Lina 107
film industry 57, 102, 149, 152–4, 190
Ford, Henry 50, 145
foreign policy 70–1, 76–7
foundations 28, 37, 194–5
Foxman, Abraham H. 100, 110, 119, 152
Freemasonry 49, 50, 51, 54, 140

Gaza 104, 113, 115, **116**, 148
Gazeteciler ve Yazarlar Vakfı 56
gendarmerie 149
Gezi Park Protest 169–70
Glick, Caroline 169
Granville, Edgar 13
Greeks 11, 24, 29, 46; hostility to Jews 20–2

Gül, Abdullah 103, 106, 150
Gülen, Fethullah 56–7, 111–12
Gün, Suat 45
Günzberg, Sami (Samuel) M. 23–4
Gürşen, Evren 104–5
Guttstadt, Corry 55, 128, 175–6, 192
Güven, Fahri 144

Hacker, Joseph R. 17
Hadith 52
Hakan, Ahmet 102, 197–8
Hahamb Başı 13
Haleva, Rabbi 46, 56, 57, 112, 184–5
Haligua, Avi 183
Hanafis 10
hate crimes 195–7
hate speech 127–32, **131**, **132**
Hate Speech in the Media and Discriminatory Discourse (International Hrant Dink Foundation) 129–32, **131**, **132**
Herzl, Theodor 72, 81–2
Hirsch, David 76, 78–9, 90, 140
Hitler, Adolf 112, 113, 118, 141–2, 143–4, 145, 146, 147, 151–2, 156
Hoff, Anne-Christine 111
Holocaust 2, 57, 59, 76, 83–4, 100, 104, 111; commemoration of 190–2, 212
"How did Abdülhamid make the Chief Rabbi apologize?" (Armağan) 81–2
human rights 79, 88, 197
Hür, Ayşe 141–2, 146–7

IBDA-C 143
İçduygu, Ahmet 10, 45–6
İleri 29
İnönü, Efraim Elrom 3
"Internal and external enemy, The: Jew" (Erdiş) 143
International Hrant Dink Foundation 128, 129–30, 166
International Jew, The (Ford) 50, 145
Islahat Fermani 13
Islamists 81–6
İslamoğlu, Mustafa 86
Israel 1, 44–5, 49, 50, 52, 141; affinity with the United States 55; association of Turkish Jews with 73–5, 197–200, 213; criticism of Israel 78–80, 87–8; hostility to 85; and an increase in Turkish antisemitism 166, 173–5; nationalism 76; and the PKK 90–3; relations with Turkey 57, 71, 72–8; *see also* military operations and antisemitism

Jacobs, Barry 89
Jews: association with Israel 73–5, 197–200, 213; employment in official service 23, 26, 30, 178; experiences after the *Mavi Marmara* incident 107–8, 110, 113–14; experiences during Operation Protective Edge 119–20, 122–3, **124**, 125, **126**; forced evacuations 38; hostility to 20–2, 29, 35–6; identity issues 155, 160–2; loyalty to Turkey 110, 141, 177; media and antisemitism, responses to 176–86; millet system 11–12, 13–14, 23, 27; need for keeping a low profile 179–81; opposition to Jewish neighbors 163, **163**; and Ottoman law 9–14; parliamentary representation 46–7; population figures 25; preference of, over Christians 17; recognition as a protected minority 27; religious conversion 13; restrictions on 30; security issues 47–8, 193–4, 213; social organization and status 12–13, 18–19; and sultans 17–18; trust in 164–6, **164**, *165*; and Turkish identity 155; Turkish names, use of 158–60
Joint Distribution Committee (JDC) 47
journalism 48, 51–2, 54; hate speech 129–32, **131**, **132**; Islamic journalism 83–5
justice 9, 13

Kamhi, Moshe 156
Karagöz Theater 19, 24
Karakaş, Şenol 87–8
Karakoç, Abdürrahim 112
Karaman, Salmi Sabit 145
Kavgam 145–7, **147**
kayadez 179–81
KCK Operation 92
Kekeç, Ahmet 105
Kemal, Mustafa (Atatürk) 25, 26, 82, 144
Kıran, Kenan 75
Kısakürek, Ahmet Necip Fäzıl 46, 57, 88–9, 98n94
Kıvanç, Ümit 87, 88
Kıvrıkoğlu, Hüseyin 80
Kocabaşoğlu, Yunus Emre 80
Korkut, Ege Berk 113–14
Kortun, Vasif 156
Köse, Faruk 119, 176, 198
Kressel, Neil J. 188
Küçük, Yalçın 126–7, 149, 203n40
Küçükcan, Talip 3, 80, 173–4, 200

230   Index

Kurds 26, 90–3, **93**
Kürk Mantolu Madonna (Ali) 3
Kurtlar Vadisi-Filistin (film) 153–4
Kuvayi Milliye Derneği 89

laicism 69
Landau, Jacob 42
language 4, 15, 28
Lausanne, Treaty of 25–6, 26–7, 28, 37, 38, 189
Lavie, Yigal 80
law 4; inconsistent enforcement of 15–16; Kanun 17; Ottoman law 9–14; Sharia law 9, 10, 13, 16, 17
Law no. 2762 37
Law on Foreign Language Education 28
Law on Foundations (1935) 37, 185, 194
Law on Professions and Services Assigned to Turkish Citizens in Turkey (1932) 37
leftists 87–8
Leftists and Red Ones (Türkan) 148
Levi, Avner 30, 44
Levi, Mario 120, 171, 180
Levy, Moshe 81–2

Maariv 52
Macit, Bilal 185–6
Margulies, Roni 183
Mavi Marmara 2010 74, 75, 81, 107–14, **109**, 187
media and antisemitism 140–211; animosity to Jews 140–1; antisemitism directed at Israel and Zionism 141; awareness of antisemitism, reflections of 186–201; books 145–51, **147**, 157; daily life 157–66, **158**, **159**, 163, **164**, *165*; depiction of Jews as linked with 'other' or 'evil' groups 141; education 157; entertainment 151–7; Erdoğan's discourse as reflected in the media 167–76; hate speech 129–32, **131**, **132**; hostile approach to Turkish Jews 141; Jewish responses 176–86; newspapers 141–5, 187; petitions 187–8
Mein Kampf (Hitler) 43, 88, 141–2, 143–4, 145, 146, 147
"Mein Kampf and the protocols of Zion" (Hür) 141–2
Merhaba Asker (Mungan) 144–5
Mert, Nuray 91, 102
Milat 120, 122
Milli İnkilap 42, 43
military operations and antisemitism 100–39; hate speech 127–32, **131**, **132**; *Mavi Marmara* 2010 74, 75, 81, 107–14, **109**, 187; Operation Cast Lead 77–8, 101, 103–7; Operation Pillar of Defense 113–14; Operation Protective Edge 46, 73, 88, 114–27, **115**, **116**, **121**, **124**, **126**, 183; Second Lebanon War 2006 100–3
millet system 11–12, 13–14, 23, 27, 30n1
Milli Gazete 80, 144
Molinas, İvo 4, 128, 178, 179, 180, 182, 191, 192, 194, 195
Mungan, Murathan 144–5
Municipality Law (1930) 37
murders 10, 20, 35–6, 51, 58, 89–90, 125, 127–8, 193
Musa Dağ (Atilhan) 43
Musa'nın AK Parti'si (Poyraz) 150
Musa'nın Çocukları (Poyraz) 149
Musa'nın Gülü (Poyraz) 149, 150
Musa'nın Mücahiti (Poyraz) 150
museums 156

Nahum, Haim 26
nationalism 25, 26, 37–8, 82–3; and antisemitism 88–90; Israel 76; neo-nationalists 126–7
Navaro, Leyla 182
Nazism 36, 40, 42–3, 104, 118, 126, 188
newspapers 29, 35–6, 44, 46, 48, 51–2, 54, 71, 130, 140, 141–5, 187
Niego, Aliza 35–6

Of the Turk: Researchers Regarding the Turkic Race (Akansel) 148
Oktar, Adnan 58–60
Öktem, Emre 46, 89–90, 107–8, 195
Olmert, Ehud 101, 103
Önal, Ayşe 186
Öniş, Ziya 151
op-eds 212
Operation Cast Lead 77–8, 101, 103–7
Operation Pillar of Defense 113–14
Operation Protective Edge 46, 73, 88, 114–27, 183; grassroots actions by Turkish society 119–27, **121**, **124**, **126**; political and politician stratum 114–19, **115**, **116**
Organizational Regulations of the Rabbinate 12
Orhon, Orhan Seyfi 162–3
Orhun 38
Ottoman Empire 144; communal administration 22; Greeks and Christians 20–2; Jews and sultans

17–18; modern times 23–4; non-Muslims, status of and restrictions on 9–11, 13, 15–16, 18–19; Ottoman law and the Jews 9–14; Tanzimat reforms 23; taxation 9–10, 11, 12, 15–16, 22; tolerance 10–11, 13, 14–17, 22; violence 14–17; war of liberation 24–5; Western travelers' impression of 13; and Zionism 72–3
Ovadya, Silvyo 106, 107, 152, 190
Özel, Soli 183

Palestinian Authority 76–7
Palestinian Liberation Organization (PLO) 87
pan-Turkism 43
Passport Law (1938) 37–8
Patrini, Alberto 113
Peker, Recep 45
Peres, Shimon 78, 103
petitions 187–8
Pianist, The (film) 102–3
Pirzade, İ. H. 49–51
PKK 90–3
places of worship, prohibitions on construction and renovation 10, 16, 74, 194
posters **53**, 158, **158**, **159**, 181
Poyraz, Ergün 126–7, 149–50
Project Aladdin 190, 191
Project Presenting Turkish Jewry and Jewish Culture (research study) 163
propaganda 36, 42, 49, 51, 83; antisemitic posters **53**, 158, **158**, **159**, 181
"Protocols of the Elders of Germany, The" (Akyol) 151
Protocols of the Elders of Zion 141–2, 144, 145, 146, 148
proverbs 19, 29

Quincentennial Foundation 83, 177
Quran 11, 52, 85, 86, 141, 200

race codes 189
Radikal 141–2, 144–5
Ratib, Osman 35
RTÜK 102–3

Şahin, Davut 4, 85–6
Salamon Fıkraları (cartoon series) 38–40, **39**, **40**, **41**
Şalom 110, 180, 182, 198
Say Stop to Racism and Nationalism (DurDe) 200–1

Second Lebanon War 2006 100–3
secularisation 26, 69–70, 188–9
segregation 16
Settlement Law (1934) 38
Shnidell, S. 47
Shoah (film) 190, 191
Şirin, Nurettin 74–5, 106–7
Sokol, Sam 180
Soma crisis 160–1
Soner, B. A. 10, 45–6
Sonyel, Salahi R. 13, 18
Soros, George 92–3
Soykırım Vahşeti 59
Soykırım Yalanı (BAV) 59
Stephen Roth Institute for the Study of Contemporary Antisemitism and Racism 59
Struma 212
Süter, Şakir 91
Suzy Liebermann, Jewish Spy (Atilhan) 43
synagogues: attacks on 119–20, 193, 201n8; prohibitions on construction and renovation 10, 16, 74, 194

Tan, H. E. Namık 110
Tan, Şahap 54
Tanyu, Hikmet 54
Tarih Boyunca Yahudiler ve Türkler I–II (Tanyu) 54
Task Force for International Cooperation on Holocaust Education, Remembrance and Research 190
Taşkıran, Ahmet 199
Tasvir-i Efkar 29
taxation 11, 12; cizye 22; poll tax 9–10, 15–16; Varlık Vergisi 41–3
Tekin, Arslan 142
Tekinalp, Munis 82–3
terrorism 51, 58; publications 143–4
Tevfik, Ebüzziya 23–4, 29
Tezcan, Fatih 144
Tezyapar, Sinem 59–60
Tilbe, Yıldız 156–7, 181
Toledo, Zali de 56–7, 101, 167–8
tolerance 10–11, 13, 22, 35, 56; and violence 14–17
Tunay, Faik 74, 170–1
Türkan, Reha Oğuz 148
Turkey 24; from 1923–1933 35–6; from 1933–1943 36–40; 1980s–1990s 57–60; antisemitic publications 29, 38, 38–40, **39**, **40**, **41**, 42–3, 44, 45, 46, 48–51, 51–2, 54, 56–7, 58–60, 126–7, 157; antisemitism, discrete nature of 2–4;

Turkey *continued*
  constitutions 4, 28, 44, 48; first years of the republic 25–8; Jewish population figures 25; late 1960s–1970s 48–57; minority rights 25–6; nationalist ideology 25, 26, 37–8; and the Palestinian Authority 76–7; parliament 46–7; post-war to the late 1960s 44–8; relations with Israel 57, 71, 72–8; restrictions on Jews 30; social liberalization 58; unified Turkish society policy 28–30
Turkey and its Jews (Pirzade) 49–51
Turkification 24, 28, 44, 82–3
Turkish Consumers Union 106
Türkmen, Füsun 46, 89–90, 107–8, 195
Türköne, Mümtazer 3, 120

Ulema's 16
Ülken, Hilmi Ziya 45
Ünal Selçuk 110–11
United States 55, 57, 71, 81, 90, 93, 102, 111, 150, 152–3
Uzer, Umut 77
Üzmez, Hüseyin 142

Vakit 142

Valley of the Wolves: Iraq (film) 149, 152–4
Varlık Vergisi 41–3

Washington Post 151
Weiss, Adina 44, 55–6
"Why antisemitism" (Dalkılıç)

Yahudi Meselesi (*the Jewish Problem*) (Ülken) 45
Yahudi Psikolojisi (Yayaoğlu) 148; definition 1
Yahudilik ve Masonluk (Oktar) 59
Yahya, Yasef 193
Yalçın, Soner 126–7, 148–9
Yayaoğlu, Recai 148
Yeni Akit 46, 92–3, 119, 152, 160, 198
Yeni Asya 187
Yıldırım, Bülent 119, 122
Yıldırım, Murat 117
Young Turks 25, 72

Zaman 187
Zionism 21, 49, 50, 141; and the AK Party 72–8; anti-Zionist writings 52; leftist view of 87–8; as a threat 54; view of, as a scam to conquer the world 82–5